Mobilizing Knowledge in Healthcare

Mobilizing Knowledge in Healthcare

Challenges for Management and Organization

Edited by
Jacky Swan, Sue Newell, and Davide Nicolini

OXFORD
UNIVERSITY PRESS

Great Clarendon Street, Oxford, OX2 6DP,
United Kingdom

Oxford University Press is a department of the University of Oxford.
It furthers the University's objective of excellence in research, scholarship,
and education by publishing worldwide. Oxford is a registered trade mark of
Oxford University Press in the UK and in certain other countries

© Oxford University Press 2016

The moral rights of the authors have been asserted

First Edition published in 2016
Impression: 1

All rights reserved. No part of this publication may be reproduced, stored in
a retrieval system, or transmitted, in any form or by any means, without the
prior permission in writing of Oxford University Press, or as expressly permitted
by law, by licence or under terms agreed with the appropriate reprographics
rights organization. Enquiries concerning reproduction outside the scope of the
above should be sent to the Rights Department, Oxford University Press, at the
address above

You must not circulate this work in any other form
and you must impose this same condition on any acquirer

Published in the United States of America by Oxford University Press
198 Madison Avenue, New York, NY 10016, United States of America

British Library Cataloguing in Publication Data

Data available

Library of Congress Control Number: 2015959830

ISBN 978–0–19–873823–7

Printed in Great Britain by
Clays Ltd, St Ives plc

Links to third party websites are provided by Oxford in good faith and
for information only. Oxford disclaims any responsibility for the materials
contained in any third party website referenced in this work.

About this Book

As with many innovations, the idea for this book followed a series of rather haphazard, informal conversations among colleagues, visitors, and friends of IKON (the Innovation, Knowledge and Organizational Networks research unit) at Warwick Business School in the UK. We recognized that we were each ploughing our own knowledge mobilization furrows, that we had a wealth of (too much!) rich empirical material, and that we shared a common skepticism about the merits of traditional, linear "transfer" approaches to closing the so-called "research-practice divide" in healthcare. We shared the view that knowledge mobilization is essentially social and arises, not from the accumulation and transfer of never-ending quantities of new evidence, but from connections between people, ideas, and practices. Informed by research in organization and management studies, we were each in our own ways (and sometimes together) trying to develop practically relevant understandings of the dynamic, social, and political processes entailed. We also observed that work advocating this approach to knowledge mobilization in healthcare (including our own) tends to be scattered across a wide number of different journals and outlets, and across disciplines. We decided, then, to draw together our different studies in order to develop a new "project" for knowledge mobilization—one that would combine theoretical insights with practical understandings, drawn from rigorous research studies, of the challenges for management and organization that knowledge mobilization presents.

The themes and chapters in this collection are the result of this project. Our book does not attempt to develop a new monolithic "grand theory" of knowledge mobilization, nor does it prescribe universal "best practice" recipes on "how to do it." This would be at odds with our assumption that knowledge is social and contextual in its very nature. Rather, the main aim of this book is to provide a research-led, empirically grounded, state of art "review" of how knowledge is actually mobilized in healthcare settings, focusing on the particular challenges this poses for management and organization and on how these could be overcome.

Following our introduction, that lays out our knowledge mobilization agenda and sets the scene for the chapters that follow, the collection is

About this Book

organized according to four, thematic sections. These take, as their primary focus, different social agents and domains where actions to mobilize knowledge happen. These four themes ask, respectively: "How do healthcare managers mobilize knowledge in their practical, everyday work?"; "How do organizations develop capabilities needed for knowledge mobilization?"; "How is knowledge mobilized through networks connecting different practice and professional domains?"; and "How does knowledge travel across space and time?".

We hope that our book is useful for, and used by, scholars and students with interests in healthcare management, knowledge and innovation management, and, more broadly, in management and organization studies. We also believe that the book offers important insights for managers and healthcare practitioners interested in closing the 'research-practice divide' by paying serious attention to the social practices, and divisions of practice, that create this divide in the first place.

Jacky, Sue, and Davide

Acknowledgments

Each chapter includes its own acknowledgments. In addition, the Editors would like to acknowledge the National Institute for Health Research (NIHR) Health Services and Delivery Research (HS&DR) Programme (project numbers: 09/1002/36 Nicolini et al.; 09/1809/1075 Scarbrough et al.; 08/1808/244 Swan et al.; 12/5002/20 Swan et al.), and the NIHR CLAHRC West Midlands who provided partial funding for the research that provided us with insights for the book and the editorial sections. We would also like to thank those that contributed to these funded projects for their much valued input into discussion, debate, and project execution—Emmanouil Gkeredakis, Sarah Evans, Marco Marabelli, Daniela D'Andreta, Maja Korica, Bart Johnson, Rachel Manning, Claudia Roginski, David Sharp, John Powell, Aileen Clarke, Harry Scarbrough, and Sian Phillips. Details of these research projects can be found on the website for the Innovation, Knowledge and Organizational Networks (IKON) research unit—<http://www2.warwick.ac.uk/fac/soc/wbs/research/ikon>. We have been learned a lot from our regular discussions with the practitioner-members of IKON's Knowledge and Innovation Network (see <http://www.ki-network.org>). Finally we would like to thank Dawn Coton, the IKON projects co-ordinator, for her invaluable support and assistance.

Disclaimer: The views and opinions expressed therein are those of the authors and do not necessarily reflect those of the HS&DR Programme, NIHR, NHS, or the Department of Health.

Contents

List of Figures xi
List of Tables xiii
Notes on Contributors xv

Introduction—Knowledge Mobilization in Healthcare 1
Jacky Swan, Sue Newell, and Davide Nicolini

Theme 1. Understanding How Managers Mobilize Knowledge

Introduction 19

1. "Epistemic Fit" and the Mobilization of Management Knowledge in Healthcare 23
Gerry McGivern, Sue Dopson, Ewan Ferlie, Chris Bennett, Michael Fischer, Louise Fitzgerald, and Jean Ledger

2. Objects and Monitoring Practices: Understanding CEOs' Information Work as Mundane Accomplishment 41
Maja Korica and Davide Nicolini

Theme 2. Developing Organizational Capabilities for Knowledge Mobilization

Introduction 61

3. Enhancing Absorptive Capacity of Healthcare Organizations: The Case of Commissioning Service Interventions 65
Charlotte Croft and Graeme Currie

4. Creating and Sustaining the Right Kind of Space for Organizational Learning in Primary Healthcare 82
Trish Reay, Kathy GermAnn, Ann Casebeer, Karen Golden-Biddle, and C. R. (Bob) Hinings

Contents

Theme 3. Mobilizing Knowledge through Networking

Introduction   103

5. Knowledge Mobilization across Inter-organizational Healthcare Innovation Partnerships: A Network Ambidexterity Perspective   107
   Eivor Oborn, Karl Prince, and Michael Barrett

6. Knowledge Mobilization in Healthcare Networks: The Power of Everyday Practices   132
   Sue Newell and Marco Marabelli

7. Knowledge Mobilization and Network Ambidexterity in a Mandated Healthcare Network: A CLAHRC Case Study   151
   Daniela D'Andreta and Harry Scarbrough

Theme 4. Mobilizing Knowledge across Space and Time

Introduction   173

8. Recovering the Performative Role of Innovations in the Global Travel of Healthcare Practices: Is there a Ghost in the Machine?   177
   Davide Nicolini, Jeanne Mengis, David Meacheam, Justin Waring, and Jacky Swan

9. Mobilizing Knowledge in the Ecology of Healthcare Innovation   199
   Maxine Robertson and Jacky Swan

   Conclusions—Knowledge Mobilization: Moving On...   223
   Jacky Swan, Sue Newell, and Davide Nicolini

References   231
General Index   257
Index of Names   262

List of Figures

I.1	The nested ecology for knowledge mobilization	14
3.1	A representation of absorptive capacity knowledge mobilization processes	81
4.1	Mechanisms for creating and sustaining the right kind of space for organizational learning	98
5.1	The SEARCH model for organizing knowledge mobilization	113
5.2	A CLAHRC model for organizing knowledge mobilization	117
5.3	The existing landscape of stakeholders	123
5.4	A connected healthcare platform and ecosystem	124
6.1	Timeline of events and data collection at Dooly	137
7.1	CLAHRC-NET reciprocal ties at Time 1	162
7.2	Network position of CLAHRC-NET knowledge brokers at Time 1, internal ties only	165
7.3	Network position of CLAHRC-NET knowledge brokers at Time 1, including ties to external actors	166
7.4	Network position of CLAHRC-NET knowledge brokers at Time 2, internal ties only	167
7.5	Network position of CLAHRC-NET knowledge brokers at Time 2, including ties to external actors	168
8.1	Chronology of the development of RCA in the USA, UK, and Australia	191
8.2	The travel of RCA	192
9.1	The drug development process	211
9.2	Ecological model of healthcare innovation	220

List of Tables

I.1	Practical implications of "evidence utilization" and "knowledge mobilization" approaches	8
1.1	Comparison of the key features of management knowledge mobilization across the six cases	36
2.1	External sources of information consulted by CEOs (via interviews, supplemented by observations; in no particular order)	50
2.2	Accessing information as part of keeping "in the know": A summary of key practices, including relations and objects	57
5.1	Knowledge mobilization for network ambidexterity across health innovation partnerships	127
6.1	Data collection	138
6.2	Examples of power of ongoing practices	143
7.1	Network ambidexterity metrics for CLAHRC-NET at two time points	160
8.1	An ideal model of the RCA process	182
8.2	Root Cause Analysis in practice	182
9.1	Models of the innovation process	202
9.2	The timescape of the healthcare innovation ecology	215

Notes on Contributors

Michael Barrett is Professor of Information Systems & Innovation Studies at Cambridge Judge Business School. His research interests span innovation, social theory, and organization literatures. He has held editorial roles in a number of leading journals including *Information & Organization, MIS Quarterly*, and *Information Systems Research* and is a member of the Editorial Board of *Organization Science*.

Chris Bennett is an independent research psychologist. Previously at Warwick Business School, most of her research has involved aspects of change within the NHS and other public sector bodies. Current work concerns the effect of perceptions of risk on decision-making about patient safety.

Ann Casebeer is an Adjunct Professor at the O'Brien Institute for Public Health, University of Calgary, Canada. Her research has targeted: advancing experiential learning platforms in education and practice; broadening the stakeholder base for health system decision-making to include patient and citizen perspectives; and, evaluating team and networked based innovation.

Charlotte Croft is Assistant Professor of Healthcare Improvement at Warwick Business School. Her research focuses on issues of organizational behavior, leadership and identity in professionalized settings. Her work has recently been published in journals such as *Organization Studies* and *Public Administration*.

Graeme Currie is a Professor of Public Management at Warwick Business School. He researches leadership, knowledge mobilization, and strategic change, commonly in the empirical setting of healthcare. Recent work has been published in *Academy of Management Journal, Organization Studies, Leadership Quarterly, Human Resource Management,* and *Public Administration Review*. In a previous life, before becoming an academic, Graeme worked in organization development roles for a major car manufacturer and the National Health Service in England.

Daniela D'Andreta is a Research Fellow at IKON, Warwick Business School. She has conducted research and evaluation on mandated networked forms of governance that span academic-health-industry domains, to investigate the implications of these structures for innovation and leadership. Her methodological specialism is in blending Social Network Analysis (SNA) with qualitative, comparative case-study methods.

Sue Dopson is Professor of Organizational Behaviour at Saïd Business School, University of Oxford. Her research centers on transformational change and knowledge exchange in the public and healthcare sectors. She currently represents the University of Oxford as Non-Executive Director of the Oxford Health NHS Foundation Trust.

Notes on Contributors

Ewan Ferlie is Professor of Public Services Management at King's College London. He has published widely on themes of organizational change in public services settings, including healthcare and higher education, held research grants from the National Institute of Health Research and other funders. Ewan is an Academician of the Social Sciences.

Michael Fischer is Senior Research Fellow at the University of Melbourne and Visiting Scholar at the University of Oxford. His research focuses on the organizational behavior, leadership and regulation of research-intensive healthcare organizations. He specializes in ethnographic case studies of everyday 'backstage' work and organizational change.

Louise Fitzgerald is Visiting Professor (Organizational Change) at Saïd Business School, University of Oxford and Emeritus Professor at De Montfort University. Her research and publications focus on innovation and organizational change in complex, professionalized organizations. She is an Academician of the Social Sciences.

Kathy GermAnn is an independent health services researcher and evaluator, and an adjunct professor at the School of Public Health, University of Alberta. Her main interests are organizational and inter-organizational processes of collaborating, learning, and changing and the organizational determinants of employee wellbeing.

Karen Golden-Biddle is the Questrom Professor in Management at Boston University's Questrom School of Business. She has two related streams of work: articulating imaginative work in theorizing; and organizational change, especially the cultural and relational processes constituting and motivating engaged efforts that foster human and organizational development.

C. R. (Bob) Hinings is Professor Emeritus, Strategic Management and Organization at the University of Alberta, Canada. He is also a Fellow at the Judge School of Business, University of Cambridge. His broad research career includes studies of organizational and institutional change with particular attention to power dynamics, organizational design and field level configurations.

Maja Korica is an Associate Professor at Warwick Business School, University of Warwick. Her scholarly interests lie in the "backstages" of organizational life, particularly relating to how the work of senior executives and boards of directors is accomplished, as well as in mundane practices of coordination, leadership, governance, and accountability.

Jean Ledger is a postgraduate researcher at King's College London, Department of Management, specializing in health policy, public management, and qualitative research. She has worked on a number of large-scale projects and grants examining knowledge flows within healthcare systems.

Gerry McGivern is Professor of Organizational Analysis at Warwick Business School. He has published research in leading social science journals and lead ESRC and NIHR funded research projects relating to professionals' knowledge, practice, identity, leadership, and how they are affected by regulation and organization, primarily within healthcare.

Notes on Contributors

Marco Marabelli is Assistant Professor at Bentley University. His research philosophy involves a critical and practice-based approach to social dynamics associated with knowledge management and innovation, mostly at the network level. Marco holds a joint appointment at Warwick Business School, in the Information Systems Management (ISM) group.

David Meacheam is a senior lecturer in the School of Business, University of New South Wales, Canberra, at the Australian Defence Force Academy. David's research interests include assessing the impact of organizational type on knowledge management practices.

Jeanne Mengis is Associate Professor of Organizational Communication in the Faculty of Communication Sciences at the Università della Svizzera Italiana in Lugano and director of the Institute of Marketing and Communication Management. She conducts research on cross-disciplinary collaboration, knowledge integration, the role of objects and materiality in boundary work, and evidence-based learning. Her work has appeared in international journals such as *Organization Science, Organization Studies, Organization and Social Science & Medicine*.

Sue Newell is Professor of Information Systems and Management and Head of the Department of Business and Management, at Sussex University. She has a BSc and PhD from Cardiff University. Her research focuses on understanding the relationships between innovation, knowledge, and organizational networking, primarily from an organizational theory perspective.

Davide Nicolini is Professor of Organization Studies, as well as Co-Director of the IKON Research Centre, both at Warwick Business School, University of Warwick. Widely published in major international journals, his current research focuses on the development of the practice-based approach and its application to phenomena such as knowing, collaboration, innovation, and change in organizations.

Eivor Oborn joined Warwick Business School in October 2012 as Professor of Health Care Management. She has published research on topics including healthcare leadership, change management and technology adoption and use. She received her PhD as a Gates Scholar from Cambridge Judge Business School in 2006.

Karl Prince completed his PhD in 2006 and subsequently worked a number of years in industry managing innovation. He is currently a research associate at Cambridge Judge Business School and recently held an NIHR CLAHRC funded research position at Warwick Business School. His research interests concern the dynamics of innovation, and particularly the relevance of knowledge translation and the role of information and communication technologies.

Trish Reay is Associate Professor, Strategic Management and Organization at the University of Alberta, Canada, and holds a partial appointment at Warwick School of Business. Her research interests include institutional and organizational change, professions and professional identity; her multi-level research has primarily been conducted in healthcare organizations.

Maxine Robertson is Professor of Innovation and Organisation in the School of Business and Management, Queen Mary University of London. Maxine's research

Notes on Contributors

interests focus primarily on three inter-related areas: networked innovation processes and practices, knowledge work, and professional identity. She has explored these domains in a variety of sectors and contexts, notably in the biomedical, IT, UK legal sector, and also within expert consulting firms.

Harry Scarbrough is Professor in Information Systems and Management at Cass Business School, City University London. He has carried out a number of studies on learning, innovation and technology funded by the major UK Research Councils and the National Institute of Health Research. His interests span information systems and organization studies, and include work on "knowledge translation" in healthcare, and the development and diffusion of innovations in computer games. His work has been published in journals such as *Social Science and Medicine*, *Organization Studies*, and *Information Systems Research*.

Jacky Swan is Professor of Organizational Behaviour at Warwick Business School, University of Warwick, joint founder and Co-Director of the IKON Research Centre. Her research links innovation and networking to processes of creating, sharing, and managing knowledge in complex organizational contexts, including healthcare. She recently completed a major funded study of the use of evidence-based knowledge in healthcare commissioning management.

Justin Waring is Professor of Organizational Sociology and Director of the Centre for Health Innovation, Leadership & Learning at Nottingham University Business School. His research is concerned with the social organization of expert work, with a particular focus on how new organizational forms impact upon the practices, cultures, and governance of professionals, and how these institutions can inhibit change. His recent work aims to develop a distinctly sociological analysis of healthcare quality and safety improvement.

Introduction—Knowledge Mobilization in Healthcare

Jacky Swan, Sue Newell, and Davide Nicolini

The so-called "knowing–doing gap" is a persistent problem in healthcare—significant new knowledge is created but only some of it is shared and even less is used (Gkeredakis et al., 2011). As a consequence, many innovative ideas fail to change practice in healthcare settings. This research–practice divide has led to a growing concern—amongst academics, practitioners and governments alike—with new ways of mobilizing knowledge in healthcare. For example, in the UK, the Cooksey Report (2006) identified the gap between new clinical discoveries and their use in practice as one of the biggest challenges to healthcare improvement, so providing impetus for a number of major new, policy-led initiatives aimed at closing the so-called "translational gap" in healthcare. Such initiatives are reinforced by the widely cited social and economic costs of *not* using research-based evidence in practice (e.g. Darzi, 2007).

However, initiatives to improve knowledge translation have met with very mixed results (Ferlie et al., 2013; Fitzgerald and Harvey, 2015). This has been blamed, in part, upon flawed assumptions about knowledge itself and how it is mobilized (Swan et al., 2010). Thus, despite using the term "knowledge translation," mainly policy makers, practitioners, and academic alike, still tend to frame the problem as one of transferring knowledge (and technologies) from producers to users through a linear sequence of steps (e.g. knowledge production, knowledge transfer, knowledge use—Cooksey, 2006). Knowledge, within this technocratic view, is treated as an entity, or as "thing-like"; objective facts (e.g. "best evidence") must be established and spread before being implemented in practice. Within healthcare, the Evidence-Based Medicine (and, more recently Evidence-Based Management) movement, as well as implementation science streams of research, are heavily imbued with this view. It is now recognized, however, that this linear model greatly underestimates the socially situated nature of knowledge and the challenges of mobilizing knowledge across boundaries created by different kinds of practice (e.g. professions, occupational groups, and organizations—Ferlie et al., 2012; Greenhalgh and Wieringa, 2011). These challenges are particularly acute in the complex, interactive setting of healthcare, where such boundaries seem to be very pronounced and claims as to what counts as "best" or "valid" knowledge are hotly contested (Oborn, Barrett, and Racko, 2013).

Given this, there is increasing interest in how knowledge is circulated and negotiated among those involved in healthcare (including patients) and in how practice is actually transformed. In this book we use the term "knowledge mobilization" to capture these processes. Thus we define knowledge mobilization as a proactive process that involves efforts to transform practice through the circulation of knowledge within and across practice domains. In this definition we share (with many others) the view knowledge is not a thing that people "have" that can be simply passed around, but is part of what people do and who they are (Cook and Brown, 1999; Waring et al., 2013).

The collection of chapters brought together in this book examine the dynamics of knowledge mobilization and focus, in particular, on the challenges these pose for organization and management; challenges that have received much less attention than those concerned with clinical practice in the healthcare setting. Linear views that see the process of the circulation of knowledge and innovation in terms of a rather mechanical sequence of production, transfer, and utilization are especially ill-suited when trying to understand managerial work (Scarbrough et al., 2014). This is because healthcare managers operate in conditions that are complex, fluid, and subject to competing demands and pressures and shifting knowledge claims (Ferlie et al., 2013). The activity of managers takes place at the encounter between multiple organizational and professional domains. Their work is often discursive in nature and lacks the reassuring foundation of a corpus of disciplinary knowledge and professional tradition. Pressure to act fast, and the continuously shifting context, prevent the use of traditional modes of validating knowledge (e.g. via scientific method). As a consequence, what counts as "knowledge," "evidence," or "best practice" is always open to multiple interpretations and contestation, and is increasingly exposed to public scrutiny (Gkeredakis et al., 2014). Pipeline-like models that think only in terms of transfer from producers to rather passive users, and do not pay heed to the complex conditions of managerial work, cannot account for what is going on. Perhaps worse, the belief that it is indeed possible to transfer knowledge can become the basis for poor decisions and wrong initiatives, or costly initiatives that are doomed to fail (Swan et al., 2010; Ferlie et al., 2013). Rather, to address the "knowing–doing gap" we need accounts that embrace the utilization of knowledge *in practice* via negotiated interaction among agents "within the specifics of an organizational reality" (Fitzgerald and Harvey, 2015: 199).

Building on the collective scholarship of some of the most prominent academics in this area, this collection examines in detail how knowledge is mobilized in healthcare organizations, how practice is affected, and what enables or constrains knowledge mobilization efforts within and across contexts. We do so by, first, adopting an *ecological view*; that is, a view which recognizes that how knowledge is mobilized, and to what ends, is the result of multiple, nested processes rather than a single, sequential chain of actions. We suggest, second, that these processes are driven by a variety of purposeful *agents* that include, but also go beyond, individuals. These include networks, institutionalized collaboratives, professional associations, formal organizations, and institutions. All these agents work concurrently to trigger, sustain, or constrain processes of knowledge mobilization and one kind of initiative is always "nested" in conditions prepared by other agents and/or by prior (or future) initiatives. Third, we suggest that much is to be gained if we study knowledge mobilization as the result of a nexus of interconnected *processes and practices*. It is by following processes and practices "in situ" that we can actually start to produce realistic and useful accounts that help policy makers, practitioners, and researchers understand how knowledge mobilization actually works and design initiatives accordingly.

These three guiding assumptions—nested ecology, agency, and process/practice—run through the chapters and themes in this collection. It is a claim of this book that taking into account agency—the capacity of an "entity" to act—in this complex, nested ecology is fundamental to providing sufficiently nuanced explanations of how knowledge is made to count at the point of action. If we are to foster and facilitate the processes that underpin knowledge mobilization in healthcare management, then this is a necessary departure point from (much) previous work. The aim of this book is not, however, to provide a monolithic "grand theory" of knowledge mobilization—we have no such grand theory to offer. Our more modest objective is to exemplify the nature, complexity, and working of this complex ecology for knowledge mobilization through a number of theoretically-grounded empirical studies, organized around four themes. Each chapter will illustrate in detail how knowledge mobilization works, what the challenges encountered by the process are, and how such challenges can be, or have been, overcome in practice. Chapters are then grouped according to four-themes that take as their focal point different "domains of action"; the work performed by managers, organizations, networks, and wider trans-local regimes.

Through putting together these different chapters, this book embraces a practical sensitivity. This suggests that to understand the complex social phenomenon of knowledge mobilization, we are better off accumulating the insights and wisdom derived from multiple, well-designed, in-depth case studies, rather than developing an abstract theory that covers too much and ends up explaining very little. Accordingly, the book describes new forms of organization that facilitate knowledge mobilization (e.g. collaborative working, networks, and networking) and discusses organizational capabilities (e.g. for learning and knowledge absorption), and management practices that make a practical difference to knowledge mobilization. Moreover, since all knowledge mobilization takes place under specific policy and institutional conditions, some of the chapters will explore how that context shapes the development of these organizational forms, capabilities, and practices. Before describing what the reader should expect to find in the book, some clarifications on what we mean by knowledge mobilization and how we approach the topic are in order.

I.1 What is Knowledge Mobilization?

The idea of "knowledge mobilization" was introduced in the mid-2000s, as a contrast to the prevailing linear model of knowledge production and utilization, to underscore the interactive, social, and interpretive nature of the process, whereby individuals, teams, and organizations co-create, absorb, and put to work knowledge (Levin, 2008). Still today, debates on the role of knowledge and, in particular, "evidence," in healthcare organization and management remain sharply polarized around two alternative views that differ significantly in terms of their theoretical underpinnings, lexicon, and practical implications. At one extreme are those (scholars, consultants, policy makers) who believe in the possibility of extending the principle and practice of evidence-based medicine (Sackett et al., 1996)—whereby robust, scientifically proven evidence is implemented in practice—to healthcare management issues (Walshe and Rundall, 2001; Kovner, Fine, and D'Aquila, 2009; Rousseau, 2006). At the opposite extreme are those who, like the authors of this book, contest this rationalistic approach and suggest that organizational realities seldom map unproblematically onto their idealized "evidence-based" representations (e.g. Dopson et al., 2002; Dopson and Fitzgerald, 2005; Learmonth, 2006; Learmonth and Harding, 2006; Morrell, 2008). As an alternative, they propose a view that sees knowledge as entangled in organizational and managerial processes that are social, political, and sensitive to context and institutional conditions and forms of agency.

The former group considers the use and spread of knowledge largely as a utilitarian problem of efficiently circulating, assimilating, and utilizing "best available information." They use the lexicon of production, diffusion, and utilization of evidence and describe barriers and enablers to the "push" of evidence and its "pull" by users. At its core is the idea that managers who use evidence are in a better position to deal with their everyday challenges and achieve their organizations' goals (Rousseau, 2006; Rousseau and McCarthy, 2007; Chalkidou et al., 2008). This is because evidence can inform managers of "what works and what doesn't" (Kovner and Rundall, 2006).

Traditionally, this group of scholars have focused on how knowledge products (e.g. research outputs, evidence-based guidelines) can be utilized to make efficient decisions that "would not have been made otherwise" (Landry, Amara, and Lamari, 2001: 297; Estabrooks, 1999). Three forms of utilization are considered. Instrumental utilization captures instances when there is a clear correspondence between an identifiable piece of research and a specific decision or intervention. Conceptual utilization refers to "where knowledge of a single study provides new ideas, new theories, and new hypotheses leading to new interpretations about the issues and the facts surrounding the decision-making contexts without inducing changes in decisions" (Landry, Amara, and Lamari, 2001: 297). Symbolic utilization involves the use of a piece of research as a persuasive or political tool to legitimate a position or practice (Beyer and Trice, 1982).

Other work in this "knowledge utilization" camp focuses on various aspects of the decision-making process and enablers or barriers to implementation. Advocates endorse the view that new evidence-based models of organization and management diffuse within a population through a communication-based process of social contagion (cf. Rogers, 2003). The success of diffusion depends on the idea itself, its perceived added value, and how it is communicated, with adopters being depicted as largely rational decision makers. The focus here is on responsive adaptive behavior; the driving force behind the diffusion of managerial evidence being the perception that adopting and implementing the model will yield efficiency gains (Strang and Soule, 1998; Van de Ven and Hargrave, 2004).

Thanks to its contiguity and compatibility with the discourse of modern neoclassical economics, the knowledge utilization approach has become dominant among managers, policy makers, and researchers, even breeding its own field of scholarship on "implementation science." Speaking in terms of production, diffusion, and utilization of managerial knowledge seems rather normal and down to earth. This is accompanied with the belief that innovations and best practices necessarily prevail when sufficient evidence of their superiority is publicly available and when barriers to their implementation and take-up are removed and enablers put in place.

Opponents of this approach suggest that this knowledge utilization model is based on a number of unwarranted assumptions (Rich, 1997; Rich and Oh, 2000; Ward et al., 2011). For example, the idea that knowledge can be considered as an input to a decision-making process, such that it is possible to trace the relations between one and the other, is seen as overly simplistic. The model ignores the fact that "decisions generally do not represent a single event [and they] must be viewed longitudinally" (Rich, 1991: 331). Accordingly, it is almost impossible to predict when, or where, a specific knowledge "input" is likely to have an effect on a particular decision "output" and the same "piece of knowledge" can have multiple effects in different contexts. Similarly, the model ignores the fact that the utilization of knowledge can have negative and unintended consequences for certain groups of healthcare professionals. Therefore, rejecting, or actively ignoring, some information can be a fully rational response to a politically charged situation.

These criticisms are echoed by scholars who are skeptical of the possibility of adopting an evidence-based approach, grounded in medicine, for healthcare management. Questioning the possibility of universally applicable evidence to deal with complex management issues, these scholars suggest that the presumption that science alone is efficacious for managerial problem-solving is deeply problematic (Learmonth, 2006; Learmonth and Harding, 2006; Scarbrough et al., 2014). Accordingly, they dispute the notion that "what works" can be defined irrespective of the values, beliefs and socio-political interests of the researcher/manager (Gkeredakis et al., 2014). The rhetoric of science is a "mask for the politics of evidence" (Learmonth, 2006: 1089) that obfuscates the fact that the politics of organizational life play a decisive role in what evidence is used, how, and why (Dopson et al., 2002; Fitzgerald and Harvey, 2015).

Other critics from organization studies question the whole idea of knowledge that underpins the traditional model. Cook and Brown (1999) thus accuse this view of adopting what they call an "epistemology of possession," which conceives knowledge as a type of substance, resource, or asset, that can be accumulated, fixed (e.g. as guidelines), transmitted, and utilized. This privileges explicit knowledge over more tacit forms and the knowledge possessed by individuals over that shared among social groups. In so doing, it offers a view of knowledge that is severely under-socialized. Also, in emphasizing the never-ending production of new knowledge (more is better), it may actually reinforce, rather than close, the "knowing–doing gap." They argue, rather, for an "epistemology of practice" that sees knowledge (or knowing) as socially situated and produced through (rather than before) doing. Thus people acquire shared meanings, know-how, and identity through their interactions within a "community of practice" (Brown and Duguid, 2001; Lave and Wenger, 1991); knowledge is not something people "have" but rather what they "do" and who they "are" (Waring et al., 2013).

The social, contextual, and political nature of knowledge and (what comes to be accepted as) evidence in healthcare was confirmed by a well-known study by Gabbay and Le May (2010). It is perhaps not surprising that these scholars became notable in the healthcare field as their study was itself evidence-based, drawing from an observation of knowledge utilization in primary care. Contrary to the precepts of the knowledge utilization model, they found that explicit evidence was rarely used by doctors in their daily clinical decision-making. Rather, clinicians used tacit "mind-lines" which they defined as "collectively reinforced, internalized tacit guidelines" (Gabbay and Le May, 2010: 2015). While mind-lines built on the doctors' early training and experience, and were at times informed by short readings, they largely resulted from the interactions with other clinicians and stakeholders (opinion leaders, patients, and pharmaceutical representatives). Similar findings have emerged from studies on knowledge circulation in "communities of practice" (Lave and Wenger, 1991) and "networks of practice" (Brown and Duguid, 2001), which question equally the emphasis on explicit knowledge at the expense of interactive, social processes, and collective sensemaking.

In order to stress the social, historically situated, and complex nature of the processes whereby knowing is entangled in the doing of management work, scholars and practitioners alike have started, more recently, to use the term "knowledge mobilization." According to Levin (2008) "mobilization" is preferred to "utilization" or "translation" because it emphasizes the multifaceted, longer-term, and often political nature of the work in comparison to earlier terms "that seem to imply a one directional and linear move from research to practice" (Levin, 2008: 11). Adopting a knowledge mobilization perspective implies, among other things, that:

- Knowledge is essentially social in character; it resides in mind-lines, in communities of practice, in networks of practice and other types of collectives which sustain, legitimize, and transform it through social processes.
- At any point in time the mobilization of knowledge is purposefully pursued by multiple individual and collective actors. Understanding agency is therefore fundamental to knowledge mobilization.
- Agency operates across multiple contexts, or "domains of action" (e.g. management teams, organizations, networks, policy regimes). What happens in one domain is nested within, and shaped by, what happens in another.
- How, what and when knowledge is mobilized is a result of the complex interactions among agents which take place in very specific historical and material conditions—often referred to as the institutional context.
- The nature and structure of social networks (formal and informal) matter to the mobilization of knowledge. Brokers and boundary spanners acquire fundamental importance.

- Political considerations, peer pressure, legitimacy-seeking and vested interests play a central role in knowledge mobilization. The social position and social capital of agents constitute major factors in determining whether research is exploited in practice or not.
- Knowledge does not travel untouched through social interactions; it is modified in the process. Knowledge mobilization is therefore necessarily a process of transformation. This allows for the same content to be used differently in different social and cultural contexts (Nicolini, Powell, and Korica, 2014).

It is worth underscoring at this point that this paradigmatic shift is much more than a simple lexical substitution—a word game so to speak. The "utilization" and "mobilization" approaches, in fact, suggest profoundly different views of what can be done practically to support and improve knowledge mobilization. This is because they make different assumptions about what causes the research–practice divide in the first place. These differences are summarized in Table I.1.

It is important to note that the knowledge mobilization view does not discount the role of evidence in decision-making, or the importance of timely and efficient access to information. Rather, evidence and information are seen as forms of codified knowledge that can be powerful resources, but whose

Table I.1. Practical implications of "evidence utilization" and "knowledge mobilization" approaches

	Evidence Utilization	Knowledge Mobilization
The research–practice divide stems from:	Not having sufficiently robust evidence or from not being able to diffuse and implement it.	Differences in social practice (among managers, clinicians, researchers) that generate different ways of knowing and doing.
It is closed by:	Creating, through research, universal, propositional knowledge;	Facilitating and leveraging social processes whereby knowledge can circulate;
	Training managers to develop skills needed to be able to search, evaluate and apply evidence in their organizations;	Connecting across knowledge boundaries created by divisions in practice (e.g. between researchers, managers and clinicians);
	Making sure the best available evidence is sourced in an efficient and timely manner;	Understanding and changing the ways in which non-human artifacts are entangled in the knowledge mobilization process;
	Creating a research culture within organizations such that, managers, just like doctors, strive to cure their organizational ills by drawing upon a large body of authoritative, formal knowledge.	Recognizing the realities of the political and institutional conditions within which the process unfolds so that evidence (and other forms of information) does not "speak for itself" but must be advocated by social groups and opinion leaders.

meaning and relevance depends on the particular context within which they are put to work. For example, the results of a scientific study may assume different meaning and relevance when considered in the context of a commissioning decision as compared with a clinical one. How evidence participates in, and is constructed through, managerial action thus becomes an empirical problem that needs to be explored, rather than a normative assertion about how managerial action should happen.

I.2 Opening the Black Box of Knowledge Mobilization

The notion of knowledge mobilization opens a new and interesting window on the challenges faced by healthcare managers and organizations in making their work more knowledgeable and evidence-based. The actual process of knowledge mobilization, and how this happens in practical settings, remains, however, a "black box" that needs to be opened. This book should be considered as a modest contribution to the collective effort in this direction. Hence, it presents a series of rigorous, theoretically grounded empirical studies that study in depth efforts to mobilize knowledge in healthcare management and organization. Before introducing the chapters, we will summarize the key guiding assumptions that underscore the content and structure of the book.

I.2.1 *To Study Knowledge Mobilization You Need to Start from Where the Agency Is*

One guiding assumption of a knowledge mobilization view is that agency drives the process. However, we should remain open to the issue of where the agency lies. The received wisdom of the utilization view—including its more socialized version (e.g. Rogers, 2003)—is that knowledge is circulated thanks to the agency of individuals (e.g. managers) and the structures they create (e.g. information systems). Accordingly, you need to study the rational intentions of individuals and/or the general fabric of social structures of which they are part (e.g. their role positions as "managers," "nurses," or "librarians"). In other words, the locus of agency (the response to the question: where is the impetus for knowledge mobilization?) is the more-or-less rational decision-maker constantly looking to maximize the quality of his or her decisions within a particular social structure and set of resources. In practical terms, this translates into the instrumental strategy of asking "which system can support the information needs of the decision maker" or, more often, the "spray and pray" strategy of "if we disseminate it widely enough an idea will come to the attention of decision-makers by virtue of the sheer force of its superior quality." The latter, of course, rarely happens (as attested by the many studies of failures to adopt evidence-based guidelines—Swan et al., 2012).

On the contrary, the approach purported here suggests that much is to be gained if we accept that, because knowledge is mobilized for a variety of aims, interests, and purposes, many more "actors" are interested in—and involved in—the process. For example, knowledge is mobilized rather naturally in communities of practice—both spontaneous and designed ones—as this is the very nature of these forms of sociability (see Nicolini, Scarbrough, and Gracheva, 2015, for a discussion). Groups and teams have, similarly, been shown to be capable of learning and becoming conduits of knowledge (Edmondson, 1999). Mandated networks (such as the UK Collaborations for Leadership in Applied Health Research and Care—CLAHRCs) mobilize knowledge by design because this is inscribed in their mission (see chapters in Theme 3 of this book). Professional associations and regulatory bodies actively mobilize knowledge as this is critical to their project of maintaining control over their knowledge jurisdictions (Swan, Newell, and Robertson, 1995; Robertson and Swan, Chapter 9 in this book). Organizations as a whole often put in place complex processes of knowledge acquisition, development, and learning in order to resolve their particular issues (see chapters in Theme 2). In short, agency can happen in multiple domains, in multiple ways, and for different purposes. Moreover, one kind of agency may be helped or thwarted by agency in a different domain. For example, in chapter 9 by Robertson and Swan, we see how a commercial firm's mobilization efforts, aimed at developing new drugs, are sometimes thwarted by the agency of regulatory groups, which is aimed at ensuring new knowledge does not harm patients.

I.2.2 Knowledge Mobilization in Healthcare Unfolds in a Complex, Nested Ecology

Acknowledging that multiple kinds of agency and actors are involved at *the same time* in knowledge pursuits, leads to our second guiding assumption; knowledge mobilization always takes place in a complex, and nested, ecology. This consists, not just of "knowledge producers" (e.g. researchers) in flat-line relationships with "knowledge users" (e.g. managers), but of multiple agents operating in different domains of action (e.g. management decisions, clinical projects, regulatory systems...) and with different degrees of authority and/or influence over the actions of those in other domains. The very existence of this complex ecology makes linear and rational processes the exception rather than the norm (Dougherty and Dunne, 2011). The co-existence of all these agents, each pursuing their own practical objectives and interests, and with their own language and history, almost certainly creates all sorts of boundaries and barriers to the sharing, interpretation and use of knowledge (Carlile,

2002). The chances that knowledge can travel unchanged across these boundaries (as depicted by the traditional linear view) are rather slim.

Moreover, what happens in one domain of action (e.g. developing a new policy, or establishing a new network aimed at innovation) becomes the context for what happens in the others (e.g. deciding which particular project to prioritize). Thus the ecology for knowledge mobilization has a "nested relationality" (Nicolini, 2012; Jarzabkowski, Bednarek, and Spee, 2015). The expression "nested relationality," from practice-based studies scholars, captures the idea that complex phenomena—such as a global markets, fashion, or scientific progress—emerge from the connections among several sites of practices. At each site the local practice both depends upon, and contributes to, the practices in the other sites. Although each site is nested among others, there is no need to assume that a higher level of reality exists (e.g. "the environment") which controls such connections. Of course, not all the sites have equal influence, but why this is the case can be explained empirically without recourse to unexplained external forces.

The same view can be applied to knowledge mobilization. As seen, knowledge mobilization takes place in a variety of locales and is promoted and supported (or opposed) by a variety of actors. We refer to these locales as "domains of action," emphasizing the agency that drives practice. Although, figuratively, we can refer to actors as being located at different "levels" (individuals, groups, organizations, inter-organizations, institutions) these levels are not hierarchically organized—they are not like Russian dolls one inside the other. Rather, the actions taken in each tends to become "the context" for the others. Changes in knowledge mobilization in the corporate domain may thus affect processes in the individual or policy domains. This view makes it possible for causality to flow in multiple directions. For example, a shift in global discourse (e.g., toward "evidence-based care") is likely to affect which knowledge will be considered legitimate and when, although how this happens is open to empirical scrutiny. Conversely, the birth of such a new form of discourse can itself be studied empirically as emerging from ordinary actions of specific individuals, groups, and organizational actors (Scarbrough, Robertson, and Swan, 2016).

I.2.3 *Processes and Practices are Meaningful Units of Analysis*

Given the complex, nested ecology a focus on processes and practices is important for understanding and improving knowledge mobilization. It is useful to examine processes as they link domains of action in the ecology—for example, the process of commissioning a new mode of service delivery connects local management decisions with inter-organizational change within a professional context. Practice-based studies are also useful as they foreground the importance of activity, performance, and work in all aspects of organizational life (Nicolini, 2012; Nicolini and Monteiro, 2016). While they leave ample space for individual agency (practices need to be performed each time anew) they invite us to focus on existing—and emerging—regimes of activity and routines, how these are constituted, their history and composition. Taking processes and practices as a unit of analysis when talking about knowledge mobilization has a number of benefits—many of which will become apparent when reading the chapters in this book.

First, thinking in terms of processes and practices forces us to stay close to the "coal-face" of management and organization; knowledge mobilization is conceived as something that takes place through sayings, doings, interactions, and things. Seeing knowledge mobilization as something achieved with words and deeds make us sensitive to aspects that other approaches tend to background, including, for example, the role of material artifacts and peoples' values, interests, or desires. The success or failure of knowledge mobilization is likely to depend, then, not just on big strategic initiatives (e.g. the establishment of knowledge translation networks such as CLAHRCs—as seen in Theme 3), but also on the cumulative effects of small mundane, everyday events, such as the lack of space to meet. Staying close to what actually happens, and paying attention to ordinary things, is important to understand, not only what happens in the room of an individual manager (see Theme 1), but also how organizations behave (Themes 2 and 3) and how ideas travel globally (Theme 4).

Second, thinking in terms of processes and practices helps us to shift the focus from (individual) actors and their personality/style to the activities and organizational conditions that encourage or hamper the mobilization of knowledge. This is important and practical because processes, practices and organizational conditions are all "things" within the reach of managerial interventions. In other words, these are things about which something can be done (albeit not always easily).

Third, examining processes, practices, and routines allows us to talk about how they conflict or compete with each other for time and attention, how well new processes align with established ones, and whether they pull in opposite and at times contradictory directions. This helps us to understand how practices might be better orchestrated across the complex ecology of organizations and actors such that change is actually sustainable (Dougherty and Dunne, 2011; Swan, Robertson, and Newell, 2016). By addressing the issues of change in terms of practical things that actually need to happen, it also helps to avoid the tendency to attribute failures to utilize evidence and knowledge simply to the incompetence, or moral failures, of individuals/groups. Because each of the chapters in this book draws from robust empirical accounts that say something about processes and practices, they can provide more practical answers than moot appeals to be, for example, "more sharing" or to develop an "evidence-based culture."

Finally, analyzing processes and practices helps us to operationalize the ubiquitous presence of so called "contextual" conditions in ways that eschew the traditional idea that the context is some kind of passive background to the real event. When organizational phenomena are seen in terms of practice, context becomes simply a useful shorthand to describe the complex array of things that were (or were not) said and done in the past, or said and done in other domains, and that spill over to the here and now. Context thus conditions and manifests itself in what is sayable and what we are expected to say; what is doable and how we understand what we should do; in the history of relationships we have with others and who we talk to; in the tools that are used; in rules, regulations, and ways of evaluating work; in the expectations about the communities we serve, and so on. Like everything else, "context" becomes tangible and within reach, rather than an ineffable background that is difficult to act upon.

I.3 The Themes of the Book and How Each Chapter Contributes

Our guiding assumptions for the book, discussed in section I.2, are summarized, albeit schematically, in Figure I.1 and are reflected in the structure of this book. First, all chapters draw their contributions from detailed qualitative empirical studies that provide rich insights into processes and practice. Second, the premise that knowledge mobilization happens in a complex ecology and is driven by multiple sources of agency is reflected in the organization of chapters into themes. Each theme, and the chapters within, takes as its focus particular forms of agency taking place in a particular domain of action.

Theme 1 focuses on the domain of managerial action and looks at the question of how managers mobilize knowledge. In Chapter 1, McGivern and colleagues look at how, and under what circumstances, managers (general managers and clinical managers) use management knowledge, research, and evidence, including Evidence-Based Management research. Drawing on six-case studies, and theory on "epistemic stances," they develop the idea of "epistemic fit," showing how clashes between the norms, interests, and epistemic stances of different communities critically influence managers' knowledge mobilization. Interestingly knowledge brokers are found to have a key role to play in "fitting" knowledge within context but their ability to do so depends on organizational conditions, as explained in the chapter. In Chapter 2, Korica and Nicolini tackle the question of how top executives keep informed so that they can do their work, when faced with so many, often conflicting, demands. Using a practice-based approach, the chapter

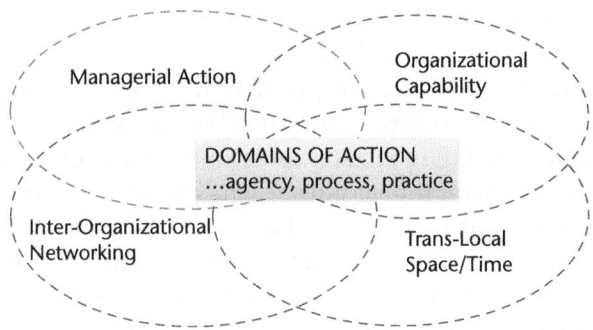

Figure I.1 The nested ecology for knowledge mobilization

reports on a detailed ethnography of the daily work of Chief Executives running National Health Service (NHS) trusts in England, showing how they make themselves practically informed in their everyday decision-making. CEOs' knowledge mobilization specifically aims at "keeping in the know" in order to handle the very varied, practical challenges of their day-to-day job. What counts as "evidence", and what objects are relied upon, are tightly bound up with the CEOs' ever-changing practical concerns in situ.

The chapters in Theme 2 turn to the domain of organizational action and look at how healthcare organizations develop and sustain capabilities that enable them to acquire, share, and use knowledge to improve learning and service delivery. Building on theory on "absorptive capacity" which identifies critical features of the knowledge mobilization process (acquisition, assimilation, transformation and exploitation—e.g. Zahra and George, 2002), Chapter 3 by Croft and Currie explores the absorptive capacity of healthcare commissioners who are responsible for planning and budgeting healthcare services. They identify the critical organizational capabilities required for building such absorptive capacity, including systems capabilities, socialization capabilities, and coordination capabilities. The latter are found to be especially important to the improvement of knowledge mobilization in healthcare, given the complex, interactive nature of the ecology, and can even help overcome limitations in the former. In Chapter 4 Reay and colleagues continue with the theme of organizational capabilities by asking how knowledge mobilization can be facilitated through the development of "space"—the social and relational context that evolves as people interact and share knowledge—for organizational learning. Drawing from a study of managers, physicians, and other health professionals in ten primary healthcare innovation sites, these authors characterize different types of space—generative, inert, and toxic—and identify four kinds of strategies (social practices) that are important in creating the right kind of space for organizational learning and knowledge sharing to occur. These entail assembling the right people, developing positive social relationships, focusing the conversation, and managing setbacks and frustrations.

Theme 3 considers the domain of inter-organizational action and the ways in which agency can be exercised through network relationships. In many countries, policy makers have mandated the establishment of formal network initiatives aimed at speeding the translation of knowledge into practice by establishing novel, more collaborative, forms of organization. Yet, as seen, these have had mixed results (Ferlie et al., 2013; Crilly et al., 2013). The chapters in this theme focus on how these new networked initiatives actually develop, the major challenges they face, and what seems to lead to success. One ongoing challenge for these networks is to achieve what has come to be known in the literature as "ambidexterity"; that is, a balance between exploration (the ability to create and acquire new knowledge by linking a wide number of diverse partners and forms of knowledge) with exploitation (the ability to exploit and embed created/acquired knowledge in practice—e.g. Andriopoulos and Lewis, 2009). Drawing from in-depth case studies of three different inter-organizational healthcare networks, Oborn and colleagues, in Chapter 5, focus on the different ways in which diverse stakeholders manage their work in order to achieve ambidexterity. While ambidexterity was achieved differently in each case, there were four common processes that leaders and managers needed to develop. These were: (i) to carefully engage the appropriate stakeholder members; (ii) to develop workable funding strategies; (iii) to mediate between competing priorities of the diverse stakeholders involved and; (iv) to deal with the political challenges of knowledge in innovation.

Chapter 6, by Newell and Marabelli, presents findings from a longitudinal case study of a networked healthcare initiative in Canada that was trying to deliver coordinated care for children with complex health needs by mobilizing knowledge across the various agencies involved. The chapter specifically addresses the nature of agency in such networked initiatives by asking how, and in what forms, power mobilizes knowledge. A key issue is how the changes inspired by the initiative can be made durable. Recognizing that hierarchical and resource-based forms of power are necessarily limited in networked settings, the authors take a practice view to ask how everyday practices acquire the power to mobilize knowledge. They identify the myriad of everyday, sociomaterial practices—including talk, text, and objects—that "make things happen" in network settings and sustain improvements in knowledge mobilization.

The topic of ambidexterity is revisited in the chapter by D'Andreta and Scarbrough in Chapter 7. Drawing from social network theory (e.g. Reagans and McEvily, 2003), and using novel social network analytical techniques, they explore how a policy-mandated network with a specific remit for knowledge mobilization (the UK CLAHRC) achieves ambidexterity through an informal social network structure that combines brokerage (links across diverse professional groups) and closure (tight-knit social groups that helped to embed new knowledge into changes in healthcare practice). Moreover, ambidexterity in the informal social network needed to be supported by a formal management structure that coupled formally appointed "Knowledge Broker" roles that helped to create diverse linkages, with thematic, project-focused work groups, providing a focus for the embedding of new ideas. This has important implications for the design of such mandated networks. Rather than being funded and then "left to happen" (which is often the case), the informal social dynamics need to be carefully considered and supported by appropriate formal management structures.

Theme 4 turns to the domain of wider, trans-local social spaces and practice regimes that shape the mobilization of knowledge in local settings. The chapters here address the question of how innovation happens within and across institutional contexts. In Chapter 8, Nicolini and colleagues help to address a well-known problem in the complex healthcare ecology, which is that many innovations fail to spread (Ferlie et al., 2005). By exploring practices for improving patient safety that *did* spread globally, they show how the circulation of knowledge was facilitated and sustained by the construction of a discursive "package" of "anxiety-reassurance." This worked to both spread and reconfigure knowledge of patient safety, first, by raising public and professional anxiety about existing practices to manage patient safety, and second, by creating reassurance through a new management "solution" to the problem. Finally, Chapter 9, by Robertson and Swan, moves debate into the realm of healthcare innovation in the commercial arena. Theorizing drug development as a complex, networked innovation process (Dougherty and Dunne, 2011), this chapter uses a longitudinal case study to examine in detail how practices embedded within the organizational ecology shape knowledge mobilization. Building on research that has identified key features of the institutional "landscape," the authors introduce, also, the notion of an ecology "timescape" to more fully explain the problems of knowledge mobilization in healthcare innovation projects. This comprises the different temporal orientations held by agents within the ecology—including commercial firms, clinicians, regulators, and financiers—that guide their decision-making and the pace of their activities, often creating significant constraints on practice. The chapter highlights the importance of overcoming these challenges through appropriate forms of governance.

The chapters and themes in this collection are guided by a common interest in knowledge mobilization in healthcare as a proactive process of transforming practice in a complex, nested ecology. They build upon the corpus of existing research by examining, in depth, what these processes and practices look like, how they unfold in particular domains, and to what ends. The chapters are also diverse in terms of theory, research site, and the practical challenges for management and organization addressed. We do not intend to unite them with some kind of grand, unifying theory—we do not believe that such a project is feasible or desirable. Nor do we impose a strict common template on how they tell their stories—we believe that each should speak in its own voice as is appropriate to the subject matter. Rather, as you read on, you will hopefully find that "the devil in the detail" offers much more to our understanding of what knowledge mobilization concretely is, and how it can be performed in such a way that it helps, rather than hinders, improvements in healthcare.

Theme 1
Understanding How Managers Mobilize Knowledge

Introduction

The focus in healthcare research is often on clinical practitioners (doctors, nurses, paramedics, etc.) and the ways they use (or do not use) evidence-based medicine. However, many healthcare organizations are very large and have a cadre of managers (with or without a clinical background) who play a crucial role in mobilizing knowledge within and across the organization. This first section of the book focuses on how (if at all) knowledge is mobilized in management practice and decision-making, on what kinds of knowledge and evidence healthcare managers deploy in practice, and on how they come to decide what counts as valid or relevant knowledge. Thus, in this first section, the domain of action that is in focus is the work performed by managers. Of course, given the idea of a "nested" ecology, managers do not practice in isolation from the overlapping agencies of their organizations, networks, and trans-local contexts. In this sense, the two chapters in this section simply bring to the fore the agency of the managers, simultaneously recognizing that the agency of these managers is constrained and afforded by the organizations in which they work, the professional networks with which they engage, and the broader trans-local context of healthcare management.

In relation to clinical practitioners, Rousseau (2006) describes medicine as a "success" because, she argues, it was the first area of practice to institutionalize the idea of evidence-based practice. In clinical practice, then, while there continues to be variation in terms of the use of evidence, the "ideal" of the practice is, Rousseau declares, accepted—clinical decisions should be informed by evidence of what works and clinical guidelines, protocols, and pathways are continuously being defined and diffused in line with this view of what constitutes "best practice." On the other hand, Rousseau (2006), among others, finds that in relation to managers (including healthcare managers), not only do practitioners rarely use evidence to decide on their practice, the idea of using an established social science evidence-base is not even widely accepted.

Understanding How Managers Mobilize Knowledge

We have already seen in the Introduction why this view of rationally using "evidence" may be problematic, but for those who believe in the linear view of the diffusion of knowledge (the contagion model), the fact that in relation to management evidence-based practice is not followed is seen to be a "problem" that needs to be addressed. To overcome this "problem" some of the management literature suggests how to promote evidence-based management through better management education (Rousseau and McCarthy, 2007) to try and encourage managers to become more like scientists. However, as you may have anticipated given the perspective taken in this book, the chapters in this section do not adopt this view, but, rather, problematize the idea that managers *should* or even *could* rationally produce, diffuse, and reuse evidence that can work across all contexts. Thus, rather than bemoaning the fact that healthcare managers do not use evidence to make decisions, the two chapters in this first section instead look at what knowledge and information managers actually *do* use in their everyday work and why. In doing this, the chapters problematize the idea that there is some kind of singular, universally applicable evidence-base and instead show how managers adapt evidence from their local context and their established normative understandings and practices. In this sense, the chapters illustrate that what counts as "evidence" is locally produced, rather than simply defined by a set of universal facts, and that, moreover, given that practitioners are invested in their practices, even a clear "proving" that something works will be insufficient to ensure that it is adopted.

Turning to the two chapters, Chapter 1 explicitly considers the question about the circumstances in which managers use research-based management knowledge (that they call Evidence-Based Management or EBMgt) in their decision-making. Not surprisingly, given what we have said about knowledge mobilization, they found that the use of EBMgt was very rare and where it was used, this was done very selectively. The interesting issue, then, is what and when evidence *is* used by healthcare managers. The research reported in this chapter suggests that knowledge, as evidence, is mobilized when it supports the managers' own "identity work" and when it fits with the dominant "epistemic cultures" at play in a particular community. This, of course, illustrates the point that we have made in Introduction—that knowledge is always related to the complex array of contextual and institutional conditions, so that what counts as evidence depends on the values and interests of those involved. The selective approach to using EBMgt, then, attests to the inappropriateness of assuming that it is possible to amass and transfer a set of management approaches that will be adopted across healthcare contexts, even healthcare contexts that appear to be very similar (see also Newell et al., 2003).

Chapter 2 focuses on senior healthcare managers, specifically CEOs (Chief Executive Officers) of UK NHS (National Health Service) trusts, and considers how these managers know what they need to know (which of course is indeterminate) to keep their trusts running smoothly. Here they identify the different relational practices and objects that support this ongoing knowing, in the face of huge amounts of complex information that could be accessed. Thus, again, the chapter demonstrates the selectivity of what these individuals do to keep "in the know," not systematically considering or even scanning all the sources of evidence that are potentially available, but instead exhibiting patterns of practice related to the relationships that they have cultivated and the material objects that they systematically make use of. This, therefore, means that other relationships and objects are systematically ignored, not because they could not provide potentially valuable information, but simply because they are not part of the ongoing practices of the particular individuals. These practices had emerged over time, not because of some rational plan, but rather as an outcome of a complex array of past and present doings and sayings. Of course, in the "rational" knowledge transfer literature it is recognized that people have limited attention and so have to be selective, but here we see how this selection is the outcome of emergent practice rather than a result of the cognitive limitations of the human (and material) actors involved. Knowledge mobilization then, as it relates to using evidence to make managerial decisions, exhibits the characteristics that we have outlined previously—it takes place in everyday practices, practices that are themselves nested in a wider ecology of practices, is emergent, and is socially and historically situated.

1

"Epistemic Fit" and the Mobilization of Management Knowledge in Healthcare

Gerry McGivern, Sue Dopson, Ewan Ferlie, Chris Bennett, Michael Fischer, Louise Fitzgerald, and Jean Ledger

CHAPTER SUMMARY

This chapter discusses the mobilization of management knowledge in healthcare, drawing on six qualitative case studies in a diverse range of healthcare settings. Drawing on theory about management knowledge and practices' "fit," and emergent theory about "epistemic stances," it explains how cultural/institutional, political, and epistemic fit and clashes between the norms, interests, and epistemic stances of different communities affected knowledge mobilization in these settings. It also highlights the key role of knowledge brokers in "fitting" knowledge within contexts as part of their own identity work. Yet the chapter also notes that knowledge brokers' ability to mobilize and fit knowledge depended on having a senior role or senior level support, and credibility/legitimacy with dominant communities. It suggests that the novel concepts of "epistemic fit" and "fitting" are useful in explaining the process of knowledge mobilization, particularly in complex pluralistic healthcare contexts containing multiple epistemic communities which produce, use, and value knowledge in different ways.

1.1 Introduction

What kinds of management knowledge are mobilized in healthcare, how does this happen, what supports and what inhibits this process? The traditional perspective on the diffusion and adoption of management knowledge, innovations, and practices is that they happen for rational reasons, related to their technical efficiency and advantages compared with alternatives. However, rational accounts may overlook the way innovation and diffusion happens *in practice*, often revealing more variation at organizational level, affected by a wider range of factors (Ansari, Fiss, and Zajac, 2010; Sturdy, 2004).

The concept of "evidence-based management" (EBMgt) draws on a rational perspective, advocating using the best and most appropriate management practices, as established through rational review and evaluation of knowledge, research, and evidence. EBMgt is modeled on evidence-based medicine, which is viewed as legitimate and widely practiced in healthcare. Healthcare therefore provides an important context in which to examine EBMgt (Rousseau, Manning, and Denyer, 2008; Walshe and Rundall, 2001).

Yet a rational process may not be wholly followed, even in evidence-based medicine. For instance, clinicians have been found to evaluate new clinical evidence by drawing on "mindlines," that is, internalized tacit guidelines, influenced by the opinions of their professional communities, rather than rational assessment of evidence (Gabbay and Le May, 2004). Furthermore, management is more subjective and contextually situated than clinical science, which is something the EBMgt movement has been critiqued for overlooking (Ardnt and Bigelow, 2009). This may explain why, in the limited research on the implementation of EBMgt in healthcare, few instances of "gold standard" EBMgt have been found in practice (Reay, Berta, and Kazman-Kohn, 2009). A broader perspective on the adoption and diffusion of management innovation, knowledge, and practices may be required to explain why this is so.

We draw on a recent research project (Dopson et al., 2013) examining (general and "hybrid" clinical) managers' use of management knowledge, research, and evidence, including the potential use of EBMgt, in six diverse healthcare settings. Based on our empirical findings, and building on the work of Ansari, Fiss, and Zajac (2010), we suggest that a key factor affecting knowledge mobilization is the "fit" between knowledge and the contexts in which it is mobilized.

The healthcare organizational context contains multiple professional communities with different "epistemic stances" (Chakravartty, 2011; Fayard, Gkeredakis, and Levina, 2016 forthcoming) in relation to what constitutes valid knowledge (Ferlie et al., 2005; McGivern and Dopson, 2010), and often affected by wider "epistemic cultures" (Knorr-Cetina, 1999). Accordingly, we draw attention to one aspect of fit, "epistemic fit," which we suggest is particularly important in healthcare but has so far been largely overlooked in this setting. We explain the importance of "epistemic fit" with the prevailing epistemic stances of key communities within the knowledge mobilization process, and highlight the important work of "knowledge brokers" (Dopson and Fitzgerald, 2005; Lomas, 2007) in developing epistemic fit with the healthcare context.

In Section 1.2, we review literature on the adoption, diffusion, and "fit" of management knowledge, innovation, and practices and then theory about epistemic cultures, epistemic stances, epistemic communities and boundaries, and finally knowledge brokers. Next we outline the qualitative research methods used to collect and analyze data discussed in this chapter, and then provide a brief overview of the six case studies we analyzed; an independent charitable trust providing specialist clinical services; an Academic Health Sciences Centre (AHSC); a NHS (National Health Service) Primary Care Trust (PCT); a management consultancy project in the NHS; a healthcare policy "think tank"; and a Collaboration for Leadership in Applied Health Research and Care.

We then discuss our findings, first in relation to influences on managers' use of management knowledge in general and then as demonstrated in the six case studies. Finally we explain our theoretical stance relating to "fit" and "epistemic fit" and how knowledge brokers engage in "fitting" knowledge with its context.

1.2 The Diffusion, Adoption, and "Fit" of Management Knowledge

Sturdy (2004) contrasts the rational view of the adoption and diffusion of management knowledge ideas and practices with alternatives, including political (relating to power, conflict, and interests), cultural (relating to prevailing cultures and norms), and institutional (affected by notions of and the search for legitimacy) views. Social, cultural, and institutional accounts explain how the adoption or diffusion of management knowledge and practices may depend on their social legitimacy and whether they conform to group norms, pressures, and normative cultural pressures. Political accounts show how power, politics, and the interests of those involved affect the process (Sturdy, 2004; Ansari, Fiss, and Zajac, 2010). Knowledge is "at stake," inscribed with the interests of its creators (Carlile, 2004), who need to maintain their credibility within their wider communities (McGivern and Dopson, 2010), so actors are therefore likely to mobilize knowledge reflecting their interests and resist knowledge that goes against them (Sturdy, 2004; Ansari, Fiss, and Zajac, 2010).

Ansari, Fiss, and Zajac (2010) argue that the "extensiveness" and "fidelity" of the diffusion and adoption of management practices depends on their "fit" with wider rational, cultural, and political contexts. *Rational fit* relates to practices being seen as more technically or rationally efficient or useful than alternative practices in particular contexts. *Cultural fit* relates to practices conforming to legitimate social, institutional, cultural, and group norms. *Political fit* relates to practices reflecting prevailing power dynamics and political interests. Accordingly, depending on their technical, cultural, or political fit, management practices may be extensively or narrowly diffused in ways that closely or loosely resemble their original form.

Indeed practices, knowledge, and evidence often require customization and "tailored adaptation" (Ansari, Fiss, and Zajac, 2010) to make them meaningful and suitable within specific organizational contexts (Robertson, Swan, and Newell, 1996; Dopson and Fitzgerald, 2006). Managers have been found to implement management knowledge in ways that suit their own purposes and only narrowly resemble the original ideas they were based on (Zbaracki, 1998). However, Gkeredakis and colleagues (2011) suggest that variations in the implementation of management knowledge are more commonly due to the creativity and workarounds necessary to make knowledge fit local circumstances, be practically intelligible, and workable.

Accordingly, knowledge mobilization in healthcare often relies upon "knowledge brokers" (Dopson and Fitzgerald, 2006; Lomas, 2007) who are able to make appropriate adaptations because they understand the communities involved (McGivern and Dopson, 2010; Currie, El Enany, and Lockett, 2014; Martin, Currie, and Lockett, 2011). In healthcare, such knowledge brokers may frequently be "hybrid" clinical-managers, with a clinical background working in a managerial role. Hybrid managers have been found to play a key role in mobilizing managerial knowledge and practices into healthcare contexts, often doing so as part of "identity work," aligning their personal identity, profession, and organizational contexts (Ferlie et al., 2013; McGivern et al., 2015). "Identity work" is the work of forming, repairing, maintaining, strengthening, or revising constructions that produce a coherent and distinctive sense of self, which is particularly necessary during transitions and disruptions that change actors' relations with a profession or organizational context (Sveningsson and Alvesson, 2003).

Healthcare contains a range of "epistemic cultures" (Knorr-Cetina, 1999: 1), defined as "amalgams of arrangements and mechanisms—bonded through affinity, necessity, and historical coincidence—which, in a given field, make up how we know what we know." Knorr-Cetina (1999) sees epistemic cultures as "creating and warranting knowledge," with "epistemic machinery" relating to the production of knowledge.

However, there may be variations in the influence of epistemic cultures within medical science and between clinical, managerial, and other communities in healthcare. "Epistemic clashes" (Albert et al., 2008; McGivern and Dopson, 2010) and impermeable boundaries between epistemic communities have been found to undermine knowledge mobilization and the diffusion of innovation in healthcare. Examples include boundaries between various clinical professions (Ferlie et al., 2005); clinical and social scientists (Albert et al., 2008); academics, practitioners, and policy-makers involved with healthcare (McGivern and Dopson, 2010; Swan et al., 2010); health service researchers and organization scientists (Currie, El Enany, and Lockett, 2014); and those commissioning and governing healthcare (Martin, Currie, and Lockett, 2011).

Chakravartty (2011) and Fayard, Gkeredakis, and Levina (2016 forthcoming), both drawing on the work of Van Fraassen (2002), discuss the notion of "epistemic stances," defined as "a cluster of attitudes, commitments, and strategies relevant to the generation of factual beliefs... [which] determine how agents go about making claims about the world. Stances are not believed, but adopted, held, and expressed in human action" (Chakravartty, 2011: 38). Epistemic stances are enacted attitudes toward the pursuit of knowledge, reflecting onto-epistemological beliefs, affecting whether knowledge, practices, and evidence are valued and considered worthwhile investigating and developing (Fayard, Gkeredakis, and Levina, 2016 forthcoming).

A key difference between epistemic stances and epistemic communities relates to the level of analysis. Epistemic cultures are whole fields of scientific knowledge production (like high energy physics or molecular biology), which can only be understood through extensive participation or ethnographic immersion in scientific cultures (Knorr-Cetina, 1999). Epistemic stances are more localized phenomena, which become visible in concrete situations in relation to novel problems, or the evaluation of new forms of knowledge or evidence (Fayard, Gkeredakis, and Levina, 2016 forthcoming). Therefore examining epistemic stances may be useful in the studies of specific examples of knowledge mobilization in healthcare.

Drawing on theory about the fit of management knowledge and practices, epistemic communities, boundaries, clashes, and epistemic stances, we explore six empirical case studies of management knowledge mobilization in healthcare in Section 1.5.

1.3 Research Design and Methods

We examined managers' use of management knowledge, research, and evidence (produced by management academics, "gurus," and consultants) in six healthcare settings (given pseudonyms), purposefully sampling a diverse variety of healthcare settings in order to study the impact on organizational contexts on this process. The organizations involved in the case study sites were:

- "Beechwell"—a health policy "think tank";
- "Elmhouse"—a global management consultancy;
- "Firgrove"—an AHSC;
- "Mapleshire"—a Collaboration for Leadership in Applied Health Research and Care;

- "Oakmore"—an independent charitable trust providing specialist clinical services;
- "Willowton"—an NHS PCT.

Our research study involved interrelated phases of data collection. First, we interviewed forty-five general and "hybrid" clinical managers across the six cases, all identified as having an interest in using management knowledge and research. Using semi-structured interview questions, developed from a review of literature on research utilization and knowledge mobilization (Crilly, Jashapara, and Ferlie, 2010), we explored their motivation to seek knowledge, their search strategies, sources they drew on, how they used management knowledge and research in their day-to-day work, and how their careers influenced the way they did so.

In the second research phase, we conducted six qualitative case studies (Eisenhardt, 1989; Yin, 2003; Golden-Biddle and Locke, 2007) examining how research-based knowledge was used in the different organizational settings, focused on a knowledge "tracer" derived from a management text and associated management theories. The six case studies involved a further ninety-two semi-structured interviews across the sites (making a total of 137 interviews conducted during the overall project). Interviewees were asked the same questions across the case study sites to enable comparison of findings. We collected further data through documentary analysis and observation.

Individual interview data were coded and analyzed drawing on iterative qualitative methods (Miles and Huberman, 1994; Strauss and Corbin, 1998; Eisenhardt, 1989). Case studies were organized around case narratives (Golden-Biddle and Locke, 2007; Eisenhardt, 1989), with members of the wider research team working in pairs to gather and analyze data for each case. We then compared overall case narratives (Golden-Biddle and Locke, 2007; Eisenhardt, 1989) across the six cases, interrogating data based on core project research questions. New themes, including epistemic fit, emerged from the cross-site comparison. We then explored the literature reviews to see which theories explained findings, looked at new theories, and then discussed how results might extend, develop, or refute pre-existing theory.

1.4 Research Findings: Influences on Managers' Use of Management Knowledge

During the first phase of the project we asked interviewees to complete a short survey about key influences on how they used, selected, and utilized knowledge. A previous literature review (Crilly, Jashapara, and Ferlie, 2010) suggested that managers might be influenced by personal experience, immediate communities of practice, training courses, and experiences of research, management books, and international management experts or "gurus," academic research published in journals, financial pressures, or remote group influences (e.g., norms in wider professional communities).

Our survey results suggested that managers were least likely to be influenced by academic management research, particularly academic management journals, and more oriented toward knowledge drawn from their own experiences, immediate (epistemic) "communities of practice" or research-based knowledge discovered during training courses or (particularly postgraduate) academic management studies. These suggested that knowledge mobilization is less about the *rational* evaluation of evidence and more about *personal* experience and managers' membership of particular communities.

1.5 Research Findings: The Six Case Studies of Knowledge Mobilization in Healthcare

In this section we examine the evidence in our cases relating to "fit" and "epistemic fit" and how knowledge brokers engage in fitting knowledge with its context. The first two cases, Oakmore and Firgrove, demonstrate settings where good "fit" and knowledge brokering enabled effective knowledge mobilization. In the next two, Willowton and Elmhouse, knowledge mobilization was less effective over the course of the study, with varying contextual conditions causing "clashes" as well as "fit." The final cases, Beechwell and Mapleshire, are discussed in less detail, as in these examples conditions for knowledge mobilization were unfavourable. The section ends with a summary table enabling comparison across the cases on a number of different parameters.

1.5.1 *Oakmore: An Independent Charitable Trust Providing Specialist Clinical Services*

The most successful example of knowledge mobilization we studied was in "Oakmore," an independent charitable trust providing specialist clinical services. This was an interesting example of a healthcare provider operating outside of the NHS. While affected by wider clinical epistemic cultures, Oakmore had relatively recently introduced a number of management-orientated directors and non-executive directors at board level who encouraged the acquisition and use of new forms of knowledge and innovative thinking. Thus Oakmore's epistemic stance was "open" to new management knowledge. We examined the implementation of the "balanced scorecard" (Kaplan and Norton, 1993), and related Key Performance Indicators, within Oakmore.

Oakmore's CEO (Chief Executive Officer) (and Medical Director) had a successful academic medical career but was also interested in management. The CEO can be seen as a "willing hybrid" medical-manager, engaged in transforming clinical professional norms and healthcare organizations (McGivern et al., 2015). The CEO employed people with business backgrounds at senior level within Oakmore, attempting to make the organization more "business like" and "blend" medical and managerial knowledge and ways of thinking.

A senior Oakmore manager had written their MBA dissertation about the balanced scorecard, which the CEO read and consequently became interested in implementing in Oakmore to focus staff on performance outcomes. The balanced scorecard fitted with the organizations' traditionally open and increasingly business-like epistemic stance and culture. Oakmore's CEO also had personal and professional credibility and the top job in the organization, providing referent and legitimate power, respectively (see French and Raven, 1959), to drive its implementation and persuade staff of its utility for the organization. The CEO was personally invested in using management knowledge, as part of professional identity work, and there was also a political fit between the balanced scorecard and the prevailing power, politics, and interests of the CEO and other powerful actors in Oakmore.

Thus, with cultural, political, and epistemic fit, the balanced scorecard required little adaptation in order to be successfully mobilized in Oakmore, though it should be noted that the CEO's earlier work in developing Oakmore's more business-like epistemic stance and selection of and decision to implement management knowledge that fitted with it were also essential.

1.5.2 *Firgrove AHSC*

A second case of successful knowledge mobilization was in "Firgrove," an AHSC, established by a major NHS Foundation Trust, linked to a teaching hospital and associated university. The AHSC's purpose was to transform healthcare by narrowing the gap between basic and clinical science.

The tracer for this case was a strategic initiative to build a "coaching culture" and promote "coaching conversations" in the wider AHSC, drawing on the work of Edgar Schein (1969). Firgrove was described as having an organizational culture in which people were "open" to collaboration and plural forms of knowledge. So while Firgrove's clinical epistemic stance favored rational-analytic evidence, based on hard data, it was also receptive to "softer" qualitative forms of knowledge and actively supported multiple epistemologies. Thus there was not simply a cultural and epistemic fit between Firgrove and coaching knowledge but implementing this management knowledge exemplified Firgrove's culture and epistemic stance.

A key knowledge broker in this case was a Research Director, based in Firgrove's Organizational Development Unit, who had completed a PhD drawing on Schein's ideas and was personally invested in and drove the mobilization of this management knowledge. The Research Director was supported by the university Dean and hospital CEO, who sponsored, role-modeled, and promoted coaching conversations, providing a "distributed leadership team," which has been found to underpin organizational change in other healthcare research (Fitzgerald et al., 2013; Ferlie et al., 2013). Hence we also see political fit between the mobilization of this management knowledge and the prevailing power, politics, and interests of key actors.

The Firgrove case provides another example of management knowledge being successfully mobilized into practice, requiring little adaptation, because it fitted (exemplified) Firgrove's open, innovative, pluralistic, and collaborative culture, epistemic stance, and the political agenda and interests of powerful actors. While there was perhaps technical fit between coaching cultures and Firgrove, we found less evidence of actors evaluating this knowledge/evidence to establish technical fit. We also see that knowledge mobilization was again driven by a key knowledge broker, personally invested in the knowledge and its implementation as part of their own identity work.

1.5.3 *Willowton PCT*

"Willowton" PCT was a primary care organization responsible for commissioning healthcare services for its local population. Willowton was undergoing structural change from a PCT to a Clinical Commissioning Group (CCG) during this case study.[1] Here knowledge mobilization varied as the organizational context and predominant epistemic stance changed.

We examined the mobilization of a "whole systems" learning initiative within the PCT, drawing on ideas outlined in a book written by a GP Clinical Director working for the PCT, based upon the GP's doctoral research. The book framed healthcare organizations as complex adaptive systems and accordingly advocated facilitating service improvement through organizational learning and "grass roots" involvement in change. The GP Clinical Director was heavily personally invested in whole systems thinking and the initiative and acted as the key knowledge broker in the case, initially with the support and sponsorship of the PCT CEO.

Wider clinical and medical epistemic cultures common in primary healthcare affected Willowton PCT's organizational culture and epistemic stance, but the PCT was open to multiple forms of knowledge. The whole systems learning initiative was seen to provide a solution to a problem the PCT was facing: getting disparate and independent GPs working together to improve local primary healthcare services. Thus, initially, there was cultural, epistemic, political, and (unsubstantiated claims of) technical fit between the knowledge the initiative was based on and its organizational context and objectives.

However, in the post-2008 financial crisis era, Willowton switched focus to making management cost reductions and accordingly developed a "hard" epistemic stance, valuing audit, outcome measures, and performance management. The PCT CEO, who initially supported the initiative and acted as a steward of the PCT's previous culture and epistemic stance, then left the PCT. As the initiative lost fit with the PCT's new harder epistemic stance and sponsorship from its CEO, the GP Clinical Director came under pressure to demonstrate that time and resources committed to the initiative were producing a measurable financial return. In theoretical terms, the GP was asked, for the first time, to show evidence of a technical fit between the initiative and the PCT's objectives. Adapting whole systems learning to fit the metric and short-term performance outcome-dominated organizational stance proved too difficult and the initiative was "summarily executed." Thus we see here a loss of political, cultural, epistemic, and rational fit between the initiative and the PCT.

Here, again, we see the importance of both fit between management knowledge and the prevailing culture, politics, and epistemic stance within the organization, and input from a key knowledge broker in fitting knowledge into the organization. However, in this case we also see how cultural and political contexts and epistemic stances can radically change, with the consequence that management knowledge and knowledge brokers can fall out of fit if they are unable to adapt. This case also provides an interesting example of how lack of technical fit may be used to justify the nonmobilization of knowledge that does not fit organizations in a wider range of ways.

1.5.4 *Elmhouse Consulting*

Another mixed example of knowledge mobilization was in our case study of an NHS project run by "Elmhouse Consulting," a global management consultancy. Management consultancies are increasingly drawn upon by healthcare organizations to advice on strategy and to help implement organizational change (Saint-Martin, 2004), so we were keen to examine the impact of management consultants and consulting knowledge on healthcare.

Our knowledge tracer was the implementation of an Elmhouse change model during a consultancy project in an NHS Strategic Health Authority (SHA) and associated PCTs. Elmhouse partners developed the Elmhouse model; one was working on the project we studied. The model drew on evidence from Elmhouse's previous consulting work, as well as ideas from the Partner's Business-School-based PhD. This particular Partner was therefore a key knowledge broker in the case study, although other Elmhouse consultants working on the project also played important knowledge brokering roles.

Senior SHA managers commissioned, supported, and sponsored Elmhouse to implement their model in the regional NHS with the aim of redesigning healthcare services and making major efficiency savings. Elmhouse's model was seen to have "fitted" the SHA's "strong delivery focus," "structured" approach, and "tight timescales." So there was epistemic and political fit between the Elmhouse model and the SHA's epistemic stance, culture, and interests. One SHA senior manager noted they "never saw [the Elmhouse model] as empirical evidence, it just came across as folk who knew what they were doing." So again, we saw no evidence of attempts to establish technical fit between the Elmhouse model and the SHA's objectives.

While Elmhouse's change model was readily mobilized within the SHA, there were political, cultural, epistemic, and rational clashes between the model and local PCTs. PCT NHS managers and clinicians were less concerned about Elmhouse's "high level" analysis of cost savings than the day-to-day impact of service redesign on patients and the need to develop clinical buy-in to change. The end of our case study coincided with a government announcement (Department-of-Health, 2010) that SHAs and PCTs would be abolished, with SHA and PCT managers facing losing their jobs. This complicates our ability to assess the project. However, PCT managers and clinicians appeared to struggle with understanding or accepting Elmhouse's analysis for service redesign and efficiency savings. Accordingly, while Elmhouse consultants were brokering and fitting their knowledge to the local NHS context there was some progress mobilizing the Elmhouse model; but after the project ended, and consultants left, knowledge mobilization and related service redesign stalled.

In this case we see a mix of fit and clashes between the rational, political, cultural, and epistemic stances of the groups and organizations, with variation over time. Actors focused on challenging the technical fit between knowledge and organizational context, while political, cultural, and epistemic clashes were not overtly discussed. Significant technical, cultural, political, and epistemic clashes between the Elmhouse model and its context meant that this knowledge would need to be heavily adapted to be mobilized. However, we question whether Elmhouse's model could be adapted to fit PCTs because its consultants were more focused on "persuading" clients to mobilize their model and "fixing the context" so that it was receptive to Elmhouse's epistemic stance and model. Finally, knowledge mobilization progressed more quickly while the Partner and Elmhouse consultants were brokering knowledge, but dramatically slowed when they left the client site. This is an important finding, which suggests that knowledge brokers may need to be *personally* invested in knowledge and its implementation and *permanently* embedded in the contexts in which it is mobilized.

Finally in this section, we give brief resumes of our other two cases, in neither of which was knowledge effectively mobilized.

1.5.5 *Beechwell: A Health Policy Think Tank*

"Beechwell" was a health policy "think tank" aiming to improve UK healthcare through health policy analysis, research, and leadership development. Beechwell was organized into separate divisions, with distinct epistemic stances affected by wider epistemic cultures. For example, the policy division drew on, valued, and produced "rational" academic knowledge, while the Organizational Development division was oriented to "softer" developmental knowledge, such as leadership development. We examined knowledge flows between Beechwell's divisions, using the tracer of an economic analysis of the post-2008 financial crisis healthcare context produced within the policy division.

In principle, the analysis was adopted across Beechwell as a "strategic" cross-departmental theme. In practice, the economic analysis failed to attract "natural synergy," so was not mobilized. This was largely due to limited epistemic fit and cultural differences between the policy division's analysis and the OD division. Furthermore, key actors in Beechwell, a high profile Chief Executive and Director, were oriented toward the external public rather than focused on internal issues; the absence of internal knowledge brokering also undermined mobilization of this knowledge.

1.5.6 *Mapleshire CLAHRC*

"Mapleshire" was a Collaboration for Leadership Applied Health Research and Care (CLAHRC) situated within a university research department and partnered with an NHS Trust, SHA, and a local authority. CLAHRCs were established across the UK to conduct and translate applied health research into practice to benefit patients. Mapleshire CLAHRC involved a diverse range of epistemic communities, including social science and business-school-based academics, clinical academics, and NHS practitioners, each with distinct interests and epistemic stances, affected by the wider epistemic cultures.

The tracer for this case study was the "X-change programme" (a pseudonym) encouraging involvement in the CLAHRC, sharing of data and analytical perspectives, extracting common themes from research projects and fostering communication, sharing, and spread of information. The X-change programme was based on theory about "communities of practice" (Wenger, 1998) and cultural change in the NHS (Bate, 1994). A key knowledge broker was the CLARHC's initial Director, a successful academic social scientist, with a track record in health services research.

Differences between local communities' epistemic stances and interests significantly slowed knowledge mobilization. In particular, clinical communities did not engage with the X-change programme, which drew on ideas more congruent with the epistemic stance of business school and social science academics. Low epistemic fit between the X-change programme and clinical communities undermined knowledge mobilization in this case. Finally, Mapleshire lacked a knowledge broker with a clinical background (and thus sufficient understanding of the clinical epistemic culture and interests), so accordingly was unable to adapt the X-change programme to fit the clinical epistemic stance and engage clinical communities.

In Table 1.1 we highlight and compare the key findings across the six cases: In this table we display and compare six features of our six cases: (1) the management knowledge being mobilized; (2) the main communities in the case contexts; (3) whether there was a political, cultural, epistemic, or technical fit or clash between the knowledge being mobilized and these communities; (4) the key knowledge broker in the case; (5) the knowledge broker's source of power/authority; and (6) the work the knowledge broker engage in fitting knowledge to context.

1.6 Discussion

1.6.1 *"Fit," "Epistemic Fit," and Management Knowledge Mobilization in Healthcare*

In all six case studies, we found that "fit" (Ansari, Fiss, and Zajac, 2010) between the management knowledge being mobilized and the prevailing cultures, (political) interests, and dominant "epistemic stances" (Chakravartty, 2011; Fayard, Gkeredakis, and Levina, 2016 forthcoming) in organizational contexts significantly affected knowledge mobilization. As we have noted, healthcare is a particularly complex context, containing plural professional and epistemic communities, defined and based on particular bodies of knowledge, with distinct "mindlines" (Gabbay and Le May, 2004) and epistemic stances affecting what is seen to be valid and valuable knowledge (Ferlie et al., 2005). For example, in medicine the "gold standard" of knowledge and evidence is the randomized control trial (RCT) (Timmermans and Berg, 2003) whereas in management, RCT-based knowledge is rare (Reay, Berta, and Kazman-Kohn, 2009) and even inappropriate (Ardnt and Bigelow, 2009). While acknowledging the importance

Table 1.1. Comparison of the key features of management knowledge mobilization across the six cases

	Oakmore: Charitable clinical service provider	Firgrove: AHSC	Elmhouse Consulting	Willowton PCT	Mapleshire CLAHRC	Beechwell Think Tank
Knowledge mobilized	Kaplan and Norton's "balanced scorecard"	Schein's "process consultation"	Elmhouse's organizational change model	GP Clinical Director's model of "whole systems learning" in healthcare	Wenger's "communities of practice" and Bate's cultural change model	Beechwell's analysis of healthcare quality after the financial crisis
Communities involved in case context	Clinicians, academics, and managers	Clinicians, academics, and managers	Senior SHA managers and local healthcare managers and clinicians	Primary health clinicians and managers	Clinical, social science, and business school academics, healthcare practitioners and managers	Policy analysis and leadership development
Fit or clash	Fit: Cultural, political, and epistemic fit	Fit: Cultural, political, and epistemic fit	Mix: Political, cultural, and epistemic fit with SHA; Political, cultural, epistemic, and technical clash in PCTs	Mix: Political, cultural, and epistemic fit in first time period; Political, cultural, epistemic, and technical clash in second time period	Clash: Cultural, political, epistemic, and technical clash	Clash: Cultural and epistemic
Knowledge broker	CEO and Medical Director (Personally invested in the knowledge)	OD Director (Personally invested in the knowledge)	Consultancy Partner (Personally invested in the knowledge)	GP Clinical Director (Personally invested in the knowledge)	CLARHC Director (Not invested in the knowledge in the long term)	Think Tank Director (Disinterested in knowledge mobilization)
Power and authority from	CEO role, personal and professional credibility	Hospital CEO and University Dean sponsorship	SHA CEO sponsorship	PCT CEO sponsorship, personal and professional credibility (Initially)	Director role (Lacking clinical background and credibility)	Director role
Fitting work	Hybrid CEO blending clinical and managerial knowledge to create more "business like" clinical organization	OD Director mobilizing ideas from their own PhD into organizational practice	Elmhouse persuading SHA, PCT managers and clinicians to adopt their model during a short-term project	Clinical Director mobilizing whole systems learning, drawing on ideas from their own book and MD.	Less personal and short-term mobilization (academic rather than translational focus)	Less personal mobilization (academic rather than translational focus)

of institutional/cultural, political, and, to a lesser extent, technical fit (Ansari, Fiss, and Zajac, 2010), we make a contribution by highlighting the importance of what we refer to as "epistemic fit" between knowledge and its organizational context within the knowledge mobilization process in healthcare.

In our two most positive cases of knowledge mobilization, Oakmore and Firgrove, the organizations' epistemic stances were "open" to new (including managerial) knowledge. In Oakmore, medical and managerial knowledge were "blended" to create a more performance-oriented and "business-like" healthcare organization, and the balanced scorecard fitted Oakmore's epistemic stance. Firgrove actively promoted plural epistemologies, so "coaching conversations" not only fitted but also exemplified Firgrove's epistemic stance.

Elmhouse and Willowton provided cases of mixed fit and clash and varying management knowledge mobilization over time, affected by the organizations' and their associated communities' epistemic stances and changing power dynamics. In Willowton, whole systems learning initially fitted the PCT's epistemic stance, cultural and political dynamics. However, this management knowledge then lost fit with in the post-2008 financially constrained era, and could not be adapted to fit this new organizational context. While lack of technical fit between whole systems learning and the PCT's performance objectives was ultimately used to justify pulling funding for the Initiative, we argue that this was more a consequence and function of lack of political and epistemic fit.

Elmhouse's change model fitted the SHA's epistemic stance, SHA managers' mindlines and political agenda but was not readily mobilized to the PCT. This was due to cultural, political, and epistemic clashes between Elmhouse's model and the managerial and clinical communities within the PCT. As in Willowton, we again see arguments about lack of technical fit, being used (here by PCT managers and clinicians) to challenge the mobilization of management knowledge, while lack of political, cultural, and epistemic fit was less openly discussed. Yet we suggest that the non-mobilization of this form of management knowledge was determined less by its lack of objective fit with organizational issues/problems and more by clashes with a priori political interests, institutional/cultural norms, and epistemic stances.

In Mapleshire and Beechwell, incommensurability between management knowledge and the epistemic stances of communities into which it was being mobilized fatally weakened the process. This supports the findings of previous research (Ferlie et al., 2005; Albert et al., 2008; McGivern and Dopson, 2010; Swan et al., 2010) showing how boundaries between epistemic communities can undermine innovation and knowledge mobilization.

1.6.2 Knowledge Brokers' Roles in Management Knowledge Mobilization in Healthcare

A second key finding from our cases relates to the important role of knowledge brokers in developing fit between management knowledge and organizational contexts, which echoes findings from research on the mobilization of *clinical* knowledge (Dopson and Fitzgerald, 2006; Lomas, 2007). Oakmore's CEO, Willowton's GP Clinical Director, Firgrove's Research Director, and the Elmhouse Partner all played vital roles in mobilizing management knowledge they believed fitted problems the organizations in our case studies were facing. We saw less emphasis on the "tailored adaptation" of management knowledge to fit organizational contexts as described by Ansari, Fiss, and Zajac (2010). Instead, these knowledge brokers fitted knowledge by, first, selecting management knowledge culturally/institutionally, politically and epistemically appropriate to organizational contexts, and, second, shaping the epistemic stances of the organization and associated local communities to be receptive to this knowledge.

The most successful knowledge brokers in our case studies were *personally* invested in management knowledge they were mobilizing, drawing on it to construct their sense of self and mobilizing it to transform organizational contexts as a form of "identity work" (also see Ferlie et al., 2013; McGivern et al., 2015; Fischer et al., 2015). For example, the implementation of the balanced scorecard in Oakmore reflected its CEO's "hybrid" medical-managerial identity and the more "business-like" clinical organization he was developing. Firgrove's Research Director, Willowton's GP Clinical Director, and the Elmhouse Partner had all been interested in the management knowledge they were mobilizing since doctoral studies. However, where knowledge brokers were only temporarily invested in mobilization in organizational sites the process was less effective. For example, after the Elmhouse project ended, and the management consultants left the NHS organizational site, mobilization of their change model slowed. In Mapleshire and Beechwell, where knowledge mobilization was least successful, knowledge brokers appeared neither personally nor permanently invested in the knowledge being mobilized. So management knowledge mobilization in our cases was personal, occurred indirectly through knowledge brokers, and often took time.

Management knowledge may be mobilized more on the basis of liking, trusting, and believing in knowledge brokers, than on that of understanding the knowledge being mobilized or the evidence behind it; so knowledge brokers needed personal and professional credibility. For example, some Willowton managers we interviewed struggled to articulate what "whole systems thinking" was but supported the whole systems learning initiative because they liked and respected the GP Clinical Director who was leading it. By contrast, the

Mapleshire CLAHRC Director, as a social scientist, lacked the clinical authority and credibility to influence powerful doctors to adopt the X-change programme.

Finally, knowledge brokering and mobilization requires power but also increases knowledge brokers' power where successful. For example, Oakmore's CEO drew upon hierarchical authority and professional credibility to make the organization's epistemic stance more receptive to management knowledge and to impose the balanced scorecard on it. In doing so, Oakmore became aligned with the CEO's own agenda and the CEO's power base was increased. Firgrove's OD Director, the Elmhouse Partner, and Willowton's GP Clinical Director (initially) were supported in their efforts to mobilize knowledge by CEOs in their respective organizations. However, the Willowton and Elmhouse cases show how changing structural power, loss of senior level support, and fit with dominant organizational epistemic stances affect knowledge mobilization. So epistemic fit reflects, affects, requires, and confers organizational power.

1.7 Conclusion

In this chapter we have discussed the "fit" between management knowledge and organizational context (Ansari, Fiss, and Zajac, 2010) in healthcare. Healthcare is a particularly complex context, containing plural professional and epistemic communities, defined and based on particular bodies of knowledge, with distinct epistemic stances on what is valid and valuable knowledge. Drawing on six diverse case studies of the mobilization of *management* knowledge in healthcare, we highlighted the importance of "epistemic fit" between the management knowledge being mobilized and the dominant "epistemic stances" (Chakravartty, 2011; Fayard, Gkeredakis, and Levina, 2016 forthcoming) in the sites we examined.

Knowledge brokers play a key role in mobilizing knowledge into healthcare. This has been discussed before (Dopson and Fitzgerald, 2006; Lomas, 2007), but our cases point to some novel aspects of knowledge brokering. First, the most successful knowledge brokers were *personally* invested in the knowledge they brokered and its implementation *in the long term*, so knowledge brokering can be seen as a form of identity work. Second, knowledge brokering can be understood as involving "fittingwork," developing technical, cultural/institutional, political, and epistemic fit between knowledge and context. However, in our cases knowledge brokering was less about adapting management knowledge to context than selecting appropriate management knowledge and developing organizations' epistemic stances to be "open" to it. Finally, knowledge brokering appears to rely upon the individual having power but can also provide and enhance their power. Thus, while fitting may require sufficiently sharing the epistemic stance and interests of those with most power, it can also increase knowledge brokers' power by aligning their own fit with that of their organization.

Acknowledgments

We would like to thank the National Institute for Health Research Service Delivery and Organization (NIHR SDO) program for funding this research project (ref: 08/1808/242) and the anonymous organizations and individuals who participated in it.

Note

1. PCTs were abolished following the "Equity and Excellence" White Paper (Department of Health, 2010) replaced by Clinical Commissioning Groups.

2

Objects and Monitoring Practices

Understanding CEOs' Information Work as Mundane Accomplishment

Maja Korica and Davide Nicolini

CHAPTER SUMMARY

This chapter builds on an observational study of seven top managers of sizeable healthcare organizations in England, to examine the objects and practices by which they accomplished information work and how they made themselves practically informed in their work tasks. In particular, it "zooms in" on what the CEOs oriented their attention to every day (i.e., on the objects of information work), as well as on how such information came to practically matter (i.e., on monitoring practices). It was found that rather than scanning or sourcing in largely targeted ways, executives seemed preoccupied with "keeping in the know," making informating a constant aspect of their daily activity. This capacity was achieved in mundane ways by combining a very personal assemblage of objects of information work with a number of recurrent monitoring practices. The regular employment of these objects and practices, underpinned by certain informal rationales influenced by experience and evolving practical concerns, actively constituted a personal consultative horizon that reflected CEOs' personal preferences and idiosyncrasies, but also suggested potential weaknesses.

2.1 Introduction

Perhaps one of the most basic questions in management is the following: how do managers and executives know (or come to know) what they need to know? Or, put differently, how do they keep practically informed as part of their everyday work, and, relatedly, what does this tell us about the nature of their work itself? Such questions have become more prominent in recent decades, given notable policy interest in knowledge mobilization as a means of ensuring appropriate take-up of evidence-based insights by practitioners (see Crilly, Jashapara, and Ferlie, 2010), as well as the growing evidence-based management movement, which argues that managers incorporating "good evidence" in their work is critical to ensuring positive outcomes and improving management in a meaningful way (Walshe and Rundall, 2001; Pfeffer and Sutton, 2006; Rousseau, 2006, 2012; Kepes, Bennett, and McDaniel, 2014). In spite of the acknowledged centrality of information in managerial work, however (see Mintzberg, 1973; Pfeffer and Salancik, 1978; Stewart, 1984; Penley et al., 1991), and the above-mentioned wider interest, the ways in which managers, and top executives in particular, deal with information and knowledge has received relatively little empirical attention (Auster and Choo, 1993; de Alwis, Majid, and Chaudhry, 2006; Anderson, 2008). This contrasts, for example, with the considerable attention paid by scholars and practitioners to issues such as knowledge management, organizational learning, and information management at an organizational level (Easterby-Smith and Lyles, 2011; Hislop, 2013).

Furthermore, when studies of how managers deal with information have been conducted, they tended to focus on very specific aspects, namely what sources managers use and where they direct their scanning efforts (de Alwis, Majid, and Chaudhry, 2006). This absence has been partly addressed by scholars working to advance a social approach to knowledge mobilization (e.g., Dopson and Fitzgerald, 2005; Swan et al., 2012), who have conducted detailed empirical studies bringing into question traditionally functional understandings of knowledge mobilization, with its unproblematic understanding of what counts as information or "evidence," and a linear process of informational sourcing and exchange. For instance, McGivern and colleagues (Chapter 1) conducted an in-depth, interview-based study of general and clinical managers in six healthcare settings in the UK, which highlighted the rare use of scholarly management texts by practicing managers, a high reliance on personal experience, and adaptation of "evidence" to local contexts and understandings as a necessary part of what knowledge mobilization entails in practice (see also Dopson et al., 2013). In particular, the study allowed them to advance the notion of "epistemic fit," which puts an emphasis on epistemic communities and the work of individual "knowledge brokers" in making evidence "fit" in a meaningful way across professional groups characterized by different normative understandings.

The work of top executives, as distinct organizational actors whose use of evidence could be seen to have significant impact beyond their immediate work alone, however, has not thus far received similar attention. As a consequence, we lack accounts that provide a full vista of the information work of top executives: a more comprehensive account of the various ways in which keeping themselves informed, as part of their everyday work, is accomplished. Furthermore, asking this question is particularly relevant in the context of healthcare settings, like the UK National Health Service (NHS). Such contexts are characterized by complex accountability relationships, multiple actors and professional domains, often-overlapping institutional structures, high public visibility, and intense media interest, particularly when things go wrong. In other words, they represent both exceptionally rich contexts in which to explore such activity empirically, and also settings in which, practically speaking, executives being appropriately informed may matter in particularly acute and impactful ways. The latter is evident, least of all, in the plethora of evidence-oriented publications, organizations, and fora focused on providing appropriate information to facilitate their work, from the think tank King's Fund publications and regulator reports and guidelines, to interventions by sector bodies like NHS Leadership Academy and NHS Providers (the Association of NHS Foundation Trusts and Trusts).

This gap is addressed in this chapter by building on an in-depth longitudinal ethnographic study of seven CEOs (chief executive officers) running NHS trusts in England. Employing a practice-based analytical sensitivity (Miettinen, Samra-Fredericks, and Yanow, 2009; Feldman and Orlikowski, 2011; Nicolini, 2012; Vaara and Whittington, 2012), we tackle that core question of "how do CEOs come to know what they need to know" by examining the non-linear, relational practices and mundane objects by and through which the CEOs kept themselves practically informed as part of accomplishing their work. More specifically, we consider in rich detail the following: how was the pertinent information or "evidence" of their daily information work accessed or engaged, and what kinds of information or "evidence" were or were not a feature of this work for individual CEOs observed, with what possible consequences? In other words, we explore what was the CEOs' attention oriented toward, and how were individual orientations toward certain information practically accomplished. Crucially, we suggest that these are highly related aspects of the same practice. Separating the *what* (objects of information work) from the *how* (monitoring practices) is thus an analytical distinction we make for the sake of clarity, not an expression of distinct empirical reality. Similarly, though we recognize that these two aspects, making up what is traditionally termed information "sourcing" or "scanning," are but one part of a more nuanced understanding of information work (see Nicolini, Powell, and Korica, 2014), due to limitations of space we necessarily focus here on the question of which sources, when, and how, while acknowledging this is but part of a far more complex whole.

In particular, in our study we found that the established idea of scanning, predominant in the management literature (de Alwis, Majid, and Chaudhry,

2006), captures only in part the information work of top executives. According to our observations, the main concern of the studied CEOs was instead that of *keeping "in the know"* for all the practical purposes of their day-to-day job. As such, what counted as "evidence," or relevant insight and information, was thus tightly bound with the CEOs' mundane practical concerns in situ. Put differently, the nature of the CEO's work at the time, coupled with certain priorities and tasks, and also the CEO's own distinct ways of working meant that certain sources and materialities and certain relational doings, which together made up the information work of that CEO, were made prominent and accorded most attention and practical value in specific instances. In so doing, certain other sources and ways of keeping informed were at the same time downplayed or dismissed. As a result of such practices, each CEO's ways of keeping "in the know" were notably distinct, which reflected in part the ever-changing practical concerns of their work. Notably, such an understanding of knowledge mobilization—as highly contextual, practically oriented sociomaterial practice—implies a further challenge to traditional models discussed in the knowledge mobilization literature, as we outline in the following sections.

The chapter proceeds as follows. We begin by reviewing the literature on managerial information behavior, and introduce practice-based studies as a valuable theoretical underpinning of our empirically driven contribution. This is followed by a review of our study, highlighting its rarity in observing directly and for sustained periods what executives do, rather than relying on post-hoc accounts, surveys, or diaries. We then present our findings and introduce the distinct *objects* and *monitoring practices,* which jointly accomplished the situated practices of keeping "in the know" for individual NHS CEOs.

2.2 What We Know about How Managers Deal with Information

As outlined in Section 1.2, we commence our engagement by briefly examining the literature on how managers, and particularly top executives, deal with information and knowledge. Our suggestion is that much is to be gained if we integrate the traditional approach focused on scanning behaviors and informational sources used by managers with a broader attention to the actual practices through which executives makes themselves knowledgeable, and the relational and material sites within which these practices take shape.

Historically, the interest in how managers deal with information has centered on two specific issues: strategic scanning and source preference and utilization (Abebe, Angriawan, and Tran, 2010; de Alwis, Majid, and Chaudhry, 2006). In particular, according to de Alwis, Majid, and Chaudhry

(2006), empirical research on the former has focused on three aspects: the nature of scanning processes, effects of environmental scanning on organizational strategy and performance, and environmental contingencies of environmental scanning. Regarding the latter, the question here has been "where do managers source their information, the assumption being that 'good' information leads to 'good' decision-making, so source matters?" (de Alwis, Majid, and Chaudhry, 2006: 364). Relatedly, most studies, which follow the seminal work of Aguilar (1967), found that managers' source preference has changed relatively little. Managers still use people and informal social networks to access information they need (McDonald and Westphal, 2003; Anderson, 2008), although in recent years the Internet has also assumed a prominent role (El Sawy, 1985; Trinh and Mitchell, 2009). In terms of why managers give preference to one source over another, the picture remains unclear, with some emphasizing ease of access and level of effort (Zmud, 1978; Taylor, 1986), and others highlighting source quality.

While useful in stressing the importance of such considerations, most studies in this field remain notably limited. Firstly, many still use a very narrow concept of information, namely what is transmitted between a source and a receiver as per the classical approach to information (see Buckland, 1991). This narrow view contrasts with the shift toward embracing a much more comprehensive understanding of information as "difference that makes a difference" (Bateson, 1972: 253; see Bates, 2007, 2010). The shift marks a move toward a more dynamic engagement that posits that "information" needs to be understood processually, in relation to and as part of an activity. Any distinction between information, knowledge, and evidence, for instance, is here also seen as an empirical, not an analytical, question. Secondly, many studies in the managerial literature still subscribe to an instrumental view of information. What this ignores is the complexity characterizing processes of knowledge mobilization (Rich, 1991), and other uses of information, for instance as symbols of legitimate decision-making (Feldman and March, 1981). Finally, management scholars pay scarce attention to the actual work practices of managers. When they do so (with exceptions like McGivern and colleagues highlighted in Section 1.2), they tend to consider information scanning as a well-identified activity separate from day-to-day activities. In spite of researchers lamenting the fact "that we do not understand how managers actually gather information, particularly in realistic settings" (Anderson, 2008: 52), observational studies of how managers deal with information are rare, with most existing studies based on either surveys or post-hoc accounts (Fidel and Green, 2004). As a result, we know less about what managers do, and more about what managers think is most important, what they should do, or what they believe the researcher is seeking (de Alwis, Majid, and Chaudhry, 2006: 374).

2.2.1 *The Promise of a Practice-Based Approach to Managerial Information Work*

To address this gap, we engage with practice-based studies (see overviews by Schatzki, Knorr-Cetina, and von Savigny, 2001; Nicolini, Gherardi, and Yanow, 2003; Miettinen, Samra-Fredericks, and Yanow, 2009; Vaara and Whittington, 2012; Nicolini, 2012) and their application to the field of information behavior in particular (Tuominen, Savolainen, and Talja, 2005; Savolainen, 2007; Bates, 2010). The practice-based approach focuses on the joint accomplishment of work through the organization of social interaction, and the use of supporting technologies and artifacts. Such studies urge that attention be paid to the discursive, relational, material, and contextual interactions at a given time and place, in order to understand both the rich granularity of everyday interactions and how these are informed by institutionally mandated meanings and conceptualizations (Nicolini, 2009, 2012). A practice-based orientation also embraces a view of organizational knowledge as a form of social expertise and collective knowing, situated in the historical, social, and cultural context from which it arises. Knowing is thus seen as the situated capacity to draw distinctions, exercise judgment, and decide what should be done in the current course of discursive or material action; knowing what to say and what to do manifest in practice and through practice (Nicolini, 2012). Taking such an approach implies that in management, just as in clinical work or policy decision-making, knowledge is thus necessarily "knowledge-in-practice-in context" (Gabbay and Le May, 2010). While this approach has been meaningfully engaged in the study of information and knowledge processes at an organizational level (Brown and Duguid, 2000; Orlikowski, 2002; Nicolini, Gherardi, and Yanow, 2003; Levina and Vaast, 2005; Gherardi, 2006; Feldman and Orlikowski, 2011), it has thus far remained largely absent in the study of executive managers.

As such, the practice-based approach also offers a number of guiding insights to the study of information behavior, in contrast to the traditional approaches recounted earlier. In particular, it encourages empirical studies of actual organizational environments, and of everyday, situated ways, and objects through which managers engage with information (Tuominen, Savolainen, and Talja, 2005: 338). In addition, the approach can also be mobilized to explain the preference for (and relevance of) certain sources, and how these become habitualized. For example, concepts such as "small worlds" suggest that information seeking should be examined as a dialogical and discursive co-achievement,[1] but also that what and how sources are sought and identified can only be understood as part of work practices in context (Savolainen, 2007). Above all, a practice-based approach suggests that we stop relying on second-hand, post-hoc accounts, which in this setting have revealed themselves to be particularly unreliable (Fidel and Green, 2004). Instead, it directs researchers toward observation-based studies that allow us to better appreciate situated realities, and the relational and object-based arrangements, within which information work unfolds. This is what we sought to do.

2.3 The Study

In particular, between March 2011 and May 2013 we conducted an in-depth ethnographic study of seven healthcare CEOs. The study combined shadowing of individual CEOs with interviewing and documentary analysis, with both authors involved in fieldwork and data analysis.

2.3.1 Sample

Our sample was composed of seven CEOs of acute and mental health NHS trusts in England. The CEOs managed organizations that included multiple hospitals (e.g., three large hospitals), annual budgets exceeding 500 million pounds ($800 million), and up to 10,000 staff. We chose to study these executives as their organizations sit at the crossroads between the private and public sectors, and are tasked with meeting multiple and often competing performance demands and other expectations that come with such a position. We reasoned that their informational landscapes are acutely complex, and therefore would constitute an ideal case to explore the intricacies of how CEOs deal with information daily. Although in this section we refer to the CEOs as male for reasons of anonymity, the sample included an almost even ratio of men to women (3:4). This was an intentional choice to maximize analytical diversity. For the same reason, we also selected CEOs with diverse professional backgrounds (NHS management, private sector, nursing, and medical), and at different junctures in their careers, in terms of both tenure in the present post and overall experience at CEO level. The sample also included organizations with different performance levels according to regulator indicators (e.g., financially sound vs struggling).

2.3.2 Data Collection

Our primary method was shadowing (McDonald, 2005; Czarniawska, 2007; McDonald and Simpson, 2014), which involves a researcher closely following an individual as they go about their working day, and observing as much of it as possible. This enabled us to understand the various nuances of daily information work as it happened. Executives were observed for five or more weeks each (except one, where observations lasted 3.5 weeks). We were able to document most aspects of work, other than occasional one-to-one supervisory meetings with junior colleagues, HR (human resource)-related meetings concerning individuals, and private meetings with patients. When evening or particularly sensitive events would occur, post-hoc accounts were collected. The same method was used to collect information about the work the CEOs did at home or when commuting. Field notes were taken "in vivo" using tablet computers, or shortly after when appropriate.

Such shadowing-based observations were supplemented by interviews. In particular, we conducted five formal, semi-structured interviews with CEOs toward the end of observations. They lasted between thirty-eight and sixty-five minutes, and were recorded and transcribed verbatim. The two remaining CEOs were interviewed informally, as part of daily observations. These ethnographic interviews were also transcribed and used in the analysis. In addition, we conducted two formal interviews with two different personal assistants, which were recorded and lasted approximately half an hour each. A final key source of data constituted documents, including meeting papers, articles referenced by the CEOs, and copies of publications consulted. Given the nature of each CEO's work, particularly the number of large formal meetings attended, but also the level of comfort of each CEO with regard to sharing internal documents, the number of documents gathered for each site varied greatly, from thousands of pages to approximately a hundred. These were supplemented by externally available information, like annual trust reports and regulator documents.

2.3.3 *Data Analysis*

The analysis was carried out as a reiterative, abductive process that proceeded in parallel with the study (Yanow and Schwartz-Shea, 2006; Golden-Biddle and Locke, 2007; Mantere and Ketokivi, 2013). Abductive research aims to move away from the binary of inductive versus deductive research, and is oriented instead toward "[giving] rise to speculations, conjectures, and assessments of plausibility rather than a search among known rules to see which one might best fit the facts" (Weick, 2005: 433). In particular, we first worked independently. In line with the abductive openness toward analytical surprises (see Locke, Golden-Biddle, and Feldman, 2008), no set analytical categories were identified prior to fieldwork. Both of us regularly read and reflected on their field notes, including before each return to the field, and wrote analytical notes. These were eventually converted into extended analytical memos, which synthesized emerging insights and enabled cross-case comparative analysis. We then moved to the joint analysis. We worked inductively, interrogating the data for emergent contents and interactional patterns, and recursively going back and forth between transcripts, original recordings, and field notes (Yanow and Schwartz-Shea, 2006). We jointly developed a list of emerging first- and second-order analytical categories. This was discussed and refined through regular meetings. In addition, members' validation further informed and enriched the analysis (Sandelowski, 1993), via consultations with the project's scientific Advisory Panel, the feeding back of provisional results individually to participant CEOs, and two policy workshops attended by fifteen current or former CEOs.

2.4 The Information Work of CEOs: Objects in Practice

The first aspect of acquisition or sourcing work, as our particular focus here, that we suggest is meaningful to consider in order to comprehensively understand managerial information work in situ is, "*what* are the sources of information or 'evidence' that are accessed and brought to bear by observed NHS trust CEOs in order to accomplish their everyday work?" As a framework for a more detailed discussion to follow, Table 2.1 summarizes the major reported sources of external information in particular, and the reasons why each was seen as more or less pertinent by the CEO.[2]

Importantly, as Table 2.1 demonstrates, the CEOs did not only cite written documents or publications as a key source of relevant information. Events, like Institute of Directors (IoD) seminars and meetings of groups of CEOs, but also people, like management consultants, and the informal network of "people of integrity" used by a mental health (MH) CEO, were highly pertinent. Indeed, what quickly became apparent, once we compared the interviews with our observations, was that CEOs consulted more different sources of insight than the evidence-based or traditional knowledge mobilization movement would suggest. These included some sector publications based on evidence, like King's Fund reports, but also "gossip" emails, "quirky little meetings" with external organizations without immediate relevance, sessions with personal coaches, and informal phone calls with a former Action Learning set, to name but a few.

Equally of interest, however, were also the notable absences with regard to CEOs' external sources of information. In particular, we recorded only one reference to NHS Evidence (NHSE) as the epitome of a gateway enabling evidence-based practice in healthcare. We also did not observe any CEOs consulting scholarly journals, with the exception of the *Harvard Business Review* (*HBR*), which aims to simplify and filter scholarly work for easier "consumption." Equally, with the exception of one particularly learning-oriented CEO,

Table 2.1. External sources of information consulted by CEOs (via interviews, supplemented by observations; in no particular order)

CEO of Large Acute	CEO of Medium Acute	CEO of Large Acute	CEO of Small Acute	CEO of Medium MH	CEO of Medium MH	CEO of Large Acute
Harvard Business Review ("for leadership issues")	Health Service Journal (HSJ)	Internal IT system (Organizational strategy based on "accurate, timely information"; allows managing on "factual basis")	FTN pieces and summaries ("I'll always read those")	NHS Confederation pieces	Today Programme, Radio 4 (every morning, "consciously started the day reflecting on […] the main headline story and then that's helping frame […] the kind of wider system")	Local newspapers (PA marks health stories with post-its)
The Week, the Month ("just to sort of make sure I've got a sense of the world out there")	Strategic Health Authority meetings (with fellow CEOs)	Ward visits ("If you want to see what's happening on the ground…")	Legal firms ("they do good summaries")	HSJ reports	Local CEO group ("incredibly valuable source of data" regarding policy and comparative standing)	Radio (on in the background in the mornings)
Health Service Confederation abstracts ("useful")	HSJ journalist (gains insights while correcting a trust-related story)	HSJ ("flick through once a week")	SHA event on quality (normally good speakers)	FTN documents	"People of integrity" (e.g., a chair of a networking group; "gives me the flavor of what's the politics like in the system")	Books
The Association of UK University Hospitals ("very useful source")	BBC News digest	FTN, NHS Confederation, AUKUH pieces ("I'll skim through it")	"Maintenance stuff" (e.g., Monitor, FTN, Care Quality Commission) ("because you need to keep up to date")	SHA correspondence	HSJ ("what it tells me is not the truth but what current powers that be in the NHS think and do […] I don't necessarily think that's the real world")	Health Investor
The Times	Management consultants	The Week and the Month ("send it around my team and assume one of them will flash things up, I don't read it")	"Work-specific stuff" (e.g., "wanting to bone up on M&A")	Websites ("I tend not to look at a lot of websites unless I'm chasing something specific")	Health Investor, NHSmanagers.net ("it's challenging to any status quo")	Reports (e.g., annual report of the National Hip Fracture Database)

Monitor and Foundation Trust Network ("less useful… I need to know what they're up to but doesn't have so much resonance […], doesn't help me in my world")	*Books* (e.g., Atul Gawande's *The Checklist Manifesto*)	*Particular group of trust CEOs* ("I'd get better information out of that")	*HSJ* ("just sort of a scandal rag and I actually didn't find the professional articles particularly enlightening")	*IoD events and other talks* (e.g., CEO of Tesco) ("I get some of my know-how through them")	*Harvard Business Review* ("prompts me to think about my management practice as a manager")	*HSJ* (via the website, frequently)
HSJ ("increasingly irritated…just tabloid journalism for me")	*Articles* (e.g., by Kaplan on how to solve cost crisis in healthcare)	*Slides from external sources* (e.g., Department; wordy, unclear, so difficult to follow through)		*Books* (e.g., Jack Welch autobiography)	*Regulator websites* ("I often scan Monitor, just to see and I do look at the benchmarking data and I'm very often on CQC")	*Twitter* (useful for keeping up to date)
Additional sources: NHS Confederation summaries, King's Fund report, SDO documents (part of "train pile"); Documents from NHS Confederation annual meeting; management consultants, etc.	**Additional sources:** NHS Institute documents (e.g., Helen Bevan slides on change); one-to-one phone calls with network of peers; Department of Health email digest, etc.	**Additional sources:** Emails, national meetings, phone calls with colleagues, etc.	**Additional sources:** External meetings (e.g., with PCT cluster head, Clinical Commissioning Group (CCG), NHSE, management consultants, solicitor, phone calls with regulator, etc.	**Additional sources:** *Harvard Business Review*, *HSJ*, site visits, visits to other CEOs, etc.	**Additional sources:** Other trust websites, *Guardian* "Society" section, Management Focus, SHA data (anything benchmarking related "quite useful"), events (e.g., The National Institute for Health and Care Excellence); "quirky little meetings" at local Council, CCG events, coach, etc.	**Additional sources:** Emails, *Guardian* "Health Network" section, LinkedIn discussion boards, FT Development Agency folder, informal Action Learning set, blogs, talks with Chair, etc.

whose steady organizational context enabled dedicated time for exploratory sourcing, we observed few instances of CEOs accessing external guidelines and processing these themselves. More commonly, if these were accessed, they were distributed to other staff as part of an ongoing conversation, for them to mobilize further. Similarly, management scholarship was rarely referenced, with the exception of the same CEO, who mentioned a piece of research as "good emerging evidence" regarding how medics and managers learn differently. Notably, this insight was originally obtained via a conversation with a colleague, rather than the CEO reading the actual study. In line with work of McGivern and colleagues (Chapter 1), as well as others, this again brings into question evidence-based movement's reliance on external, written, research-based, directly accessed information as the sole "evidence" appropriate for "best practice" sourcing. As we found, everyday practices of NHS CEOs reveal a much more complex and multifaceted picture.

A key part of this more nuanced picture was the various criteria we observed being employed to judge a source or insight as more or less relevant. In particular, what struck us was the greatly differing bases for decision-making, which reflected both practical concerns at that moment given the task at hand, and also personal preferences for accessing information. For instance, as one acute trust CEO noted, "[regarding Monitor and Foundation Trust Network, they are] less useful...I need to know what they're up to but it doesn't have so much resonance [...], it doesn't help me in my world." Here, the CEO saw Monitor and FTN as less pertinent because they "don't help [him] in [his] world." In other words, because there is little perceived contextual relevance, the information itself was simply irrelevant. Similarly, an MH CEO commented elsewhere that he visited websites mostly as part of a specific search, depending on the task. In his words, "I tend not to look at a lot of websites unless I'm chasing something specific." In other words, the particular context and task at hand mattered greatly in determining whether a source was accessed or information considered as potentially germane.

Indeed, as we will see in Section 2.5, different sources of information were accessed at different times, for different purposes, and toward different ends. Notably, experience played a significant role regarding what sources CEOs found useful and accessed regularly. As one MH CEO noted, "I think it's quite limited, my sources of information. [...] And I suppose I've honed it over the years." We observed that CEOs learned over time what sources "worked for them," and tended to rely on a "trusted few" making up their particular approach to keeping "in the know." Though CEOs did reflect on these and change or adjust them as they went along, we saw that certain sources appeared simply as "theirs": always consulted, like a habit. The twin matters of purpose and experience are important because a key suggestion of the

Objects and Monitoring Practices

evidence-based movement is that the take-up of "evidence" is chiefly determined by the inherent qualities of the "evidence" itself, most notably its scholarly credentials, format, and perceived timeliness. Instead, we observed CEOs judging sources more or less relevant for many different reasons, all of which contributed toward a personal "ranking" making up a CEO's own preferred consultative horizon. *How* then was sourcing accomplished, as the necessary other side of this information work coin, is therefore what we turn to next.

2.5 The Information Work of CEOs: Monitoring Practices

Having therefore considered the distinct sources consulted (or not) by CEOs in their daily work, we next detail their varied practices of making themselves "in the know" in order to accomplish their work. In particular, we found that this transpired through four types of sociomaterial activities (which we call *monitoring practices*): practices of intentional seeking for specific information; practices of deliberate monitoring; practices of undirected heedful monitoring; and unanticipated finding.

2.5.1 *Monitoring Practices: CEOs as Information Seekers*

We noticed that CEOs occasionally did indeed occupy themselves with *actively seeking* specific pieces of information as suggested in the literature, as also mentioned earlier. The time devoted to seeking was, however, very limited, and intentional information-seeking was rare. Active information-seeking was usually prompted by the emergence of a specific problem or in view of a specific need (for example, making a decision). As an acute trust CEO noted in an interview, "I mean, there's a maintenance job to be done, isn't there, making sure you're professionally up to date but then there might be a specific job of work to be done and for me it's, you know M&A [mergers and acquisitions], where I'll say okay, if there's something coming up, [I'll attend an event specifically on that issue]." The direct search for information was thus typically supported by three sub-tasks. First, in few, rare occasions CEOs actively searched for information themselves. This was done during quiet times, after meetings or in evenings. More often, however, the CEOs operated by proxy. The CEO would walk out of his room, wander to a collaborator's office and ask them if they could "take a look" or "find out for me about this." Finally, a third practice was for the CEO to mobilize his network. In this case, the intentionality was not in seeking information, but rather in seeking the source that could satisfy the need.

2.5.2 Deliberate and Non-Directed Heedful Monitoring

As we noted in Section 2.5.1, however, conventional seeking occupied a small part of CEOs' time. Most often, they were engaged in the mundane "background" of daily work, until some exception or anomaly was detected; that is, until some piece of information was considered as a "difference that makes a difference" (Bateson, 1972). In particular, our observations suggested that CEOs then engaged in two types of monitoring practices with different levels of intentionality and premeditation: deliberate monitoring, and heedful, non-directed monitoring.

Deliberate monitoring was associated with a number of familiar organizational practices, like overview of key performance indicators, and periodic review meetings. For example, one CEO consulted his corporate information system first thing in the morning to check how the organization was doing against key performance indicators. Similarly, all the organizations studied featured a plethora of highly ritualized events like weekly team meetings, monthly board meetings, and individual monitoring conversations. The monitoring effect was obtained by a mix of temporal periodicity (if you talk about the same thing every week, variations become immediately noticeable); linguistic practices (most such meetings started with temporal accounts of "what happened since we last met"); and tools (documents and graphs to demonstrate a before/after effect). A typical technology used during these meetings (apart from one organization where electronic reporting was particularly advanced) was the "exception report," which was used both to monitor progress and to focus attention in the interest of time ("green" issues were often skipped). One characteristic common to all such occasions was that information emerging from and discussed in such settings was often broader and only parenthetically linked to its declarative scope. For example, during a performance management meeting with the Financial Director, the CEO "deviated" from the supposed task to encourage the Director to present a frank and comprehensive state of their strengths (and weaknesses) with regard to financial performance.

This tendency of monitoring to emerge from unplanned sources was especially evident in the third set of practices, whereby the CEOs gathered information while *heedfully participating* in activities that ostensibly had other objectives. As one acute trust CEOs put it, "what I do is I attend meetings that I've been booked into [...] and I use that as another data source... But the really valuable bit for me is being in a room with peers and just chatting about what your current issue is, and then you get a real sense of where we sit, as kind of benchmarking data." Such meetings thus served a variety of purposes, as an information opportunity and an "informational ground" (see Pettigrew, 1999: 811). Indeed, all CEOs engaged in and even engineered a number of events that they knew from experience could become useful

Objects and Monitoring Practices

information grounds. For example, they made a deliberate effort to chair internal events and occasions, participate in all sorts of national forums, and speak at meetings and public events, and often chaired them, which implied extra work. This was done for the dual purpose of both raising their personal and institutional profile, and collecting information because these occasions often became great opportunities for doing so (occasionally purposeful, but mostly as a unidirectional process). As we were told repeatedly, the most useful aspect of these events was often "the informal chats before and after the formal meetings and in between presentations."

An ordinary yet critical means employed by CEOs, which facilitated such practices internally, was to operate an "open doors policy," as well as to engage its counterpart—"popping by" unannounced to other people's offices. The policy, often institutionalized through specific conventions (e.g., "door open" means "feel free to come in"; "door ajar" means "do not disturb") actively turned the CEOs' offices, their doorways, and the spaces immediately outside into critical information grounds, where significant information work was carried out. Interestingly, keeping the door open not only operated as an authorization to enter, but often acted as an invitation, even an injunction. Another common activity that sustained heedful monitoring as a practice was arranging walkabouts and visits to the "front line." One of the CEOs, for example, devoted a few hours a week to work in the wards as a way to staying in touch with staff, but also to capture information that would have been otherwise filtered by the organizational hierarchy.

Finally, all CEOs also engaged in other forms of heedful monitoring. These included browsing the press and listening to the news (mostly a range of habitual outlets), using social media, and remaining open to information. As one acute trust CEO told us, "I use Twitter to keep up-to-date [...]. If you follow the right people you'll see most of the news coming through. And if there are articles in the broadsheets, someone will post the link to them on. You could miss one Tweet of course about a specific article but if it's causing a bit of noise you always see it. So yeah, I find that very good for keeping up to date." Twitter was thus a way to gather information without any particular need or goal in mind. CEOs often replicated such postures in personal encounters. They would do so at any possible opportunity by steering even the most ordinary social conversation (e.g., meeting someone while walking to the coffee shop or in the corridor) in this direction by using relatively mundane, but powerful discursive devices, such as "Good to see you! How are you? And what is new?"

2.5.3 Finding Unexpectedly

Finally, openness toward information and surprise characterized our fourth and final type of monitoring practice, which we call *unanticipated finding*. This somewhat residual category covers all the occasions when CEOs encountered information in the course of a seemingly unrelated working task. Examples would include overhearing conversations in public spaces, hearing "gossip" while fetching a coffee, or noticing things while walking to a meeting. Holidays and time off were also occasions when CEOs would pick up information that they had not solicited or expected, but that presented itself to them, or that others felt appropriate to share. One CEO, for instance, told us that the idea of service improvement came while walking through a village on holiday.

In summary, our observations suggest that monitoring conducted at different levels of focal awareness was pervasive in the work of the CEOs we studied. In many ways, the CEOs never switched off: work was information work, and information work was work. Rather than representing a distinct stand-alone task, monitoring as part of information work thus constituted a central dimension of everything they did. We thus termed the practice through which CEOs carried out their information work "monitoring practices," rather than seeking or scanning, to underscore that the overall preoccupation and goal was not that of responding to a question or making a decision as traditionally framed, but satisfying specific practical need of *keeping "in the know"* in order to accomplish work. Our analysis is summarized in Table 2.2.

To this end, it is important to note that our distinction between monitoring practices was introduced for analytical purposes only. Most of these in fact served multiple purposes and often took place at the same time. For instance, even when seeking something specific, CEOs frequently ended up finding pieces of information that they could use for purposes that exceeded those originally implied. Two things in particular struck us about these. First, they were mostly relational and discursive in character. Second, the practices, or mix of practices, we observed were fundamentally different from those assumed in many of the normative texts in the decision-making and evidence-based literature. In particular, contrary to the prevailing romance of leadership depicting CEOs like heroic captains, while CEOs occasionally actively and purposively sought information, this was an exception rather than the norm. CEOs are thus better described as gatherers of scattered insights and cultivators of information gardens they have grown in particular ways, rather than sole hunters of distinct pray.

2.6 Discussion and Concluding Thoughts

In this chapter, we adopted a practice-based approach (Schatzki, Knorr-Cetina, and von Sevigny, 2001; Nicolini, Gherardi, and Yanow, 2003; Miettinen, Samra-Fredericks, and Yanow, 2009; Nicolini, 2012) to study of information work of CEOs in the English NHS. In particular, unlike McGivern and

Table 2.2. Accessing information as part of keeping "in the know": A summary of key practices, including relations and objects

Monitoring Practices	Most Frequent Related Information	Most Observed Activities	Most Influential Relations (With and through Whom?)	Most Used/Relied upon Objects (With the Mediation of What Tools?)
Intentional Problem-Driven Information Seeking (seeking specific information to satisfy a clear need or problem; information seeking as focal task)	– External reports on key strategic issues (e.g. mergers and acquisitions) – Expert views on how issues should be approached (e.g. phone call to lawyers)	– Individual search (rare) – Delegating – Establishing contacts with an expert/friend	– Close collaborators (members of the TMT or executive staff) – PA – Immediate personal network (old colleagues, professional friends)	– Ad-hoc reports – Internet – Phone – Email
Deliberate Monitoring (gathering information on the state of the organization and its environment)	– Internal operational info (e.g., exception reports) – Informal, verbal insights from senior executives	– Periodic internal meetings – Monitoring key performance indicators – Review meetings – one-to-one conversations	– TMT – Personal network – Chair of the board of directors and other Non-executive director	– Company reporting system/dash board (paper based vs online) – "Train pile" of readings compiled by PA
Heedful/Non-Directed Monitoring (gathering general information within purposively accessed information grounds but without a clear need or problem to solve)	– Informal "benchmarking data" regarding how the organization compares – Verbal information and "gossip" from internal and external sources, often during events – "How things really are"	– Conversations – "Open door" and "popping by" – Creating expectations – Attendance to institutional events/conferences – Visits and travel to other institutions/abroad – Walkabouts (wards, services) – Newspaper browsing	– Other CEOs (individually or in organized groups) – Chair of the board of directors – Consultants – Governors (members of public) – Patients	– Email – Internet – Social media (scarce) – Publications (rare)
Unanticipated Finding (encountering information while pursuing a different task)	– Informal insights – Reports (at an external conference stand, Twitter) – Verbal reports	– Informal conversations – Byproduct of sending emails or browsing the Internet – Gossip – Mental and material notes	– All stakeholders	– External events (documentation sourced there)

colleagues (Chapter 1), who focused on epistemic communities as collective relational settings in which "evidence" is given particular meaning, we focused on the mundane work through which individual CEOs gathered, engaged with, and made relevant distinct information. We found that such processes, which are frequently portrayed as psychological, are in fact the result of a number of observable sociomaterial practices. Specifically, *information work*, the generic name we have given to this type of activity, transpires through a number of relational doings, including distinct *monitoring practices*, which are carried out in relation to distinct *objects of information work*, including specific sources of attributed significance.

In particular, our findings coincide with the observations of other scholars who foregrounded the centrality of information work in CEO jobs (e.g., Gioia and Chittipeddi, 1991; Weick, Sutcliffe, and Obstfeld, 2005; Nag and Gioia, 2012). We suggest, however, that the traditional idea that when it comes to information behavior CEOs are mainly or most importantly scanners is an over-simplification. Scanning assumes a strong intentionality on part of executives. It also implies that information is collected in view of its utilization, either immediate or "for future courses of action." Our data suggests, however, that the time devoted to actively seeking information was quite limited. CEOs rarely went to events or meetings with an explicit, single-objective-focused "finding out" intent. Further, the "finding out" appeared closely related to a distinct form of information, namely a report on or specific insight into a distinct topic of present interest. Indeed, certain modes or orders of monitoring practices were often oriented toward certain objects of information work, like reports on M&A, which were actively sought by an acute trust CEO about to commence such a process in his organization. Such active seeking practices, however, made up a small part of the CEOs' information work. Instead, the CEOs' attention was always "on," via different monitoring practices, in relation to a broader vista of what constituted information and evidence as "what matters or could matter." Through such distinct practices, CEOs thus performed certain ways of being (and remaining) practically knowledgeable in order to accomplish their daily work.

Our observations thus suggest that the main preoccupation of CEOs was keeping oneself *"in the know"* for all the possible requirements of the job at hand. This preoccupation, which permeated all moments of their working day, descended directly from a central feature of their job, that is, their being accountable for the effective running of their organization. As one CEO nicely put it, "the worst thing for a CEO is to find yourself asking after the fact: how could this happen without me knowing?" In this sense, our findings corroborate and substantiate the speculative intuition put forward by Feldman and March (1981: 182), who suggested that most managers operate in a surveillance, rather than a decision, mode.

As such, it could be argued that CEOs are, at the everyday level of "keeping in the know," much like other managers. Though our empirical focus on CEOs alone does not allow us to provide first-hand comparative insight, we would argue, however, against the suggestion that there is nothing qualitatively different about the work of CEOs compared to other managers. In particular, our analytical focus here has placed in the background the intensity of the activity which comes with the CEO's role as the "nerve centre" of organizations, and also the considerable external and internal accountability demands placed on CEOs as accountable officers. The latter implies that failing to "keep in the know" is not just potentially an operational problem, but also an occasion for intense public scrutiny and regulatory involvement. Put differently, more than other managers within their organizations, healthcare CEOs in the NHS are *expected* to "be in the know," and often in particular ways (see, for instance, King's Fund, 2011). This means that while the constitutive everyday activities by which this is accomplished may be different, the practices are not. This is because practices are more than "just doing." They are instead situated activity in relation to distinct aims, tools, multiple negotiations, meaningful others, and varied social and historical conditions within which such activity unfolds (Sandberg and Tsoukas, 2011; Nicolini, 2012; Schatzki, 2012).

Relatedly, the shift from scanning to *keeping "in the know"* is much more than a mere semantic trick. The idea of keeping "in the know" suggests in fact that information work is less a mental activity and more, in line with the practice-based approach we suggest, something that the CEOs do with others and among a carefully choreographed array of things, in relation to distinct, at times habitual sources and objects of information work. It also underscores that such work is part and parcel of their daily activity, and a tacit skill developed in distinct ways. As we have argued in detail elsewhere (see Nicolini, Korica, and Ruddle, 2015), this practically means that CEOs can also work to continually adjust their practices to match their constantly evolving needs, through a reflective and structured process, rather than relying on habitual practices and sources which may no longer be appropriate to their work at present. Finally, it necessarily also highlights the wide range of insights which constituted the "difference that makes a difference," that is, relevant information in the work of CEOs. This is in contrast to the traditional evidence-based management focus on published "evidence" as most meaningful. Indeed, in line with other colleagues exploring knowledge mobilization as social practice (Swan et al., 2012; Dopson et al., 2013), including McGivern and colleagues (Chapter 1), our findings add to growing questions regarding evidence-based management's prevailing models, premised on the idea that positive consequences will ensue if managers make organizational decisions informed by research, rather than relying on personal experience only (see Baba and HakemZadeh, 2012; Rousseau, 2006; Walshe and Rundall, 2001). Our study offers instead a more complex and perhaps nuanced picture, which recognizes that while such sources are made useful in practice by CEOs in particular ways, toward particular practical concerns, they are but one source, way, and concern making up the broader practical-oriented of each CEO keeping "in the know" every day.

Disclaimer: The views and opinions expressed therein are those of the authors and do not necessarily reflect those of the HS&DR Programme, NIHR, NHS, or the Department of Health.

Acknowledgments

This project was funded by the National Institute for Health Research (NIHR) Health Services and Delivery Research (HS&DR) Programme (project number 09/1002/36) [the chapter draws in part on the empirical material contained in its final report published in 2014].

Notes

1. Small worlds have been defined as social environments where individuals live and work, bonded together by shared interests, and where everyday information seeking and sharing is oriented by generally recognized norms (Burnett, Besant, and Chatman, 2001).
2. While this was possible for some sources, for others we were merely able to observe their use (or not) as part of everyday work. In other words, we were not always able to detect the specific relevance as understood and given by each CEO to distinct sources.

Theme 2
Developing Organizational Capabilities for Knowledge Mobilization

Introduction

While the previous section focused on managers, this section focuses on organizations as the domain of action. Thus, the quality of healthcare depends on the ability of organizations to learn, in order to not repeat mistakes and to improve practices where there is scope for this. This section, then, examines how healthcare organizations develop and sustain capabilities, including absorptive capacity (the ability to acquire knowledge from outside the organizational boundary and learn from this knowledge) and generative spaces (the ability to form spaces where practitioners can learn from each other), that enable those involved to acquire, share, and use knowledge to improve learning that can help to support service delivery. A particular aspect of this need to learn relates to the importance of working more collaboratively, both within a particular healthcare organization (e.g., specialists from different backgrounds working together in a hospital setting), and across healthcare organizations (e.g., healthcare commissioners working with hospitals, GP (general practitioner) services, and social services). What is clear from the two chapters in this section is that organizational learning may not "just happen," but, on the other hand, that it can be encouraged by managerial efforts that support the development of capabilities (coordination capabilities in the words of Croft and Currie, Chapter 3) and create an environment (a space, in the words of Reay et al., Chapter 4) that will facilitate learning. This involves more than just getting people to come together; it also involves generating the emotional energy that will encourage people to want to contribute, for example, through conversations that can promote new ideas for working more effectively together.

Even from this brief introductory paragraph to this theme, it should be clear that, while the focus is on organizational learning, this is nested within the domain of action of individuals (managers and other practitioners) with their particular, and sometimes conflicting, goals, interests, and aspirations. However, to consider only this individual-level agency is insufficient to do justice to the findings that are evident in the two chapters that follow. Rather, the different organizations that are "at-play" in the particular settings of interest—including their histories, cultures, structures, and processes—influence the practices that we see emerging that either restrict or afford the organizational learning that is achieved. This is why it is essential to focus on the organizational domain of action, rather than simply the individual.

An important issue that is highlighted in the two chapters that follow is that developing capabilities that promote knowledge mobilization is not a one-off effort, which once established will last forever. Rather, developing learning capabilities is an ongoing accomplishment that requires continuous effort—it requires ongoing practice. Any of us who have learnt but then not practiced a skill (like playing the piano) will understand this, since once we return to play after a few years, we will most certainly not be able to do so at the level of skill we had reached previously. And just as this is the case for our own individual learning, it is also the case for organizational learning.

The idea that a capability needs to be developed and sustained over time is first taken up in Chapter 3. The authors apply the concept of "absorptive capacity," which relates to an organization's ability to take new ideas from beyond its own boundary and integrate these ideas with existing organizational knowledge to create new products, services, or processes that can improve performance. Absorptive capacity, as traditionally used, aligns very much with the knowledge as possession view, discussed in Introduction. In Chapter 3, however, absorptive capacity is viewed as an ongoing practice of translation rather than as a simple process of transferring knowledge from the outside to the inside. And just as all the other chapters, the chapter considers this particular aspect of knowledge mobilization in relation to a specific context—here in relation to commissioning service initiatives that are aimed at preventing hospital admissions of older people who could be better looked after elsewhere. In examining this issue, the chapter considers how the unique healthcare context impacts the particular capabilities that influence the absorption of external knowledge. For example, the highly defined regulatory environment of healthcare leads systems capabilities narrowly focused on ensuring compliance with rules and standards, while the professional demarcations that are strongly entrenched in healthcare settings negatively influence socialization capabilities. These limitations of systems and socialization capabilities, in turn, negatively influence the access to and utilization of external knowledge. On the positive side, however, the study does show how certain social networks can counter-balance these limitations in absorbing new knowledge. More specifically, it demonstrates how links between commissioning agencies and both GPs and patients, which help to bolster coordination capabilities, can provide some counter-balance to the more limited systems and socialization capabilities. This is because this type of coordination capability provides access to local, experiential knowledge that is otherwise absent, leading commissioning agencies to make decisions that are not suited to the specific needs of the population they are designing services for.

The importance of building connections between people who can then share with each other is also illustrated in the Chapter 4, which identifies three different outcomes from a common initiative to promote inter-organizational learning communities. All three initiatives started off with good intent (as well as with some legacy resentments between the different organizations involved—policy makers and healthcare practitioners) but not all managed to sustain the initiative and, indeed, in some of the cases the initiative "went toxic." And while they did not show this, it is also possible that some of the cases that they describe as "generative" could easily dissolve and become "inert" if not "toxic" if those involved do not continuously work to promote the conditions (the space) that facilitate learning and knowledge mobilization. Thus, in this chapter the authors stress "the importance of managers' hands-on and relatively continuous attention to positive social relationships." This illustrates the point that knowledge mobilization does not just happen and is not a one-off event; rather it is a practical accomplishment that must be continuously re-enacted to foster the ongoing learning that will support an organization's ability to sustain improvement into the future. This chapter also emphasizes the importance of building spaces that encourage networking across different communities. The importance of networking, as a specific form of agency implicated in mobilizing knowledge, is taken up more centrally in the chapters in Theme 3. Next we turn to the two chapters that illustrate the importance of different types of organizational capability and their influence on knowledge mobilization.

3

Enhancing Absorptive Capacity of Healthcare Organizations

The Case of Commissioning Service Interventions

Charlotte Croft and Graeme Currie

CHAPTER SUMMARY

Knowledge mobilization occurs within overlapping processes, which can be conceptualized as acquisition, assimilation, transformation, and exploitation. These processes are influenced by combinative capabilities. Systems capabilities, that is formalized data sets/ IT system, can limit the type of knowledge acquired and used to guide service interventions. Socialization capabilities, represented by power differentials between professional groups, can limit knowledge sharing between more and less "credible" groups. Coordination capabilities can overcome barriers of systems and socialization capabilities, encouraging more flexible approaches to the four stages of knowledge mobilization. In particular, this chapter highlights the importance of clinician involvement in knowledge mobilization in healthcare settings, and identify the untapped potential of patient involvement, which could further enhance knowledge mobilization.

3.1 Introduction

The quality of services delivered by healthcare organizations is improved when the organizational capacity for knowledge mobilization is developed, encouraging the integration of diverse forms of knowledge (Damanpour and Schneider, 2009; Moynihan and Landuyt, 2009; Salge, 2011; Salge and Vera, 2009, 2012). However, within complex healthcare settings, whilst different forms of knowledge may be acquired, its use in driving quality improvement is limited (Berta et al., 2010; Easterby-Smith et al., 2008;

Ferlie et al., 2012; Harvey et al., 2010; Walshe et al., 2009). This challenge can be conceived as the "absorptive" capacity of an organization to acquire and utilize knowledge (Cohen and Levinthal, 1990). Absorptive capacity conceptualizes knowledge mobilization as occurring within four non-linear, overlapping processes: acquiring information; assimilating or analyzing that information to make it relevant to the setting; transforming information into service design; and exploiting knowledge by scaling up services, or by altering services to improve quality (Cohen and Levinthal, 1990; Zahra and George, 2002).

Whilst developed in private sector settings, there has been recent application of the absorptive capacity concept in healthcare settings to offer insight into how organizations can improve service interventions by enhancing knowledge mobilization processes (Berta et al., 2010; Easterby-Smith et al., 2008; Ferlie et al., 2012; Harvey et al., 2010; Salge and Vera, 2012; Walshe et al., 2009). Our study offers an empirical departure from those previously carried out by focusing not on healthcare providers, responsible for delivery of services, but upon absorptive capacity of healthcare commissioners, who plan and budget for healthcare services. Readers might note that recent reforms in the English NHS (National Health Service) mean the central government budget for healthcare is not allocated directly to healthcare providers, but instead to commissioners, who negotiate with healthcare providers on funding for existing services and new services. These commissioners are locality-based, typically covering 500,000 potential patients, and are called "Clinical Commissioning Groups" (henceforth referred to as CCGs), which bring together a wide range of stakeholders in a commissioning network consisting of various professionals, managers from different organizations, and patient representatives. Commissioners' ability to acquire and utilize knowledge to inform the planning and budgeting of healthcare services is crucial in ensuring a healthier population in England, but existing research suggests that knowledge mobilization processes by commissioners are ineffective, and the knowledge acquired may not translate into service design or delivery (Imison, Curry, and McShane, 2011; Smith et al., 2000; Swan et al., 2012).

Our chapter begins with a conceptual outline of absorptive capacity, followed by discussion of its antecedents ("combinative capabilities"), and how they might play out in healthcare organizations. After outlining our specific research questions we detail our empirical research design. Our findings drive a discussion regarding the role of co-ordination capabilities to enhance knowledge mobilization within commissioning networks, supporting use, as well as acquisition, of knowledge for quality improvement. Finally, we conclude with a synthesis of the application of our findings to both theory and practice, and outline avenues for further research.

3.2 Absorptive Capacity—a Conceptual Outline

Zahra and George (2002) derive two interacting elements to absorptive capacity: (1) Potential Absorptive Capacity—the ability to acquire and assimilate knowledge; and (2) Realized Absorptive Capacity—the ability to put newly acquired knowledge into action within the organization through transformation (the development of an intervention) and exploitation (scaling up of that intervention). Whilst they identify that both of these elements are essential for innovation, they note that the majority of research focuses upon knowledge acquisition processes, thus ignoring assimilation, transformation, and exploitation. This distinction is important given that it is the variance between potential and realized absorptive capacity which explains, and determines, variance in performance amongst organizations.

Van den Bosch, Volberda, and de Boer (1999) go further to identify that combinative capabilities are an important antecedent to developing realized absorptive capacity. Van den Bosch, Volberda, and de Boer delineate three combinative capabilities: (1) systems, (2) socialization, and (3) coordination capabilities. Systems capabilities refer to formal knowledge exchange mechanisms, such as written policies, procedures, and manuals designed to facilitate transfer of codified knowledge, but also to environmental incentives that shape priorities. Socialization capabilities refer to cultural mechanisms that promote shared ideology and collective interpretations of reality within organizations. Coordination capabilities refer to lateral forms of communication such as education and training, job rotation, cross-functional interfaces, and distinct liaison roles.

Empirical studies in private sector settings show that different combinations of combinative capabilities have different impacts on absorptive capacity (Van den Bosch, Volberda, and de Boer, 1999). The traditional interaction of systems and socialization capabilities are thought to stymie absorptive capacity. Van den Bosch, Volberda, and de Boer also show that coordination capabilities mediate their effects, and so enhance absorptive capacity. The different balances between combinative capabilities are critical to understanding the absorptive capacity of healthcare organizations. It is therefore clearly important to understand these combinations further, particularly the positive effect of coordination capabilities upon absorptive capacity.

Working from the effect of coordination capability in private sector settings (Van den Bosch, Volberda, and de Boer, 1999), Hotho, Becker-Ritterspach, and Saka-Helmhout (2012) suggest that policy-makers and managers of public services, wishing to promote knowledge mobilization, need to attend to coordination capabilities, such as development of learning relationships through establishing internal and external networks; staff development and training; appropriate leadership; organizational strategy; investment in information support systems; participation in decision-making (also see Harvey et al., 2010). Since coordination capabilities are likely to have the biggest and most positive effect on absorptive capacity they offer a valuable starting point for further attention. However, it is important not to lose sight of how environmental incentives and professional organization also affect absorptive capacity. Within healthcare settings, the influence of centralized performance measures and the multiple hierarchies and power differentials of professional organization impacts knowledge mobilization processes, as detailed empirically in Section 3.3 (Easterby-Smith et al., 2008; Jansen, Van Den Bosch, and Volberda, 2005; Lane, Koka, and Pathak, 2006; Volberda, Foss, and Lyles, 2010; Zahra and George, 2002). As such, healthcare organizations provide an illuminating context from which to explore the influence of combinative capabilities on knowledge mobilization.

3.3 Research Design

To explore how CCGs can enhance their absorptive capacity for acquisition and use of knowledge, we followed a tracer study (Hornby and Symon, 1994), that of commissioning interventions to reduce avoidable admissions of older persons into hospitals. In the study we gathered data from nine CCGs in the English NHS. Within each CCG we undertook semi-structured interviews and asked respondents to describe the commissioning process, focusing on the four processes encompassed within knowledge mobilization, embedded in an organization's absorptive capacity (acquisition, assimilation, transformation, and exploitation), and their antecedents, or combinative capabilities. We did not directly invoke technical terms, such as absorptive capacity and capabilities, but asked more general questions, such as: how do you acquire data and information about hospital admissions? How do you use such data and information? What are the barriers to using data and information? How are these barriers mediated? Our sample of interviewees from the CCG-led commissioning networks represented stakeholders who were seen to be central to the commissioning process, including patient representatives and clinicians, and those that carried some "managerial" responsibility for commissioning, from healthcare and other organizations (e.g., public health, social care). With assistance from the relevant CCG Chief Operating Officer in exploratory interviews designed to engage CCGs in our study, we identified some respondents a priori, and then followed a snowball sampling pattern (Biernacki and Waldorf, 1981), until the themes emerging from interviews were theoretically saturated. Further to this, to reflect the ongoing politicized nature and top-down control which characterizes healthcare contexts, we interviewed those overseeing the performance of CCGs at national and regional levels. A total of

109 participants were interviewed. Interviews lasted between forty-five minutes and one hour and were audio recorded and transcribed. Coding was carried out by one member of the research team, and analysis was guided by searching for in-vivo codes related to combinative capabilities, as set out in Section 3.4.

3.4 Combinative Capabilities in CCGs for Mobilizing Knowledge

We present our empirical data within the four processes of knowledge mobilization that constitute an organization's absorptive capacity: acquisition, assimilation, transformation, and exploitation. These processes are non-linear and overlapping, but we present them in four distinct sections to explore the influence of combinative capabilities on knowledge mobilization by CCGs, outlining how the limitations of systems and socialization capabilities may be mediated by the development of coordination capabilities.

3.4.1 *Acquisition*

Formal data acquisition mechanisms can be conceptualized as representing systems capabilities, whereby information is collated by the CCG through standardized reporting systems:

> We automatically receive data from a number of providers, such as community doctors, the ambulance service, the hospitals, as well national level data. (CCG D—Interview 11)

Theoretically, the data acquired guides commissioning decisions. However, our interviewees suggested that, rather than enhancing acquisition of data, systems capabilities had the potential to inhibit acquisition. They said this was due to gaps in the type of data being collected, with some data missing that was likely to prove more relevant to their needs:

> There's a mass of data floating around in the system, but people aren't collecting the right data. Further, they're not asking the right questions of the data so they're not therefore deriving the right answers from that data that they have, and so passing on less relevant data to us. (CCG E—Interview 5)

In addition, acquisition of information was limited due to the influence of central government regulation on systems capabilities. For example, centralized barriers between social care and healthcare services—in their priorities, methods of data collection, and funding arrangements—had the potential to limit acquisition and knowledge mobilization:

> The division between social and health is difficult... They've both got their pots and they both want to protect their money and "No, that's not my job, that's health." "No, that's not us, that's social care."... they've got different pressures and they won't share information across the system which makes it difficult to care for the patients doesn't it? (CCG G—Interview 9)

Although more explicit in relationships between health and social care teams, central government regulations were seen as limiting knowledge mobilization, due to the influence on systems capabilities, in a wide range of settings. However, interviewees in this study suggested that coordination capabilities, in the form of the involvement of community doctors (General Practitioners [GPs] in the English NHS) or patient and public representatives ("Patient and Public Involvement [PPI]" in the English NHS), could overcome the limitations of systems capabilities, and so enhance acquisition of knowledge. For example, the involvement of GPs as a coordination capability was particularly highlighted in examples where standardized acquisition systems, such as risk profiling tools for patients at risk of admission, were not perceived as comprehensive. Involving GPs in further identification of "at risk" patients subsequently enhanced the scope of knowledge available to guide decisions:

> My experience is that the people that it [existing standardized systems] throw up are not all of the people that we need to discuss. So the GPs will bring up other people that haven't been thrown up by the risk profiling system which they know are ongoing cases that we're all involved with and we know are possibly at more risk of going into hospital than others. They don't come up in the system but the GP knows about them. (CCG G—Interview 3)

In other words, knowledge mobilization was enhanced due to the acquisition of more experiential knowledge, which supplemented the "hard" data acquired externally, overcoming the "gaps" in information from standardized data collection services. In another example, the acquisition of information from a patient representative group supplemented formally acquired information about attendances in accident and emergency departments, leading to an understanding about the need to develop x-ray services outside of accident and emergency:

> And so one of the things we [patient representatives] did was an audit of people who attended accident and emergency... we asked them questions about what alternatives to accident and emergency they had explored, such as a walk-in centre [a lower level emergency service located in the community],?... We found something like 25 to 30 percent of people who attended accident and emergency actually just needed an x-ray and because we didn't have x-ray facilities available outside of accident and emergency all the time then we were pushing people to go to accident and emergency unnecessarily... people themselves were able

to identify that "I just need an x-ray. I know I don't need accident and emergency...I've broken my arm. I know it's not badly broken, but I just need an x-ray to confirm it and a plaster." (CCG E—Interview 3)

These examples highlight that, whilst acquisition can be inhibited by systems capabilities, coordination capabilities enacted through GPs or patient representatives can overcome these limitations. By facilitating access to more experiential forms of knowledge, coordination capabilities enhanced knowledge mobilization by contributing to a more "complete" picture of information available to commissioners. However, acquisition is only one element of the knowledge mobilization process, as the data acquired now needs to be analyzed through assimilation.

3.4.2 Assimilation

Assimilation refers to the process by which the knowledge acquired is turned into a form which can be analyzed and used by commissioners. During the assimilation process, both internal and externally acquired information need to be brought together to develop an integrated picture of service performance and guide future decisions. However, integration of information can sometimes be problematic. As outlined by those interviewed, those with relevant pieces of information are not always brought together:

> We've got some soft information here from the community health teams around some of the follow-up to those older patients attending accident and emergency. Community teams often have to pick up a mess because somebody's been discharged inappropriately and then they go back into hospital. There is no consistency regarding who receives this information, to supplement our formal data, yet we need that integration of on the ground intelligence to prevent re-admission of older patients to accident and emergency. (CCG E—Interview 8)

As with acquisition, GP involvement and PPI mediated the assimilation problem. The involvement of GPs encouraged different interpretation of the "numbers" acquired through formal data collection processes, developing a more in-depth understanding of the data:

> I can work the numbers and I can tell you statistically that's a big number or that looks very odd, but I can't always give an informed explanation as to why that might be or is that a good thing.... as soon as you start moving into some of the clinical areas just being able to work with somebody who knows their stuff, it adds something to our understanding. (CCG D—Interview 5)

GP involvement therefore added a new dimension to assimilation processes, and was used to "make sense" of external sources of information. Similarly, information from patient representatives was used by commissioners to triangulate quantitative data acquired, allowing a more comprehensive understanding of the quality of services:

> So we've tried to assemble all the various pieces of patient feedback and patients' experience surveys that have been done in the past couple of years and I'm trying to triangulate the quantitative with that qualitative patient experience to actually make a slightly more valuable kind of recommendation to inform our service intervention to reduce admissions of older people to hospital. (CCG F—Interview 6)

However, direct involvement of patient representatives in assimilation process was limited. Patient representatives were not involved in the process of "making sense" of the data, and often reported that they felt under-utilized at this stage:

> You see, when I asked them what kind of research could I do as a member of that group...he couldn't say. He didn't discourage me from doing research, but he couldn't say if I could do some sort of research into [specific group]...that a layman like myself could carry out something. (CCG F—Interview 1)

Indeed, the perceived "importance" of the information acquired and assimilated from PPI groups was seen as lesser than that from clinicians or managers. Professional groups with higher levels of social legitimacy, such as managers, could undermine the knowledge sharing with less powerful groups, such as patient representatives.

> I think them feeling involved is probably the best that we can do on that and seen as being open and honest about our decision-making. They don't necessarily have all the information or the knowledge and experience to make the decisions that we would make as health professionals...it's really peripheral stuff to be honest. (CCG A—Interview 7)

Whilst the influence of power differentials between groups was most pronounced on limitations on knowledge sharing with patient representatives, some interviewees also noted similarly limitations between managers and clinicians, where clinical knowledge was perceived as more "important" than managerial information:

> For me to go in as a manager and try and argue a case with a dozen clinical directors, with the best motivation all I can do is argue the numbers, the philosophy, present a management argument to why we should do this or we should do that...they don't see that as credible. (CCG B—Interview 3)

In conclusion, the influence of power differentials between professional groups, representing socialization capabilities, had the potential to limit knowledge mobilization, due to the perceived credibility or appropriateness of their involvement.

3.4.3 *Transformation*

Once different types of information have been assimilated for locally relevant knowledge, there remains the need for its transformation into a service intervention to be commissioned. However, for commissioners attempting to design services, integrating perspectives and demands from multiple organizations was seen as problematic:

> It's challenging to get that shared interpretation of what the information actually means for actual service design because clearly there are different interpretations you can apply to the same information. From a commissioner perspective, we will see a problem or challenge from one particular perspective, but healthcare providers will see a very different challenge, and so we will support different service interventions. (CCG D—Interview 12)

In essence, the challenge for knowledge mobilization during transformation processes was one derived from socialization capabilities, within which different perspectives and power differentials between organizations and professionals were embedded. CCGs were commonly small organizations, which were seen as less influential than hospitals, the latter dominated by powerful groups of doctors, who had been accustomed to patterns of resource allocation around which they resisted any change, whatever the "evidence" might suggest. However, those interviewed once again noted that the involvement of GPs had potential to mediate limitations of socialization capabilities. The involvement of GPs acted as a coordination capability by encouraging integrated working with clinicians in secondary care organizations, and involving them in service design discussions:

> When we involved GPs, we saw negotiation moved away quite dramatically from the old style negotiation which was all about finance and activity to a discussion that focused on quality outcomes and patient pathways ... the GPs were able to bring a level of reasonableness into that room with their medical colleagues that had previously not been there, with hospital doctors viewing us managers with some suspicion. GPs brought in the perspective of a practitioner dealing with patients on a day-to-day basis, which hospital doctors accepted and which really altered the dynamic in the room. (CCG B—Interview 10)

The involvement of GPs encouraged knowledge mobilization across doctors in different organizations derived from a shared professional background, and ability to bring in a patient-focused perspective to integrate with managerial or financial considerations.

In other interviews, commissioners also noted how older people were admitted to hospital in the absence of effective collaboration across healthcare and social care organizations. Where there existed integrated care pathways between the different organizations, this acted as coordination capability, encouraging knowledge mobilization across sector boundaries:

> It [an integrated health and social care pathway] represents a smoother pathway for the patient. In the past the older patient would have been taken into hospital, the patient discharged, and community social care teams have little contact with what's going on. The older patient may then be subsequently re-admitted to hospital because the social care support wasn't there. Because we're integrated now we can see two sides, the need for social care, as well as health care, for the patient, and so prevent re-admission. (CCG G—Interview 5)

However, whilst patient-focused care was at the center of integrated relationships between health and social care, enhancing transformation, involvement of patient representatives in the transformation process was again limited. PPI acted as a coordination capability by encouraging patient-focused design of services, but commissioners acknowledged that knowledge mobilization of information from patient representatives was focused on setting a strategy direction in a more general way, rather than involving patients in the development of specific services; that is, in their transformation:

> They're more about, you know, "I've got complex problems and I get bounced around between different services and it gets confusing, it makes me anxious, I don't know where I'm supposed to go next. It's very lengthy, it's uncomfortable because I have to go on public transport for two bus rides and it takes a whole day to go to an appointment and then when I get there they haven't got my notes." It's those sort of softer things which are not amenable to a single fix, but tell me where we need to go in terms of strategy. (CCG F—Interview 11)

In summary, coordination capabilities during transformation processes were represented by GP involvement to mediate what might prove a sticky relationship between managers and hospital doctors, thus overcoming some of the barriers associated with socialization capabilities. In addition, the encouragement of integrated relationships between health and social care organizations, with the needs of the patient held at the center of service design, enhanced transformation processes. However, similar to their role in assimilation, PPI represented an under-developed coordination capability in the transformation process.

3.4.4 *Exploitation*

Research on absorptive capacity in the private sector suggests exploitation is related to the ability of organizations to use the knowledge derived from small local pilots or projects, to develop wider-scale product or service change. Within the context of healthcare, this is perhaps difficult to examine,

Enhancing Absorptive Capacity

particularly given the local nature of commissioning organizations. However, we can also conceptualize exploitation as the way organizations are able to use any feedback from commissioned services to constantly improve their services, adapting them to maximize their potential effectiveness, in our study to further reduce avoidable admissions of older people to hospitals. In our study, interviewees noted how systems capabilities, or the standardized systems through which they collected feedback information, could limit this process:

> There's no underpinning intelligence around how that service runs, or what the experience of those patients is in those services we have commissioned. (CCG D—Interview 16)

Interviewees suggested that gathering feedback on an ongoing basis about services was difficult, due to systems capabilities. A particular challenge related to how they might measure the effect of *absence* of the service intervention they had commissioned to reduce avoidable admissions of older people into hospital:

> I think some of the difficulty is capturing what doesn't happen. Sometimes you will put in a service to prevent avoidable hospital admissions or perhaps deterioration in the health of an older person that might eventually lead to admission. However, there's a real dilemma about how you evidence the impact of the new service, what would have happened if it wasn't there. Our data management systems aren't sophisticated enough for this. (CCG G—Interview 2)

Exploitation represented the most under-developed process of absorptive capacity across all nine CCG cases without exception. Indeed, across all nine cases, it was difficult to identify any exploitation of knowledge. However, in one CCG, information obtained from patient representatives enhanced exploitation. First, acquiring information about patient experience increased the scope of data acquired to inform exploitation; that is, it was a key dimension of the knowledge used to make a decision about whether to continue and scale up a service intervention to reduce avoidable admissions of older people to hospitals. Second, by involving patients (or their carers) in service development, or in decisions about discontinuing services, interviewees suggested that a sense of ownership could be generated amongst those experiencing services, which helped spread knowledge of an isolated service intervention in other geographical localities. Third, such involvement adapted the service intervention to local context as it spread beyond its pilot:

> They'll go and say to other patient representative groups and GPs, "This is a good thing. We helped with the design of this and this is the reason why it's good," and that helps any new service spread quite quickly as others want to take it up. We had an issue. It was at a public meeting somewhere, where somebody was having a go at our CCG over something and one of the guys from the patient group stood

up and defended it because he'd been in on the inside and said "You've totally got this wrong. They're doing it this way, and it does work." (CCG C—Interview 4)

However, and similarly noted earlier, socialization capabilities limited knowledge sharing with patient representatives, and the involvement of patients was seen as underutilized, and at times tokenistic:

> I'm still feeling somewhat tagged on.... Tokenism is what I often say... I just wonder what my contribution is and do they really want somebody... a bloke (to) sit back and say nothing. (CCG F—Interview 10)

In conclusion, exploitation is the most under-developed of knowledge mobilization processes associated with absorptive capacity for CCGs. However, knowledge mobilized through patient representatives represents coordination capability during exploitation processes. Patient involvement encouraged feedback of information not supplied by existing systems capabilities, developing a sense of ownership amongst the public and patients for the service intervention to which they are subject, potentially informing scale-up and adaptation. Despite this potential enhancement of knowledge mobilization, socialization capabilities, in the form of power differentials between different groups, had the potential to undermine patient involvement, limiting the exploitation process.

3.5 Discussion

In this chapter we have considered the influence of combinative capabilities on the four processes of knowledge mobilization that inform an organization's absorptive capacity. Contextualizing the findings empirically within healthcare has enabled us to develop some insights into the influence on knowledge mobilization in complex, professionalized settings. In doing so, this chapter addresses calls for more research into how organizational antecedents impact knowledge mobilization, taking account of organizational context, the role of individuals and groups, and associated power and politics (Easterby-Smith et al., 2008; Jansen, Van Den Bosch, and Volberda, 2005; Lane, Koka, and Pathak, 2006; Volberda, Foss, and Lyles, 2010; Zahra and George, 2002). Existing research into knowledge mobilization in healthcare organizations highlights that acquisition of external knowledge is less of a problem than actual use (i.e., assimilation, transformation, and exploitation) of that evidence to drive quality improvement (Berta et al., 2010; Easterby-Smith et al., 2008; Ferlie et al., 2012; Harvey et al., 2010; Walshe et al., 2009). We now draw on our findings to explore the influences and limitations on knowledge mobilization for commissioning decisions.

In our empirical study, we highlighted how systems capabilities had a limiting influence on the acquisition of external information, as standardized systems conform to centralized systems of performance measurement and policy compliance (Nicolini, Waring, and Mengis, 2011). Healthcare organizations represent a distinctive context compared to private sector R&D (Research and Development) contexts, in which much of the empirical work around absorptive capacity has taken place (Easterby-Smith et al., 2008). As such, the influence of systems capabilities on knowledge mobilization in this setting was more explicit than in research into private sector organizations. First, healthcare organizations are subject to New Public Management reform that frames performance through financial incentives and regulation. Encompassed within systems capability, such government policy affords access to external resources, and directs and formalizes acquisition and assimilation of knowledge. However, it narrows the search for new external knowledge and scope for processing that knowledge, as managers in healthcare organizations "gameplay" to ensure compliance with policy requirements around their governance (Lavertu and Moynihan, 2013; Moynihan, 2006; Moynihan and Hawes, 2012). Pulling in external knowledge within healthcare organizations toward quality improvement appears particularly directed toward compliance with government regulation and performance management (Nicolini, Waring, and Mengis, 2011), in a way likely to limit the search and utilization of external evidence, limiting knowledge mobilization. Subsequently, systems capabilities can narrow the breadth of external information acquired and assimilated by healthcare organizations, or available for service exploitation.

In addition to systems capabilities, the influence of socialization capabilities on commissioning processes was also more evident than in private sector settings. Healthcare organizations exemplify the professional bureaucracy archetype (Mintzberg, 1979), within which professional organization is likely to represent a key influence upon socialization capability, limiting knowledge mobilization as follows. External knowledge interacts with strong organizational cultures and structures, so that socialization capability within healthcare organizations restricts knowledge mobilization (Van den Bosch, Volberda, and de Boer, 1999). As such, power and status linked to professional roles is likely to impact healthcare organizations' ability to exploit new knowledge (Ferlie et al., 2012; Harvey et al., 2010; Walshe et al., 2009). For example, Berta et al. (2010) note the role of doctors in subverting an organization's learning capacity, in relation to the adoption of new clinical guidelines, based upon formal evidence, into practice. Similarly, Ferlie et al. (2005) note that deeply ingrained organizational structures and social networks within healthcare organizations engender institutionalized epistemic communities of professional practice, which exist in silos, relatively decoupled from one another. Again, these stymie the search for external knowledge that lies outside current ways of thinking amongst powerful professional groups. Thus, the acquisition and use of internal knowledge, as well as that external to the organization, seems important in the healthcare setting.

Due to the professionalized context of commissioning organizations in this study, socialization capabilities had the potential to limit the transformation or exploitation of services. Our empirical findings indicated that socialization capabilities influenced knowledge mobilization in two ways. First, integration of PPI during transformation and exploitation processes was limited, and at times seen as tokenistic. Whilst information acquired from patient representatives was used to supplement externally acquired information, patient representatives were not involved in the assimilation, transformation, or exploitation of services. In this case, the potential of PPI as a coordination capability was undermined by the socialization capability of the organization, which perpetuated power differentials between professionals and users of service, and did not integrate PPI into the commissioning process.

Secondly, socialization capabilities had the potential to limit transformation of knowledge into service design, due to competing demands and priorities of the multiple stakeholders involved in the commissioning process. This reflects the context, characterized by institutionalized professional silos, limiting communication and knowledge sharing between different organizations (Ferlie et al., 2005). However, those same professional silos appeared to enhance the involvement of GPs as a coordination capability, as they were able to communicate directly with medical peers in hospitals. This facilitated the sharing of information and integration during transformation processes, overcoming inter-organizational or inter-professional barriers experienced by managers within previous commissioning structures.

To mediate the limitations of systems capabilities, our study identified how coordination capabilities, notably in the form of GP involvement or PPI, facilitated exposure to different, experiential types of knowledge. Accessing this local, experiential knowledge enabled CCGs to "patch up" the gaps informed by systems capabilities, encouraging the integration of both external and experiential knowledge. We highlight the role of GPs, and to a lesser extent patient representatives, in mediating the effects of socialization and systems capabilities is particularly relevant to professionalized organizations.

GP involvement is a coordination capability of CCGs which bridges the limitations of systems and socialization capabilities in all four processes of knowledge mobilization. GP involvement allows integration of internal, tacit knowledge with the external information acquired from "hard" data collection systems. It also encourages integration of knowledge across organizational barriers, overcoming previous limitations of socialization capabilities. Therefore, GP involvement in commissioning processes is an important coordination capability and should be encouraged by CCG managers.

In contrast, whilst the importance of PPI was noted throughout our empirical findings, it was only explicitly integrated into acquisition processes. During acquisition episodes, PPI had an important role in overcoming systems capabilities, providing a new type of information for assimilation. However, during transformation and exploitation processes, PPI was less explicit, due to the limits of the organizational culture, or socialization capabilities. In highly professionalized organizations, socialization capabilities may limit the value attributed to "lesser" forms of information or external knowledge (Todorova and Durisin, 2007). PPI was not felt to be embedded in the "culture" of CCGs, suggesting that this is a coordination capability which is underdeveloped, but has the potential to further enhance absorptive capacity. Managers within healthcare organizations should work to further integrate PPI mechanisms into all four aspects of knowledge mobilization to improve their absorptive capacity, enhancing the quality of commissioning decisions.

3.6 Conclusion

Our study, which provides insight into absorptive capacity, is particularly relevant to healthcare settings currently. Healthcare settings globally are subject to financial parsimony, and as such need to be smarter about knowledge mobilization, in particular how acquired knowledge informs the planning of, and funding for, service interventions, not least given burgeoning demands due to the increasing demands from older patients on hospital services (in the English NHS, for example, around 50 percent of hospital beds may be occupied by older patients). For example, a healthcare organization may invest significant resource in IT (information technology) capacity to acquire information, but if this information is then not used intelligently to inform service development, then investments will merely result in potential absorptive capacity, rather than realized absorptive capacity (Zahra and George, 2002), without patient, financial, or competitive advantage. At the same time, we note our analysis is not limited to commissioning care of older people, since application of the absorptive capacity concept allows theoretical generalization to other domains of healthcare, both delivery and commissioning of services, and indeed other public services characterized by professional organization and central government intervention (Eisenhardt, 1989).

Our study highlights the importance of coordination capabilities in enhancing absorptive capacity and knowledge mobilization in public services organizations. First, coordination capabilities enhance capacity for integrating externally acquired information with more local, experiential information, overcoming the limitations of systems capabilities embedded in standardized reporting systems. Second, the involvement of professionals within public services organizations, in our study GPs, can overcome socialization capabilities by encouraging knowledge mobilization across organizations. However, we have also identified how the socialization capabilities of highly professionalized organizations can also inhibit enactment of coordination capabilities, in our study PPI, due to power differentials across patients, managers, and professionals, and more generally, an unsupportive organizational culture.

Detailing this further, an initial problem to be addressed is that of the acquisition of knowledge. It may be that too little or the wrong type of evidence might be acquired. Coordination capability may help ensure that a wider range of relevant evidence is acquired, including, for example, patient experience evidence. In assimilation processes, different sources of evidence need to be brought together, and decision-makers need to ensure they are weighted appropriately, for example, ensuring that the patient voice is not rendered marginal as decision-making around service change ensues. During transformation, when evidence is turned into a service intervention, decisions about what constitutes an appropriate intervention should incorporate a wide range of relevant perspectives. Decision-makers must consider what the service looks like from a professional's, manager's, and patient's perspective. During the final processes of absorptive capacity, exploitation, when the service intervention is scaled up, decommissioned, or adapted, decision-makers need to fully examine what's working, from whose perspective, what might they adapt as they scale up. All these challenges require coordination capabilities. Our study identified three coordination capabilities—professional involvement, client involvement, integrated service delivery models. How such coordination capabilities play out is summarized in Figure 3.1.

The model outlines how evidence and knowledge takes the form of information from a diverse range of sources, including research, patient involvement, clinician and managerial knowledge. Facilitating, or inhibiting, knowledge mobilization are the three combinative capabilities: systems, socialization, and coordination capabilities, which are antecedents to the four overlapping processes of knowledge mobilization that underpin absorptive capacity. However, socialization and systems capabilities have the potential to inhibit absorptive capacity, limiting the breadth and type of information acquired and used to guide service decisions. The three types of coordination capability identified in this study—clinician involvement, PPI, and integrated services—work to overcome the limitations of systems and socialization capabilities. In particular, the coordination capabilities have the potential to enhance exploitation processes, an area which is underdeveloped in healthcare organizations. Enhancing exploitation encourages the scaling of service intervention in response to knowledge mobilization of information from a wide range of sources, and is an area where healthcare organizations should seek to develop their capacity, improving decision-making and quality of services.

Enhancing Absorptive Capacity

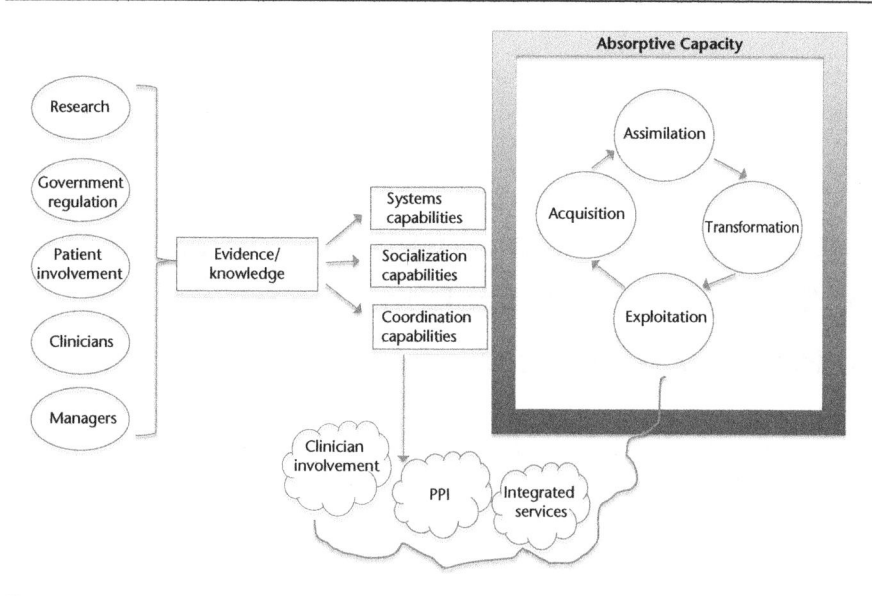

Figure 3.1 A representation of absorptive capacity knowledge mobilization processes

Finally, in terms of further research, coordination capabilities within healthcare organizations have been identified within the literature as represented by the following: the development of learning relationships through the establishment of internal and external networks; staff development and training; appropriate leadership; organizational strategy; investment in information support systems; participation in decision-making; and, more generally, social relations inside and outside the organization (Harvey et al., 2010; Walshe et al., 2009). Whilst our empirical study has highlighted professional involvement, client involvement, integrated service delivery models, others may wish to examine possibilities offered by other forms of coordination capability.

Acknowledgments

The findings in this chapter were drawn from a study funded by the NIHR (National Institute for Health Research), HS&DR (Health Research Health Services and Delivery Research) stream. The conclusions presented in this chapter are the opinions of the authors and do not represent the views of the NIHR. Currie's work on the chapter is partly funded by NIHR CLAHRC (Collaboration for Leadership Applied Health Research and Care) West Midlands.

4

Creating and Sustaining the Right Kind of Space for Organizational Learning in Primary Healthcare

Trish Reay, Kathy GermAnn, Ann Casebeer, Karen Golden-Biddle, and C. R. (Bob) Hinings

CHAPTER SUMMARY

This chapter investigates how knowledge mobilization can be facilitated within organizations by focusing on the development of "space" for organizational learning. The authors studied how managers, physicians and other health professionals in ten primary healthcare innovation sites attempted to create and sustain space for learning as part of an initiative to improve primary healthcare. By "space" they mean the social and relational context that develops and evolves as people interact and share ideas to create new ideas and knowledge. The chapter contributes to the literature by identifying three different types of space: generative, inert, and toxic. Its findings draw attention to the importance of managerial actions in supporting organizational learning. Four strategies are identified that are important in creating the right kind of space where organizational learning and sharing of knowledge can occur: (1) assembling the right people, (2) developing positive social relationships, (3) focusing the conversation, and (4) managing setbacks and frustrations.

4.1 Introduction

Healthcare organizations are increasingly expected to find better (higher quality and often lower cost) ways of providing services. In order to improve services, organizations must draw on existing knowledge and learn to accomplish work in new ways. Our chapter addresses this book's topic of *knowledge mobilization* (how existing knowledge is locally used to change healthcare

Creating Space for Organizational Learning

practice) by focusing on a particular conception of knowledge generation and use—*organizational learning* (OL)—a process through which organizations improve their capabilities by gathering and using knowledge to move up the learning curve (Argote, 1999).

We take a social perspective to organizational learning by highlighting the importance of interactions and conversations among people as a key mechanism through which knowledge is generated and used (Antonancopoulou and Chiva, 2007; Easterby-Smith, Crossan, and Nicolini, 2000; Williams, 2001). Although researchers have pointed to the organizational importance of the "space" where interactions and conversations occur (Bouwen and Hosking, 2000; Nonaka, Toyama, and Byosiere, 2001), there has been less attention to the nature of this space and its role in supporting (or not) organizational learning. Similar to Croft and Currie (Chapter 3), we study the development of processes internal to organizations that can facilitate the recognition and use of available knowledge in ways that improve the quality of services provided. In addition, we focus on conditions under which health professionals can collectively develop and implement new ideas about better ways to provide care.

We became interested in what actually happens in the space for organizational learning through our research investigating the development of new primary healthcare sites in western Canada. As part of government initiatives to improve healthcare, special innovation sites were established with the goal of learning new and better ways to provide primary healthcare. Physicians and other health professionals were challenged to work together, develop new programs, learn from their implementation experiences, and use the learnings to continually improve service provision. We were fortunate to begin the field component of our research at the time when these innovation sites were just starting up. We used a comparative case study approach, following events and interviewing key individuals in each of ten sites over a three-year period.

As our study progressed, we observed that although each site started out much the same, by the second and third year of our study, only six sites were viewed in positive terms. In these sites, new, innovative programs were developed and implemented, and seemed to be working well. People talked about their sites in very positive terms, and we labeled the space for learning as *generative*. In the other four sites we saw a different picture. In two sites we heard about space that we characterized as *inert*. Here, people felt disconnected from each other and described the initiative as stalled; few if any new programs were in place. In the other two sites, we heard about space that we labeled *toxic*. People were angry and seldom even spoke to each other. The development of new programs had been abandoned, and people were not even talking about trying anything new. In this chapter, we attempt to understand how people in some sites developed *generative* (or positive, enthusiasm-rich) spaces for organizational learning, and what they did differently compared to sites where *inert* or *toxic* spaces developed.

4.2 Space for Organizational Learning

Research in organizational learning has shown the importance of learning processes within organizations (Easterby-Smith and Araujo, 1999; Spender, 2008) and given attention to the overall changes in how organizational members "see things and behave in pursuit of [organizational] goals" (Williams, 2001: 68). This focus on the process of organizational learning rather than the outcome (Bapuji and Crossan, 2004) has arisen largely through a social perspective on learning—one that gives particular attention to people and their interactions (Easterby-Smith, Crossan, and Nicolini, 2000). This is an important foundation because it underscores the view that organizational learning occurs through the dynamic processes of conversing and relating with others (Brown and Duguid, 1991; Cook and Yanow, 1993; Gherardi and Nicolini, 2000).

Although there have been studies that reveal ways in which conversations form the basis for organizational learning (e.g. Cunliffe, 2008; Yanow, 2004), we know relatively little about the space where organizational learning occurs. Most notably, Edmondson and colleagues (Edmondson, 1999; Tucker, Nembhard and Edmondson, 2006; Tucker, Nembhard, and Edmondson, 2007) studied team psychological safety—the shared belief that one's team is "safe for interpersonal risk taking" (Edmondson, 1999: 350)—in numerous settings, including healthcare. They showed that psychological safety, grounded in mutual trust and respect amongst team members was an essential condition for team learning because people needed to feel safe before they would admit to "not knowing" about something or having made a mistake. Nembhard and Edmondson (2006: 947) found that leader inclusiveness—"words and deeds by a leader or leaders that indicate an invitation and appreciation for others' contributions"—supports learning in teams characterized by differences in status.

From a somewhat different perspective, Nonaka and colleagues developed theory about knowledge creation that relied on the concept of *ba*—the "shared space that serves as a foundation for knowledge creation" (Nonaka and Konno, 1998: 40). Nonaka, Toyama, and Byosiere (2001: 492) developed a model of organizational learning focused on the importance of interactions among individuals in an organization and the space (*ba*) where these interactions occur. This space can be a mental, virtual or physical place (Nonaka, Toyama, and Byosiere, 2000), but it is where various forms of knowledge are shared, created and integrated into practice as individuals interact with each other (Nonaka, Toyama, and Byosiere, 2001). Through conversation and other interactions, knowledge is re-created and amplified by the collective (Nonaka, Toyama, and Byosiere, 2001; Nonaka and Konno, 1998). *Ba* is somewhat ephemeral—its boundaries and characteristics are fluid as people come and go, and it is itself changed through the processes of knowledge creation and organizational learning. *Ba* is not a passive space; it requires energy for the active creation of knowledge (Nonaka, Toyama, and Byosiere, 2001).

Other researchers have also proposed that space is critical to understanding learning. Fahy, Easterby-Smith, and Lervik (2014) investigated ways in which aspects of space and time impacted learning in organizations. Drawing on the distinction between *conceived*, *perceived*, and *lived* space (Beyes and Michels, 2011), Fahy, Easterby-Smith, and Lervik (2014) found that the way people see themselves as members of a particular space influences their actions within that space. Bouwen and Hosking (2000) built on Winnicott's (1971) notion of "transitional spaces" as "potential spaces or intermediary worlds involving the interplay of inner and outer experiences, actors and third parties, in between past and future, where social realities are in the making" (2000: 273). They drew attention to the importance of places where different groups could gather and share views as an important part of learning. Somewhat similarly, Edenius and Yakhlef (2007) showed the impact of physical space, and Baker (2002) developed the concept of "receptive spaces" for conversational learning. Similar to Edmondson (1999), these studies highlight the importance of safety and respect for colleagues. Baker, Jensen, and Kolb (2005) expanded these conceptualizations to describe the nature of the space in which conversations occur suggesting that "conversational learning as a self-organizing entity cannot exist without a receptive space to hold it" (Baker, Jensen, and Kolb, 2005: 424).

A review of the works cited above reveals that the notion of "space" can be viewed in various ways. Our focus in this chapter is specifically on what we call "relational space"—the social context that develops and evolves as people interact and share ideas to create new ideas and knowledge. This conceptualization is consistent with Edmondson's (1999) notion of psychological safety, Baker's (2002) "receptive spaces," and Nonaka, Toyama, and Konno's (2000) notion of *ba*.

The concept of relational space is also consistent with positive organizational scholarship (POS) and its focus on learning through social interaction, including the importance of the space where interactions among people occur (Cameron, Dutton, and Quinn, 2003; Cameron, Bright, and Caza, 2004; Spreitzer et al., 2005). This body of research adds two important points to the organizational learning literature. First, it draws attention to the importance of positive relationships, and second it shows that a positive work environment can be associated with exceptional organizational outcomes.

Research has shown that organizations or departments with a carefully developed and sustained positive atmosphere have achieved extraordinary individual, work unit, and organizational outcomes (Dutton and Ragins, 2006). For example, the development of a positive workplace atmosphere led to significantly improved outcomes for a billing department (Dutton, 2003). Similarly in a restructured healthcare organization, key leaders took action to develop a sense of mutuality, positive regard, and respect for others. People working there reported being enriched and energized by these positive relationships, and drew on them to enable the achievement of successful organizational outcomes even in difficult circumstances (Golden-Biddle et al., 2007: 291). Other researchers suggested that the energy produced in positive relationships could ignite eager investment in ongoing, coordinated actions with others, and serve as a resource in addressing organizational challenges (Quinn and Dutton, 2005). In addition, studies by Gittell and colleagues showed how positive organizational outcomes were achieved by fostering the development of mutual respect, shared understanding and shared goals (Gittell et al., 2008; Gittell, 2001).

So, what is the role of managers in creating and sustaining relational spaces in which organizational learning can occur? Edmondson (1999) found that manager coaching and support along with contextual supports (e.g. information, funding) contributed to team psychological safety, and thus improved learning. Nonaka, Toyama, and Byosiere (2001) proposed that managers (and middle managers in particular) were critical to organizational learning because they could bring together knowledge assets (people) and *ba*. Leadership style (transactional or transformational) and organizational learning were found to be linked to the characteristics and atmosphere of the organization (Jansen, Vera, and Crossan, 2009; Nemanich and Vera, 2009). Hannah and Lester (2009) also investigated leadership and proposed that effective managers engaged in orchestration—creating an appropriate climate by continually encouraging individuals to create an atmosphere for learning, who similarly encourage others.

POS researchers have also given attention to managerial action. For example, leaders or managers were found to provide continual and relentless attention to the day-to-day atmosphere, allowing processes of learning to be embedded in the culture (Golden-Biddle et al., 2007). Similarly, leaders have been identified as key agents in developing a positive organizational atmosphere (Cameron, 2008) or more specifically in finding ways to support knowledge work or organizing activities based on compassion (Kanov et al., 2004; Pittinsky and Shih, 2004).

While the literatures on organizational learning and POS have given attention to the space where people interact, and the importance of developing and sustaining such a space to facilitate learning or organizational improvement, both have largely ignored space that is less than positive. POS purposefully adopts a biased focus in order to learn from "positive examples" (Cameron and Caza, 2004). The empirical literature on OL tends to be biased toward successful examples because most researchers find cases of organizational learning and "work backwards" to try to understand how it has occurred.

There are, however, reasons why negative outcomes should be expected and considered. Even in settings where open conversations are encouraged, the processes of relating and conversing can be both complex and fragile. Many conversations within organizations do not contribute value (Gratton and Ghoshal, 2002). People at different levels and locations in the organization often see the organization in very different ways, and this diversity can threaten the learning process (Yanow, 2004). Potential participants may come to the conversation with a history of unsatisfactory or conflicting relations with other participants. Status differences among group members and divergent political interests can shut down the learning process by privileging some voices (and meanings) at the expense of others (Blackler and McDonald, 2000; Marshall and Rollinson, 2004; Yanow, 2004). Space that is characterized by a lack of reciprocity and/or an authoritarian culture can cause individuals to guard, rather than share, their knowledge (Edelman et al., 2004). Stress, threat, and being treated disrespectfully may produce a defensive clinging to what is known rather than openness to new ideas and perspectives (Baker, 2002: 2). And unskilled facilitation of learning processes can "bring painful hurt and embarrassment, sever communication, and sometimes relationships, block the possibility of hearing how other people see the same situation quite differently, and block learning" (Baker, 2002: 102). At the other end of the spectrum, strongly held group norms and assumptions may also impair critical examination of accepted ideas and solutions by shutting down generative conversations before they can begin (Janis, 1972).

To summarize, researchers have identified the importance of creating space for organizational learning. However, even though there is a strong knowledge base showing that effective conversations and supportive social environments are important, there has been little attention given to how different types of space impact learning, and how supportive space can be facilitated. Thus our research question: *How do people in organizations create and sustain the right kind of space for organizational learning?* We use the term "organizational learning" from a social constructionist perspective following from the work of Brown and Duguid (1991), Cook and Yanow (1993), and Gherardi and Nicolini (2000) that is based on the assumption that "learning occurs and knowledge is created mainly through conversations and interactions *between* people" (Easterby-Smith, Crossan, and Nicolini, 2000: 787) and that organizational learning can be recognized by the development of new organizational capabilities (Bohmer and Edmondson, 2001).

4.3 Research Settings and Methods

We studied the development of 10 different primary healthcare innovation sites in Western Canada. Each site was established in response to calls for increased integration, coordination and improvement of primary healthcare services as part of ongoing initiatives to improve the effectiveness and efficiency of the Canadian healthcare system. Primary healthcare (PHC) is the term used to describe all health services available in community settings as the first point of contact. Most typically, this is the type of care patients receive in family doctors' offices, but it also includes services provided by other healthcare professionals such as public health nurses, rehabilitation therapists, mental health providers or dieticians.

Each PHC site's mandate was to "be innovative" and learn how to provide services in better ways. They were expected to rely on interdisciplinary teams and develop new programs that were particularly suited to people living in the geographic area. In short, they were expected to engage in organizational learning by mobilizing knowledge to create new ways of working. We followed events and interviewed key informants in each of the 10 sites over a period of three years (2005 to 2008). In total, we conducted 170 semi-structured interviews with managers, family physicians, and other healthcare professionals. In addition to qualitatively analyzing these interviews, we also collected and reviewed archival data related to the PHC initiatives, such as business plans, annual reports and promotional brochures.

In the second and third year of our study, we observed variation across sites in terms of learning to work collaboratively and engage in new practices. In six sites, interviewees told us proudly about new programs that were already implemented. In two sites, we heard about a few advancements but people were more focused on their frustrations with lack of participation and enthusiasm. And in the two other sites, we consistently heard about difficulties in moving forward and frayed relationships within the site. In considering similarities and differences across our 10 sites, we focused on how key actors in each site attempted to encourage the development of new ideas and practices that could lead to improved PHC.

4.4 Creating Space for Organizational Learning

We wanted to understand how the "right" conditions for organizational learning were developed and sustained over time. In all our study sites, the desired outcome was that participants in the interdisciplinary teams developed new, innovative approaches based on available knowledge and know-how. We saw that some sites were moving ahead with initiatives better than

Creating Space for Organizational Learning

others. In all sites, we asked about "how things were going." Their descriptions were interesting to consider in light of the concept of space or *ba* (Nonaka and Konno, 1998), where people come together to engage in conversation and share knowledge. In the six sites where new approaches were actually being implemented, the atmosphere and sense of ability to improve services was positive and hopeful. We termed this type of space "generative." In two sites, we heard that a few new programs were being planned or were in place, but interviewees were relatively unengaged with initiatives and were not sharing ideas with each other to develop new approaches. We labeled these spaces "inert." In the two other sites, the atmosphere seemed to be poisoned with negativity and bitterness. Little, if anything, was being done differently from the past and team members were either unhappy or angry. We called these spaces "toxic." Below we explain each of the types of space.

4.4.1 Generative Space

In six sites where organization learning appeared to occur, interviewees told us about their passion for working together in interdisciplinary teams that they believed provided a much better way of providing care. Their enthusiasm was infectious, and in conducting interviews we were always impressed with the positive and energetic atmosphere we felt. People felt good about the work they were doing and their passion was easily apparent. We characterized the space they had created within their site as *generative* because it seemed to foster an ever increasing sense that team members could collectively combine their knowledge to make meaningful advancements. The following quotations illustrate this enthusiastic and developmental space:

> We're really learning the process of working as a team. We've now got a midwife and a pharmacist, as well as other health professionals—and it's working out extremely well. We still need more physicians, but all of us docs are growing in the sense of learning teamwork. Some of the things we've been able to accomplish are just incredible. [Physician]

> Our teams have really expanded over the last year, and it's all on the clinical side. We're still working on our abilities to increase the team, but we're definitely getting better at it. We can now bring new professionals onto the team, and we know how to introduce them into the setting. We know how to focus on relationship building. We're seeing that we're building strong relationships among professionals—including physicians, and that seems to be the key to success. [Health manager]

4.4.2 Inert Space

In the two sites where people told us that only minimal (at best) advancement was occurring, we were given somewhat emotionless accounts of how people were working. We heard about projects that "still hadn't got started" or those that had been stalled. Interviewees also told us about meetings that were scheduled, but not enough people attended. People reported that they were still "working in parallel with other health providers" rather than in an interdisciplinary team. We did not feel the sense of enthusiasm that was so apparent in the sites described above where we labeled the space as *generative*. Instead, there was a sense that little was happening. We characterized the space created in these sites as *inert*. As the following examples illustrate:

> We just kind of stumble along. Some things are just energy suckers. I see that this model might end up being abandoned because of the cost or the weightiness of it. [Health manager]

> We've taken very small steps so far. The amount of work involved has been big, and then we've had difficulty with hiring staff—it's a long process. [Physician]

4.4.3 Toxic Space

In the other two sites people not only told us that advancements were minimal or non-existent, we also heard very clearly that negative relationships had developed. Meetings were set, but physicians did not attend. Healthcare managers were angry because they could not move ahead without physician participation. Physicians told us that the healthcare managers were not listening to them, and that they were expecting physicians to take on extra work when they were already too busy. Other health professionals were discouraged by physicians' disinterest. Everyone we interviewed told us that the process was mired in difficulty. No one used the word "we" when talking about the PHC site. Instead, we consistently heard stories about "us and them." In characterizing this space as *toxic*, we drew on work by Frost (2004) who identified toxic workplaces where relationships among individuals were extremely poor to the point where they "poisoned" the work environment and impeded employee performance. We suggest that the "space" in these sites was similarly toxic—poisoning the work environment to the extent that relationships failed. The quotations below show this toxicity:

> Things aren't working well. Changes may not even be helpful. [Physicians here] just see the investment in money—and they don't seem able to see the benefit. We developed a lot of stuff, and the physicians didn't even come to meetings. [Health manager]

> Today I went where we were supposed to be meeting. I looked around. I sat there a few minutes, and then I thought—"you know what, I don't think anybody else is coming." So I went back to my office. It's really too bad, because I think that people have lost sight of the fact that in order to work well, we need to spend time working together. [Health professional]

4.5 Creating Generative Space for Organizational Learning

We were particularly interested in understanding how the six sites developed and sustained a generative space that seemed to be associated with organizational learning. We also wondered how they had been able to avoid the situations experienced in other sites that became characterized by inert or toxic space. At the start in all ten sites, diverse groups of people (physicians, other health professionals and RHA managers) were brought together to design and develop implementation strategies for innovative approaches to PHC. The overall structure and systems were relatively similar across all sites. But what was identified as most crucial by our interviewees, was the efforts taken to establish meaningful conversations and relationships among the various stakeholders. People responsible for organizing the sites with generative spaces told us how they intentionally and conscientiously sought to develop relationships among participants, believing that they provided a critical space for conversations that would lead to organizational learning. In our analysis of the data, we identified four micro-level strategies that were important in developing this generative space for organizational learning: (1) assembling the right people, (2) developing social relationships, (3) focusing the conversation, and (4) developing mechanisms to manage setbacks. In the sites where we identified generative space for organizational learning, we saw that all four strategies were used consistently. In the sites where inert or toxic space developed, not all strategies were implemented, or they were implemented but not sustained. Below we explain each of the four strategies.

4.5.1 *Assembling the Right People*

In all ten sites, people responsible for starting up the initiative told us they invested a great deal of energy into bringing physicians, managers, and other health professionals together to begin the planning process. They believed it was critical to bring all of the right participants together, and while that was reasonably easy for RHA employees, it was very difficult to convince busy physicians to attend meetings. Physicians were disinclined to attend planning meetings, since their financial compensation was normally based on the number of patients treated (fee for service) and meetings used up time that could otherwise be revenue generating. Thus, finding ways to get physicians to assemble with others received high priority.

Senior RHA leaders and one or two physicians with particular interest and expertise in primary care took responsibility for bringing other people on board. Interviewees often referred to these initial assemblers as "visionaries," "early adopters," "champions," and "enthusiasts." Interestingly, in almost every case, these leaders adopted an inclusive recruitment strategy. Rather than hand-picking a select group of individuals, they approached as many people as possible and tried to convince them all to attend meetings.

In some cases, RHA managers approached physicians, but more typically, champion physicians recruited other physicians. One strategy was to encourage physicians based on their desire to improve the services available for their patients. This approach was designed in response to physicians' frustrations with existing practices, gaps in services, and dreams for making things better; but it was time-consuming and difficult. As one physician champion noted:

> The painful part along the way is convincing your colleagues that this is the way to go. I spent hours and hours talking with them—and I haven't always succeeded. [Champion Physician]

Financial incentives were used to try and bring physicians to the table. Physicians who worked on a fee-for-service basis told us that funding for meeting time was an important factor in encouraging their participation. They explained that because they were already feeling overworked, exhausted, and underappreciated, they were reluctant to "volunteer" their time, especially when, as they commonly reported, "Everyone else at the table was being paid." Managers seemed to accept that this financial incentive was necessary to encourage physicians in joining the planning processes.

> Physicians are very busy, and for them to take time out of their practice was financially very unrewarding for them. So this [extra funding] created an opportunity for two parties to come together and not have to worry about money. [RHA manager]

Assembling the right people remained an ongoing process because physicians in particular seemed to drift away. Physicians repeatedly told us that they inherently disliked meeting time—even when the compensation system facilitated it. Thus, in sites where generative space was developed, we observed ongoing actions to bring people together. As the innovation sites progressed, new members were integrated into the conversations, and others stepped away. Over time, site directors took on increasing levels of responsibility for planning and day-to-day operations and senior RHA managers became less involved. As one RHA Vice President described:

> I was the first one, I was absolutely there. You need to get those wheels going, you need to get traction. For me as a VP, it's like: How is this going? Is this the right approach? [...] Finding out all the challenges, all the pitfalls, certainly being very, very close to the letter of intent, and business planning [was] key for me. And since then, I've been able to back right off and let others carry the ball. [Senior RHA manager]

We observed that this micro-process of *assembling the right people* was the first step in creating a space for organizational learning. All ten sites engaged in this micro-process in the early stages. But in the two sites where we identified the development of toxic space, in spite of supportive remuneration, physician attendance at meetings became lower and lower to the point where meetings no longer occurred. In the two sites where we observed the development of inert space, the right people were initially assembled and they continued to meet, but little energy or enthusiasm was evident. However, in the six sites where we identified generative space and organizational learning seemed to occur, assembling people on a regular basis continued and was viewed as important. Thus it seems that assembling the right people is an important continual process that helps to create the right kind of space for organizational learning. Without assembled people who are committed to developing new and better ways of providing services, relationships between them are unlikely to form and organizational learning is unlikely to proceed.

4.5.2 Developing Positive Social Relationships

Bringing people together was an important first step, but we also heard from interviewees about the importance of developing trusting social relationships—especially between physicians and RHA managers. Historical circumstances led to some sense of distrust between physicians and managers. However, PHC innovation and additional funding demanded that the two work together. The goal of innovation site organizers was to develop new working relationships as a foundation for further initiatives.

Interviewees from the six sites that developed generative space for learning spoke at length about the ongoing development of more positive, respectful and trusting relationships between physicians and RHA members. Long standing taken-for-granted assumptions meant that people needed to step back and meet each other under new circumstances. We heard from interviewees about how relationships evolved over time as members of the innovation sites began to plan, dream, and problem-solve together. People found ways to get to know each other and develop an appreciation for each other's work. These dynamics relied heavily on the involvement of "neutral" facilitators who were neither physicians, nor RHA employees. It seemed to be important to create a sense of something new, where old relationships could be considered a thing of the past. One site manager explained it as follows:

> So I was the one neutral body that came on board. I wasn't [RHA] and I wasn't a physician. I was an external resource that was used to develop processes that were collaborative to develop the business plan. I was their "in-between" really, Switzerland, in a lot of ways. I didn't represent all of the regional needs and requirements. I didn't represent all the physicians' needs and requirements.

People told us it was crucial to provide a middle ground where physicians and RHA managers could meet and begin to develop trusting relationships:

> We came to the conclusion that it couldn't be the RHA, neither could it be the physicians leading the business planning process. It needed a third party. So we hired a project manager and that was absolutely crucial. It really works better if you've got somebody in the middle. And we've learned that that's a very crucial piece. [RHA manager]

Encouraged by the neutral facilitator, people spent time talking with each other and began to learn more about each other, not just as professionals, but also as people. And through this, they began to trust and respect each other, as noted here:

> I think it was something that happened gradually. First of all we would set 15–30 minutes at the beginning of meetings and basically talk with each other. Gradually learn more about each other, and we saw each other as individuals—not as an RHA person, or physicians. And I think what happened is, this grew into respect and trust in each other. I think this is the most important thing that's been going in the months that I have been involved in it. [RHA Manager]

As they talked and worked together, people began to see each other in new ways. Several RHA managers, for example, described their surprise in learning that physicians genuinely cared about their patients. This led to new insights about why physicians behaved as they did.

> In all honesty (and I see now that it clouded my view) I thought that all physicians care about is money. What I learned is that they really do care about the people that they treat; they really do. I was surprised to hear that they are worried the RHA will take their patients away. I still remember when I was at a conference with Dr. X and I said, "You really do care about these people, don't you?" And he says, "Well, yeah, I do." [RHA Manager]

> It's a long process and collaboration involves compromise. And compromise means you really have to listen, and it means seeing doctors in a new way for me. I had to learn to actually listen to what physicians were saying and try to empathize. And I think it's been the same way for them. They're now seeing us as more than holding the money bags for the RHA. They're seeing us as struggling with how to deliver quality care as well. So I think that's been a real learning for everyone. [RHA Manager]

Building social relationships as part of starting up the innovation sites was primarily about building mutual trust and respect such that people were able to express their ideas and concerns and be open to those of other people. Thus it nurtured a generative space for conversations that facilitated development of innovative ideas. In the majority of our sites, people reported that they began to truly listen to each other, they began to see the system from different perspectives, and they came to understand different peoples' ways of working in the system. However, in the two sites where a toxic space developed, interviewees continued to talk about "us" and "them." In our final round of interviews it was evident that positive social relationships had not developed. Thus we suggest that the development of social relationships among individuals is an important component of creating a space for organizational learning.

4.5.3 Focusing the Conversation

In addition to *assembling the right people* and *developing social relationships*, interviewees also identified the strategy of *focusing the conversation* as critical (and difficult). In the sites with generative space, key individuals took particular efforts to direct the conversation and attention onto a small number of projects while putting others on the backburner. This was not a simple task since most individuals were particularly interested in one or two favorite programs or projects. And since the innovation sites began with wide-open agendas, focusing in on a few initiatives meant that some people could potentially become disengaged if attention to their favorite was delayed or ignored.

Many interviewees spoke about the importance of finding common ground. Although they described this in various ways, including, "having a shared vision," "unity of direction," "shared goals," "being on the same page"—all were consistent in noting that being on common ground, although requiring compromise, was fundamental to working and moving forward together. As one manager noted:

> It's really neat that we've been able to at least sit down and talk about it, and work toward understanding each others' goals. And then figure out what we will tackle first.

It was critical that people found a way to reduce a large number of potentially good ideas down to a manageable number. However, in some sites it was difficult to narrow in on a small number of initiatives because there were far more good ideas than could reasonably be tackled at one time. A physician explained this as follows:

> Well, after the first few meetings it was clear that we had developed about ten great ideas for improving primary health care. But [the executive director] was chairing the next meeting, and really made a good case for developing a priority list—even though some people would be disappointed that their idea had to wait. I think that [he/she] was quite convincing. And we all agreed to limit our first efforts to two initiatives—and try to make sure that these two were successful. It's a good thing we did, because we didn't realize how hard it would be just to work on the two.

In the two sites characterized by a toxic space, we observed that in one case plans were developed by managers but without much input from other health professionals, including physicians. This meant that the number of initiatives being considered at any one time was relatively small and manageable, but it also meant that the free-wheeling brainstorming sessions (with excitement and engagement) we heard about in some of the other sites did not occur.

In the other site where toxic space developed, there was initially a decision to take on nine strategic initiatives—identifying a champion for each and expectations that all would significantly move ahead within a year. Interviewees reported that each of the initiatives was important and could potentially contribute to the improvement of primary healthcare services in the area. However, when faced with funding delays, it became difficult to maintain any enthusiasm. We heard from interviewees that in hindsight, they believed they would have been more successful if they had agreed to focus on only a few initiatives early in the process.

In focusing the conversation, we observed that key individuals engaged in an important strategy to support organizational learning. By narrowing the options, people found ways to prioritize and then worked together on the highest priorities. People appreciated the guidance provided by site managers—although not always initially. This focus helped to achieve success on one or two initiatives so that people could feel energized to take another step forward.

4.5.4 Managing Setbacks and Frustrations

In each of the innovation sites we followed, there were delays or setbacks from time to time. Some sites coped with this much better than others. For example, delays in gaining government approval for business plans led to more difficulties in some sites. But in other sites, people found ways to manage the delay and minimize any resulting problems. In one site, physicians and other key individuals became so frustrated that they walked away from the process. Long periods of seeming inactivity appeared to take away enthusiasm, and in some sites getting started again proved to be very difficult.

In addition to time delays, another challenge was navigating what several people referred to as "two cultures"—*physicians* who tended to be very action-oriented and preferred to "just do it," and RHA *managers* who were accustomed to lengthy planning processes. Finding ways to bring these cultures together required excellent facilitation efforts, and there were varying degrees of success. In the sites where generative spaces were created managers found ways to keep people engaged by generating a sense of progress. They were able to identify small interim projects that could be accomplished even if larger projects were delayed. Managers also reported that it was critical to have the authority to make decisions at the table, rather than having to seek permission from someone higher up. This delegation of authority enabled the planning process to proceed more expeditiously. Similarly, site managers told us that bringing things of value to the table, and not waiting until everything was "100 percent perfect," but rather adjusting along the way, was helpful in developing mechanisms for managing delays or setbacks.

The importance of having an individual dedicated to the planning process became most apparent in those sites where there was no full time manager, or where an individual left the position. The lack of a manager made it very clear how critical leadership was in maintaining forward momentum and keeping interest and enthusiasm up, even in the face of setbacks:

> When we lost [the manager position] we really saw the need for somebody who has a good overall understanding and could be constantly working with the broader group to keep them moving. We found that if it's left among the broader group, they're so busy on a day-to-day basis, that no one champions the process through. There wasn't anyone there to pick up the pieces, and to keep it moving along. [RHA manager]

In the six sites where generative space was developed, site managers found effective ways to manage setbacks and keep people focused collaboratively on big picture goals. In the sites where inert space developed, managers seemed unable to keep people engaged. And in the sites where toxic space was created, managers found that they were dealing with overwhelming levels of negativity that prevented any sense of looking forward.

Overall, we observed that in sites where generative space developed, the managers engaged in all four strategies and continued to renew their efforts over time. In the other four sites, we saw that managers engaged in only some strategies, and their engagement was short-lived. In the two sites with toxic space, there was initial attention to assembling people and developing relationships, but when setbacks and delays occurred, there did not seem to be any mechanisms to overcome the frustration.

4.6 Discussion and Conclusions

We wanted to understand how healthcare professionals and managers created and sustained conditions that encouraged organizational learning—that is, how to develop the right kind of space. Although we did not initially set out to focus on the work of managers, our interviewees consistently told us about the importance of managerial work. In sites where organizational learning seemed to occur, we heard about the efforts of site managers to create a space that people described in terms of positive feelings of enthusiasm and

[Figure 4.1: A flow diagram showing boxes labeled "Assembling the Right People", "Developing Social Relationships", "Focusing the Conversation", leading to "GENERATIVE SPACE", with "Managing Setbacks & Frustrations" feeding back into the process.]

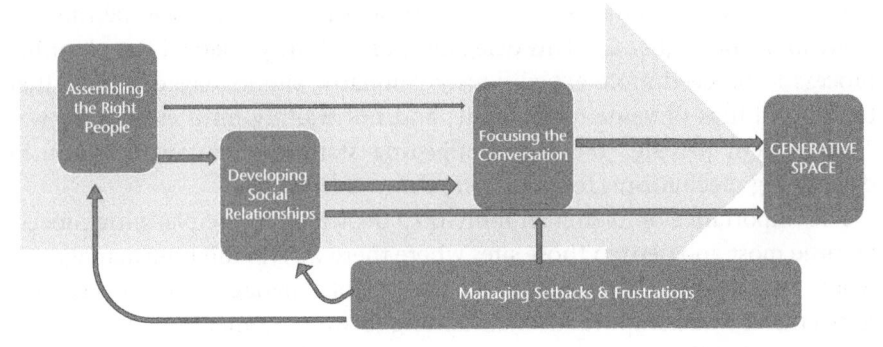

Figure 4.1 Mechanisms for creating and sustaining the right kind of space for organizational learning

accomplishment. Managers helped to create this generative space by consistently engaging in all of the following four strategies: (1) assembling the right people, (2) developing positive social relationships, (3) focusing the conversation, and (4) managing setbacks and frustrations. In other sites, managers engaged in some but not all of these strategies, or they initially engaged but were unable to sustain their efforts over time. These were the sites where space was *inert* or *toxic*.

Figure 4.1 provides a schematic representation of our findings about how the right kind of space for organizational learning can be created. The cases we studied suggest a strong role for managers in terms of engaging health professionals through the four strategies we identified: assembling the right people, developing positive social relationships, focusing the conversation, and managing setbacks and frustrations. It was through the ongoing accomplishment of these strategies that managers were able to facilitate the creation of space for organizational learning.

Our study contributes to theory about organizational learning and knowledge mobilization in several ways. First, we show that the nature of space for learning matters. Our study supports and builds on previously developed theoretical concepts about the importance of social relationships and conversations as an integral foundation for organizational learning (e.g. Bouwen and Hosking, 2000; Nonaka and Konno, 1998; Nonaka, Toyama, and Byosiere, 2001). By engaging in a longitudinal research study, we were able to observe a variety of cases and thus able to develop a typology of space for learning (generative, inert, and toxic) that includes both positive and negative space. This is an important difference from previous studies that have mostly ignored the negative. Nonaka and colleagues developed the concept of supportive *ba* by focusing only on situations where organizational learning occurred. Other studies (e.g. Baker, 2002; Edenius and Yakhlef, 2007) have similarly focused on understanding how successful organizational learning occurred. Although we identified the development of different types of space, we admit that we too were most interested in understanding positive cases and how generative space was created and maintained. We suggest that future research should further investigate cases of inert or toxic spaces. It would be both interesting and important to better understand whether such negative spaces, once created, tend to become entrenched or whether particular strategies can transform them from negative to positive.

The second way in which we contribute theoretically is by turning the focus inward to better understand the experiences of people who are involved in the process of organizational learning. We identified four strategies that were critical to developing the right kind of space for learning, expanding on trends in the organizational learning literature to shift attention from outcomes to process (Bapuji and Crossan, 2004). Our study draws attention to the importance of the perspectives and perceptions of individuals inside organizations. With consideration of POS approaches, we developed a better understanding about the importance of positive social relationships as a foundation for organizational learning. We also observed the problems that can occur when positive relationships are not present. Our interviewees told us how their perceptions of the space influenced learning. Consistent with the POS literature (e.g. Cameron, Bright, and Caza, 2004; Spreitzer et al., 2005), people told us that social interactions were critical to learning, and when such learning occurred there was a sense of enthusiasm and accomplishment that spiraled upward.

This perspective on space for organizational learning provides additional richness and new dimensions to the concept of *ba*. Where Nonaka, Toyama, and Byosiere (2001) developed a model that dissected space for learning into sections where different components of knowledge translation occurred, our focus allowed us to understand this space in terms that held particular value for people attempting to engage in learning. We suggest that when people believe they have positive relationships at work, they can move forward with processes of organizational learning. On the other hand, when there is a general feeling of apathy, lack of energy, or even hostile feelings among people in the workplace, organizational learning is less likely to occur. Our findings suggest that in addition to the importance of psychological safety (Edmondson, 1999), the right kind of space for organizational learning needs to be characterized by positive emotions such as enthusiasm and confidence that become contagious—encouraging everyone involved to mobilize existing knowledge and generate new ideas in ways that advance organizational capabilities.

Our third way of contributing to theory is by highlighting the importance of managerial work to promote organizational learning. The strategies designed and implemented by managers (or lack thereof) can: create generative spaces for learning, leave learning suspended (in inert spaces), or destroy learning (in toxic spaces). It is through managers' purposeful actions that people can be brought together to develop positive social relationships that foster organizational learning; without such actions, or with inadequate managerial efforts, the requisite relationships are unlikely to occur. Our findings build on those of Hannah and Lester (2009) in that we observed the importance of intermingled leadership and managerial skills (not one or the other). In addition, we found that effective managers used their leadership and managerial skills to modify their own actions in response to changing circumstances and unexpected turns of events. For example, when delays occurred or when key individuals left the organization, managers provided leadership in revising interim goals and activities. They also engaged in multiple conversations with health professionals to continually build team relationships and maintain enthusiasm.

While others have found that managers are critical to the knowledge creation process, less has been said about *how* managers support learning. For example, Nonaka, Toyama, and Byosiere (2001) identified a crucial role for managers in learning but did not describe this role in detail. Edmondson (1999) identified manager support, coaching, and role modeling as important, and Nembhard and Edmondson (2006) found that leader inclusiveness supported learning in teams characterized by status differences. But these authors did not identify specific practices that constituted "supporting," "coaching," "role modeling," or "inclusiveness." By focusing on the people involved, we were able to identify critical strategies in which managers engaged. In particular, our study highlights the importance of managers' hands-on and relatively continuous attention to positive social relationships.

Our study answers some questions and raises others. We do not know what kind of learning, if any, occurred in the inert and toxic spaces. We have focused on the organizationally beneficial outcomes associated with generative spaces (i.e. innovations in primary healthcare delivery), but this does not preclude the possibility that some other type of learning occurred in the inert or toxic spaces. For example, people who find themselves in inert spaces might be learning how to conserve new knowledge and innovative ideas for use when circumstances are more supportive; or, people in toxic spaces may simply be learning how to survive in undesirable situations. In addition, and consistent with Croft and Currie's (Chapter 3) suggestions, the impact of power dynamics across professions may lead to particular types of hierarchical relationships that support different styles of learning. These considerations could lead to interesting new insights in terms of developing working relationships and collaborative efforts that best support knowledge mobilization and organizational learning.

We do not know how widely our findings are generalizable, but we believe they provide transferrable lessons for others trying to improve the use of knowledge and generation of innovations in similar jurisdictions. The people we interviewed were all from publicly funded healthcare organizations where mobilizing knowledge and learning to provide services in better ways were part of their mandate. Based on our previous work and conversations with managers of other organizations, we believe that similar processes occur at least within the public sector. We note that while three years is a relatively long time to follow organizations, it can still be far too short to understand all aspects of organizational learning initiatives. Longer term research projects would be helpful in understanding more about the creation and maintenance of the right kind of space for organizational learning. We hope that future research will provide further insights and continue to expand our collective knowledge base in this area.

Acknowledgments

The authors thank the Canadian Institutes for Health Research and the Alberta Heritage Foundation for Medical Research [CIHR Grant # 78710] for funding that supported this research.

Theme 3
Mobilizing Knowledge through Networking

Introduction

In this section, the domain of action that is in focus is the networking that links the different organizations and professions that are involved in improving treatments and delivery of treatments in healthcare. Healthcare managers, academic scholars, and policy makers alike recognize the importance of cultivating better interactions among different healthcare professionals and researchers in order to speed up the translation of knowledge into practice. As a result, there are now a large number of formal initiatives aimed at establishing novel, more collaborative, networked, forms of organizing that will mobilize knowledge across the research–practice (or knowing–doing) divide. This is the theme of the three chapters in this section, with each focusing on how new forms of networked organization, established to create the type of collaborative relationship between researchers and practitioners that can generate and mobilize knowledge, actually emerge and are sustained over time. In doing this each chapter examines a set of critical challenges that arise in such network settings and analyses how these challenges were (or were not) overcome. Moreover, in line with the idea of multiple overlapping agencies, the three chapters in this section treat networks not as simple channels through which information and knowledge flow, but rather as agents that are part of the complex healthcare ecology, influencing the ways knowledge is mobilized (or constrained).

Traditionally, the research–practice divide has been seen either as a problem caused by researchers (academics undertaking research that is not practically relevant—"ivory tower" research) or as a problem caused by practitioners (clinicians and other practitioners not having the time or inclination to keep up-to-date with new advances in knowledge that indicate a practice change would be helpful). Both of these views of the problem, however, are based on the assumption that knowledge can be generated in one place/time and then transferred and relatively easily implemented in another, if only those involved would not be so resistant and wedded to the existing processes. As we have seen, this view is problematized in this book. In its place, we have emphasized that a more realistic (and more effective) view of how new knowledge is generated and mobilized to support healthcare is that researchers and practitioners need to work together in an iterative and continuous cycle of idea generation, development, and implementation. In this section we examine the challenges associated with this process in network initiatives; that is, initiatives that attempt to formally bring together diverse individuals and organizations on the assumption that this will increase collaboration and knowledge sharing and so improve the uptake of research evidence into practice (and so improve healthcare and its delivery).

Chapter 5 characterizes the knowledge mobilization challenge in network settings in terms of the simultaneous need for knowledge exploration and exploitation, noting that these two knowledge processes, while complementary, can also be antagonistic in practice. The authors relate this to the idea of ambidexterity, which is the capability to deal with the tensions between knowledge exploration and exploitation. They report three different network initiatives and show how the tensions between exploration and exploitation played out in each case, allowing them to suggest three different modes of dealing with network ambidexterity. For example, in one case, even while the focus was on network ambidexterity, the initiative attempted to develop individuals who could bridge the research–practice divide through training to become "practitioner-scholars." In another case, knowledge brokers were used as a bridge between those undertaking the research and those engaged in practice. In the final case, a hub organization was used to broker relationships between the various organizations involved.

While the three cases in Chapter 5 use different approaches to overcome the research–practice divide, all illustrate the political nature of moving toward more collaborative and networked modes of organizing and all stress the importance of social networks. These issues are taken up in the following two chapters in this themed section, with Chapter 6 focusing on the power of everyday actions for mobilizing knowledge across a network, and Chapter 7 focusing on how social networks emerge and influence network level knowledge mobilization based on mandated formal structures.

In Chapter 6 the authors consider the power of everyday "work" that initiates and sustains a project that is designed to encourage increased coordination and collaboration amongst all the various organizations and individuals involved in the care of a particular, clinically vulnerable population. In considering the power of everyday talk and text, in combination with the power of objects, they show the work that is needed over time to mobilize knowledge in a network

Mobilizing Knowledge through Networking

settings where it is not possible to impose or mandate change (this in contrast to Chapter 7, which shows mandating some structural changes was possible once the network initiative was formally established).

Turning to Chapter 7, the authors, like those of Chapter 5, use the term "network ambidexterity," but since they focus on social networks, they use the term to describe the simultaneous conditions of brokerage (to connect disconnected groups and so close "structural holes," thus encouraging exploration) and closure (that produces cohesive communities that allow knowledge to be embedded in practice, thus encouraging knowledge exploitation). The important aspect of this chapter is that it demonstrates how network ambidexterity can be virtuously produced through the creation of formal structures (in this case, organizing around themes that bring together people from different backgrounds) and brokering roles (in this case, knowledge brokers whose remit is to reach out to ensure that the research being done within the themes is accessible to those for whom this is relevant). These formally designed network structures influenced the social networks that developed over time, facilitating the network ambidexterity that promoted the knowledge mobilization that was sought. These authors do acknowledge that while their case demonstrates a virtuous cycle of formal structuring and the emergence of productive informal social networks, there may also be situations where a vicious cycle could be produced. Given the various boundaries that must be overcome in network settings, this is of course an important word of caution and attests to the idea that facilitating effective knowledge mobilization in formal network initiatives requires significant organizational work by those involved, echoing the conclusions in Chapter 4.

In combination, then, the three chapters in this section demonstrate the difficulties but also the opportunities that derive from the effective mobilization of knowledge in network settings. More importantly, they demonstrate the significant work that is required to set up and maintain such network forms that can facilitate knowledge mobilization over time. Knowledge mobilization does not just happen, even when the appropriate structures, roles, and incentives are put in place to provide knowledge sharing linkages between the organizations and individuals involved. Proactive work is involved and this means that the outcomes of formal initiatives to facilitate knowledge mobilization across the research–practice divide will also be emergent, and outcomes will not always be as intended. The chapters in this section illustrate some of the practices that can facilitate outcomes that are positive but it should be clear by now that there are no simple solutions given the variety of agents involved and the diversity of practices and vested interests in the healthcare ecology.

5

Knowledge Mobilization across Inter-organizational Healthcare Innovation Partnerships

A Network Ambidexterity Perspective

Eivor Oborn, Karl Prince, and Michael Barrett

CHAPTER SUMMARY

Research since 2005 has furthered our understanding of mobilizing research knowledge into practice with a focus on appropriate ways for health organizations to address the "knowledge gap." This chapter examines how knowledge mobilization is performed in inter-organizational healthcare networks, and how different stakeholders work together to achieve a balance between research knowledge production and implementation in three different network initiatives. In particular, it explores how network ambidexterity—the balance between exploration and exploitation—is achieved to facilitate knowledge mobilization. The findings reveal four key challenges common across the case studies: managing and engaging stakeholders, managing appropriate funding strategies, managing competing priorities, and the politics of knowledge in innovation. The chapter reveals how network ambidexterity is developed differently across each inter-organizational initiative in light of these challenges and contribute to the literature by developing a classification of ambidexterity in inter-organizational networks that may prove useful in illuminating knowledge mobilization practices.

5.1 Introduction

The healthcare landscape is becoming increasingly complex. For example, organizations with expertise and capabilities in inpatient care, community-based care, health research, commissioning and purchasing, technologies, patient advocacy, and supporting online communities are becoming involved in enabling better patient care (Zachariadis et al., 2013; Swan et al., 2010; Barrett, Oborn, and Orlikowski, 2015). As such, rather than the historical tendency for health organizations to work in relative isolation, organizations are cognizant of being part of a wider health ecosystem that can work together in synergistic and collaborative ways.

The purpose of this chapter is to take an in-depth look at three very different inter-organizational partnerships which were set up with the explicit goal of knowledge mobilization. Each partnership sought to bring together diverse skills needed to develop and use healthcare-related knowledge in improving patient care, yet sought to accomplish this goal through relatively different activities and strategies. Thus, whilst previous chapters have examined how organizations work to improve their own capabilities to support knowledge mobilization, here we take a wider view of how organizations might rely on each other to develop value across a network by balancing and complementing their different capabilities. Some organizations and groups focused more on identifying new knowledge (e.g. research) whilst others sought to implement and exploit this knowledge in health service delivery contexts, requiring knowledge mobilization across the network partnerships to ensure an adequate balance of these different capabilities. Knowledge mobilization, as a general process of transferring research into practice and informing research through practice, can be regarded as constituting both open explorative learning and the more exploitative process of implementing knowledge in healthcare practices. In essence, exploration underpins the knowledge generation processes of health research whilst exploitation underpins service improvement and implementation activities.

As emphasized in literature on innovation and creativity (e.g. Miron, Erez, and Naveh, 2004; Amabile, 1996), open exploratory processes of knowledge creation which include problem identification and accessing background disciplinary know-how are generally stimulated in contexts that are different from the managed performance of service efficiency. Given the immediate pressures of meeting performance targets, those working in service delivery often have little spare capacity or organizational slack to engage in reflexive reading or research seminar attendance so as to stimulate their learning. In meeting these challenges, leaders seek to stimulate new forms of value such as developing new knowledge. While there are a number of possible ways, we know little about how diverse stakeholders arrange and work together (or not) across a diverse partnership to create value, whether through exploratory knowledge development or through the exploitation of implementing novel ideas into work practice.

This chapter seeks to contribute to our understanding in this area by examining how knowledge mobilization enables different modes of achieving ambidexterity across a network. Complementing D'Andreta and Scarborough's Chapter 7 in this volume, which examines network structures and brokerage, this chapter examines how inter-organizational partnerships achieve a balance between exploration and exploitation through developing innovative knowledge mobilization network initiatives. We argue that achieving this balance through what we call *network ambidexterity* is key to managing the multiple demands of the diverse requirements, stakeholders, structures, and processes involved in the practice of mobilizing knowledge. In accomplishing network ambidexterity, leaders in our three cases needed to carefully engage the appropriate stakeholder members, develop workable funding strategies, mediate between competing priorities, and deal with the political challenges of knowledge in innovation.

5.2 Literature Review

Our approach is informed by innovation scholarship (Turner, Swart, and Maylor, 2013; Lavie, Stettner, and Tushman, 2010), which emphasizes the importance of enabling ambidexterity through integrating the exploration and exploitation activities associated with health-related research and healthcare delivery (Oborn et al., 2013). The primary goal in innovation is to draw on explorative and exploitative processes to enable new forms of value (March, 1991). Yet these processes are often in tension (Benner and Tushman, 2003). Exploration involves searching, flexibility, experimentation, and discovery. The outcomes of exploration are essentially to develop potentially radical new ideas and can be regarded as potentially disruptive to the status quo (Lewin, Long, and Carroll, 1999). Exploitation is concerned with seeking an increase in efficiency and productivity by reducing variance as well as limiting the range of alternatives for decision-making and execution (Turner, Swart, and Maylor, 2013). Rather than seeking new knowledge and the introduction of new ideas, exploitation is about building on existing knowledge bases, refining and extending existing competencies and processes.

While both of these foci are necessary for organizational success (Rivkin and Siggelkow, 2003) they are inherently contradictory and difficult to balance (Tushman and O'Reilly, 1996). Although often referred to as dichotomous options, exploration and exploitation might be viewed as a continuum, as is often observed in practice (Lavie, Stettner, and Tushman, 2010). Similarly, exploration and exploitation are linked by a transition where the ability to acquire new knowledge can be dependent on existing knowledge within an organization (Cohen and Levinthal, 1990), so that without prior exploitation of knowledge within an organization it may be not be possible to seek out suitable knowledge for future innovation. Numerous scholars, particularly in the field of innovation, have examined how to balance exploration and exploitation within organizations and revealed how balance might be achieved at various levels—such as firm, team or individual levels—as well as across domains, and over time (Lavie, Stettner, and Tushman, 2010; Turner, Swart, and Maylor, 2013).

A key theoretical construct which describes the connection between exploration and exploitation and the ability to manage the tensions between them is ambidexterity (Simsek 2009). Organizational ambidexterity can be achieved through architectural ambidexterity, where separate strategies, structures and processes are focused on differentially supporting *either* exploration *or* exploitation (Gupta, Smith, and Shalley, 2006). Alternatively, contextual ambidexterity might be achieved where exploration and exploitation are integrated though social and behavioral means (Gibson and Birkinshaw, 2004) to develop an organizational context and culture that, for example, promotes aspects of both creativity and efficiency across teams and individuals. To facilitate contextual ambidexterity, socialization and team-building practices might be used to foster shared values and aid coordination (Andriopoulos and Lewis, 2009).

At the level of an organization, Andriopoulos and Lewis (2009) develop some guidelines as to how ambidexterity might be enabled. First, they posit that a multiple levels approach is necessary to manage the tensions. For instance, it is necessary to deal with both strategic concerns at the firm level and the personal drivers at the individual level. A key advantage of this approach is that the management of ambidexterity becomes the responsibility of actors across an organization. Second, engaging both integration and differentiation may be a useful tactic for developing ambidexterity. Integration attempts to highlight the importance of both exploration and exploitation rather than a "defensive" reaction to selecting either as a preferred option, while differentiation helps to focus actions, aiming to maximize the benefits of either exploration or exploitation. Third, the learning synergies enabled by exploration and exploitation can maintain ambidexterity. The mutual reinforcement between knowledge creation (supported by exploration) and the utilization of existing knowledge (supported by exploitation) is central to realizing ambidexterity (Smith, Collins, and Clark, 2005).

The research focus to date has been to examine ambidexterity at organization, team or individual levels (Turner, Swart, and Maylor, 2013; Lavie, Stettner, and Tushman, 2010; Andriopoulos and Lewis, 2009). However, there remains a paucity of research and examination of how ambidexterity might be enabled in inter-organizational networks and what different strategies might be applied to forming appropriate structures and contexts (Im and Rai, 2008; Stadler, Rajwani, and Karaba, 2014).

Networked settings are particularly challenging since knowledge is distributed amongst the various actors, their interests may be diverse and power within the network may be more widely distributed (Swan and Scarbrough, 2005; Prince, Barrett, and Oborn, 2014). Further, networks may be less stable as members enter and leave while knowledge flows may also be limited by cliques (Dhanaraj and Parkhe, 2006). Stadler, Rajwani, and Karaba (2014) proffer that a network level of analysis can contribute to our understanding of how ambidexterity is accomplished through, for example, the social ties between actors as well as the processes and combination of different structural and temporal solutions.

5.3 The Empirical Cases

The knowledge mobilization case studies draw on in-depth field studies with which the authors have been involved. The first case, which draws on thirty-nine semi-structured interviews, focuses on a regional multi-stakeholder learning and capacity development program. The second case, drawing on 106 semi-structured interviews concerns a user-driven health research program set up by the UK Department of Health. All three authors were researchers in CLAHRC organizations. The third case draws on a series of 35 semi-structured interviews regarding the set up and planning of a collaborative inter-organizational network aiming to integrate and exploit (big) data available across sectors and organizations in a regional health context.

5.4 Case 1. Search Canada: A Knowledge Mobilization Program for Building Capacity and Evidence-Based Practice

Following a number of healthcare reforms and reorganizations across the provincial healthcare system, a large provincial research funding organization in Canada decided to launch and support a new learning program around knowledge mobilization for healthcare professionals. This innovative residential learning program provided a select group of healthcare professionals from across the province with competencies and social resources necessary for effective mobilization of healthcare knowledge from research publications into practice. As such, the partnership focus in enabling ambidexterity was on improving their understanding of exploratory research in order to enable better exploitation of these findings in their practice. With a particular emphasis on addressing the capacity building concerns of smaller, rural health regions, the knowledge mobilization learning program attracted between twenty-five to twenty-seven healthcare workers from across the province biannually. Over time, the program was enhanced with a unique web technology-based network of knowledge resources, incorporation of a provincial network of targeted knowledge mobilization support and a more coordinated, team-based and user-responsive instruction.

> One of the things [we] have always tried to do is to create a learning space that was safe but also allowed people to test and risk in a way they might not in their own team... [or] in an academic classroom where they're being graded. So it was important, philosophically, to bring them together, to create, so that they knew each other and could trust each other. (Senior academic)

Established in 1996, the program was a leader in knowledge mobilization capacity development, and an innovation in the field for well over a decade. Several members from the CLAHRCs (described in the second case) went to Canada between 2008 and 2010 to study and learn from the SEARCH program.

5.4.1 *Managing Engagement*

In the local health regions at the time, those clinical and managerial stakeholders closely linked to universities or urban teaching hospitals were more likely to engage with emerging research or have social connections with researchers who could inform their practice. However, most areas of the province were rural and remote. A key goal in the partnership was to bring isolated rural clinicians and managers into contact with a wider social network so that they could learn from each other, become more aware of research evidence and thereby improve their capacity to use research evidence in their clinical practices.

> So my goal was also to create a more open environment where new comers could really engage... So creating [knowledge mobilization program] with the particular governance structure... that it was not just a nice idea, it was actually part of a strategy to create this institutionalisation of the commitment to research use in the province... that's why we wanted more sectors, we wanted the universities and we wanted regions... (Senior Manager)

A critical emphasis in the SEARCH model was to develop strong relationships between program participants from different regions, sectors and professional backgrounds. Seeking to overcome the traditional hierarchies prevalent in healthcare organizations, for example between clinical academics and community-based nurses, an emphasis was given to learning from each other. This was explained by one participant as follows:

> [The program] is like a spider web. It is all connected, everybody knows what other people are doing. There is no hierarchy, anybody can talk to anybody at any point in time and be treated as an equal. It is hard to describe. But I mean you would

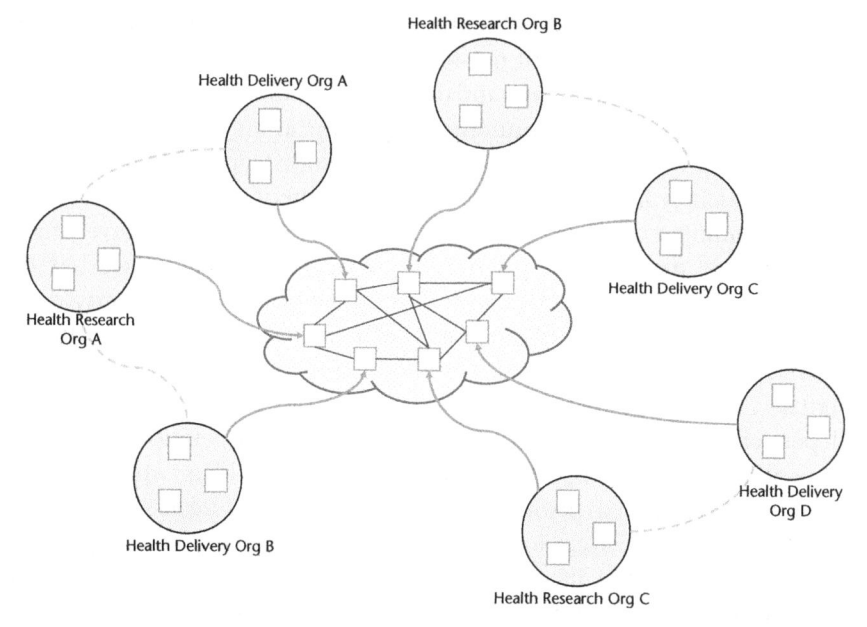

Figure 5.1 The SEARCH model for organizing knowledge mobilization

have a first year [participant] who might be a health records person in a health region who would just email a professor and say I need help on this and it would happen. That is not normal, in our world. (*Healthcare executive*)

Figure 5.1 is a diagrammatic representation of how SEARCH organized knowledge mobilization and engaged with various stakeholders across the network.

5.4.2 Managing Funding

The partnership was initially funded through a modest government health research grant. This grant covered the fixed administration costs, venue rental fees, program materials, and a portion of academic time given to teaching. As health delivery organizations became involved in the program, they also contributed toward the costs of program delivery. Contributing to the funding encouraged them to increase their ownership of the program content. Thus, as the program developed, regional units were increasingly interested in having input into the research topics being learned by the clinical staff from their units. On the other hand, a number of universities objected to the program funding, believing that this would reduce the funds available to them for medical research.

Originally established and funded by the Research Foundation, the knowledge mobilization partnership was transformed over time from a small administrative unit run in collaboration between a manager and a group of academics into an independent not-for-profit corporation with a more differentiated organizational structure and diversified funding. A key reason for this change was the significant withdrawal of provincial funding that supported the partnership with a rationale of making the knowledge mobilization partnership financially independent from the government.

Whilst a number of private organizations expressed interest in investing in the knowledge mobilization partnership, several key stakeholders felt the partnership mission was at odds with developing intellectual property rights on their learning program and open methods of collaboration and exchange. Yet in order to attract investors, commodifying the learning program was essential. This created a complex dilemma for the program; in order to acquire independent funding they also needed to change their operational mandate, goals and culture. An appeal from numerous stakeholders who had been significantly influenced through the program over its years of operation yielded a barrage of letters to funders in an attempt to keep the program alive and unchanged in its open learning mandate. Though this tactic was initially successful, the funding eventually atrophied and the program closed.

5.4.3 Balancing Competing Priorities

A primary challenge was freeing up academics' time so that they could support the learning program and develop its content. In the formative stages of the partnership, the number of stakeholders was small; those individuals who became involved were already invested in the mission of knowledge mobilization as an ideal. These motivated individuals were able to either convince or work around the bureaucratic demands of their host (university) organizations in order to participate in the partnership. For example, a number of academics were interested in teaching evidence-based practice skills, such as how to critically appraise research papers or make sense of systematic reviews. Yet their host departments were not necessarily supportive of their activities, seeing this partnership program as a possible competitor to their own university-wide research and teaching agenda. Some administrations felt it took individuals away from developing their research publications, a key metric of university department performance. Nonetheless, given the high levels of autonomy held by most academics, a number of keen researchers and teachers became centrally involved.

Over time, as an independent legal entity evolved, the corporation established a Board of Directors that was accountable to the shareholders (i.e. health organizations and universities). These had to engage in contractual relations with various regional and national governmental agencies. However, aligning these multiple stakeholders with very different goals, modes of operation and interests in intellectual property associated with the learning methodology and program made it difficult to also maintain the open, flat hierarchy associated with the ethos of the program. Though private funding was potentially available, aligning the multiple interests of the stakeholders was not feasible in the available time frame.

5.4.4 Managing Knowledge Politics

Early on in the program, academics—knowledgeable in systematic review methodologies, evidence-based evidence synthesis and knowledge mobilization principles—were in charge of learning content. Thus the learning program emphasized strong capacity building in understanding the research process and gaining literacy in appraising journal papers. However, over time more program stakeholders became vocal about the program's learning topics and attendee participants became particularly interested in more supported learning in regards to specific service changes. For example, epidemiologists favored statistical evidence and clinical academics favored rigorously controlled clinical trials whilst nursing and management practitioners and scholars highlighted the merits of qualitative inquiry, action research and evaluation studies. This highlights the multiple perspectives on what is useful evidence and what is good research. Thus over time, program content became negotiated across stakeholders rather than given by academics.

Another challenge was how to identify and select the ideal program participants who would benefit from the capacity development offered by the program. Should it be geared to the established opinion leaders and boundary spanners in organizations, who had already established an enthusiasm and skill in knowledge mobilization? Such program attendees were more likely to reflect well on the learning potential derived from the program. Initially these high-profile and enthusiastic individuals were recruited to the program, and they helped establish the program as a flagship in the country and internationally. However, over time this exclusivity was questioned, in favor of a needs-based approach. Thus several stakeholders suggested it would be better to also educate laggards who could potentially benefit more from the learning process. This shifted the learner cohort into a more mixed group with respect to their receptivity toward the program content.

5.5 Case 2. CLAHRCs UK: Knowledge Mobilization in Health Service Research

Nine CLAHRCs were set up in 2008 in England as a pilot program funded by the Department of Health to bridge the research to practice knowledge gap.

Matched funding was provided by organizations participating in the partnership. Whilst multiple activities related to enabling knowledge mobilization were important, a heavy emphasis on exploration through conducting and publishing new research was at the centre of the endeavor. CLAHRCs organized themselves into research and implementation themes and then developed governance mechanisms that enabled organizations to bridge and coordinate the efforts of academics across different departments and the provider organizations. Most of the partnerships involved more than one university department as well as health (e.g. NHS—National Health Service) and social service providers and occasionally other stakeholders (such as business sector, police, or public and patient representatives). In 2013, 13 CLAHRCs were (re)funded for another five-year period.

5.5.1 *Managing Engagement*

Whilst the nine individual CLAHRC arrangements were complex in that each entity organized their partnership in unique ways, CLAHRCs have been consistently organized around a lead university department and a lead NHS hospital provider around which a central management team structure was set up. The primary objective of the partnership was to conduct applied health service research that the participating provider organizations would find useful for informing its clinical services or management. As such, university partners were central to the collaboration as they were needed to conduct or oversee research that could be both published in peer-reviewed journals as well as having impact once implemented in some area of the local or national NHS.

University academics organized and led their exploratory research activities through numerous research teams, some working in multidisciplinary fashion across several university departments. In order to develop research projects that might have reasonable impact and utility to service providers (e.g. nurses, midwives, and doctors), representatives from provider organizations participated in the research team activity. Thus the CLAHRC emphasis on translating knowledge was in producing new (research) knowledge that health service providers would find useful and relevant and thus would exploit. Ambidexterity was sought through a new approach to research so that the exploratory findings were more relevant for being exploited by a wider group of stakeholders.

> This is the most radical thing the NIHR has ever [funded]. I have never done research like this before... it is completely different. (*Senior Academic lead*)

Thus, control over the research program and exploratory activity in the CLAHRCs was shifted away from being solely in the purview of academic researchers and the research questions they found interesting, to include the

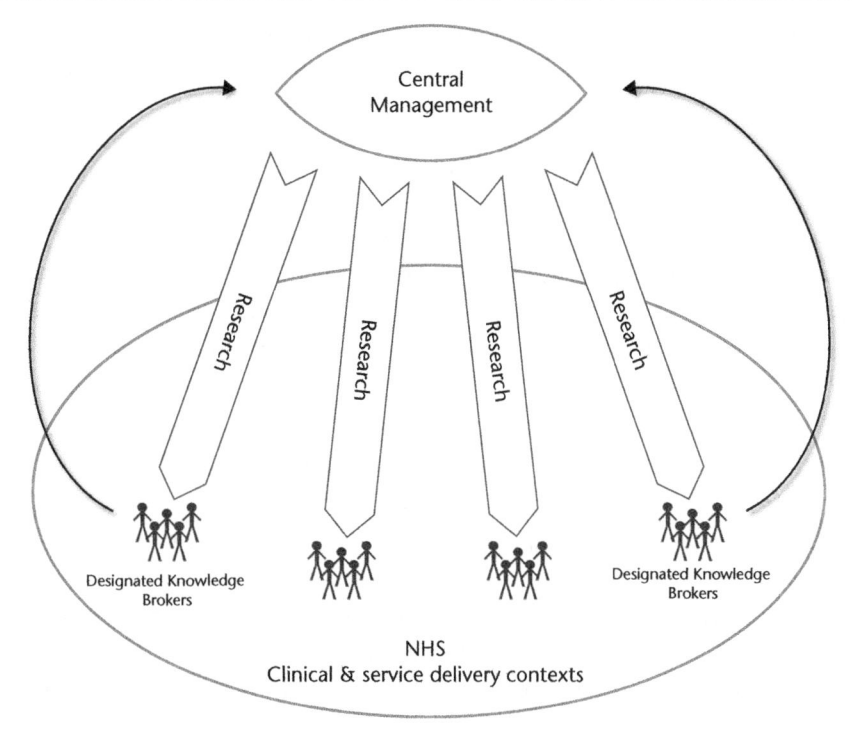

Figure 5.2 A CLAHRC model for organizing knowledge mobilization (Oborn et al., 2013)

views and interests of other stakeholders. Given the large number of CLAHRCs this resulted in numerous new forms of research collaborations. For example, numerous partnerships developed explicit roles for boundary spanners, or knowledge brokers—i.e. those designated individuals who could broker knowledge between the research and service provider communities. These individuals were often staff from provider organizations who spent time with the research team, so that they were able to represent provider interests in the research project, learn to understand the research process better as well as being made aware of research findings. An example of how this was organized is shown in Figure 5.2.

> We are trying to fully integrate [knowledge brokers] into our [research] team so that they know what stage we are at with the research. They helped write the implementation component for each of our proposals and we also have used an implementation contact to work alongside our [boundary spanner], so they do a bit of education and teaching and support with the [boundary spanners].
> (*Theme leader*)

Given the large number of CLAHRCs, there were other ways of organizing that they developed (see Oborn et al., 2013 for more detail). For example, some partnerships sought to incorporate members from provider organizations or service users onto the research team. Such individuals would then be encouraged to develop research skills, increase their research literacy, often assist with collecting research data and take a central role in facilitating the implementation of the research findings. Some research teams sought novel methods for conducting research, such as action research approaches, or involving researchers from other disciplinary areas, such as business schools or sociology, to participate in research process. Still other CLAHRC research teams were made to bid for projects involving specified service evaluation, thus focusing their research activities on researching the implementation and exploitation of various service forms.

> We used to stand outside and look in at [the research process] but now you have opened up the windows and let us in ... [it is great] to participate in the research [process]. (*Senior manager, service provider*)

These diverse forms of exploration sought to develop new knowledge that would both be more useful to partner organizations and which would be more accessible. Rather than service providers (managers or clinicians) needing to search extensively to find answers to important questions in their practice, they were able to learn directly from the researchers about findings that they might find useful.

5.5.2 Managing Funding

Each CLAHRC partnership was funded approximately £10M through a national research funding body. However the collaboration also needed to show that partners were willing to match this amount through their own in-kind investment. This in-kind investment did not need to be in cash, but rather could be accommodated through building space or staff time (e.g. during participation in research or learning activities). In-kind contribution from partner organization served to increase their commitment, helping to ensure involvement was maintained. Researchers also augmented the research funding by using these funds to support further grant applications, for example, by using CLAHRC funding to complete pilot phases of a research protocol.

5.5.3 Balancing Competing Priorities

A number of competing priorities emerged, particularly in relation to investing resources into research activities or implementation activities. Researchers are clearly rewarded for high quality research publications through the university system. To be internationally competitive and receive standing, academic researchers need to publish in designated top tier journals. Whilst researchers were generally keen to make their findings accessible to service providers, this was not their primary interest. Furthermore, they were not often skilled at communicating their findings to the appropriate target audience, neither did they have jurisdiction to impose changes to clinical practice. Many academics also felt that one study did not provide sufficient evidence to justify service change, but advocated a more robust approach of multiple confirming studies.

Managers and busy clinicians on the other hand equally had many competing priorities, juggling multiple "targets" and reorganizations imposed by the government. Thus the new "research findings" were often only a small aspect of what they needed to focus on. This was particularly the case if any of their designated targets were at risk of being breached (which may incur a fine from the government), as this then absorbed the majority of their energy. A large number of providers (both health and social care organizations) were also involved in significant government reforms, and expressed "change fatigue" in relation to yet another innovation, such as implementing service change in relation to research findings. Amongst the managerial staff there was also considerable turnover, thus those individuals who had been supportive of the research initially had often moved on to another post and dropped out of contact with the research team with their new priorities.

5.5.4 Managing Knowledge Politics

Whilst universities are equipped for setting up approval for research projects, service organizations are not equally streamlined to facilitate research activities. Challenges in gaining research approval were particularly acute when non-service provider staff (e.g. university-based researchers) needed to interview clinical or managerial staff or patients in relation to the research intervention. As the research was most commonly of an applied nature (such as action research-based) and exploratory in relation to particular host organization queries (such as the evaluation of a stroke service) contextual and inter-organizational aspects of the research were often important. Yet the research ethics or governance processes, initially set up to protect patients during clinical trials and from invasive techniques, were difficult and time consuming (forms often exceeding seventy-five pages), generally requiring exact interview questions (difficult for open-ended qualitative techniques) and who was going to interviewed (difficult before the researcher has been able to gain access to identify key informants). Further, each individual provider organization needed to give their own approval, such that researchers generally needed to pursue several separate approval applications in tandem for each project. In practical terms this meant that most research projects took a year to gain approval, though the projects were often identified as priorities by the provider organizations themselves. This was complicated by junior research staff turnover, as the research approval process was in relation to designated, named individuals, and if they left, new approval often needed to be obtained. The ongoing challenge of research approval was persistent for the second refunding of the CLAHRCs where research teams were often waiting past one year for gaining approval to initial data collection, which underutilizes the (paid) researchers' time.

A further challenge was regarding data protection of patient records. Numerous research collaborations involved social services and social service staff. However, the records held by social services and health services could not be easily shared. Nor could healthcare staff access their (electronic) patient records off site, due to data security issues. Nonetheless, these services often delivered "integrated" care within the community, though staff were challenged in being able to access and share appropriate information. Consequently, this became an acute problem for research teams examining the implementation of community-based or "integrated" services.

5.6 Case 3. TechFirm: Knowledge Mobilization through Big Data Integration

Given the rapid development of digital data repositories and health-related data sources there is potential value in integrating healthcare-related data across public and private organizations in ways that build knowledge and add value to their often disparate goals. TechFirm, a global technology and consulting firm, sought to create an innovation partnership across the healthcare sector in the UK that could potentially redefine the health ecosystem. The aim of the partnership was to focus on data integration and data analytics for the diverse organizations involved and thereby develop new knowledge regarding healthcare operations, clinical efficiency and effectiveness as well as support medical research. As such the aim was to both explore and exploit, with the latter being the primary way of funding the former.

In this third case, the central technology stakeholder worked for a two-year period to establish a partnership between multiple public and private organizations which could mutually benefit from sharing data. However, after initial investments over the two-year period, the partnership did not materialize in practice, but rather remained as a good idea that all potential ecosystem stakeholders agreed needed to be pursued. The case outlines the overall knowledge mobilization strategy, based on big data integration and the challenging process of attempting to set this up.

5.6.1 *Managing Engagement*

TechFirm recognized the increasing opportunities that data had begun to play in the healthcare sector. It had noted that there were many different information systems and "gadgets" with increasing amounts of data being collected, but minimal integration of these across the wider health field. Rather than aim to only add to the pool of knowledge and technological innovations already in the market, TechFirm felt they could maximize value as a central integrator by creating a technical platform that linked the multiple technologies and their data sets across the healthcare sector so as to generate new knowledge, and new forms of value, through information integration.

> I think the biggest challenge in terms of data is the ridiculous legislative hurdles... There are so many. So much bureaucracy there... that people are concerned... we're certainly doing stuff at the moment [where we ask] "is this legal?"... we're not entirely sure... So it's fiendishly complicated and I don't think anyone really understands it well enough. (*Healthcare provider, clinical researcher, and data analyst*)

TechFirm decided to enlist the help of a boundary spanner in the form of university-based researchers to facilitate access to health stakeholders and explore opportunities. University researchers could help to map the existing knowledge landscape, using an explorative strategy to examine how stakeholders could be accessed to create an integrative platform to facilitate knowledge mobilization and innovate across an emerging ecosystem. TechFirm could also, together with its university collaborators, explore directly the potential of its ideas and begin to determine what steps were needed in the innovation effort.

Any data-related innovations in healthcare need to deal with the regulatory constraints, particularly in relation to data privacy. Thus the partnership sought to include regulatory stakeholders to inform the process, so they could provide updated, relevant knowledge regarding evolving regulatory requirements. This was key to ensuring that any innovation could ultimately be exploited. TechFirm also wanted to bring patients (service users) and members of the public as stakeholders into the intended ecosystem, yet this encountered a challenge regarding the ownership of healthcare data. While TechFirm wanted to push the concept of a patient owning their own data, and to be key stakeholders, it became clear that that doctors controlled primary patient data. Doctors thus became important stakeholders to enroll as gatekeepers in controlling access to knowledge repositories involving primary care data. They would have to be engaged as part of both exploration and exploitation processes. TechFirm, however, continued to push for public involvement due to the increasing use of health and wellness data tracking devices, for example mood apps, medication reminders and wearable fitness monitors owned by public. But the challenges in working with healthcare data were recognized as significant.

Secondary and community healthcare knowledge repositories were controlled by other stakeholders such as hospitals and community health workers. A significant observation was that these knowledge repositories (primary, secondary and community) remained unconnected with few NHS stakeholders able to broker any knowledge exchange across internal or external boundaries despite the technological feasibility.

> Possibly I think the problem is there's a lot of different things going on at the same time and certainly one of the challenges we've had locally is the fact that there's national programmes going on, so there's things like [System A] which wants to expand to be a national programme. But at the same time there's another thing called [System B] which is a way of sucking data out of all [general practice] systems across the whole [country]... So you know which system do you go for or do you create local systems?... There's not really a co-ordinated approach at the moment.
> (*Healthcare provider clinical researcher and data analyst*)

While a connected healthcare data platform could offer ways to further address some technological concerns, it was clear that TechFirm would have to make compromises to get existing stakeholders to share knowledge effectively by forging links between these diverse organizations.

The exploration of existing stakeholders also revealed a range of technology and consulting organizations directly involved in the healthcare data initiatives. Further, significant innovation appeared to be occurring through smaller companies developing data analytic tools to aid healthcare professionals to improve healthcare outcomes. However, most of these efforts were fragmented and their effectiveness questionable on the national and regional scale of knowledge integration, though offering improvements on the local level. TechFirm could see an important role for other sensor companies (e.g. medical device) in a connected healthcare data platform as collectors and providers of data. Both healthcare providers and technology companies could benefit from more effective knowledge mobilization between domains. Success of the integration platform would not only depend on exploiting the knowledge of individual stakeholders but also getting stakeholders to exploit their collaborative ecosystem.

The existing landscape of actors (Figure 5.3) therefore consisted of a number of stakeholders whom were already connected in knowledge exchanges, while others were unconnected but had relevant knowledge and growing interest in healthcare data integration.

The goal of the partnership was to transform the relationships between these stakeholders through an innovative IT platform. Such a platform could integrate data between relevant stakeholders so they could create new forms of

Knowledge Mobilization across Healthcare Partnerships

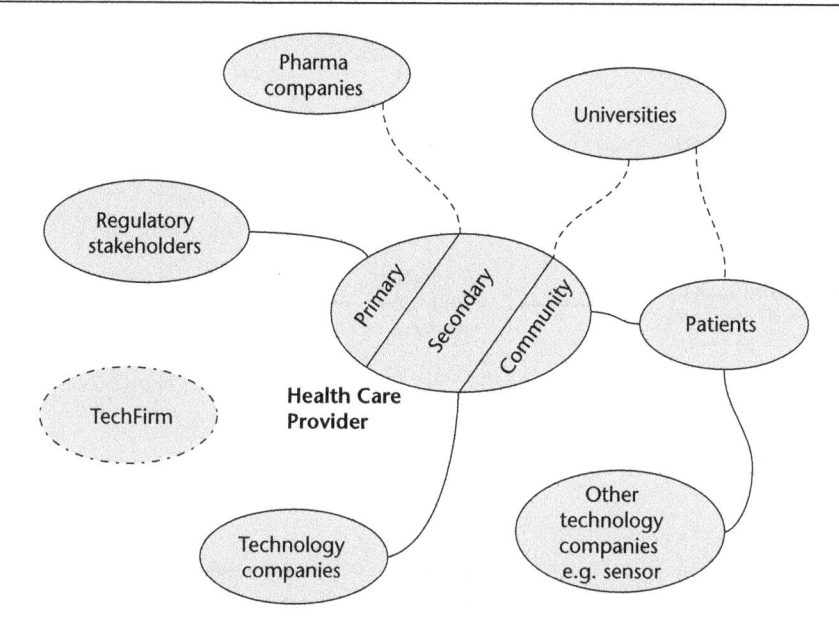

Figure 5.3 The existing landscape of stakeholders

value, such as following patient care records between primary and tertiary sectors, or between hospitals (which in the current system each have their own independent data storage and retrieval) or patients' wearable tracking devices to their primary care record. Integrating these data sources would enable the different providers to manage healthcare in better ways, and create a collaborative ecosystem. Figure 5.4 represents how TechFirm began to envisage an ecosystem that could connect these stakeholders.

5.6.2 Managing Funding

A significant barrier to exploiting any innovation in creating the underlying platform technologies and the ecosystem was the issue of cost. As a private company TechFirm could not justify a significant upfront resource allocation to create an integrative healthcare data platform technology on its own. Existing data technology companies saw little advantage in investing in a potentially rival system at this early stage and smaller companies did not have the slack resources to contribute.

TechFirm's board also wanted some assurance that TechFirm would remain a central actor in the newly established ecosystem before investing in developing an integrative technology platform. TechFirm attempted to negotiate directly with the multiple (public) healthcare providers to agree that any initial investment in prototyping could be matched with assurances that the

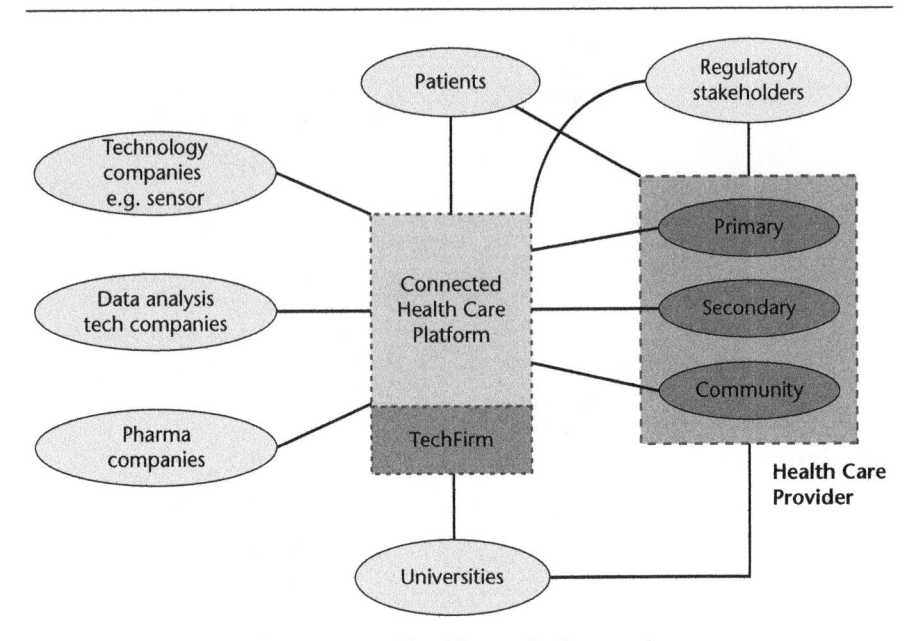

Figure 5.4 A connected healthcare platform and ecosystem

platform would be adopted once proven successful through multi-year contracts. However, the health providers do not have a forum for negotiating common strategic initiatives amongst themselves and generally work as competitors in patient care, making multi-party discussions difficult to orchestrate.

Pharmaceutical companies were identified as key stakeholders who could provide funding, given their available resources and expertise, especially if they were motivated by the new research opportunities available through the big data sets. These include developing new services such as adherence-based services to assist patients in taking their drug medication in terms of prescribed quantities and frequency. Yet, pharma companies traditionally worked separately and in isolation, investing heavily in research to develop products. The knowledge they generated was seldom shared and what knowledge exchange took place with external partners was tightly controlled. Getting pharma companies to fund an ecosystem where relatively open knowledge mobilization would be key to success required a significant shift in how they operated.

5.6.3 Balancing Competing Priorities

Having learnt that the public healthcare providers could not be treated as an amorphous organization with single, clear points of contact, TechFirm faced competing priorities with regards to which stakeholders to focus their engagement and with whom to negotiate. TechFirm thus chose, for example, to focus on how to engage with doctors and clinic practice managers who were often regarded as gatekeepers to their patients' healthcare data and therefore key in being able to exploit an integrative data platform. TechFirm spoke with doctors to determine how they currently worked with patient data and what improvements they thought could be made to using patient data for healthcare improvements. They also outlined to doctors how the idea of a connected healthcare platform could work in order to gauge their response. Doctors could see benefits but were concerned that they would lose control over data. Doctors felt that integrating data now could possibly bring adverse risk in data usage in the future as new stakeholders became involved. Their relations with private sector companies have a legacy of mistrust, with data exploitation for monetary gain being a lingering concern.

TechFirm also believed it could demonstrate to doctors and other healthcare providers the advantages of an integrative system that encouraged knowledge mobilization between the disconnected health providers by involving other technology providers. Yet engaging with technology companies already working with the public provider was proving difficult as there was little incentive for them to collaborate. Given their position, these companies were less keen to exchange knowledge in an open manner, preferring to keep to more formalized sharing. TechFirm hoped that if an ecosystem partnership was able to draw together enough of these companies, they would be able to develop system prototypes that could demonstrate the power of a collaborative platform, encouraging established firms to cooperate more closely.

5.6.4 Managing Knowledge Politics

A number of challenges were hampering efforts to innovate and make efficient use of existing healthcare data and information. The first challenge was the lack of system-level structures for collaboration amongst the diverse (NHS) health organizations. Efforts were often disparate and many organizations were attempting to solve problems they individually identified as important and were doing so in ways that were unconnected with what others in the health sector were doing. As a result, little patient-related knowledge was being shared across boundaries and between the various NHS organizations due to the politics involved in defining data ownership and creating a common structure for the healthcare provider. A second challenge was the interconnected relationship between national, regional and local healthcare environments which meant that it was difficult to identify the flow and control of data, difficult even for individuals based within the current healthcare providers. A third challenge was the lack of knowledge mobilization between sectors, for example, healthcare environments, social care, and technological innovators as each defined their own political turf and generally answerable to different government sections.

This was further complicated by the various legacy systems that constrained a wider rollout of connected data-related technologies across the public healthcare providers. These knowledge repositories were deeply embedded and difficult to engage. This was not only technological in nature but also raised the issue of supplier contracts and intellectual property. Many of the existing suppliers of legacy technologies had for years built up strong relationships with the healthcare provider and had contracts in place which cemented these relationships. This hampered the introduction of new relations since it was difficult for new entrants to propose new ideas in areas controlled by these suppliers. Table 5.1 summarizes our key findings on knowledge mobilization strategies across the three different case studies.

5.7 Discussion

The three cases reveal very different network approaches to achieving knowledge mobilization in inter-organizational health innovation partnerships, as each sought to achieve an ambidextrous balance between exploratory knowledge creation processes and more exploitative learning of how to improve current practices. Explorative activity involves valuing, assimilating and applying new external knowledge (Cohen and Levinthal, 1990). This may entail identifying appropriate knowledge sources, for example, databases, journal publications or knowledgeable individuals with the right skillset for the task at hand. In the healthcare field, exploration has traditionally taken the form of bench science or clinical trials, though more recently this has expanded to include more action-based forms of applied research. As our Cases 2 and 3 suggest, inter-organizational networks might also enable novel exploratory methods as traditional alliances and modes of interaction are expanded. Exploitative processes focus on implementing and refining existing practices, and have been associated with quality improvement techniques (Benner and Tushman, 2003) and increased levels of centralized control (Marabelli, Frigerio, and Rajola, 2012). In the context of healthcare, exploitation also entails producing knowledge in the form of best practice guidelines (Oborn et al., 2013).

Both exploration and exploitation entail identifying the appropriate forms of knowledge that will provide new value (e.g. to the health service) or that can refine existing practices. Our cases reveal that an important underpinning challenge in enabling exploration and exploitation stems from being aware of and engaging relevant stakeholders to facilitate knowledge mobilization across knowledge boundaries; boundaries often being founded in contrasting

Table 5.1. Knowledge mobilization for network ambidexterity across health innovation partnerships

	Managing engagement	Managing funding	Balancing competing priorities	Managing knowledge politics
Case 1: *SEARCH knowledge mobilization and learning program*	Program participants develop strong ties and search strategies for knowledge to solve current concerns. Establishing weak ties between organizations promotes exploration of problem solving around common challenges.	Source of funding influenced the focus of exploitation; stakeholders sought to promote specific projects for participants' exploratory efforts to then exploit in service context.	Challenge to support exploitation of individual's knowledge mobilization skills by releasing them from normal responsibilities.	Exploitation can enable focus on particular perspectives and enablers of knowledge mobilization. Identifying and targeting the ideal learners highlights the ambidexterity challenge of choosing the appropriate leaders.
Case 2: *CLAHRCs user-driven health service research*	CLAHRCs structured to enable engagement between designated research teams and possible user domains. Broker roles mediate across these groups to facilitate and target knowledge mobilization.	Stable government funding enables relatively long-term research projects Matched partner contributions focuses stakeholder engagement across network.	Temporal and structural separation of researchers, who prioritize discovery, and service providers who prioritize meeting targets, promotes ambidexterity across network. Exploiting research findings in practice constrained by contextual factors e.g. focus on targets, staff turnover, change fatigue.	Research governance requirements constrain flexibility of explorative approaches and types of data gathered. Data ownership limits exploitation across inter-organizational networks.
Case 3: *TechFirm big data integration*	Neutral boundary spanners key in enrolling network members, revealing key actors, their motivations and incentives to join and contribute. Strong ties needed at local levels for system-level integration.	Exploration is inherently risky and actors look to the promise of exploitation to assess investment decisions. Risk sharing challenged by cross sector norms of isolation and competition.	Synergistic collaborative exploration across the network sought amidst competing organizational mandates for exploitation. Requires new contextual culture of openness and trust.	Data ownership limits both exploration (through limited research) and exploitation (lack of sharing). Legacy systems and lack of established system-level structures constrains knowledge mobilization.

meanings ascribed to particular knowledge claims, or more fundamental political differences and priorities held by the stakeholders involved (Carlile, 2002; Swan et al., 2007a; Oborn and Dawson, 2010). Our case findings therefore additionally highlight the importance of knowledge politics, in particular, the constraints that various stakeholders and structures can place on the exploration of data innovation opportunities as well as the exploitation of available knowledge. Knowledge mobilization is dependent on the underlying data and knowledge politics is a key influencing factor in how (and what) knowledge flows across inter-organizational healthcare networks. Qualifying what counts as knowledge and how it legitimately should be produced will be influenced by the epistemic community of the groups involved (Currie, El Enany, and Lockett, 2014; Knorr-Cetina, 1999). Furthermore, we have shown the challenge of managing competing priorities as well as funding strategies is central to network ambidexterity. Here our focus on inter-organizational healthcare partnerships emphasizes the diverse priorities of those within the networks, how they can "pull" the focus from exploration to exploitation and vice versa to suit their own needs and how the resultant ambidexterity develops out of this interplay. Funding is fundamental to support exploration and ambidexterity is necessary at the network level to balance the generation of new knowledge and forms of value whilst also ensuring that stakeholder benefit from knowledge outputs (Gupta, Smith, and Shalley, 2006; Dhanaraj and Parkhe, 2006). Though the aim for inter-organizational networks is to develop appropriate ambidextrous partnerships to support knowledge mobilization (Benner and Tushman, 2003), our findings show that this can be accomplished in numerous ways and can use multiple strategies. In our cases, different foci were given to structural and temporal arrangements as well as influencing contextual features of the networks. Building on scholarship that outlines diverse modes that organizations can use for coping with the conflicting demands of exploration and exploitation (Lavie, Stettner, and Tushman, 2010; Stadler, Rajwani, and Karaba, 2014; Ambos et al., 2008) we outline three modes of achieving network ambidexterity in healthcare innovation partnerships. Modes for achieving network ambidexterity can vary in the focus on the level they seek to influence (e.g. individual, teams or systems), structural and temporal separation as well as the contextual behaviors they aim to influence.

In Case 1 the inter-organizational effort to create a knowledge mobilization program was performed through a focus on developing strong connections between diverse, individual stakeholders. The specific aim here was to develop the capacity of individuals to exploit relevant research in published literature, facilitating the identification of relevant knowledge and promoting research utilization. We suggest that this case represents a *"contextual"* mode of balance between exploration and exploitation. In this mode the knowledge mobilization network focuses on nurturing social elements to develop the "practitioner scholars" with appropriate values and culture of integrating research and practice (Gibson and Birkinshaw, 2004). Additionally, at the individual level there is a specific aim to engage and skill people to develop stronger social networks to enable greater network ambidexterity by targeted knowledge mobilization between research and healthcare delivery. A key challenge for this contextual mode of ambidexterity with a focus on the individual level is the potential for ambidexterity to be constrained systemically. In Case 1 for example, we observe how overall exploration in the inter-organizational network is less effective since funding is shifted to a focus on individual learning. The result is that some individuals, in this case academics, experience a tension between their need for explorative research (to support their academic goals) and their need to support others in the exploitation of their research.

In Case 2, the CLAHRC inter-organizational network operated a mode of *"process separation"* where the ambidextrous balance is achieved by both a temporal and structural separation between exploration- and exploitation-focused processes. We base this concept of process separation on the combination of both the domain and temporal separation modes proposed by Lavie, Stettner, and Tushman (2010) where exploration and exploitation may be prioritized at different times (such as research first and then implementation) and between separate organizational domains in charge of areas respectively. Ambidexterity in this instance is brought about by separating the research process (discovering and generating knowledge) and the implementation process (getting knowledge shifted to practice environments) in general, resulting in exploration and exploitation processes occurring in separate network entities and at different times. The key for the network members is to focus on the process most relevant to their capabilities. This is performed at the team level where research teams and implementation teams operate as different groups, each with their main focus on exploration and exploitation respectively. A key requirement here is the need to have bridging ties between these teams to ensure knowledge flows are enabled (Stadler, Rajwani, and Karaba, 2014). In our case this was accomplished by the designation of knowledge brokers to perform this bridging. A result of this bridging is that teams which focused (in the main) on exploration and exploitation remained aware of each others' processes and requirements, adjusting their own processes to facilitate knowledge mobilization e.g. researchers directing future research to accommodate implementation efforts of practitioners (Simsek, 2009).

In Case 3 the mode of ambidexterity is *"structural integration"* where there is an attempt to ensure system-level integration between organizations with expertise and access to data on different aspects of health research, service performance and patient care. This structural integration may be coordinated, as in our case, by a central hub organization which acts as a network broker, integrating the various organizations and facilitating knowledge flows between them (Dhanaraj and Parkhe, 2006). As the central orchestrating role of the hub firm is key to its own success (e.g. as a profit-making organization), securing the legitimacy of its position and enrolling the right stakeholders to maximize new knowledge flows is paramount (Prince, Barrett, and Oborn, 2014). Given the lack of hierarchy in network contexts (Swan and Scarbrough, 2005; Nambisan and Sawhney, 2011), creating such network integration poses a number of challenges. In order to act as an orchestrator in the network, a position of centrality needs to be obtained (Dhanaraj and Parkhe, 2006) as illustrated in Figure 5.4. Further, funding is difficult as system integration costs are typically significant and the central organization has to convince others of an appropriate business model and display of commitment, which requires significant legitimacy (Prince, Barrett, and Oborn, 2014). This requires strategic action from core actors to form and maintain a network and to extract value from it (Powell, Koput, and Smith-Doerr, 1996; Dhanaraj and Parkhe, 2006).

In addition to enabling knowledge mobility across the network, Dhanaraj and Parkhe (2006) suggest that integrating hub firms need to support network stability and appropriate uptake of knowledge by relevant stakeholders, thereby exercising a subtle form of network leadership. However, achieving network ambidexterity through a mode of structural integration could enable both exploration and exploitation to occur simultaneously, as data and information can be continuously integrated in real time analyses to inform service operations. Despite the structural integration of exploration and exploitation-focused organizations, there may be significant issues in knowledge sharing, as organizations can remain focused on their own goals. Additionally, individuals and teams may be less aware of other parts of the network as the ambidexterity here is at the network level.

Three key knowledge mobilization capabilities have been highlighted, namely: improving research capacity amongst service providers; producing (greater) relevant research findings; and changing service provision in accordance with research knowledge (Oborn, Barrett, and Racko, 2013). By integrating knowledge exploration associated with research activity, and knowledge exploitation associated with implementing existing knowledge, the network initiatives in our case studies aimed to increase productivity and inter-organizational effectiveness. However, other such ambidextrous inter-organizational partnerships may choose to focus on these capabilities to varying degrees, and may accomplish this in very different ways. Furthermore, different stakeholders within the networks will have different resources to contribute to meeting these objectives as well as different views on which capabilities they are most interested in investing. Future research could investigate how ambidexterity is developed differently given these different foci and resource arrangements, seeking to illuminate how the varying balance of exploration and exploitation deliver knowledge mobilization in inter-organizational networks.

5.8 Conclusion

In this chapter, we have highlighted a network ambidexterity perspective as valuable to understand how knowledge mobilization is achieved across inter-organizational healthcare innovation partnerships. Our cases suggest implications for managers and leaders who are seeking to develop knowledge mobilization partnership; highlighting the multiple tensions of conjoining very different types of practices, inter-organizational goals and stakeholder interests, competing priorities as well as finding appropriate ways to fund the endeavor. We suggest that leaders of knowledge mobilization initiatives need to consider and communicate a vision which does not focus on "research and knowledge production" as merely an output and "what it can do." Rather, it should be understood as a set of practices geared to achieve an appropriate balance of exploration and exploitation.

Future work could usefully consider the level of analysis in understanding how ambidexterity, as a link between exploration and exploitation (Stadler, Rajwani, and Karaba, 2014), is performed as a process of integrating and differentiating these different types (Andriopoulos and Lewis, 2009). In particular, we agree with Stadler, Rajwani, and Karaba (2014) who point to the potential of social ties to explain how initiatives can enable knowledge exchange through what we have termed network ambidexterity. Our case studies bring to light examples of how this occurs in practice, revealing an individual-level network focus, a team-level network focus as well as network-level focus. Such future developments build on the work of Lavie, Stettner, and Tushman (2010) who draw on the wider literature to show how exploration and exploitation may be effectively balanced.

Acknowledgments

This chapter presents independent research funded by the National Institute for Health Research (NIHR) Collaboration for Leadership in Applied Health Research and Care West Midlands as well as (former) Cambridgeshire and Peterborough. The views expressed are those of the authors and not necessarily those of the NHS, the NIHR, or the Department of Health.

6

Knowledge Mobilization in Healthcare Networks

The Power of Everyday Practices

Sue Newell and Marco Marabelli

CHAPTER SUMMARY

This chapter focuses on practices aimed at supporting knowledge mobilization to improve coordination across a network of organizations that are each involved in the care of children with complex health needs. Improving knowledge mobilization in network settings is particularly challenging because there are typically no formal hierarchical relationships that can be used to "impose" change. The chapter therefore explores the power of everyday practices that can promote changes associated with improved knowledge mobilization and overall care coordination. Using data from a longitudinal in-depth case in Canada, it demonstrates the power of talk, text, and objects to promote and make durable improved knowledge mobilization across healthcare networks. The practice view of power used in the analysis provides, as we illustrate, very different insights into what allows network change to happen when compared with the view that assumes this depends on the power and resources that can be mustered by individuals "in charge."

6.1 Introduction

Coordinating the practices of different healthcare professionals is very important, particularly when dealing with life-threatening situations such as in ER (Emergency Room) or when healthcare workers deal with severely ill patients who need speedy diagnoses (Kaelber and Bates, 2007). This coordination is especially crucial when patients have multiple diseases that require several different interventions (Abraham and Reddy, 2008). However, the different backgrounds, knowledge, and approaches to problem-solving of the various healthcare providers involved may make it difficult to coordinate practices to provide efficient and effective services for patients, families, carers, and communities (Gittell, Godfrey, and Thistelthwaite, 2013; WHO, 2010). This issue becomes even more complex when the parties involved do not all sit within the same organization. For example, medical staff in a hospital may need to coordinate not only with other hospital clinicians but also with professionals in other healthcare-related organizations, such as social services, independent physicians, psychologists, and schools. It is precisely this type of broader networked coordination that is the focus of many current strategic healthcare initiatives. Thus, many healthcare initiatives are geared towards facilitating better coordination across a network of organizations and professional groups.

Improving this type of networked healthcare coordination depends on mobilizing knowledge across the array of professional groups and organizations involved (Currie and White, 2012; Kimble, Grenier, and Goglio-Primard, 2010), and necessarily involves changes in individuals' everyday practices. Yet, as we will discuss, in networked settings, changes addressed to promoting knowledge mobilization require more than a directive to each party to "work together and share information" since there are no hierarchical power relations that can impose direction (Rodriguez et al., 2007) and a lack of physical proximity can increase the problems (Ardichvili, Page, and Wentling, 2003; Whittington, Owen-Smith, and Powell, 2009). To understand how such knowledge mobilization can be achieved we focus on the power of everyday practices because this helps illuminate "the political nature of networking and knowledge management practices undertaken by various interest groups" (Hislop et al., 2000: 401). The role of the power of everyday practices in networked settings is still underexplored. Most research that has looked at power in such settings has focused on how senior management groups manage changes from a top-down perspective (Dezso and Ross, 2012; Menz, 2012; Rodriguez et al., 2007). Here we focus on how emerging (everyday) practices can enable durable changes associated with improved knowledge mobilization in network settings, and we do so by examining the role of power.

Given the above, we address the following research question: *how do everyday practices have the power to mobilize knowledge in a networked change initiative in healthcare?*

The remainder of this chapter includes a theoretical background before outlining our research methods. We go on to present and analyze our findings before discussing them in light of prior literature. We conclude the chapter with a consideration of the implications of our study—for theory and practice.

133

6.2 Background

Mobilizing knowledge is often difficult, and this is true for a number of reasons including its stickiness (Szulanski, 1996) and its tacit nature (Polanyi, 1962). In network contexts, knowledge mobilization can be even more challenging (see e.g. Hansen, 2002; Lane and Lubatkin, 1998; Tsai, 2002). Scholars embracing the practice perspective (Gherardi, 2000; Nicolini, 2011) highlight such challenges by arguing that knowing resides in a particular socially situated and materially equipped context or site (Gherardi, 2012) and requires action, doing, or "practice," with knowing never fixed, but always in a state of becoming (Chia, 2003). Mobilizing knowledge across practice sites—necessary in network settings—is therefore, by definition, going to be difficult and will require some kind of force or power to facilitate it. Indeed, from the practice perspective, knowledge and power are interwoven since, as Foucault indicates, "the exercise of power itself creates and causes to emerge new objects of knowledge and accumulates new bodies of information" (Foucault, 1980: 52). Thus, in this chapter we focus on the power dynamics that underpin knowledge mobilization in network settings.

Power has traditionally been seen as a resource that can be used by powerful individuals to achieve the strategic objectives that they set (Dahl, 1957; Emerson, 1962; Hunter, 1963; Pfeffer and Salancik, 1974); for example, seniority in an organization gives an individual or group access to resources that they can use to enforce decisions (e.g. by using "a carrot or a stick"). This conceptualization of power draws from the philosophy of Marx. Marx sees power as a resource that is associated with economic relations. Those who own the means of production exercise power, either directly or indirectly, over those who work for the owners. Weber extends this analysis to highlight that power can be "owned" based on a position in the organizational hierarchy (legal-rational power—essentially an extension of Marx's view of the power of owners of capital) but also from a person's personality (charismatic power) or from tradition (e.g. first born to the royal family becomes the next king/queen). Others have followed suit, often building on the work of French and Raven (1959) who defined five sources of individual power—reward, coercion, legitimate, expert, and referent power.

While these views of the sources of individual (or group) power are helpful, what they lack is an explanation of how power initiates change. This is especially important because very often change happens (or does not) without any obvious use of power (or resistance) (Pfeffer, 1981). Pierre Bourdieu (1977, 1991) provided an early insight into how power is enacted in practice without this being evident overtly. Bourdieu illustrated how our position in the social hierarchy (our culture) leads us to think and see the world in a particular way such that we assume the "way things are" is natural and just (even when we may be disadvantaged by the status quo). Hence, it is often not necessary to use overt power (neither the carrot nor the stick) since power is embedded in the existing relations between social actors. In this way dominant groups can remain dominant not by overtly repressing others but because these "others" accept their position in the social hierarchy. Practices, then, can have symbolic power to the extent they are accepted by those involved as legitimate because of the existing social order. This reminds us that "resources" are multivarious and that these resources do not always need to be constantly deployed to change (or maintain) ongoing practices (Levina, 2005). Symbolic power may be particularly important to consider in network settings where authority derived from a position in an organizational hierarchy is less relevant. Other scholars (Clegg, 1989; Hardy, 1996; Lukes, 1974; Lawrence et al., 2005) similarly argue that viewing power simply as a resource that is leveraged as needed does not reflect the complexity of the construct (Dhillon, 2004).

The practice view of power, then, helps us to examine how power is enacted in everyday practices, rather than simply examining the (re)sources of power. Foucault is a key scholar in this respect, departing from the idea that power is owned by individuals or groups who use it as an instrument of coercion and instead seeing power as "embodied and enacted rather than possessed, discursive rather than purely coercive, and constitutes agents rather than being deployed by them" (Gaventa, 2003: 1). In Foucault's (1978: 93) own words: "Power is everywhere: not because it embraces everything, but because it comes from everywhere. [...] Power is not an institution, nor a structure, nor a possession. It is the name we give to a complex strategic situation in a particular society."

Latour (1986) embraces Foucault's view of power as everywhere and provides a useful example that contrasts this view with the one that sees power as deriving from the actions of powerful individuals. For Latour, from the "powerful individual" perspective, an order (described as a token) is proposed by a powerful individual (or group), and the token, according to the inertia principle, will move in the direction given by the powerful actor as long as there are no obstacles (e.g. frictions or resistances). In this view of power (the "diffusion" view), the greater the strength with which the token is delivered, the more the token will travel and overcome resistances. However, ultimately, the token will encounter resistance and this will slow down the order's pace of impact so that the original force (power) is reduced. In contrast, power can be seen as performative, and this relates to the idea that the spread of the token "is in the hands of people" (Latour, 1986: 267). Its displacement is not caused by the initial impetus (i.e. it is not dependent on the resources of the person attempting to make the change), since the token here has no impetus; instead, it is the energy given to the token by people, who keep it going. In this context, the token is not a "mandatory" order, but is something that people reshape, by "modifying it, or deflecting it, or betraying it, or adding to it, or appropriating it" (Latour, 1986: 267). Latour calls this a "translation" view of power since power relates to social processes where the change (the token) is negotiated, rather than "executed" (or spread by force). Given that change is likely to face significant resistance in network settings, since there is not a single authority to "push" (i.e. diffuse) the change across a network, we need to examine how change spreads across a network through everyday translation practices.

Latour's translation model is illustrative of the idea of power that resides in everyday practices that are imbued with particular values, cultures, symbols, and meanings in particular settings (Foucault, 1982; Bourdieu, 1977; Vaara and Whittington, 2012). Interestingly, Latour suggests that when power is explained with the translation model, the "size" of those (individuals or groups) who aim to circulate the token does not really matter (see also Fox, 2000). In other words, all "actors" can potentially enact power effectively and, as we will see, actors include material objects as well as human actors, as illustrated by the work on boundary objects (Star and Griesemer, 1989). Moreover, as previous research illustrates (e.g. Levina and Orlikowski, 2009) practices have the ability to promote change, but this cannot happen overnight; instead, power is constituted in the ongoing negotiations of practice (Bourdieu, 1977; Clegg, 1989), including in everyday discourses (Hardy and Thomas, 2014; Hardy and Maguire, 2016), as we will show through fieldwork.

6.3 Context and Methods

6.3.1 *Case Background*

The case focuses on a pilot project, which was set up to improve coordination of care for children with complex care needs at Canadian Hospital, Dooly, and between Dooly and other (external) healthcare agencies such as social services. While the need to improve healthcare coordination at Dooly emerged in 2008, it took two years to get funds for the initiative. A pilot project officially started on April 1, 2010 and a partnership was established involving the hospital and three agencies. The partnership created with the pilot project implies that all four organizations involved in this healthcare network have the same decision-making "rights," through representatives of each partner. The funding for the pilot originated from a surplus of one of the three agencies of the partnership.

Children with complex care needs were defined as children with multiple and life-threatening diseases who need to be seen by several specialists. The need to improve healthcare coordination for this group emerged when some families of these children pointed out that the different physicians (specialists)

Knowledge Mobilization in Healthcare Networks

who were taking care of their child did not exchange crucial medical knowledge with each other. As a result, the families were often overwhelmed and emotionally drained because it fell to them to coordinate the care of their child. Additionally, the external agencies (e.g. social services) were not always aware of each child's most recent health issues, and this too posed health risks. Further the hospital did not receive the most recent updates—from school or social service agencies—about their social/psychological condition. The project started with twenty children being enrolled in the pilot. A nurse dedicated to the project (nurse coordinator) and a project manager were hired, and one of the hospital doctors (who was already taking care of children with complex needs) undertook the role of full-time responsible physician. In spring 2014 (second phase) additional funds made it possible to add resources: an additional nurse (full-time) and three physicians (one full-time and two part-time) were hired. This allowed them to enroll twenty additional children (see Figure 6.1 for a timeline of key events).

6.3.2 Data Collection

Fieldwork was undertaken longitudinally (September 2010–April 2015) in situ and retrospectively (2008–10, including the review of documents) adopting an interpretive qualitative approach (Walsham, 1993, 2006). Interviews were conducted with the aim of having each participant tell us her/his "story" (i.e. their version of key events) in the style of a confessional (Schultze, 2000), allowing for uninterrupted storytelling. Thus, the data provide a holistic overview of events. Data included interviews, observations and collection of documents, with

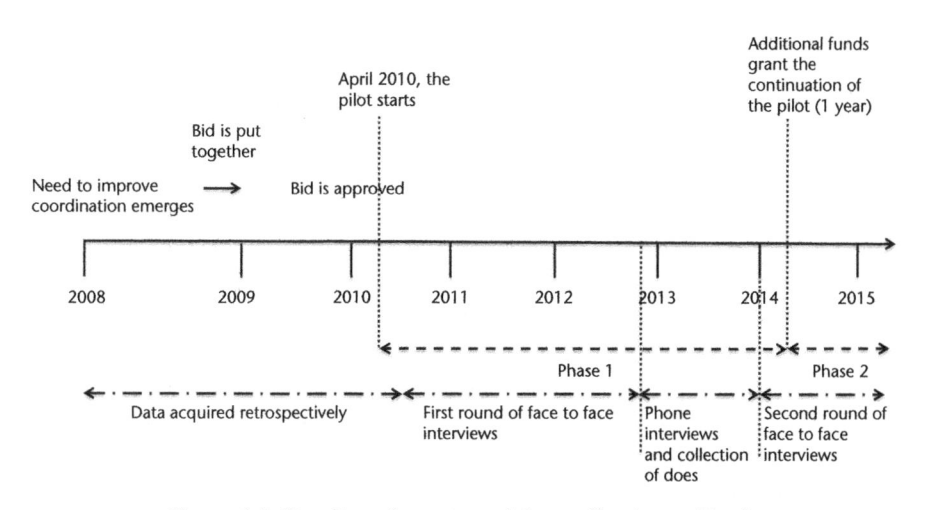

Figure 6.1 Timeline of events and data collection at Dooly

Table 6.1. Data collection

Main participants in the study	Interviews	Observations	Documents
CEO, CIO, project manager, nurses, project directors (other agencies), end users (patients/families)	43	14 (steering and working committees)	250 pages of official documents

interviews (including many repeat interviews) and observations audiotaped, professionally transcribed, and analyzed using Nvivo® (see Table 6.1).

The data analysis involved first the writing of a broad narrative of the case, aimed at identifying relevant events along a timeline. Second, we loaded all transcripts and documents into Nvivo® and singled out main themes associated with the initiative using an open-coding procedure (Miles and Huberman, 1994). Third, we conducted a more focused and theme-addressed coding (Strauss and Corbin, 1998) to identify key constructs for the emerging theoretical framing of the evidence collected, with practice, power, and knowing as the organizing constructs.

6.4 Findings

6.4.1 *From Conception to the Start of the Pilot Project (2008–10)*

Dooly hosted a family forum, giving parents the opportunity to share their experiences and feelings about their child's care. Families used the forum to highlight coordination problems they had experienced both within the hospital and between the hospital and the other agencies. Examples brought up in this forum included: a mother recalling that she had to head to the hospital three days in a row to have her child undertake the same test, but for three different specialists; a foster mother pointing to the difficulty she experiences when she needs to talk to a specialist about what another specialist said about her child; a mother indicating how she was not listened to when taking her child to the ER because of a medical emergency, with the outcome that there was a delay in deciding about treatment while the doctor looked up the medical record; a father relaying how he had put together a very short binder related to his child's health (he calls it a "cheat sheet") in order to help him remember things about his child's diagnoses and treatments when trying to communicate with different doctors. Healthcare workers were relatively sympathetic to the families' complaints, in particular in relation to sharing information with colleagues, but all prior attempts to "force" specialists to share clinical information about patients had been unsuccessful. For example, on one occasion a mother had formally complained that she had had to go to the hospital two days in a row for the same test. The chief pediatric consultant had rebuked the specialist who had requested the unnecessary repeat test and, for a short while, this specialist (and others who were aware of the incident) had notified other doctors about the tests that they were prescribing in order to avoid another complaint about wasted resources. However, this practice did not last.

While this order to improve coordination did not last, those healthcare professionals involved in the forum were moved by the families' stories and decided to try to do something about the poor coordination they were hearing about. One initial activity that was instigated was to sponsor a master's student to undertake a research project examining how coordination in healthcare had been approached in other contexts and with what effects. Another activity that emerged was that a core "team" (six in total, three from Dooly and three from three other healthcare-related agencies) involved in the care of the children began to informally meet (including dinners) to discuss how to help the families. In these discussions, they identified how they would need additional resources to improve coordination and so they decided to put together a proposal to bid for money. They informally approached the CEO who initially was not supportive, especially since resources were tight at Dooly. The core team then, on the one hand, used the evidence produced from the master's thesis to convince the CEO, and on the other hand, decided that it could be worth seeking external funds. In early 2008 the core team put together an eight-page letter addressed to the CEO where they formally asked him to co-sign a bid for obtaining funds to start a pilot project. This time the CEO agreed to advocate for the project and a year and a half later the bid was accepted and steering and advisory committees were created. The steering committee includes Dooly's CEO and the CEOs of the other agencies, plus the responsible physician and a project supervisor (VP of Academic Affairs at Dooly). The advisory committee includes the individuals who bid for the project (core team) plus two family members, representative of the "voice" of the many families in the family forum. The main role of the advisory committee is to implement the decisions made by the steering committee.

6.4.2 *The Pilot Project (April 1, 2010–April 1, 2015)*

The responsible physician arranged formal meetings to present to her colleagues about why improving coordination was important. This involved a Powerpoint presentation, which included evidence about improved coordination (e.g. taken from the master's dissertation) as well as more personal anecdotes from families. Following these meetings, the responsible physician took action to improve communication on a more permanent basis. She did this not by imposing strict, mandatory "rules" for the specialists (who would probably resist); instead, she was able to persuade the specialists of the relevance of each of them having a holistic view of each case. So, she arranged case meetings for each child, where all the specialists involved share their expertise, opinions, test results, and the like. While previous attempts to "force" doctors to share information had not lasted, these case meetings quickly became established practice.

Families attended these case meetings. However, for them, what made more difference was being able to contact the nurse coordinator, whose main role was to act as the interface between the hospital, the families, and external agencies. The nurse coordinator reports directly to the responsible physician, from whom she receives the most recent updates about each of the twenty children enrolled in the pilot. The nurse coordinator calls, on average, each family at least once a week—often just to see how the child is doing, sometimes to share a lab result, or to ask families to take the child to the hospital. The families contact the nurse coordinator about once a week, too. Most often contact is made via email, the main reason being that the families need to a refill a prescription. Other times, phone calls are made because of a "quasi-emergency," when the child does not feel well and the family struggles with whether or not a visit to ER is required. In these situations, generally, the nurse coordinator immediately contacts the responsible physician, and, if necessary, the responsible physician checks with the specialist(s), and feedback is provided to the family, avoiding needless trips to Dooly. The project manager supervises these processes, coordinates the advisory committee meetings, and is in constant contact with the families to gather feedback that is then shared with the nurse and the responsible physician.

Aside from these new staff roles and processes, the main ambition of the pilot project had been to create an ad hoc Electronic Medical Record (EMR) to allow the sharing of the children's medical records across the network of organizations involved. This is because the evidence (e.g. produced by the dissertation) had suggested that such systems were vital components of improved coordination. In fact, in 2010 the hospital already had electronic records where most clinical information about patients was stored. However, different units had their own systems and this represented a barrier to coordination even within the hospital. The external agencies did not have any type of EMR. Once the pilot project team started to look at implementing something to allow electronic sharing of medical records across the network, they soon realized that it was not feasible—"it was too expensive and too time consuming" (Project Manager).

After some deliberation the advisory board came up with the idea of developing a Single Point of Care (SPOC). The SPOC was based on the one father's practice of using a "cheat sheet." The SPOC is a short (two-page) medical sheet that synthesizes the most relevant information about each child in the pilot, providing a road map of what tests and visits will be needed when, as well as what medications and treatments a child is on. The nurse coordinator updates the SPOC when a change in a child's condition occurs and then gives this to the family, so they can bring it to different specialists, and if needed, to ER—even in other hospitals. The SPOC is also sent via fax or email to the external agencies (providing coordination across the network). The SPOC is designed to include only relevant (e.g. life-threatening) information about the child, and in a way that is specific enough to be meaningful for doctors, but easily understandable by non-clinicians (the families and other non-medical agencies like schools). The families quickly started to use the SPOC and found it very helpful, giving them legitimacy when they were discussing their child's illness with a professional, because *"it was signed by a doctor, not by a mum"* (mother of a child in the pilot).

The SPOC was also well received by the external agencies involved. Prior to the start of the pilot there had been attempts to promote communication between Dooly and the external agencies, but these attempts were unsuccessful. However, now, with additional resources (in particular the nurse coordinator) and a joint plan created at the advisory committee level and constantly revised to overcome challenges and "make things happen" (e.g. the creation of the SPOC in place of a "real" EMR), they were able to dramatically improve coordination across the partnership and with the families.

A second phase of the pilot was granted in 2014. This was based on surplus funds from the agencies involved. This second phase allowed the enrollment of twenty more children, and the associated new doctors and nurses to support the project. The families continued to use the family forum to advocate for turning the pilot into a program, providing evidence of how the project had helped them. For instance, a mother highlights the difference the pilot has made:

> *Before [Pilot Project] it was like if I was in a business, you know, but I wouldn't be the only person having to do all that work. You would have a manager, and you would have secretaries, you would have clerks, you would have a whole system of people and before the project I didn't have that, so what would happen before the project would only be related to how much energy I had or what his health is, and so that I could only advocate so far to make things happen. But now all doctors work together to talk about how it's going to work and who's going to take responsibility for pieces of making it work. It's not just a nice touchy feely this is a good idea, see you all later, but it's more okay, who's going to be responsible for which pieces. . . . and it's not left to me to run to a doctor and say well, did you do that part, you didn't do that part.*

At the end of 2014 the new Dooly CEO was actively trying to convince the provincial government that the pilot project should become a permanent program with state level funding. There are several pilot projects in Canada that are good candidates to become programs but funds are limited. Given this, the CEO was actively involved in trying to convince the Province of the merits of this program. He was doing this by sending to the province "official" documents that reflect the success of the pilot and by giving presentations about the initiative. The CEO has drawn on an independent study conducted by an external university that shows that the pilot has substantially improved service delivery. This university study concluded that most families indicate that their workload in managing their child's heath is dramatically reduced, while their child receives better support. Interestingly, an internal evaluation study conducted by the research center at Dooly was less conclusive because, using a quantitative approach it had been unable to identify any measurable improvements for the children's health or the hospital efficiency. This evaluation study is not part of the case that the CEO is using to get funding for a program. The outcome of this CEO work is not known at the time of writing, but as one interviewee mentioned—"*he (the CEO) knows people, a lot of people [and] this will hopefully help us, otherwise the families will feel that we've abandoned them.*"

6.5 Analysis

The above case illustrates the myriad of everyday practices that both initiated and sustained the network initiative involving mobilizing knowledge to improve coordination. It shows that senior management were not the instigators of the change in this case; rather it was the families—those one might assume would be "bottom of the pile" in terms of the power they could wield across a complex healthcare network. Moreover, we undertook our analysis in light of the literature on power that takes a practice perspective and highlights that power should be seen *in action* (e.g. as Foucault suggests, but also more recent literature, cf. Hardy and Thomas, 2014; Hardy and Maguire, 2016). Therefore, we were able to identify the emergence of practices involving negotiations and discourses (that we here call "power of talk"), written documents (here "power of text") and power of physical artifacts and concepts (here "power of objects"), illustrated in Table 6.2 and then further articulated.

Table 6.2 is useful because it identifies three ways in which the power of everyday practices manifests itself: talk, text, and objects. However, it is clear that these three "types" of practice overlap. For instance, a Powerpoint presentation (text) can be supported by a passionate talk, and the Powerpoint itself can be distributed via email or in printed copies, thus becoming an object that can be viewed as part of the "epistemic machinery" of change strategies (Kaplan, 2011). Therefore, below we single out themes that cut across talk,

Table 6.2. Examples of power of ongoing practices

Practice	Power of everyday practices to mobilize knowledge
Power of Talk	
Stories and anecdotes told by the families at the family forum illustrate the problems with the existing situation. These stories have significant emotional content: the parent losing their job; the parent trying desperately to get an ER doctor to listen to what they know about their child's problems and being ignored.	Emotional content of the stories leads those who listen to empathize with the plight of the families and want to do something to help them.
Holding informal face-to-face meetings among those supportive of the initiative. The advocates discuss why the change would be helpful and develop short-term tactics for supporting the change—e.g. the SPOC, as a "patch" since they were not able to create an EMR.	Talking with others supportive of the initiative helps to reinforce the "rightness" of the change being promoted without opposition. This helps to keep the momentum of the initiative going and builds consensus among the core team.
Meetings are held between the responsible physician and the specialists. The aim of these meetings is to have the specialists understand the relevance of sharing patients' information and then sharing this information in case meetings.	The responsible physician's reputation plays a key role in having the specialists take her seriously. This is also reinforced by the fact that she provides support to her claims using evidence from the literature.
Power of Text	
Writing a dissertation on the basis of literature showing how coordination improvements can produce benefits for both patients/families and the hospital.	In the field of medicine there is a strong tradition of ensuring that diagnostic and treatment protocols comply with existing "best practice" evidence. This helped legitimate the project.
Powerpoint presentations delivered during formal meetings, that use evidence from the literature and the family stories (e.g. meetings in Dooly where the pilot project is presented).	Powerpoint slides used during presentations helped to give the message durability, so that the text could continue to influence after the meeting. Moreover, slides often embed metaphors and figures that create links to concepts, and these have symbolic power.
Crafting official documents: the core team writes a long letter to ask the commitment of the first CEO; the second CEO writes to the Province.	These official documents provide a durable commitment to the project that is difficult to subsequently renounce.
Conducting and writing up results of evaluation studies: An evaluation study undertaken by the hospital was not able to prove that the project was successful because of the small sample. A second independent qualitative study, that involved interviews with the families, demonstrated the benefits of the pilot.	The CEO decided to use only the study that provided supporting results in the materials he presented to the Province. This text is important because it provides the evidence-base not simply for the effectiveness of this sort of initiative but for this specific initiative.
Power of Objects	
One example of the power of objects is the SPOC: initially the core team attempted to create a shared EMR but this was thwarted by a lack of funds and time. The core team, then devised a paper-based system. While the SPOC was circulated across the network, it were the families that were the carriers of the SPOC, having a vested interest in ensuring that professionals involved were kept fully informed about their child's problems, diagnoses and treatments.	An EMR is the established way of improving coordination across healthcare professionals—the literature review evidenced its importance. The inability to create a shared EMR could thus have stalled the project. However, those involved found a work-around by creating the paper-based information system. The SPOC itself carries information between specialists involved and is constantly updated and signed-off (by a doctor not a mum).

text, and objects and highlight how power-related practices have the ability to initiate and legitimize changes over time and make these changes durable.

The first theme is the *power of emotions*: The stories of the families (both before—horror—and after—relief) are passionate and it is their emotional intensity that helps to feed the existing narrative that improving knowledge sharing among healthcare professionals in the network can positively affect coordination to benefit sick children. Emotions are traditionally seen as personal responses to a specific situation (e.g. a situation is perceived as threatening by an individual which leads them to feeling afraid). However, from a practice perspective, emotions are produced relationally (Thrift, 2008; Stein et al., 2014)—that is, not only do relations between actors produce emergent task-related outcomes (i.e. knowings) they also produce human emotions, that can result in a particular felt quality or mood, that characterizes our being-in-the-world (Ciborra, 2006). Thus, emotions are not simply experienced as an afterthought of action that is produced by an individual's interpretation of the situation, but rather emotions are a psychosocial phenomenon that emerge from collective action and emotions are performative, themselves generating emergent outcomes (Solomon and Flores, 2003). Indeed, Dreyfus (1991) argues that a mood is always present, shaping and being shaped by our collective actions and this mood can generate a collective energy (or its opposite—apathy, for example). This is precisely what happened in the family forum, with those present "whooshed up" (Dreyfus and Kelly, 2011) by the family accounts of their struggles, leading to increased determination to enact change by those present.

What is perhaps interesting is that these emotional narratives were not only powerful in the context of the family forum where they were initially generative, but the narratives were also subsequently used by others to recreate this action-generating mood. For example, the responsible physician and the CEO both used family stories as they attempted to encourage others to not only understand but also "feel" that change was important. The power of these practices is consistent with the literature on persuasion, which highlights how emotions are often used as a deliberate strategy to get others to do something (Chen, Yao, and Kotha, 2009; DeSteno et al., 2004; Holbrook and Batra, 1987). In this sense, emotions can be viewed as instrumental (when generated in a practice context they can support task achievement). However, emotions also operate on symbolic (when there is an association between an emotion and a concept that plays a symbolic role), and aesthetic (when an aspect of the situation generates feelings of beauty—or its opposite, perhaps ugliness or disadvantage) levels (Rafaeli and Vilnai-Yavetz, 2004; Thuring and Mahlke, 2007). Thus, in Dooly Powerpoints were used that included graphical effects and pictures of "real" children in need of care that generated emotions through symbolic and aesthetic associations for the audience. In other words, this type of talk and text generated much more than simply a collective understanding of the problem; it generated feelings which themselves were performative, energizing people to take further action to reduce family stress.

The power of emotions is illustrative of the power of everyday practices that emerge through various forms of continuous interactions between individuals, and between individuals and objects. To this end, here we identify the second theme that related to the *power of continuous interactions*. For example, informal face-to-face meetings were very frequent in the pilot and were important in keeping the initiative live in the early days, before funding was secured. The importance of such supportive practices has been demonstrated by others, contributing to strengthening morale and providing a sense of identity with the project (e.g. Aube and Rousseau, 2005). The power of these continuous interactions was to help bolster the resolve of those who thought the project was important. Network change initiatives require significant work, and here we argue that this can be made easier when those involved meet frequently and reinforce the reasons for their engagement. Moreover, the power of continuous interaction was not simply related to interactions between people; continuous interactions between people and objects were also important, as evidenced by the way the SPOC gained power. The SPOC can be described as a material actor because it has agency—power to affect practice—in its own right. For instance, during its *continuous* use, the SPOC was modified several times, by adding and removing fields that, through practice, were found to be more or less important for sharing information in a professional (for specialists), synthetic (for ER doctors), yet understandable way (by non-clinicians, i.e. families). This clearly illustrates how the SPOC gained power through use and recalls Latour's translation model. The spread of Latour's "token" (in this case the SPOC) "is in the hands of people" (Latour, 1986: 267) and the energy that gives it power (initially, the adoption of the SPOC by the external agencies, for instance) lies in its use and appropriation by different actors, who make changes (reshaping it, when needed) but in so doing they preserve the essence of it (that it can be interpreted in different ways). Thinking of the SPOC as a material actor that is constantly reshaped through practice but at the same time as an object that keeps its own identity (synthetic medical sheet) suggests that it can be seen as a boundary object (Star and Griesemer, 1989), acting as a mediator that facilitates knowledge sharing across the healthcare network. It is clear that the SPOC benefitted from the power of continuous interactions. However, it also plays a symbolic role, and has power because it legitimizes certain practices for those involved (Swan et al., 2007a), as we suggest next.

The *power of symbols* is about practices that are accepted by those involved as legitimate because of the existing social order (cf. Bourdieu, 1977). The symbolic power of the SPOC, for instance, is evident when it empowers the families who carry the SPOC to the ER because it is "signed by a doctor, not by a mum." But the power of symbols can also be found in other contexts. It is relevant to note how a particular choice of words (text and talk) is important, having significant symbolic value. For example, the use of "case meetings" to mobilize knowledge had symbolic power as it is a language that chimes with clinicians' practice—calling these "strategy meetings" or "planning meetings" is likely to have had a very different impact. Seeing the initiative as "integrated care," similarly, played an important symbolic role, mobilizing a commitment to sharing knowledge among diverse participants (Swan et al., 2007a). Another example of the symbolic power of text is related to the official documents (e.g. the master's dissertation) that provided evidence from the literature about the relationship between knowledge mobilization, coordination, and improvement of healthcare. Given the perceived importance (i.e. symbolic power) of evidence-based practice in healthcare (see Chapter 1 in this book) it is not surprising that this textual evidence was drawn upon in many different practices to help promote and maintain the pilot project. Finally, Powerpoint presentations incorporating images and statements that can generate emotions can have symbolic power as well (Heracleous and Jacobs, 2008): for instance, the Powerpoint slides incorporated the graphical representations of the logos of the four organizations (used by the second CEO in presentations with the Province) was a metaphor that the four organizations are working together and have a shared sense of purpose. However, we need to acknowledge that the symbolic power of talk, text, and objects was made possible by individuals covering key roles in the initiative, so next we focus on how far reputation can affect the power of everyday practices.

The *power of reputation* can be found in several episodes at Dooly. For instance, a speech delivered by the Dooly (second) CEO had power because of the institutional role of a large hospital's CEO (so he was listened to). He uses *"all sorts of internal data, evidence from the community, families' feelings"* in his presentations to feed the narrative that the pilot project leads to improvements on several fronts. As well, the responsible physician could influence the specialists because she had been working at Dooly for several years and was well respected—and this helped to legitimate what she said. The responsible physician's signature on the SPOC is another example of how a person's reputation can give power to an artifact—in fact other doctors took the SPOC seriously not just because it was signed by a doctor, but because it was signed by *the* doctor they respect and listen to. This is why the SPOC had power, while the cheat sheet previously carried by the father of a sick child (and on which the SPOC was based) did not, at least in terms of legitimizing the father's talk with a physician. Thus, with SPOC in hand, the father could tell the physician what was needed, while with his cheat sheet he could not.

Here we have identified four key themes that cut across the three types of practices previously mentioned in Table 6.1. Obviously the various practices, as well as the themes, do not aim to represent an exhaustive taxonomy of all possible practices and associated themes—this would be not possible simply because of the emergent and unpredictable nature of the practices themselves. However, we believe that these examples can be illustrative of how the power of everyday practices can be enacted in a networked setting to promote knowledge mobilization, as we discuss next.

6.6 Discussions and Concluding Remarks

Enacting change, as we previously noted, becomes more challenging in network settings (such as the Dooly partnership we are focusing on) because of the very blurry (or absent) hierarchical structure. Above we have illustrated and analyzed how various practices helped to create and sustain such network change. Now we can return to our research question—*how do everyday practices have the power to mobilize knowledge in a networked change initiative in healthcare?* From our fieldwork it emerges that it takes a myriad of everyday practices (including talk, text, and objects) to "make things happen" in network settings. These practices involve a range of actors, not just senior executives, as much of the existing literature focuses on. These practices involve human actors (including end users) as well as material actors (objects). Latour's translation model of power, and its articulation, was extremely helpful to understand how this change happens. Clearly, this is not just a case of creating a common understanding of things, for instance, for the specialists to understand that sharing knowledge with each other will improve healthcare. Instead, Latour's model showcases how everyday practices involving a variety of actors were key, with talk, text and objects translating the coordination initiative so that it was enacted in practices that were made (relatively) durable over time (e.g. the case meetings, the SPOC).

The findings about the power of the SPOC corroborates that of Thomas, Hardy, and Sargent (2007), who highlight that the power embedded in boundary objects depends on "the co-construction of meaning among actors" (Thomas, Hardy, and Sargent, 2007: 2) "the absence of which is likely to indicate enforced compliance, rather than voluntary cooperation" (Thomas, Hardy, and Sargent, 2007: 4), which we saw did not work prior to the pilot, when the specialists were "told" to share their patients' medical information with each other. Following Latour, translation practices allowed the emergence of a SPOC that was quite different than the initial one (the father's "cheat sheet") or the planned one (the EMR). The SPOC that is currently used is the product of the everyday practices of a number of actors who suggested small (or large) modifications of its structure as well as its content that reflects its "processual plasticity" (Thomas, Hardy, and Sargent, 2007: 23). In this way, these everyday practices had the power to make durable changes. These durable changes had a positive impact on the children and families' health. However, this should also draw attention to whether, in the pilot, changes associated with knowledge mobilization produced positive consequences for the patients (and families) involved at the expense of those who were not selected. In the case of the pilot, one might argue that the responsible physician, who now provides good healthcare to the pilot children, is no longer available for those who did not meet the requirement to be in the pilot—even if they are in need of intensive care. In conclusion, in this chapter we contribute by providing an account of the power of everyday practices that promote change in a network context. In so doing we extend prior research on practices associated with power (cf. Hardy and Thomas, 2014; Hardy and Maguire, 2016; Maguire and Hardy, 2009).

The findings suggest several areas of research related to knowledge mobilization in healthcare networks that deserve further attention. First, the role of power in networked settings is very under-studied, with most research focusing on senior management groups (cf. Dezso and Ross, 2012 and Rodriguez et al., 2007). Here we showcase qualitative results about other actors who influenced change in a healthcare network, but obviously there is more work to do here, including when actors (e.g. patients) are thwarted in their attempts to influence change. Second, given the increase in online healthcare activity, it would be meaningful to learn more about how power emerges in practices that are undertaken in online organizational and network contexts, such as virtual teams and virtual communities of practice (Lave and Wenger, 1991; Dube, Bourhis, and Jacob, 2006). Third, we highlighted the relationship between emotions and power. We found that passion and emotion in advocating for a change—especially by the parents during the family forum sessions—created a collective mood that was itself generative of subsequent action. The power of the emotional narratives of the families, moreover, was able to influence even when others were telling their story. The power of the families is an example of an emergent, bottom-up way to influence top management decisions and reflects the point made by Levina and Orlikowski (2009) that "even agents who do not occupy dominant positions in a given institutional field [...] can nevertheless draw on critical resources and discursive legitimacy to influence changes within that field" (Levina and Orlikowski, 2009: 699). This is interesting because research has found that, in networks, peripheral nodes are less likely to initiate a change (Lockett et al., 2014). However, as we have seen in this case it was the family members who initiated the change. It was also a family member who provided the impetus for the creation of the SPOC that was eventually used by all agencies in the network. Thus, while the study supports the idea that central nodes are most likely to initiate change in a network (the families are certainly central in terms of the children that are the focus of the network initiative), further research is needed to unveil how bottom-up ways to influence top management decisions can emerge in networks. Here we argue that emotions-in-practice are a way to influence decisions from the bottom up, and in doing so we expand on Levina and Orlikowski's (2009) work. They found that individuals who participate in projects involving different, yet overlapping, fields of practice (or institutional contexts) gain greater visibility and authority in the organization. Here we further develop on these bottom-up processes by highlighting the role of emotions, which have not been fully explored in the practice literature. We know from psychology that "opening up" (Pennebaker, 2011) is a natural healing mechanism to get rid of "weights" that people carry; here we focus not on the individual psychological impact of emotional narratives but their power to generate a collective mood that can influence the intensity of subsequent action. Therefore, we argue that further research is needed that sheds light on the roles and effects of emotions-in-practice, including whether emotions can be as effective when leveraged by others (e.g. the CEO using the families' struggles while negotiating with the Province) or made up, in a more subtle way—this recalling the manipulation of meaning power as depicted by Hardy (1996).

Our findings have clear practical implications for healthcare managers, hospitals' CEOs, as well as policy makers. Healthcare managers should be aware that changes associated with knowledge mobilization are extremely challenging because clinicians are often reluctant to share their knowledge with each other. Interestingly, clinicians may resist changes, even though they recognize that mobilizing knowledge within a hospital has ultimately positive effects on healthcare delivery service (Gittell, Godfrey, and Thistlethwaite, 2013). Our case shows that the power of everyday practices emerges, for instance, through continuous interactions that proved to be helpful to share challenges and, at least in our case, were able to promote "reflection-in-action" (Levina, 2005). This suggests that it may be better for managers to give clinicians/specialists the space to confront each other, share opinions and elaborate on challenges (but also benefits) of such changes, rather than simply requesting them to change. Moreover, a "champion" (e.g. the responsible physician) can play the role of meeting facilitator. Most importantly, however, having healthcare workers engage with patients (or in our case families) in discussions about ways to improve healthcare may be potentially very powerful as a forum for change, not just because it exposes workers to the problems patients experience in getting good healthcare, but because of the potential mood that it generates that can stimulate further action.

High-profile healthcare decision makers (such as a hospital's CEO) can benefit from our findings by recognizing how relevant are political processes that involve long-term negotiations with institutions to obtain funds for pilot projects and all initiatives aimed at improving healthcare service delivery. CEOs need to constantly work (i.e. practice) to obtain money from institutions. Thus, as per our findings, we suggest that (a) evidence-based clinical research can help to build a strong case to legitimate changes; and (b) bringing up emotional issues while negotiating with institutions can help to address not just rational/efficiency-based benefits of a change, but also benefits that carry societal importance—for instance, the CEO talked about how the families involved in the pilot no longer have to manage their child's health and could return to work.

Policy makers too might be interested in considering the insights provided in this chapter: picking up from the previous point, we suggest that decisions related to funding initiatives should not solely consider clinical efficiencies—for instance, whether a project involves practices that can reduce admissions, therefore freeing-up beds. Social and psychological aspects are very much part of the health of individuals and our society at large. And healthcare initiatives, we argue, should be evaluated from a holistic perspective that accounts for cost-cutting practices, clinical research advances, but also social aspects that might seem to be weakly associated to healthcare efficiency in the short term but that, in the long term, can create a more (or less) "healthy" society. Therefore, policy makers should reward initiatives and pilot projects that show cohesiveness and the willingness to make substantial and long lasting changes—and indicators might be related to the source of these changes. As we saw at Dooly, bottom-up needs that escalate and "touch" the sensitivity of top management are illustrative of the power of everyday practices that can help make changes durable.

Acknowledgments

This study was partly funded by the Service Delivery Organization (SDO) of the UK National Institute for Health Research (NIHR) [SDO project 09/1809/1075].

7

Knowledge Mobilization and Network Ambidexterity in a Mandated Healthcare Network

A CLAHRC Case Study

Daniela D'Andreta and Harry Scarbrough

CHAPTER SUMMARY

This chapter explores the role of mandated networks in supporting knowledge mobilization. It applies a social network lens to one such network—CLAHRC-NET, which was part of a wider initiative within the UK's NHS. The focus of his chapter is on the ability of mandated networks to provide the combination of different network structures needed for knowledge mobilization. Such structures, which have been described in the social network literature as "brokerage," and "closure," are seen as supporting knowledge mobilization in two ways. Brokerage, which involves linking disconnected groups, is seen as valuable in knowledge "exploration"; that is, acquiring and creating new knowledge. Closure, involves the development of tight-knit groups of individuals, and is seen as helping to exploit such knowledge by embedding it within practice. In our research, by using an innovative combination of research methods, we were able to identify how CLAHRC-NET was able to achieve a balance between mutually reinforcing structures of brokerage and closure; a state we term "network ambidexterity." We further show how the emergence of these patterned social network ties was linked to the formal management structure and organization of CLAHRC-NET, with formal "Knowledge Broker" roles helping to create linkages between external sources of knowledge and information, and internal organized thematic work-groups that provided a focus for the embedding of new ideas in practice. The study thus highlights the scope for mandated networks to support knowledge mobilization through formal structures and roles that promote ambidexterity in the development of social ties. This has important implications for policy and practice in relation to the design of such networks. The chapter also serves to underline the value of a social network perspective for addressing the informal social dynamics of formally mandated networks.

7.1 Introduction

This chapter addresses one of the most critical questions concerning attempts to overcome the "knowing–doing gap" within a healthcare environment. This is the question of whether networks of collaborating organizations can be constructed to provide an effective mechanism for "knowledge mobilization" between domains of research and practice. The promise of such "mandated networks" has been widely touted in the healthcare management literature, but evidence on their ability to deliver valued outcomes remains mixed.

In this chapter, we address this question by drawing on some well-established concepts from social network theory—namely, "brokerage," "closure," and "structural holes"—to explore the capacity for mandated "knowledge mobilization" networks to enable both the exchange of knowledge and its implementation within practice. Networks that possess this capacity can be termed "ambidextrous." This property, which has been analyzed in some detail by Oborn et al. in Chapter 5 of this volume, is important since it involves the ability to simultaneously accommodate processes of exploration and exploitation. By applying a social network lens to an empirical case drawn from the UK NHS (National Health Service), we aim to address the broad question of mandated networks' support for knowledge mobilization, and in particular their ability to develop the ambidextrous capacity seen as so vital to that objective.

A further question that arises from the focus of our study is the character of the interaction between the formal structures (divisions of work and responsibility, role assignments and management hierarchy) associated with mandated networks and the emergence of informal social ties. This interplay has been recognized as important in Ferlie et al.'s recent review of networks in healthcare (Ferlie et al., 2010). This distinguishes between "mandated," "organic," and "hybrid" networks—the latter being an amalgam of the others. Beyond this initial recognition, however, as yet we know comparatively little about the interplay between formal structures and informal social ties or, most importantly given the focus of this chapter, the consequences that this may have for knowledge mobilization. A second aim of this chapter then is to seek to better understand that interplay through the use of a social network perspective.

The need to address these questions arises in part because the attention paid to social networks in organization studies has not, so far, been matched by work in the healthcare management field. Here, recent studies, with relatively few exceptions, have focused on mandated networks associated with policy interventions (Martin, Currie, and Finn, 2009; McAneney et al., 2010). Only in more recent work do we find social network analytical techniques being applied to uncovering the latent structure of informal ties between groups and individuals (Currie and White, 2012). However, given our growing understanding of the importance of social ties, coupled with recognition of the limitations of formal structures, we see a compelling need for research on informal network dynamics and how these underpin initiatives aimed at knowledge mobilization.

In this chapter we aim to show how applying a social network perspective can help us to address this need. To show the value of such a perspective we ground our research in an empirical study of a knowledge mobilization initiative in the UK, the CLAHRC (Collaborations for Leadership in Applied Health Research and Care) initiative over the period 2009–13. The CLAHRC initiative was the National Funding Body's largest investment in knowledge mobilization to date, encompassing £90 million funding for nine regionally-based CLAHRCs. The CLAHRCs were designed as environments that would speed knowledge mobilization between research and practice. They were based on partnerships between a diverse range organizations within the same geographic locality, including universities, local healthcare organizations (e.g. acute hospitals, mental health trusts, and primary care trusts), and other relevant groups (e.g. local authority, third-sector organizations, and charities). These partnerships supported collaborative projects that linked academic researchers with healthcare managers and a range of medical practitioner groups.

The chapter begins with a review of the literature on social networks as relevant to knowledge mobilization efforts. Subsequently, we outline some findings from our study of the CLAHRC iniative in the UK, and this leads to a discussion and conclusion which draw out the theoretical and practical implications of those findings. Important contributions from our study are a greater understanding of the role of different social network structures in knowledge mobilization, and insights based on empirical evidence on the value of "ambidexterity" in the development of mandated networks.

7.2 A Social Network Perspective on Knowledge Mobilization in Mandated Networks

From an organizational perspective, knowledge mobilization has been seen as requiring the development of linkages among a range of collaborating organizations. This reflects a recognition that the knowledge needed to support problem solving and change tends to be distributed within and between organizations and thus emanates from multiple disparate sources

(McAneney et al., 2010). As a result, policy-driven initiatives aimed at promoting knowledge mobilization typically involve the development of formal network arrangements. In the UK's NHS, such initiatives include including Diagnostic Evidence Co-operatives and Academic Health Science Networks. These kinds of policy interventions are typically based on the assumption that supporting new forms of highly networked collaboration will result in better knowledge sharing between professional groups and, as a result, the speedier translation of research evidence into practical applications.

As evidence has begun to accumulate on such initiatives, a recent systematic review of knowledge mobilization in healthcare organizations raised some concerns about the assumed advantages of such "managed" or "mandated" networks (Crilly, Jashapara, and Ferlie, 2013). This review found that the effectiveness of such networks rested upon the quality of the relationships that they promoted rather than their formal structure. For example, low-trust relationships in networks can lead to poorer knowledge sharing than high-trust relationships in hierarchies (Crilly, Jashapara, and Ferlie, 2013). Put simply, the review concluded that: "Relationships trump design" (Crilly, Jashapara, and Ferlie, 2013: 173). The broad conclusion of this review then, was that the benefits of managed or mandated network arrangements for knowledge translation cannot be taken for granted.

This finding is also echoed and reinforced by other work on mandated networks, with several studies highlighting the inability of such networks to overcome the constraints on knowledge mobilization posed by professional demarcations (Addicott, McGivern, and Ferlie, 2006; Currie and Suhomlinova, 2006; Currie, Finn, and Martin, 2008). One UK study of pilot projects in the genetics arena concludes that "even with structural change the same set of institutionalized boundaries adversely impact upon knowledge sharing" (Currie, Finn, and Martin, 2007). These studies tend to question the linear or mechanistic assumptions built into previous models of knowledge mobilization (Cooksey, 2006; Ferlie et al., 2012). Instead, they highlight the boundaries of *practice* (Carlile, 2004; Oborn, Barrett, and Racko, 2010), *cognition* (Szulanski, 2000), and *power* (Swan, Scarbrough, and Newell, 2010) (Carlile, 2002; Oborn and Dawson, 2010) that make it difficult to translate knowledge between distinct communities (Caplan, 1979). These hitherto neglected aspects of knowledge mobilization are given renewed attention within this section of the book and in related work: for example, in addition to Newell and Marabelli's Chapter 6, which provides a valuable focus on the role of power, certain journal papers explore in more detail relevant issues such as boundary-spanning practices (Evans and Scarbrough, 2014), and the relationship between cognition and social network structures (D'Andreta et al., 2016).

But while *formal* mandated network arrangements are seen as having limited ability to overcome these more deep-seated boundaries, evidence from the organization and management literature has increasingly highlighted the value of *informal* social ties. Such ties are seen as playing an important role in enabling the sharing of knowledge across organizational boundaries, providing a capacity for innovation and change not always available from formal arrangements alone (Currie and White, 2012). Thus, studies have highlighted the importance of network structures in shaping the flow of knowledge and information within and between organizations (Powell and Koput, 1996; Hansen, 2002) and have shown the roles played by different kinds of social ties, with weak ties being linked to the acquisition of codified knowledge and strong ties being linked to the establishment of trust and the sharing of tacit knowledge (Hansen, 1999).

While this work has shown the importance of the quality of interpersonal ties to the exchange of knowledge, an understanding of the capacity of network forms to promote knowledge mobilization rests not only the quality of the ties that they contain but also on the patterning of such ties in terms of network structures. Two structural forms which have been identified as particularly important in this respect are termed "brokerage" and "closure," and these are described in more detail in subsections 7.2.1 and 7.2.2.

7.2.1 Brokerage

"Brokerage" denotes the opportunity to span parts of a network that are unconnected. As described by Burt (2000) this disconnectivity produces network "gaps," otherwise known as "structural holes." These network "gaps" or "structural holes" may emerge where there is no tie between actors and/or there are disconnected clusters of actors. Actors located structural holes (in disconnected groups) thus have the potential to "broker" across such gaps to connect new or disparate sources of information (Burt, 1997, 2000). This might initially involve the establishment of a "weak tie" between disconnected third parties. Brokerage is, therefore, the action taken to close structural holes—in others words closing network gaps through network bridges or intermediary "between" actors (Freeman, 1977). Research suggests that knowledge exchanged as a result of brokerage across structural holes is likely to be novel (or as Burt terms it "non-redundant") precisely because it involves the pooling or cross-fertilization of knowledge from previously unconnected sources (Burt, 1997, 2000).

This strand of social network theory around structural holes and brokerage has been paralleled by developments in knowledge mobilization initiatives where "knowledge broker" (or equivalent terms) roles have been established explicitly to create links between different domains of research and practice

(Lomas, 2007; Dobbins et al., 2009; Ward, House, and Hamer, 2009). The knowledge broker role is designed so that individuals can act as facilitators of collaboration and "translators" of knowledge from one community to another, thus actively attempting to close structural holes. Indeed, as the use of interpersonal contacts and good communication skills in the context of partnerships and research collaborations is emphasized in knowledge brokering, it has been described as particularly suitable for linking up-stream research with downstream practice (Lomas, 2007). However, it is important to differentiate between knowledge brokerage as defined by social network position in a mandated network and that which is assigned by nature of one's formally mandated role; the first involves investigating the shape or structure of informal knowledge-sharing relations to assess a network's actual or potential ability to close "gaps," and the latter involves individuals purposefully enacting an organizational role that aims to support interaction between groups.

7.2.2 Network Closure

Tight-knit networks with overlapping ties are described in terms of "network closure." Such closure creates conditions of "social cohesion" or "embeddedness" (Reagans and McEvily, 2003), because dense or overlapping social circles encourage the development of trust, reciprocity, and cooperation (Coleman, 1988; Gnyawali and Madhavan, 2001). This creates a supportive environment for information sharing and problem solving (Gulati, 1995; Uzzi, 1997), which may be valuable during times of organizational ambiguity and uncertainty (Krackhardt, 1992; Kijkuit and van den Ende, 2010) and for embedding new knowledge (Coleman, Katz, and Menzel, 1966; Coleman, 1988). Though unlikely to be the locus of innovative ideas because it is less open to new, non-redundant knowledge (Burt, 1997, 2000), network closure does support the exploitation or implementation of knowledge (Hansen, 1999; Krackhardt, 1992; Reagans and McEvily, 2003). In particular, interests and perspectives in under conditions of closure are more likely to be aligned or normatively constrained, and the shared language and trust needed for close collaboration is already in place (Obstfeld, 2005).

As with brokerage, there are also parallels within the knowledge mobilization literature that seek to produce this network condition. In this case, the parallel with closure is the notion of "Communities of Practice." Explicit efforts have been made in some initiatives to develop such communities. These are seen as promoting knowledge sharing amongst individuals in a very similar fashion to network closure, but involving in addition to close social ties a shared sense of social identity (Kislov, Harvey, and Walshe, 2011; Thomson, Schneider, and Wright, 2013).

7.3 Network Ambidexterity and the Capacity for Knowledge Mobilization

Within the social networks literature then, there is an emerging consensus that brokerage across disconnected groups (closing structural holes) helps to facilitate the creation of new knowledge and idea generation, and that social closure within cohesive groups helps to implement and embed knowledge in practice (Baum, Shipilov and Rowley, 2003; Shipilov and Li, 2008; Porter, Whittington, and Powell, 2005). Closure and brokerage, therefore, offer different benefits for knowledge mobilization (Burt, 2005; Reagans and McEvily, 2008).

These conditions of brokerage and closure are normally viewed separately as discrete local network phenomena in the existing literature (Oliver and Ebers, 1998). When we consider their relevance to the local networks linked by knowledge mobilization initiatives, however, it is clear that brokerage and closure can occur simultaneously within an initiative's wider social network (Burt, 2000, 2005). It follows that network brokerage and closure can be seen as playing complementary roles by supporting both the creation and embedding of knowledge. We describe this ability to accommodate structures of both brokerage and closure as "network ambidexterity."

The value of such ambidexterity is that it enables the benefits of both brokerage and closure to be achieved simultaneously. This also avoids the risks of, for example, the new, non-redundant knowledge created at structural holes being lost or underexploited because it is not embedded in the practices of cohesive groups (West et al., 1999; Janssen, Van de Vliert, and West, 2004). Both network states are relevant to knowledge mobilization because structural holes may support idea generation, radical thinking, and theory building, whereas the closure of structural holes through brokerage facilitates practical implementation.

As an illustration of the value of network ambidexterity within the healthcare setting, consider the example of a clinical researcher in a CLAHRC who is looking for greater knowledge of recent research being used to assist patients with COPD (Chronic Obstructive Pulmonary Disease). He decides to link up with other COPD researchers both within his own CLAHRC and externally to other geographic environments. This brokerage allows him to build new contacts and widens his pool of knowledge. He then brings these new ideas back to his work team (characterized by the denser interconnected ties of network closure), and together they are able to develop a protocol on best practice, which becomes embedded in the implementation work of the team. In short then, brokerage and closure are network structures that can support knowledge mobilization efforts, though their usefulness will depend on the specific contexts of such efforts.

A number of recent social network studies support this view of the importance of network ambidexterity in knowledge mobilization efforts. Reagans and McEvily (2008), for example, argue that brokerage is needed to aid idea generation during knowledge seeking, while closure is required to ensure that information is embedded into a firm's existing routines and practices during knowledge transfer. Likewise, Tortoriello and Krackhardt (2010) use the Simmelian theory of social circles to illustrate the need for both closure and brokerage (Tortoriello and Krackhardt, 2010). Battilana and Casciaro further extend the analysis by developing a contingency model of the roles of brokerage and closure (Battilana and Casciaro, 2012). In their study of change processes in the UK's NHS, they observe that networks rich in structural holes support change that is more divergent from the status quo. In contrast, networks with high levels of closure are more resistant to such divergent change, but supportive of change aligned with the status quo.

7.4 Context for Our Study

Our own empirical study focuses on a knowledge mobilization initiative within the UK NHS, namely the CLAHRC initiative. Each CLAHRC enjoyed great flexibility in interpreting their broad remit, and this was reflected in the development of different operational and management structures, and distinctive visions for their work-program (D'Andreta, Scarbrough, and Evans, 2013; Evans and Scarbrough, 2014). In this chapter, we present a CLAHRC case study—termed CLAHRC-NET—for analysis.

The lead partner in this CLAHRC was an NHS mental health trust, and the core of the initiative built upon established academic–research links between this healthcare trust, a university hospital acute trust, and a university institution. However, one aim of this CLAHRC was to reach beyond the organizations that have traditionally been involved with research in order to build research capacity in localities further away from this core. In terms of formal structure, this CLAHRC was similar to others in that it was organized around a central management team and a set of broad themes encompassing clinical-research and implementation work-programs. These included "Mental Health," "Children and Young People," "Stroke Rehabilitation," and "Primary Care." Support was provided from shared services of health economics, statistics, implementation, healthcare commissioning, healthcare management, clinical-practice, and social-sciences insight. The CLAHRC also sought to put into practice its own distinctive interpretation of its mission centered on organizational learning. This spawned a number of features intended to embed this interpretation into its structure and practices. These included the clustering of work programs within a small number of defined clinical themes, which support the building of communities around these clinical areas. There was also resourcing of dedicated "Knowledge Broker" (KB) roles through which a selected group of practitioners would support knowledge translation from project teams to the wider NHS. Cross-cutting themes were formed with the aim of providing clinical project team members with specialist forms of expertise in areas such as knowledge translation, synthesis of evidence, external engagement and communication, and statistical support. The work programs of the CLAHRC-NET supported a range of outputs, including; sharing new research evidence to inform decisions made by local healthcare commissioners; incorporating findings into local and national clinical-guidelines; contributing to local healthcare services redesign; empirically testing and implementing new interventions to be used by NHS Trusts; and becoming a source of information for local clinical networks to support service development.

7.4.1 Methodology

To investigate knowledge mobilization using a social network lens, we adopted an innovative mixed-methods approach, encompassing, firstly, a social network study to address the informal structure of social ties manifested by the membership of our CLAHRC sample. This revealed the structure of the informal knowledge-sharing network underpinning the formally mandated network. The social network survey was sent by e-mail to a total of 109 individuals at Time 1 (January 2011) and 102 individuals at Time 2 (March 2012), with a final average response rate of 68 percent. Our aim was not to generate a network of all social ties, but to identify ties that were most important to the work of individuals within the CLAHRC. Network analysis was conducted in UCINET with visualization in NetDraw (Borgatti, Everett, and Freeman, 2002). Second, to complement this work, we carried out a qualitative investigation with a sample of individuals playing a variety of roles within the CLAHRC-NET, and interviewed these individuals at two time points. This enabled us to address the way in which knowledge mobilization was interpreted and realized over time by groups charged with realizing the CLAHRC-NET's objectives.

7.5 Findings: A Social Network Analysis (SNA) of Knowledge Mobilization

In this section we use some methods and techniques of social network analysis (SNA) to study the network structure of knowledge mobilization in CLAHRC-NET.

In doing so, we demonstrate how network ambidexterity—a balance of mutually reinforcing structures of brokerage and closure—was achieved in this formally mandated network. The first part takes the perspective that knowledge mobilization occurs by nature of people's positions in the informal network of knowledge sharing exchanges within the context of a formally mandated network and, to illustrate, we present some SNA metrics for brokerage and closure. The second part uses SNA to investigate how knowledge mobilization is influenced by the interplay between network position and organizational role—here we zoom in on individuals with formally assigned knowledge broker roles.

7.6 Network Ambidexterity: Combining Brokerage and Closure

Knowledge mobilization in mandated networks is supported by the network positions occupied by individuals in the informal social network of knowledge sharing relations underpinning that formally mandated network. To illustrate and unpack this further, we present and discuss some SNA metrics and visuals. Taking a quick glance at the scores in Table 7.1, it appears that brokerage activity reduces over time, whereas levels of closure are maintained.

We first take a look at the extent of brokerage taking place in CLAHRC-NET as conferred by the network positions of individuals at two time points. The three SNA metrics we provide tap into the extent to which individuals are acting as brokers across gaps in the network and the extent to which structural holes (gaps that are yet to be brokered) are present.

Table 7.1. Network ambidexterity metrics for CLAHRC-NET at two time points

	Network Metric	Time 1	Time 2
Brokerage	Ego Betweenness[a]	19.1%	10.7%
	G and F Brokerage[b]	50%	43%
	Structural Holes (efficiency)[c]	69%	68%
Closure	Density (network connectivity)[d]	8.6%	7.8%
	Average Geodesic Distance[e]	2.6	2.7
	Reciprocity[f]	24%	21%

[a] Proportion of individuals acting as "bridges."
[b] Proportion of dyads (pairs of individuals) who are not already directly connected.
[c] Structural holes measure based on the proportion of non-redundant ties in the ego-networks of CLAHRC members (efficiency).
[d] The number of observed ties divided by the total number of possible ties.
[e] The average number of links it takes to connect between one person and any other person in the network.
[f] Two-way ties. Scores taken at average across CLAHRC-NET and normalized relative to ego-network size.

The overall picture is that brokerage activity decreases over time for CLAHRC-NET, except for structural holes, which remain constant. The ego-betweenness metric represents the proportion of individuals acting as CLAHRC-NET brokers by nature of their position in the network as "bridges" between otherwise disconnected parties. Interestingly, this type of brokerage decreases between Time 1 and Time 2, as over time some of these bridges disappear. The structural holes efficiency score assesses what proportion of ties are "non-redundant," that is the extent to which connections are to contacts who are not connected to actors' other contacts. In this case, at both time points CLAHRC-NET members are investing their efforts in non-redundant ties (the proportion of non-redundant ties is 69 percent at Time 1 and 68 percent at Time 2), thus suggesting that these network interactions have the potential to offer fruitful opportunities for the mobilization of new knowledge and more exploratory forms of innovation.

Although brokerage supports the cross-fertilization of fresh ideas and the generation of new knowledge, closure is equally as important because it provides an effective structural environment for anchoring and implementing this new knowledge in practice. It is interesting, in this respect, that the CLAHRC-NET closure metrics do not alter much over time. We can discuss each metric in turn. Density is a measure of the overall connectedness of a network. Only 8.6 percent (Time 1) and 7.8 percent (Time 2) of all possible ties are present making CLAHRC-NET quite a loosely structured network. Reciprocity measures the extent to which relations are two-way, so that where *a* nominates *b* as a knowledge contact, *a* also names *b* in return. Reciprocity of ties is often used as a proxy for trust, which has been shown to be associated with the sharing of knowledge within a network (Dirks and Ferrin, 2002). The temporal data show that of the ties that are present in this low-density network, a quarter of these are reciprocal at Time 1, dropping to 21 percent at Time 2. Figure 7.1 provides a visual illustration of the reciprocal knowledge translation ties (in red) for CLAHRC-NET at Time 1, note how reciprocity is not evenly distributed but creates "pockets" or clusters in some parts of the network.

Finally, the geodesic distance metric measures the network distance between individuals as popularized by the term "six degrees of separation." Figure 7.1 reveals that geodesic distances are largely unchanged between time points. It takes an average of 2.6 or 2.7 links for one person in CLAHRC-NET to connect with any other person in the network. These low geodesics (short distances between contacts) positively impact the speed at which knowledge can be mobilized. This is particularly relevant because the relatively high structural hole scores and low density make it more likely that individuals are exchanging novel knowledge and information with each other (Burt, 1992).

Figure 7.1 CLAHRC-NET reciprocal ties at Time 1 (in dark grey)

7.6.1 *How Ambidexterity Worked in CLAHRC-NET*

Our data shows that for this networked initiative, over time, actual brokering reduced but levels of closure and structural holes (potential for brokerage) were maintained. More brokerage work was to be done at the early stages of CLAHRC-NET's evolution as heterogeneous teams were assembled from individuals from different backgrounds, with different sets of personal networks and professional expertise. Actual brokering activity was higher at the start of the CLAHRC and decreased at later stages. This is probably because at the start clinical themes had to scope out prospective collaborators, and individuals became connected to one another through their work in the initiative over time (thus closing gaps in the informal knowledge network). However, the proportion of structural holes remained constant over time as the nature of CLAHRC work meant that members were constantly seeking to branch out in their ties, reshaping the approaches and the networks used to achieve their work (unlike traditional organizational forms where teams may be more static). The change in brokerage activity was also influenced by the stages at which clinical themes needed to access expertise provided by specialist support services (changing over the project life cycle).

At the network level, we see that levels of closure were also maintained throughout, holding the network together. This was important in supporting CLAHRC-NET's ethos of "collaborative co-production" between academic and NHS members, and to coordinate the actual delivery of project work. The proportion of reciprocal (two-way) ties is suggestive of stronger working relations that would underpin shared understandings and mutual agreements across a diversity of perspectives. The distances from one person to another (through the network of informal knowledge ties) are low at both time points. This is conducive to the speedier translation of knowledge between members of the initiative, producing fewer silos.

7.7 Interplay between Formal Organization and Social Network Structures

We found that the informal social networks which developed within the CLAHRC were influenced by its management structure and organization. Two main aspects of this were found in our data; the influence of formal thematic groups on structuring social ties, and the impact of having designated knowledge brokers.

7.7.1 *Thematic Groups and Closure*

In relation to the first aspect, the work of the CLAHRC was organized into large teams referred to as "themes." Each theme had a specific healthcare focus and members of each theme therefore shared common reference points in terms of research and implementation goals, working practices, projects, and sometimes co-located office space. One result of this was the clustering of work activities that promoted a degree of "closure" within the themes (so that knowledge became embedded in projects, more so over time). Yet as we have seen, at the level of the initiative, CLAHRC-NET exhibited moderate levels of closure (that is, high in terms of geodesics and reciprocity but with low density), which meant that knowledge developing within themes could be brokered, or translated, at speed across the initiative whilst avoiding the "group-think" that might emerge in very closed, tight-knit network structures (Coleman, 1988; McEvily, Perrone, and Zaheer, 2003; Chung and Jackson, 2013).

An example from our data to illustrate how CLAHRC-NET formal structure influenced social network ties and knowledge mobilization work is provided by a CLAHRC-NET member with a background in adult mental health. She describes the networking and learning opportunities that membership in the initiative offered her, "Coming to CLAHRC has meant that I have been exposed to such a diverse range of people to start with... I would never have done stuff with children. I would never have learned about ADHD. I certainly wouldn't have gone into anything to do with stroke." She describes how the initiative was designed to encourage her to work with sociologists and organizational theorists, and to embark on a learning journey that as a practitioner she would not have experienced, "[CLAHRC-NET] opened my eyes to all this other potential... And exposed me to all those other things. It has exposed me to a wide range of networks, a wide range of different people, and enabled me to build different skills."

Our SNA also showed that collaboration between CLAHRC-NET themes increased over time from 40 percent (Time 1) to 60 percent (Time 2). For example, the CLAHRC-NET Stroke theme increased its proportion of ties to other CLAHRC-NET teams from 20 percent at Time 1 to 30 percent at Time 2. A member of the Stroke theme described how his outlook was focused on his project in the earlier stages of the CLAHRC, but later developed to encompass a greater emphasis on brokering to other CLAHRC-NET theme groups:

> Actually the whole process of CLAHRC has been quite interesting because at the beginning I guess I was quite evangelical about what the clinical trials have said that the service would do, and I am also from a quantitative background so I was very kind of black and white. And over time I've noticed in myself that I'm a lot more, kind of, flexibly thinking about things... So I feel like I've evolved as the project has evolved, if that makes sense. So... And again I think that was a good part of the design of the project really.... Because we've been with that team from the start when it was set up, there's a lot of nuances that the team have embedded that we know why that practice has been embedded... (Hugo, Stroke theme, CLAHRC-NET)

This account shows how Hugo was engaged in embedding knowledge within the project team at the same time as extending his wider access to knowledge through brokering (he describes how the team organized and learnt from participatory workshops). This is illustrative of network ambidexterity in practice (from closure around team based work to brokerage through networking with other CLAHRC-NET themes).

7.7.2 Formal Roles and Brokerage

As part of its knowledge mobilization strategy, CLAHRC-NET funded a cohort of 30 "knowledge brokers" (KBs) who held their roles on a part-time (roughly one day per week) basis. Those appointed to the KB role were senior clinical or managerial staff (consultant doctors, matrons, allied health professionals, and senior directorate managers). The aim of their appointment was to support knowledge mobilization by; ensuring CLAHRC-NET research was aligned with

Network Ambidexterity

the needs of the NHS; promoting the research amongst their NHS colleagues and potential participants; and supporting the implementation of emerging research evidence in clinical and managerial practice. In this next example, we use our SNA data to zoom in on individuals with designated knowledge broker roles. This enables us to show how the interplay between an individual's network position and organizational role may influence knowledge mobilization. The impact of knowledge brokers can be gauged from our social network data as summarized in Figures 7.2 to 7.5.

We first look at the pattern of informal knowledge sharing ties at data capture Time 1. Figure 7.2 visualizes knowledge sharing ties between CLAHRC-NET members and shows that KBs were typically positioned towards the periphery of the CLAHRC-NET social network (KBs visualized as red nodes). Figure 7.3 re-presents the image when we also add external (non-CLAHRC-NET actors) where the outer node spokes are CLAHRC-NET's external stakeholders. Through these visualizations, we see that individuals occupying formal KB roles are positioned at the edge of the knowledge-sharing network between CLAHRC-NET members, which puts them in between internal CLAHRC-NET colleagues and external stakeholders. This means, in effect, that the KBs were playing a true brokering role by nature of their network positions. Moreover,

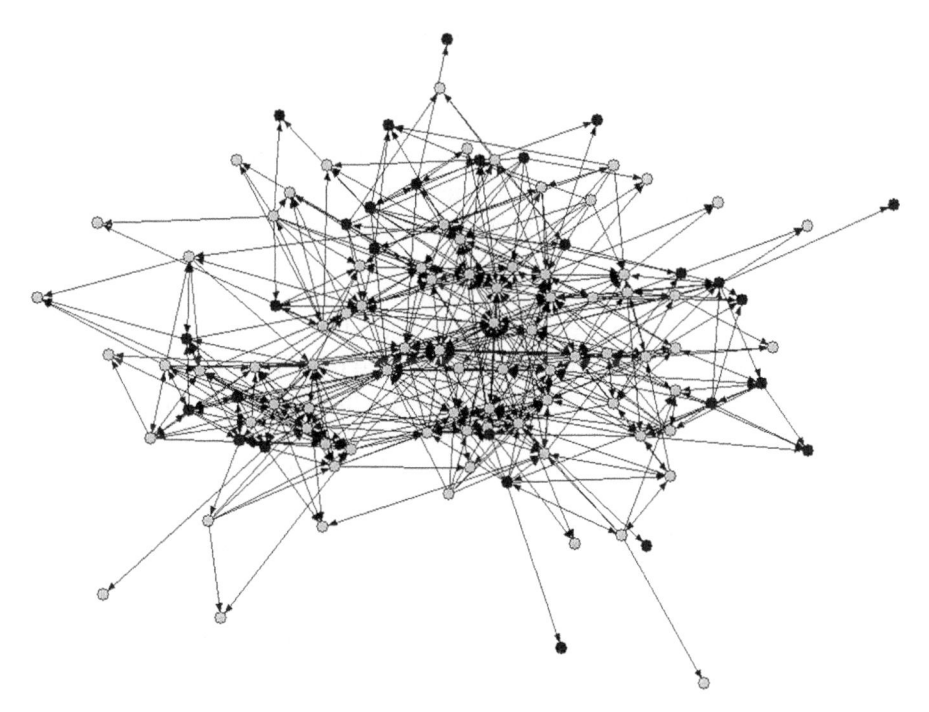

Figure 7.2 Network position of CLAHRC-NET knowledge brokers (dark grey nodes) at Time 1, internal ties only

165

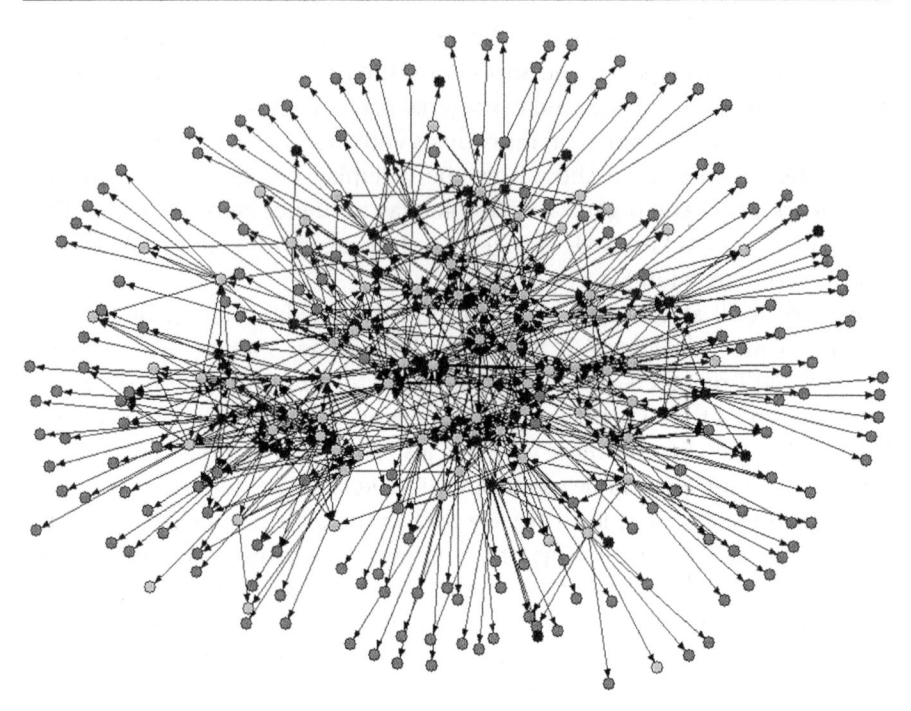

Figure 7.3 Network position of CLAHRC-NET knowledge brokers (dark grey nodes) at Time 1, including ties to external actors

the distribution of KBs across CLAHRC-NET themes (displayed as a rough circular configuration in Figure 7.3) means that each KB was tapping into different parts of the network and makes likely that they were accessing diverse knowledges.

Because their designated roles effectively positioned them at the fringes of the formally mandated network, the KBs helped to create and sustain links with external groups such as other clinicians and members of the NHS. This is important because it shows that the KBs as a group supported a specific type of knowledge mobilization role compared to other groups in CLAHRC-NET. The KBs were well positioned to be true knowledge "brokers" in the SNA sense because they occupied intermediary positions between CLAHRC-NET and its external collaborators. Moreover, because at least one KB was assigned to each CLAHRC-NET theme this capability was distributed strategically across the formally mandated network. This "in-between" position is aptly captured in the following description of the CLAHRC-NET KB program that encapsulates the internal and external facing role of the KB:

> One of the things they are doing currently is identifying the stakeholders around the areas in which we seek to make an impact. We then recruit those stakeholders

Network Ambidexterity

as members of our CLAHRC-NET.... So we take them and we work with them, engage them in the CLAHRC-NET way of doing things and what we're trying to do. And in essence that's led by the KB, and it's an attempt to try and engender community tendencies around a very specific clinical domain in which we are seeking to make an impact. (KB Program Lead)

Perhaps most surprising is the speed at which the KBs were able to mobilize into these network positions (our Time 1 data capture was at six months after CLAHRC-NET was established). This pattern of positions was largely maintained over time but with some DFs moving toward the centre of the network (see Time 2 positions in Figures 7.4 and 7.5).

This reflects a general development trend in CLAHRC-NET's knowledge mobilization activity from an expansive brokering strategy (outwardly focused stakeholder networking) to a targeted strategy (that became more internally focused on building networks around the NHS–university nexus).

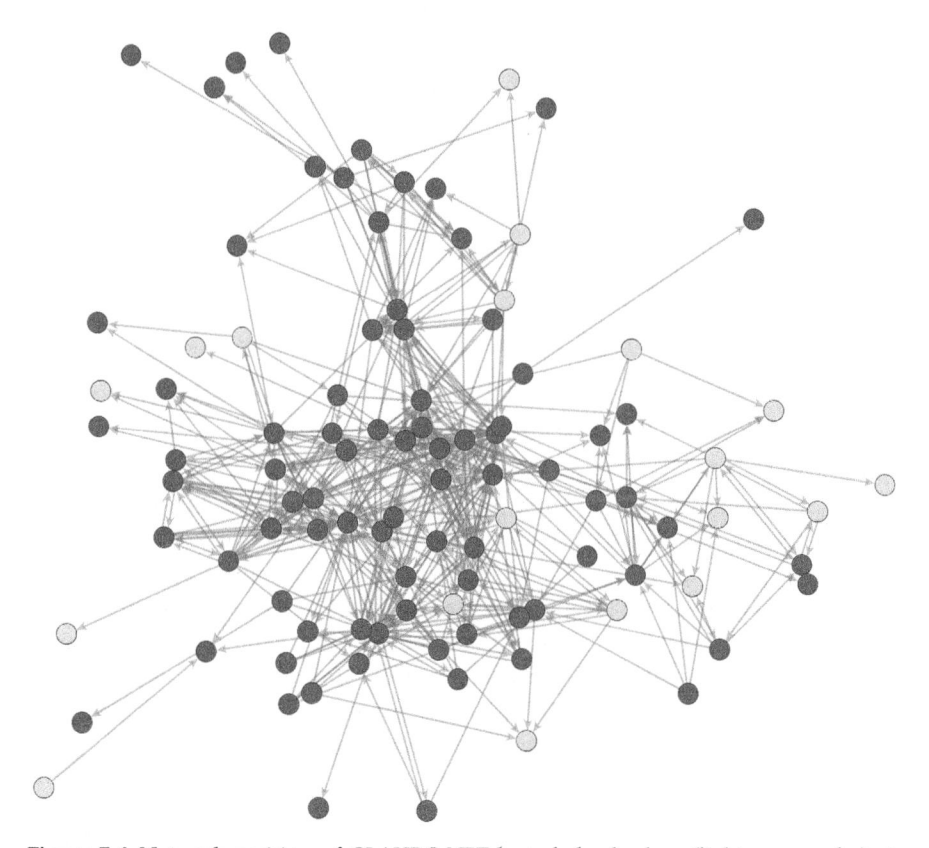

Figure 7.4 Network position of CLAHRC-NET knowledge brokers (light grey nodes) at Time 2, internal ties only

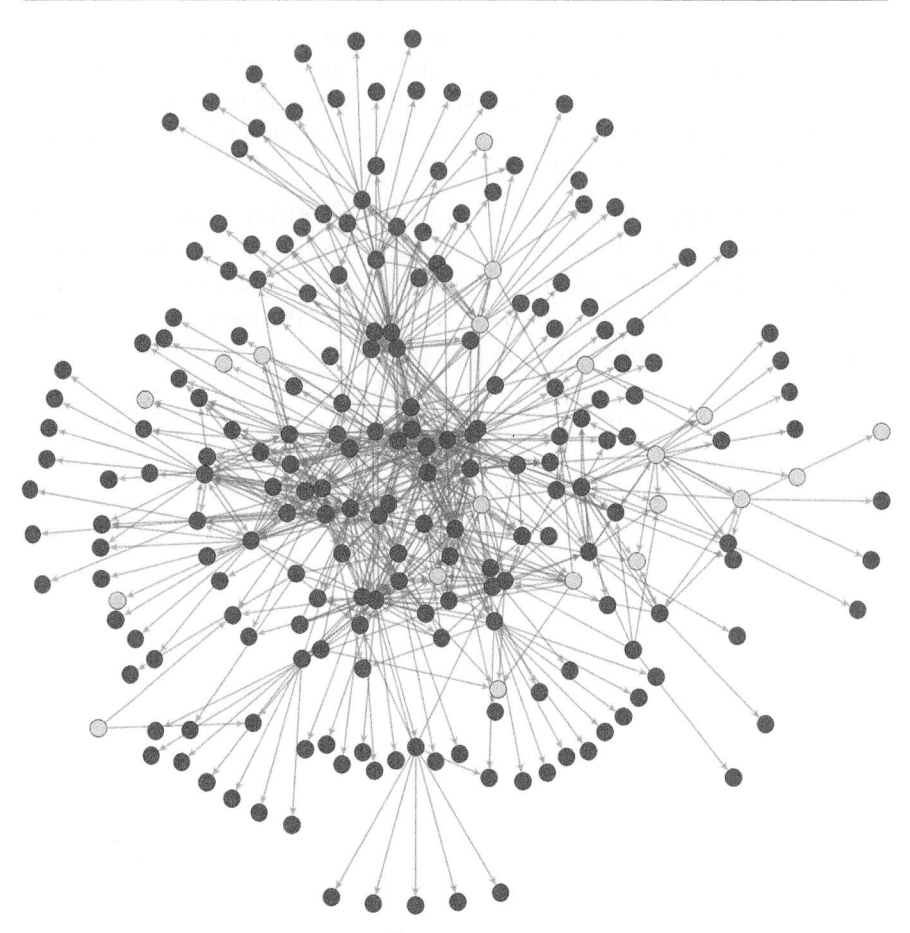

Figure 7.5 Network position of CLAHRC-NET knowledge brokers (light grey nodes) at Time 2, including ties to external actors

Our SNA revealed that at Time 1, CLAHRC-NET used an expansive information search strategy; that is to say, its knowledge networks were diverse, spanning multiple sources beyond the core NHS–university nexus (for example, to include also local authorities, central government, private industry, the third sector, and service users). In general, external contacts were important for accessing new contacts and obtaining practical advice. This branching-out supported CLAHRC-NET's strong co-production ethos that involved brokering collaboration with external stakeholders from day one. As one of our early interviewees describes:

> I think CLAHRC has forced people, researchers to expose things early before it's ready. So you're being asked to do conferences before you kind of got proper, nice findings and it's kind of a warts and all view. And I think that's a different way of working.

As the CLAHRC matured, however, this expansive networking strategy became less important. Our Time 2 SNA revealed that knowledge mobilization became more internally focused between colleagues within CLAHRC-NET itself (healthcare practitioners and university researchers) and knowledge sharing activity became predominantly based upon the exchange of scientific knowledge and on strengthening academic–health collaborations. This reduced reliance on external sources can be viewed as evidence of CLAHRC-NET becoming more self-reliant as the development of ties within the CLAHRC (through both brokerage and closure) enabled actors to access knowledge and information much more readily (and speedily given relatively low geodesic distances) from other CLAHRC members than from external contacts. There is also a sense here of groups and individuals moving from using expansive to more targeted search strategies, as the development of network ties increased their understanding of the knowledge and expertise available from different groups and individuals within the network.

7.8 Discussion

Several key findings emerge from our study that shed new light on the role of mandated networks in knowledge mobilization. Most importantly, we found that CLAHRC-NET as a mandated network was able to accommodate the qualitatively different patterns of social ties which are seen as crucial to the mobilization of knowledge. In other words, our SNA revealed that CLAHRC-NET ties exhibited both "closure," as its theme-based working helping to promote strong, interconnected ties, and "brokerage" due to the structural holes between groups and themes. The former helped ensure that new knowledge could be *exploited* effectively by embedding it in practice, and the latter enabled the *exploration* of knowledge by giving disconnected groups the potential to connect and exchange new knowledge and information (cf. Oborn et al., Chapter 5 this volume).

Second, we found an important interaction between the formal organization of the CLAHRC and its emergent social network. As noted earlier, this interaction has been noted in other studies in the NHS, with Ferlie et al. (2010) using the term "hybrid" to describe a network that grew out of pre-existing organic networks but then became mandated. In our study, hybridity was rather due to a mandated network prompting the emergence of an organic set of social ties. The direction of that interplay between formal and informal relationships, however, was less important in our case than its implications for social network structures. In particular, we found that the hybridity of the network in our case helped to enable ambidexterity. Thus, at the overall mandated network level the thematic clustering of working teams promoted the kind of network closure that supported the embedding of new knowledge and evidence into practice. At the same time, the relatively loose structure of social ties at CLAHRC level incorporated "structural holes" that provided brokerage opportunities to create and acquire new knowledge. Thus, the dual challenges of knowledge mobilization—both creating new knowledge and evidence and putting this into practical application—could be supported.

In addition, and reinforcing the link between formal structure and social network development, we found that the designation of KB roles within CLAHRC-NET made a valuable contribution to brokerage activity as individuals responded to the peripheral positioning of their role by extending the CLAHRC's external links. We saw that these positions were maintained as CLAHRC-NET became more established over time, but that some KBs moved into more central positions in the informal knowledge-sharing network in line with the overall shift in emphasis toward internally focused networking around the NHS–university nexus. Although the designation of formal brokering roles by no means guarantee that individuals will be able to perform a brokerage function, in this case the positioning of the role seems to have been important in encouraging the social ties needed to do so, but also that the enactment of formal brokering roles was influenced by the shifting distribution of ties at the organizational level.

A third, and related, finding from our study was that the persistence of CLAHRC-NET's formal arrangements over time helped to promote an ongoing dynamic of networking which helped to create new patterns of social tie formation. Thus, we found that CLAHRC-NET became more self-reliant and self-referential as a network over time; moving from using expansive (stakeholder-based) to targeted (NHS–university-based) search strategies. External knowledge ties became less important (these connections had been key for accessing new contacts and proving practical advice on knowledge mobilization work), as members became increasingly able to draw on more relevant niche, scientific knowledge from their CLAHRC-NET colleagues. In this sense, CLAHRC NET itself became the pivotal knowledge resource facility by nature of its ambidextrous networks supporting a continued ability to both access and bank the knowledge that had been mobilized through the work of its members but also for developing a specialist offering in terms of the provision of scientific knowledge.

This finding on the importance of networking activity represents a counterpoint to much previous research which has tended to view networks primarily in structural terms, as channels, conduits or "pipelines" through which knowledge is transferred (Owen-Smith and Powell, 2004), thereby neglecting their dynamic and evolving properties (Grandori and Soda, 1995). The progressive interweaving of formal organization and social ties seen in our case also underlines the benefits that arise where the formation of social networks contributes to organizational goals. Such benefits, in our case, were not limited to the knowledge mobilizing advantages of ambidexterity, but also extended to more relational forms of organizing as developing social ties enabled greater mutual knowledge and access to expertise (Cramton, 2001), coordination and problem solving (Hoffer Gittell, 2002).

One important caveat to our finding on the positive impact of the interplay between formal organization and informal ties seen in CLAHRC-NET is that this may not be generalizable to other settings, including to other mandated networks. What was observed in our study was, broadly, a virtuous circle in which formal structures and roles helped to catalyze a rich and productive combination of patterned social ties. However, it is equally possible to imagine other settings in which a vicious circle might operate where formal structures promote excessive closure in network ties, limiting the exchange of new knowledge and promoting inwardness rather than exploration. This is potentially an important topic for future research.

More broadly, our study has important implications for future research, policy, and practice in the area of knowledge mobilization. For one, it suggests that future research could usefully build upon the mixed methods approach outlined here to capture the interplay between the interpretive aspects of knowledge mobilization and the effect of shifting social network structures. In addition, important policy and practice implications arise from our study for the many mandated networks whose work involves a knowledge mobilization remit. From a practical point of view, our discussion of network ambidexterity provides a greater understanding of the need to develop formal structures that will evolve social networks that are able to accommodate both brokerage and closure, and thus sustain knowledge mobilization activity over time. Equally, consideration of the interplay between the formal arrangements of the mandated network and informal social ties highlights the possibility of both vicious and virtuous circles in their reciprocal development, leading to significantly different outcomes in each case.

These strands in our analysis not only highlight a need for greater research attention to the network dynamics of knowledge mobilization initiatives, but also highlight the significant opportunities (and risks) that attend the design of formal roles and structures in mandated networks. Although it would be a mistake to assume that formally networked arrangements necessarily secure the effective patterning of informal ties seen in CLAHRC-NET, it is clear from our study that the appropriate design and enactment of such arrangements have a significant impact on the social ties which ultimately help to realize knowledge mobilization.

7.9 Conclusion

This chapter has contributed in several ways to the broader theme of "mobilizing through networks." By applying a social network perspective, it has identified the importance of network ambidexterity as both a desirable and empirically attainable objective for a mandated network seeking to mobilize knowledge. Further, our study highlights how the choices made in the management and organization of such mandated networks—specifically, in the design of themes and the designation of broker roles—may help to promote such ambidexterity. This analysis provides a useful contribution to the debate on knowledge mobilization that has, hitherto, tended to focus only on brokerage and closure as separate network conditions. This analytical framework can thus help to inform future policy and practice as to the appropriate design and development of knowledge mobilization initiatives.

Acknowledgments

This research was supported in part by a grant from the National Institute of Health Research (NIHR) HS&DR (project: 09/1809/1075).

Theme 4
Mobilizing Knowledge across Space and Time

Introduction

In many ways, healthcare practice is treated as a universal—it is assumed that the type of drug and treatment practice that is delivered to someone with, say, asthma should be relatively standard across contexts, as enshrined in the idea of "evidence-based medicine," a theme discussed in the Introduction of this book. This is notwithstanding the more recent discussions about personalized medicine regimes, because even this is founded on the idea that how medicines are personalized can be universally defined based on our unfolding knowledge of human genes. Yet, anyone who has been treated in more than one country (or just more than one hospital or doctor's practice in the same country) will realize that the "same" treatment or healthcare practice can actually be very different in different contexts. Policy makers despair at this diversity and attempt to create a more standardized service by setting up processes and protocols that define "best practice" and assume that these can be straightforwardly diffused across contexts.

In this book, we do not dispute that some countries (and some providers within a particular country) are more successful in diagnosing and treating a particular type of patient, but we believe that it is important to understand how healthcare knowledge is mobilized across contexts, not assuming that this is a simple process of diffusing what works in one context to somewhere else. Thus, the last section of the book considers the way in which knowledge travels and spreads across contexts; that is, the domain of action that is in focus is trans-local spaces.

Corroborating the idea of knowledge mobilization articulated in this book, the two chapters in this section demonstrate again how the mobilization of knowledge is an emergent and political process, this time as knowledge circulates across much more distributed domains of space and time. Indeed, as should be clear by now, this is why we do not use the term "diffusion" or "transfer" in this book, but rather "mobilization," since diffusion and transfer suggest an unproblematic spreading of ideas across contexts, which our chapters amply demonstrate is not what happens in practice. We would also argue that it is this misunderstanding that has meant that many policy initiatives that attempt to create standard processes and practices have failed. Thus, even where ideas do become internationally popular (think of evidence-based medicine in healthcare) their uptake does not involve a simple copying, but rather a translation (Czarniawska and Sévon, 2005a; Nielsen, Mathiassen, and Newell, 2014) that reflects the ways the new idea has been shaped by the values, expectations, and practices constituting the particular context of appropriation.

Everett Rogers (2003) popularized the diffusion view of innovation, assuming that the spread of an innovation was mostly dependent on whether it created relative advantage (compared to existing solutions in a particular area). Innovations from this perspective are diffused across contexts "ready to wear" (Meyer and Scott, 1983). The Management Fashion perspective (Abrahamson, 1996) critiqued this idea, demonstrating that relative advantage was not necessarily an objective feature of the innovation but rather depended on how the particular new idea was sold and promoted by the supply side—so consulting companies and software providers have a vested interest in "proving" that a new type of EHR (electronic health record) solution is better than existing versions because this will help to garner sales for them. Simultaneously, managers are constantly looking for the new "best thing" and so can be receptive to claims on the part of the supply side, thus creating a fashion cycle, where new technologies and new management practices ride a wave of fashion (Swanson, 2012), only to, at some point, be overtaken by a new, next "best thing" so that the wave dies out. Adopters of fashions, in other words, play an active role from the fashion perspective but largely as uncritical absorbers of the latest technologies, influenced by the "organizing vision" that is created around a new idea (Swanson and Ramiller, 1997) and the never-ending search for better ways of doing something.

Yet while the management fashion perspective considered more critically the supply-push and user-pull aspects of innovation, it did not really take account of how the institutional context shapes the way knowledge is mobilized across space and time. Thus, it is not simply that managers are actively looking for new ideas; managers are also embedded and embodied in particular practices that are themselves part of a wider set of practices and these distinct practices, and the ways they interact, are continuously changing, sometimes in ways that compete and sometimes in ways that support a particular practice. A new idea will confront these existing practices and how the new idea emerges from this confrontation will be unpredictable but will certainly involve change to the new practice (as well as to existing practices).

Thus, innovations do not manifest as an objective idea but, rather, manifest in a variety of doings, sayings, and objects that will be translated and transformed as they are taken up, discarded, or changed by different practitioners with different vested interests. The two chapters in this section illustrate this by considering two different types of innovation—innovation around hospital procedures for dealing with treatments that have gone wrong and innovation around new drug development.

Chapter 8 recognizes that innovation involves transformation rather than diffusion (and so knowledge mobilization rather than knowledge transfer) but also considers how the innovation itself can be viewed as an actor shaping the way it travels and is transformed across institutional contexts. In other words, it is not just human agents that shape the way new ideas travel across contexts; the idea itself (whether a material object like a new IT (information technology) system and/or a conceptual object like a new way of enacting a particular practice) shapes the process of translation. In other words, the innovation can be considered to be a mediator in its own right (Latour, 1986); it is not just the subject of mediation (an intermediary) by the human actors that are "at play." More specifically, this chapter will look at the origins of a healthcare innovation (Root Cause Analysis, a practice that includes a set of practices, tools, and skills to identify the origin of serious clinical incidents) and how this travels globally across international contexts. It will show how two, seemingly opposite, discourses (one anxiety-creating, and one reassuring) helped to generate a wave of interest *and* urgency that allowed the innovation to travel quickly across nations and into practice, even if the outcomes of this changed practice were not always as predicted.

The final chapter in this section (Chapter 9) uses the example of the development of clinical trials research in the UK to explore the major institutional and organizational barriers to the mobilization of healthcare knowledge. It shows how deeply entrenched expectations, practices, and incentives concerning how "good" research "should" be performed can pose constraints to the innovation process and knowledge mobilization. More specifically, the chapter demonstrates how the distributed actors involved in clinical trials research have different temporal orientations ("timescapes") in relation to the development of novel drugs. More importantly, they also show how these different timescapes account for at least some of the problems associated with the successful identification and testing of new therapeutics during the clinical trials process.

The two chapters in this final section, then, show how new forms of knowledge travel across contexts, considering the particular challenges posed by different spaces and conceptions of time. They explore how practices, expectations, and values that are deeply embedded in wider, institutionalized "landscapes" and "timescapes" shape the ability to develop new forms of treatment and innovative practices. These themes are clearly reminiscent of the themes illustrated in other chapters and so also emphasize the importance of the knowledge mobilization perspective adopted in this book. Knowledge mobilization is influenced by multiple overlapping, or nested, agencies that can only be appreciated by examining the actual unfolding of particular processes and practices (the sayings, doings, interactions, and things) in a specific area of activity. The final two chapters aptly illustrate this.

8

Recovering the Performative Role of Innovations in the Global Travel of Healthcare Practices

Is there a Ghost in the Machine?

Davide Nicolini, Jeanne Mengis, David Meacheam, Justin Waring, and Jacky Swan

CHAPTER SUMMARY

This chapter discusses the global travel of practices with reference to the international patient safety movement, focusing on a specific approach to incident investigation (Root Cause Analysis or RCA for short). We assess how knowledge of the technique was mobilized, from the United States to Australia, the United Kingdom and beyond. We argue that the mobilization and world spanning circulation of this set of practices was sustained and facilitated by the construction of an "anxiety-reassurance" package. This package worked to support the mobilization of the approach through, first, raising public and professional anxiety about pre-existing management practices around patient safety, and second, creating reassurance by proposing a new management solution to solve this problem. Playing together these two seemingly opposite discourses, the innovation generated a wave of interest and urgency that it then rode and that allowed rapid globalization. Below we show how this powerful "package" actively translated the new approach in the sense of both circulating and profoundly reconfiguring it. We suggest that a focus on the innovation as a well-oiled piece of discursive machinery helps us "unpack the black box," and understand the active role of innovations in fueling their own translation. This without reverting to the old idea that innovations are "diffused."

8.1 Introduction

For the most part of the twentieth century, academics and policy makers alike endorsed the view that modes of organizing, practices, and ideas diffuse within a population or field through a more or less mindless process of contagion, usually described using the chemical image of diffusion (Rogers, 1995; Strang and Soule, 1998; Van de Ven and Hargrave, 2004). The idea of innovation and policy diffusion is based on a rational communication model and draws on the implicit principle that the knowledge is transmitted unchanged; the success of the innovation depends on the fit between the nature of the sender, the object that is translated, and the receivers. Adopters are often depicted as passive; the focus is on responsive adaptive behavior; the engine behind the diffusion of innovations is assumed to be either the acquisition of a competitive advantage or normative compliance (Johnson and Hagström, 2005).

From the 1990s this under-socialized, scarcely performative view of the circulation and take-up of new knowledge, practices and modes of organizing was problematized by a number of studies which confronted diffusion theory to posit the existence of a "ghost in the machine"[1] and brought to attention the active role of adopters in the process of innovation (Latour, 1986; Czarniawska and Joerges, 1996; Czarniawska and Sevón, 1996; Strang and Soule, 1998; Johnson and Hagström, 2005; Frenkel, 2005; Czarniawska and Sevón, 2005a; Boxenbaum and Battilana, 2005; Morris and Lancaster, 2006; Sahlin and Wedlin, 2008; Ansari, Fiss, and Zajac, 2010; Nicolini, 2010). Contrary to the prevailing diffusionist view, the Sociology of Translation suggested that the circulation[2] and take-up of innovations is better understood as a social and political process through which new ways of working actively "carve out" a space within the existing texture of practices. This is achieved by a process that allows them to become associated with a variety of different interests and goals. The more interests and goals a new practice or innovation can serve and mobilize, the more irresistible it will become. The model derives from a strong semiotic, material, and political orientation to social affairs and is based on three main claims (Latour, 1986).

Firstly, practices, policies, and modes of organizing do not actually travel and always require some type of intermediary to move in space and time. Such intermediation is usually discursive and symbolic in character. In short, it is not practices or ways of doing which travel but rather their descriptions or representations. Practice, policies, and institution are thus turned into texts, ideas, models, images, drawings, narratives, examples, and so on, which are circulated far away from the point of origin. Practices, policies, and ways of working can also be inscribed in human bodies and minds, in the form of skills and competences. In this case humans become themselves intermediaries. Finally, in certain circumstances material objects like prototypes, software, and other artifacts can also be used to convey the idea of a practice, policy, or particular new ways of working. From a research point of view the key empirical question is not only how a practice moves in space and time but how one particular new way of doing becomes relevant and compelling given that we are continuously surrounded by endless new ideas and possibilities.

Secondly, and strictly related to the former, the movement in space and time of any new knowledge, practice, or mode of organizing, is in the hands of those involved. They may accept it, modify it, deflect it, betray it, add to it, appropriate it, or let it drop (Latour, 1986: 267). The impetus must thus come from the potential users themselves who must perceive some benefits from the adoption of this new way of working. Each of these actors shapes the innovation to their own ends. Instead of a process of transfer and transmission, we have thus a process of continuous transformation (Latour, 1986).

Thirdly, because there are always several possible competing interpretations of any new way of doing things, each serving a particular type of interest, the translation process should always be regarded as a political task that takes place within specific institutional constraints and power dynamics. Organizational fields are thus the locus of tactics, strategic action, and conflict (Waring and Currie, 2009). Translating innovation is always tied to the local pursuit of specific material or immaterial interests. The receivers and (potential) adopters of innovations are thus not only active, they are politically savvy.

From the perspective of the Sociology of Translation, focusing on the characteristics of the innovation and its presumed innovativeness makes little sense and the process of translation, rather than the properties of innovative ways of organizing and practices, needs to be the focus of "diffusion" studies (Czarniawska and Joerges, 1996: 25). Innovations travel fueled mostly by the need (or desire) of actors to imitate others while pursuing their own specific interests (Czarniawska and Joerges, 1996; Czarniawska and Sevón, 2005b). Accordingly, studies in this tradition have traditionally focused on the micro-tactics and broader processes whereby interests are organized, movements created and innovations propelled (see Boxenbaum and Pedersen, 2009 for a review). However, while the previous studies documented the journey of innovative ideas and how they are made to change in the process (Ansari, Fiss, and Zajac, 2010) innovations were seen mostly as rather inert intermediaries that human individual or collective agents passed to each other. The performative power of the innovation itself was downplayed or ignored, being perceived as belonging to the alternative (i.e. diffusion) paradigm.

In this chapter we argue that by doing so the Sociology of Translation missed a chance to add a few more mediators in the world (Latour's battlecry is "more mediators and less intermediaries" see Latour, 2005: 37 and ff.) The difference between intermediation and mediation is subtle but important. Intermediaries are mediums, neutral carriers (Latour, 1994: 31). They have limited or no influence on the nature of the message or what has been exchanged. Mediation, on the other hand, implies displacement, drift, invention, and "the creation of a link that did not exist before and that to some degree modifies two elements or agents" (Latour, 1994: 31). This often requires that the message or the thing that is exchanged is modified to become more acceptable to both parties. At the end of a process of mediation both parties will end up in places that were different from where they started. Mediators are thus by definition active and consequential both on the exchange and what is exchanged.

We argue that in specific circumstances the innovation itself should be included in the explanation of its success—the innovation is a mediator in its own right. This is not because of its supposed inherent innovativeness (as in the traditional diffusion approach) but more simply because certain innovations, especially complex process innovations, are engineered to perform a specific type of (discursive) work that contributes to translation, diffusion and success. In the case of Root Cause Analysis (RCA)—a set of practices, tools and skills to investigate the origin of serious clinical incidents, the innovation itself operated as a capable, heterogeneous assemblage of human and non-human elements that actively contributed to create the context for its adoption. The package of discursive resources, tools and people (Nicolini, Waring, and Mengis, 2011) worked together to support the spread of the approach, first, by raising public and professional anxiety about the performance of pre-existing practices around patient safety, and second, by creating reassurance through proposing a new management solution to solve the crisis it had artfully created. By playing together these two seemingly opposite discourses, the innovation package generated a wave of interest and urgency that it then rode and that allowed its fast global circulation. For once, the ghost is in the machine.

This chapter is organized as follows. After briefly summarizing our research methods and context, we describe the journey whereby RCA was translated from one discipline to another and then proceeded to jump from continent to continent until it became a global phenomenon. We then zoom in on the nature of RCA and unpack its strategies and the language employed when invoking its use that explain its performative capability. We conclude by framing our findings within the broader discussion on the translation, transition, and transmission of knowledge across time and space.

8.2 Context and Methods

Our research style is based on analytic narratives (Bates et al., 2000) and process tracing (George and Bennett, 2005). Theory-guided process-tracing approaches generate explanatory models based on a limited number of historical cases.

We conducted twenty-six semi-structured interviews and a comprehensive documentary analysis in the USA, Australia, and the UK. We chart here the travel of the idea and practice of RCA (Czarniawska and Sevón, 1996; Czarniawska and Sevón, 2005a; Nicolini, 2010), examining how it was adopted as the dominant approach to learn from incidents and improve safety in the UK, Australia, and elsewhere.

Interviews were tape recorded and transcribed. Two of the authors then proceeded to create a time-ordered matrix and a number of process-event charts, working inductively to identify clear recurring patterns in the data (Levi, 2002).

8.2.1 *What is RCA?*

Root Cause Analysis refers to a family of structured methodologies for the retrospective and structured investigation of adverse incidents, near misses and sentinel events. It is aimed at helping organizations learn from their mistakes (Wald and Shojania, 2001). RCA is based on the belief that in order to prevent accidents from recurring an interdisciplinary team has to inquire not only how the event happened, but what are its underlying systemic causes to formulate corrective actions (Carroll, Rudolph, and Hatakenaka, 2002). RCA promises that organizational problems and the solutions to these problems can be identified through robust, rigorous, and rational analytical processes (Andersen and Fagerhaug, 2000).

As a process, RCA fits within a wider model of organizational learning that involves stages for knowledge sharing through incident reporting, stratification of incidents to determine their relative priority, structured investigation to determine the underlying causes and producing recommendations and service improvements to promote future safety (Nicolini, Waring, and Mengis, 2011). RCA is based on a rational choice approach to problem solving (March, 1994) and a linear view of organizational change (see, for example, Weick and Quinn, 1999). The ideal RCA process is summarized in Table 8.1.

While variations of this model exist (Bagian et al., 2002; Woloshynowych et al., 2005), there remains an enduring commitment to following a linear analytical framework (Runciman and Walton, 2007). The broad consensus is

Table 8.1. An ideal model of the RCA process (from Amo, 1998)

The seven steps for Root Cause Analysis

1. Identify the incident to be analyzed
2. Organize a team to carry out the RCA
3. Study the work processes
4. Collect the facts
5. Search for causes
6. Take action
7. Evaluate the actions taken.

Table 8.2. Root Cause Analysis in practice

What is the focus of RCA investigations?

The following is an example of a root cause analysis conducted within a Victorian (Australian) public hospital. A suicidal patient admitted to inpatient care concealed medication previously prescribed and attempted suicide via overdose. The patient survived this attempt, but subsequently succeeded in hanging themselves within the inpatient unit. The subsequent RCA investigation recommended changes in the search procedures of patients' belongings when admitted to care, revision of the guidelines for care of suicidal patients and implementing an improved anti-ligature system for bathroom doors/fittings. (State Government Victoria, Department of Health, 2014)

How does RCA work in practice?

At one of the hospital we observed in the UK the "RCA" described a facilitated group session held in one of the departments in order to further investigate and discuss an untoward accident with serious consequences for a patient. Participation was strongly encouraged but not mandatory. Usually about a dozen people attended. Statements were collected ahead of the meeting and a timeline carefully constructed. The facilitator used the incident timeline to trigger and structure a conversation in search of immediate and root causes. Other tools were utilized to give depth to the discussion, for example a fishbone analysis of contributory factors. At the end of the session the facilitators usually identified some of the "good practices" that emerged during the discussion as well as some of the lesson learned and areas that required change. A report summarizing the discussion and action point was then sent to the hospital management for approval.

that RCA represents an umbrella or toolbox of approaches rather than a single method (Andersen and Fagerhaug, 2000: 12).

Woloshynowych et al. (2005) report that more than forty RCA techniques are available, including brainstorming, cause-effect charts, change analysis, "five whys" diagrams, fault trees, and Gantt charts, providing different levels and forms of analysis at different stages of the investigation. Two examples of RCA are provided in Table 8.2.

8.3 Findings: The Global Travel of RCA

8.3.1 *The Origins: Jumping Industry Boundaries*

The modern version of RCA has its roots in the nuclear branch of the US Navy where the approach was developed as a tool to guarantee high standards of performance and reliability. After the Three Mile Island incident (1979), and subsequent enquiry, RCA was widely adopted by civilian and military nuclear industry establishments (Carroll, 1998; Wears, Perry, and Sutcliffe, 2005). Seminal publications on RCA were written by nuclear industry experts. During the 1980s and 1990s, safety professionals—usually engineers—extended the method into other industries. By the mid-1990s RCA was a cemented part of the general body of knowledge for safety professionals.

8.3.2 RCA Conquers the US Healthcare Sector

In the USA, the use of a structured method to investigate incidents was introduced in healthcare in the mid-1990s through the jointed and sometime disjointed efforts of two large agencies—the Joint Commission for Accreditation of Hospitals ("the Joint Commission") and the Veterans Health Affairs Administration (VHA) (Wears, Perry, and Sutcliffe, 2005).

The Joint Commission is an independent, not-for-profit organization formed by the merger of the largest medical associations in North America. Its primary purpose is to evaluate and provide voluntary accreditation to healthcare organizations. The VHA provides medical services for US armed forces veterans and their families. It is government funded and is the largest integrated healthcare system in the USA, serving 8.3 million customers per annum.

Both organizations became sensitized to the issue of patient safety following the Harvard Medical Practice Study (Brennan et al., 1991). The study examined 30,121 randomly selected records from fifty-one randomly selected hospitals and found that adverse events occurred in 3.7 percent of the cases (1,114 patients). In 13.6 percent of cases this lead to death (151 cases). Almost one quarter of these incidents were due to negligence.

Following the publication of the report the Joint Commission introduced an "agenda for change," including a system of voluntary reporting of critical incidents. Informants described this as highly ineffective. Under increased media attention and the report of a string of horror stories coming out of accredited hospitals, in 1995 the Joint Commission considered a punitive response, withdrawing accreditation from "error" hospitals. According to one of our informants, this policy was abandoned in favor of a more developmental approach promoted by Rick Croteau, a former NASA doctor proficient in using engineering techniques to investigate accidents and prevent their reoccurrence. Croteau, as director of the Joint Commission strategic initiative on preventing clinical errors, promoted a policy requiring all hospitals to investigate and report the causes of the most serious adverse events ("sentinel events") so that the Joint Commission could conduct cross hospital analysis and make recommendations for change. The Joint Commission developed a detailed definition of sentinel events and promoted the use of "Focus Reviews," a team based exercise modeled on Quality Circles (one of our informants described this as "RCA under a different name"). Conducting the Focus Reviews was voluntary (the Joint Commission did not have enforcing power), member organizations were motivated to adopt the practice as accreditation status would not be changed if a review was conducted. The Joint Commission however could only recommend but not prescribe how such reviews were to be conducted.

Concurrently, the VHA was following a similar path and in the early 1990s established a Patient Safety Event Registry. The process required that local experts would conduct an investigation using ten structured questions. In typical bureaucratic fashion, the report would then be sent to regional and possibly national offices. According to our informants quality was poor and the question usually attracting most attention was whether the incident could have adverse public relations effects.

Evolution hastened in the mid-1990s, when the VHA employed Jim Bagian, an ex-astronaut and safety expert at NASA. He was brought in to guide the newly established Patient Safety Improvement initiative, later to become the VHA National Centre for Patient Safety. Bagian's initial actions included establishing an Expert Panel on Patient Safety System Design with a mix of VHA employees and experts from aviation, safety engineering and psychology. The panel proposed a set of recommendations to guide the VHA attempt to improve their safety record. They examined the reporting systems used in aviation and aeronautics and in 1997 produced a series of recommendations aimed at establishing a mandatory, non-punitive system of investigation and reporting focused on learning rather than apportioning blame. At the core of the approach was RCA, understood as a structured, team based method of incident investigation that would feed the improvement process. The approach was formalized in the 1998 "VHA Patient Safety Improvement Handbook," now in its third iteration. At the same time, the two organizations (and others not mentioned here for brevity's sake but which constituted an emerging community of interest), started to meet and exchange notes. In 1996 and 1998 the two organizations gathered several hundred experts at the Annenberg Conferences where the Joint Commission shared the lessons learned through the sentinel event program while the VHA discussed their approach to learning from errors.

Matters took a further dramatic turn in 1999 with the publication of the Institute of Medicine report "To err is human." The report replicated on a wider scale the Harvard Medical Practice Study and came to the striking conclusion that about 98,000 people die each year in US hospitals as a result of preventable medical errors. As one of our informants put it:

> ...the report changed the opinion of a lot of people... From then on people could not say that medical malpractice was not a serious problem... this served to put the issue of patient safety, which previously had been invisible, on the radar screen.

Patient safety had been turned into a social problem (Kitsuse and Spector, 1973). One outcome of the report was the joint development of a Safety Assessment Code (SAC) Matrix for close calls and adverse events, bringing together the classifications used by the VHA and the Joint Commission.

Following the publication of the report, the VHA also sped up the roll out of RCA as the main approach to learn from incidents. How RCA was to be conducted in all VHA facilities, the tools to be used, when and by whom, were codified in a new version of the Handbook issued in 2000. This included diagrams, instructions on how to conduct the investigation, who was to be involved, how remedial actions were to be formulated. The initiative was a resounding success:

> We started out with less than 10% of our facilities volunteering to try this, less than 10%. In less than a month from that 10% starting to do it, the gossip mill, if you will—the conversations they would have with their colleagues... every other facility was demanding to do it immediately, and that's not an exaggeration... I had calls or emails from every director saying, "How come we are not doing this already? When do we get to start doing this?" which is a good problem to have. (Interviewee)

Concurrently, Bagian visited the Joint Commission, presented the VHA approach and showed their materials. Soon after, Dennis O'Leary, head of the Joint Commission, publicly confirmed that new Joint Commission policy was to be based on VHA's handbook for Patient Safety.

The march of RCA now was irresistible. In 2002 stakeholders across the public and private sector establish the National Quality Forum and created the first list of "never events" (very serious incidents that should never happen), and monitored their occurrence. In 2005 the Department of Health and Human Services started a national network of Patient Safety Organizations that collected and analyzed voluntary reports of adverse events. In both cases, RCA was identified as the main tool to investigate incidents, produce change, and address "the underlying system of care deficiencies" (Andersen and Fagerhaug, 2000).

Members of the two organizations differ on who should be credited for the success of the RCA. Members of the Joint Commission suggested that the VHA version of the RCA was just a modification of what they had been doing for almost two decades. The VHA claims that they should be credited for the introduction of engineering rigor and discipline:

> [At the Joint Commission] nobody knew how to do investigations. They would sit down together and look at it and say, "well, yeah, the nurse should try harder," or "I do not know, that's just a normal complication; patients died, but that just happens." So 50% of the time they get to the end saying "that just happened" while the other 50% was "try harder" or give them some training. (Interviewee)

VHA staff are happy to acknowledge that the Joint Commission had a critical role in the mainstreaming of RCA "We were acting as providers, and they were really the government oversight although we also had CMS,[3] which is another government [agency]...There's no end of government oversight, but they were the biggest of the oversight groups." If the Joint Commission speaks, the US hospitals listen.

8.3.3 *RCA Crosses the Atlantic and Takes Root in the UK*

As in the USA, institutionalized attention on patient safety in the UK started to emerge in the 1990s, the dawn of what Power (2007) describes as the age of the risk management of everything. Risk management has become a benchmark of good governance for banks, hospitals and many other organizations. Since the mid-1970s National Health Service (NHS) organizations were required to apply the Health and Safety at Work Act, 1974, subsequently safety in healthcare was forcefully brought to the fore by a series of reports from the National Audit Office in the early 1990s. In a report from 1995, for example, the National Audit Office found that "hospitals are...dangerous places for patients, staff and visitors" and that "the large number of accidents imposes a very significant burden on NHS resources which could be better spent on patient care" (National Audit Office, 1996).

Monitoring the occurrence of incidents was central to this approach. In 1991, the Department of Health (DoH) issued to all the local healthcare authorities a suite of occupational health and safety tools (SAFECODE) including IRIS, the first standardized method to report incidents implemented in the UK. The tool allowed monitoring the frequency of adverse events and provided the basis both for a number of government reports and the establishment of the still existing Clinical Negligence Scheme for Trusts, a mandatory internal insurance system. Premiums are calculated on the number of past occurrences, with significant discounts for organizations who can demonstrate that they proactively try to prevent incidents. IRIS, however, was used sporadically. As the 1995 National Audit Office report put it "we consider it unsatisfactory that, despite the NHS Executive's previous guidance, many hospitals do not have accident recording systems which provide accurate and timely information."

While the NHS was pursuing a traditional risk management approach, culminating in 1999 with the adoption of the Australian Risk Management Standard as the official NHS policy, others were following a different path. In 1995 academics and clinicians established a research unit on patient safety at University College London. The group, led by Charles Vincent, tried to adapt to the needs of healthcare settings the principles of the so called "human factor" approach to incidents (Reason, 1995). "Human factors" utilizes systemic and psychological principles to identify the communicational, cultural and contextual reasons for the occurrence of adverse events. As a founding member put it, one of the main concerns of the group was "how we could investigate incidents more systematically and produce change." While the government was mainly interested in auditing the number of incidents, internal investigations at the time were mainly used to apportion blame: "they had morbidity and mortality meetings that junior doctors and the midwives used to hate going to because they knew they were going to be hung, drawn and quartered" (Interviewee).

The group produced the CRU/ALARM protocol, a structured method for investigating clinical incidents using a combination of record review, staff interviews and a human factors checklist highlighting psychological and organizational factors (Vincent, Taylor-Adams, and Stanhope, 1998). According to an interviewee, while the protocol drew from a variety of sources, they intentionally refrained from using the name RCA. This was because RCA was perceived as a set of tools and approaches "that you apply when you are doing a systematic incident investigation" rather than a protocol that can guide the investigation. RCA was "just a label," and possibly a confusing one. As our informant stated "I think the people that were talking about Root Cause Analysis at that time were probably not people who were experts in investigation techniques." The label was as intriguing as it was vague.

As in the USA, matters in the UK took a dramatic turn in the early 2000s following yet another scandal. An inquiry conducted at Bristol Royal Infirmary in the late 1990s identified catastrophic systemic failures compounded with a culture of secrecy and collusion that had led to the preventable death of at least thirty children over five years. The resulting wave of indignation led to an investigation into the NHS capacity to learn from incidents. The results were damning. The authors of the report "An Organization with a Memory" (DoH, 2000) candidly admitted that the NHS consistently failed to learn from its errors. The experts recommended establishing a unified mechanism for reporting incidents and for ensuring that where lessons were identified, the necessary changes were put into practice. They also recommended that the NHS promote a wider appreciation of the system approach in preventing and learning from errors as well as a more open culture in which errors and service failures could be reported and discussed.

One year later, the Department of Heath published a plan to address these issues and implement the recommendations. The 2001 report "Building a Safer NHS for Patients—Implementing an Organization with a Memory" instituted explicit links between safety and clinical governance (de facto putting managers and not clinicians in charge of patient safety); also establishing an arm's length agency in charge of promoting patient safety (the National Patient Safety Agency—NPSA) and set up a national repository for reported incidents (National Reporting and Learning System) modeled on the existing Australian AIMS (see section 8.3.4). Finally, the report identified RCA as "the more in-depth approach to identifying causal or systems factors in more serious adverse events or near misses" (DoH, 2001: 37). Other homegrown systems and protocols such as SAFECODE and the CRU/ALARM protocols were ignored or subsumed under the RCA label.

Of particular interest here is that the report explicitly documents the international travel of RCA:

> There are many approaches to root cause analysis used in healthcare and in other industries. The Department of Health is participating in an Australian initiative to review a range of approaches from different countries and produce guidance on alternative methodologies that are directly relevant to healthcare. We will pilot the results of this work during 2001 and issue guidance on root cause analysis. (DoH, 2001: 38)

The "Key features of a thorough root cause analysis" discussed at page 37 of the document are taken from a Joint Commission document, itself derived from the VA handbook. The international links that contributed to the success of RCA were confirmed by other sources. Speaking at a conference after the first year of operations of the new National Patient Safety Agency, a director of the Department of Health policy unit explained that:

> Our preparations for this work began late last year by consulting experts in patient safety both in the UK and abroad. Leading patient safety proponents like Bill Runciman...and Jim Bagian...We have collaborated closely with: ECRI, the Australian Patient Safety Foundation (APSF), the Centre for Patient Safety in Chicago, the Hong Kong Hospital Authority, the US Veterans Health Administration, and with other bodies and individuals. (Knox, 2002: 230)

The conference served as the launch pad for the report "Doing less Harm" (DoH, 2001). This established the policies and practices that were to be followed by the largest public healthcare organization in the world, the NHS. The document sanctioned the discursive equivalence between investigations and RCA and translated previous approaches under the new label. Conference organizer Stuart Emslie, inventor of SAFECODE, consultant to the Hong Kong government and the NHS, explicitly reframed the ALARM protocol in RCA terms, equating the two.

Not everyone was convinced by the wholesale adoption of the RCA vocabulary, however. Two of the most prominent figures of the UCL group recall that RCA (which they call a "misnomer") became a "buzzword" at NPSA:

> I can remember Jenny Dinner (a pseudonym), because when she was initially in the post at the NPSA she gave me a call and said "do you know anything about this root cause analysis stuff?"

The informant recalls the moment when the label became institutionalized, not so much in one of the many documents that, as we have seen above, the NHS produces at a very fast rate, but in the discursive practices of the patient safety community of practice:

> Now how those "organization with a memory" people had come up with the terminology of root cause analysis I don't know...but when the first cohort of Patient Safety Managers were trained [on how to conduct investigations] the terms was institutionalized and cannot be recalled...the blind leading the blind.

8.3.4 The Burning Deck: RCA Travels Down Under (and then Takes over the World)

Within Australia the provision of public health services is primarily the concern of each of the separate eight states and territories. The story of the penetration of RCA in Australia is therefore more complex than in the two former cases. Here we recount what happened in three states: South Australia, New South Wales, and Queensland, as the story of RCA in Australia is intimately linked with—and in many ways similar to—the experience in the USA and UK.

South Australia was an early administration where attention to clinical incidents resulted in a co-ordinated attempt to record and monitor adverse events. In the mid-1980s a group of anaesthesiologists established a voluntary, anonymous reporting system (Advanced Incident Management System) which helps to collect and analyze detailed information about healthcare incidents using a classification based on most common adverse events. The AIMS-Anaesthesia database gained national attention after a serious incident with a vaporizer; clinicians identifying an array of problems with the equipment, leading to new, clearer guidelines that became a national and later international standard (Runciman, 2002; Øvretveit, 2005).

Quickly the AIMS system was expanded as a Federal initiative, to include all other specialties, providing a large, centralized repository of information on adverse events countrywide. With this data, and explicitly modelled on the 1991 Harvard Study, clinicians found that 16.3–16.5 percent of patients admitted to Australian hospitals experienced some sort of adverse event, capturing both political and popular attention (Wilson et al., 1995). A follow-up study found that about 50 percent of adverse events were preventable (Wilson et al., 1999). While the studies were later disputed for overestimating the extent of the problem they pushed patient safety to the attention of the healthcare community. Critically, the study made clear that reporting adverse events and doing something about them were two different matters.

As in the UK, the adoption of methods to actively learn from incidents—rather than only learning about them, commonly followed what one of our informants called "burning decks," that is to say crises. In interview, the generation of anxiety through the analogy of responding to the burning deck of a ship was notable.

In New South Wales that "burning deck" came with a series of accidents in a regional health authority, where whistle-blowing nurses identified adverse events in healthcare in local hospitals in the period leading up to a state election. In the ensuing public debate, state political leaders sought to allocate blame for what had been systemic public health system failures. Key health bureaucrats saw the need for a process that focused on the problem-solving aspect of RCA, rather than the allocation of blame.

Notably, one senior interviewee expressed a view that there was a pattern of the New South Wales health bureaucracy adopting US-based innovations "holus bolus" without consideration of its local appropriateness. For example, the Quality and Safety Branch of New South Wales Health initiated the adoption of RCA and a raft of other health quality techniques on the basis that the same approach had been adopted by the US VHA. In particular, Dr Jim Bagian of the VHA was considered as highly influential in the introduction of RCA, across Australia. According to our interviewees, Bagian's effectiveness springs from both his capacity to form effective relationships with key individuals, and his very persuasive use of stories. Through these stories Bagian conveys the deep cultural and behavioral patterns that underlie many medical accidents. The generally poor standards of handwashing by health professionals are a ready instance of such cultural and behavioral patterns.

In Queensland, the crisis came in 2005 when a Dr Patel at Bundaberg Public Hospital was accused of presiding over a series of poor surgical outcomes, including deaths. The event sped up the development of a State Patient Safety Centre (established in 2004) and fast-tracked both the development of RCA in Queensland and a more general patient safety management system. Drawing on lessons learned during a fellowship with the VHA in the US, Dr Wakefield, the local RCA champion, pushed forward the establishment of a comprehensive system for improving patient safety, through learning from near misses and adverse events. Rather than the blame-free emphasis of New South Wales, the recurrent theme within Queensland is upon a "just" process, linking back to the original work of Jim Bagian and reflecting a preference for procedural fairness and consistency and efforts to ensure transparency.

While, as noted above healthcare in Australia is primarily driven at the state level, the invoking of RCA has been nationally driven. Today a central body, the Australian Commission on Safety and Quality in Health Care, drives patient safety measures at the national level.

Global Travel of Healthcare Practices

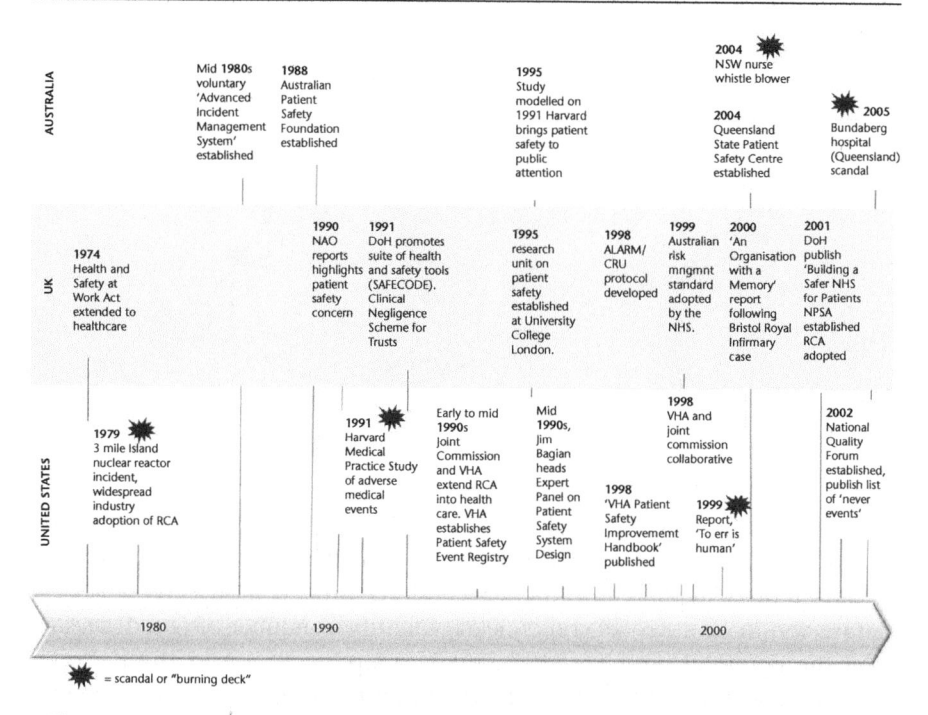

Figure 8.1 Chronology of the development of RCA in the USA, UK, and Australia

Following the adoption of RCA in Australia, the method was embraced by the World Health Organization. In 2004, the WHO launched The World Alliance for Patient Safety, putting RCA at the heart of its global campaign to promote patient safety. Training booklets on how to conduct RCA have been translated in eight languages and are fully available on the WHO website. The training material is based on the methods developed by the VHA and the UK National Patient Safety Agency (closed in 2011 as part of cost-cutting measures). RCA is now a global phenomenon. A précis of the development of RCA across the US, UK, and Australia is given Figures 8.1 and 8.2.

8.4 Analysis: An Ordinary Story of Translation—with a Twist

The story of RCA is in many ways an interesting yet quite "ordinary" case of the circulation of new ideas at global scale. It has all the ingredients of a translation rather than a diffusion story. First, RCA traveled carried by a variety of human and non-human intermediaries. In order to do so, it had to be abstracted from its original context, packaged in the form of documents, accounts, and the stories of people such as Dr Bagian. It then had to be

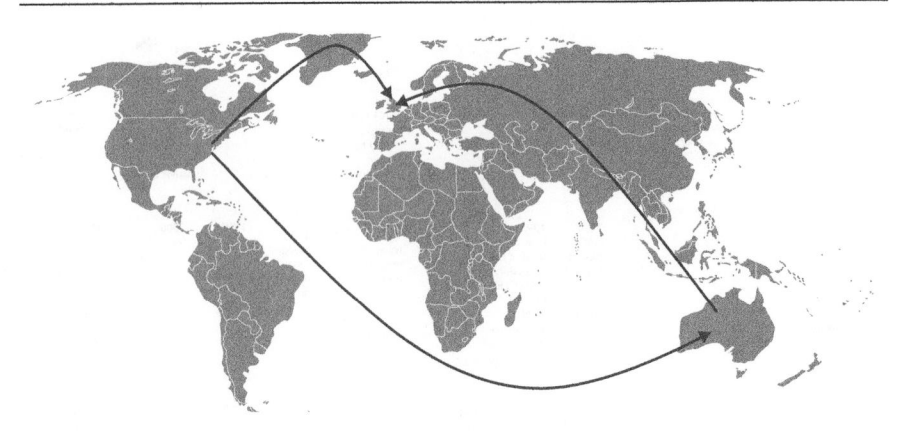

Figure 8.2 The travel of RCA

unpacked in the different localities where it was translated. Our account here is partly unique in that we could clearly trace which intermediary moved the idea from place to place and when. Second, the process was clearly of a social nature and in all cases we could clearly identify a number of (good) reasons why the potential users could benefit in adopting RCA and the personal, political, and societal benefits that would ensue from this. Finally, there is ample evidence that the idea of RCA changed as it traveled (Ansari, Fiss, and Zajac, 2010). As we have seen, RCA traveled by being translated over and over, so that at any point in time RCA was the provisional outcome of more or less a long series of prior translations, each critical for the idea to be adopted by a new audience—and therefore its travel. In the process, the RCA label "absorbed" a variety of pre-existing methods and protocols as it traveled from the NASA Space Center to the Geneva office of the WHO via the hospitals of the VHA and the NHS.

These findings accord with previous studies on the social nature of the circulation of innovation. The journey of RCA is similar to many of the translation stories recounted in Czarniawska and Sevón (2005a). In the case of RCA, we found that the circulation of the new practice was particularly facilitated by three concurrent circumstances: its theorization, interpretive flexibility, and its being sustained by a broad social network. First, authors have found that when a new idea is theorized and turned by academics and consultants into abstract models such as in Table 8.1, its capacity to travel around the world is enhanced (Greenwood, Hinings, and Suddaby, 2002). Second, ambiguity and interpretive flexibility are also well-known facilitators of circulation. Interpretive flexibility refers to the capacity for the innovation to be adapted locally so that it can appeal to a variety of users (Scarbrough and Swan, 2001). In our case, for example, because of its indeterminacy ("there are many approaches to Root Cause Analysis used in healthcare and in other industries") RCA can become the easy fix to many woes and the solution to many problems: accreditation, litigation, learning from medical adverse events. Finally, the specific dynamics in the social network that may form around an innovation also concur to determine its success (Scarbrough and Swan, 2001). In our case, for example, the travel of RCA seems inextricably linked to the emergence of a global network of people (and artifacts) that together can be held responsible for its global circulation.

Clearly, at some point RCA also acquired the status of fashion (Abrahamson and Rosenkopf, 1997; Hargadon, 2003). As we have shown above, both our UK and Australian informants made it clear that at some point RCA had become a "force majeure," with organizations adopting it as a matter of course. This happened despite strong voices against the mainstreaming of this engineering approach to healthcare. For example, in 2004, a pioneer of the CRU/ALARM protocol, the UK approach at first sidelined and then "digested" by RCA, wrote in the *British Medical Journal* that "...the term 'root cause analysis', while widespread, is misleading in a number of respects" (Vincent, 2004: 242). However, as his colleague noted, by then the term (and its focus on presumed root causes that according to Vincent rarely exist) had been institutionalized and could not be recalled in spite of its possible and well-known shortcomings. In our research, interviewees reported that in some instances of analysis, very minor case factors were exaggerated in an attempt to satisfy the presumed need to identify a root cause when in practice the adverse event had arisen from a combination of minor factors.

If one were to listen to some of our informants, most of the merit of the success of RCA should be attributed to the human actors involved. Indeed, during our interviews several of them described themselves in terms that resonate with Maguire, Hardy, and Lawrence's (2004) definition of institutional entrepreneurship ("activities of actors who have an interest in particular institutional arrangements and who leverage resources to create new institutions or to transform existing ones" (Maguire, Hardy, and Lawrence, 2004: 657)). While interviewees tried to convince us that RCA prevailed because it was superior to the other methods (a sign that they had assimilated the traditional narrative of diffusion theory), several of them seemed to be fully aware of the political and opportunistic nature of some of the events that lead to the global success of RCA. Yet the merit was all on the human side.

But is this conceivable? Was RCA really one innovation like all others? Was its success down to just something being available to fill the gap? There was nothing intrinsically new or superior about RCA that could explain its success, if nothing else because RCA had still to be tested in practice (and be found lacking: see Nicolini, Waring, and Mengis, 2011 for an in-depth discussion). Could there be other characteristics that can explain why RCA was the best bet and why the entrepreneurs went for it instead of some of the alternatives?

What happens if we open the black box of RCA and we treat it as an (active) source of performativity rather than simply an intermediary that allowed humans to align and pursue their interest?

8.4.1 Opening the Black Box: RCA as an Anxiety-Reassurance (Discursive) Package

We argue that part of the success of RCA can be explained by some of its particular characteristics, chiefly the way in which RCA is presented. RCA constitutes more than a simple toolkit to investigate incidents. In all countries we examined RCA; it was introduced as a complex discursive package built around the conflict between anxiety and reassurance. This package concomitantly highlighted and amplified the uncertainty and dangers of the medical practice and offered a reassuring solution in the form of techniques that promise some form of control of uncertainty and produce safer healthcare services. We suggest that such characteristics enhanced the capacity of RCA to recruit practitioners (rather than vice versa). In short, at some point RCA started to operate as a powerful and well-oiled recruitment machine.

We can start by noting that in all three of our cases the arrival of RCA follows what our informants described as "burning decks," a reference derived from the heroic poem "Casabianca" by Hemans. In the USA, UK, and Australia, RCA was introduced in the aftermath of some scandal or large incident, partly as a way to allay public concern. The use of scandals, inflammatory rhetoric, and scaremongering to promote policy and even product innovation is well documented (Kitsuse and Spector, 1973). Shankar and Subish (2007) for example, suggest that one of the favorite ways in which pharmaceutical companies promote their products is by "creating awareness" about illness. The resulting anxiety is then used to sell the appropriate treatment (or policy). While we do *not* suggest that RCA was artificially introduced using the same technique (called disease mongering), we argue the same basic discursive principle was operating nonetheless. Almost all the documents were constructed using the same semiotic strategy. Here is how the Under-Secretary of State Lord Hunt introduced RCA in 2001:

> Today our focus is on patient safety and with good reasons. Research carried in this country and independently in Australia and America suggests that 1 in 10 patients admitted to hospitals suffers an adverse event... at least half of these are thought to be preventable. That's 1 in 20 patients... and the research further suggests that 8% of these 1 in 20% will die as a consequence... So Learning from Experience is the answer. And to unlock the learning from experience we are looking for the real reasons—the root causes that lie behind these events. (Hunt, 2002: 3–5)

One can note the artful juxtaposition of anxiety and reassurance in the same sentence—a typical move á la Greimas that turns RCA into an actant—the hero of the story.

Once anxiety has been mobilized, RCA can then propose itself as a solution. It does so by virtue of its historic and discursive lineage. On the one hand RCA can claim to be derived from the world of engineering, where of course people are presumed to know what they are doing. If NASA used it, then it must work (let's forget about the two lost Shuttles, of course). At the same time Root Cause Analysis carries with it the reassuring idea of the possibility to get to the root of the problem, once and for all. The combination of legacy and discourse turns RCA into a suturing narrative package. Suturing narratives retell the unfolding of a crisis in terms of beginning, ending, and points in between thus restoring "a general sense of predictability" (Fine and White, 2002: 54). The redemptive nature of the narrative makes the package both seductive and convincing. It establishes direct discursive links with the modern fantasy of control over uncertainty and as such it can enroll and exploit the wider existential anxiety typical of reflexive modernity (Beck, Giddens, and Lash, 1994). In so doing, RCA latches upon what Power (2007) described as the attempt at risk managing everything. From this point on RCA starts to align and "collaborate" with other practices that are part of the same movement. Current instances are the introduction of systems of clinical governance in hospitals, and quality assurance of practitioners. Like a snowball, RCA becomes bigger and irresistible by capturing interests and actors. Unlike a snowball, part of the reason lies in the nature of its variable geometry.

Other characteristics of RCA facilitate its capacity to make proselytes. RCA is modular and therefore easy to be applied selectively, it is malleable. Experts like Vincent complain about the pick-and-choose attitude toward this approach yet this makes it particularly palatable. RCA is also easy to teach—unlike approaches that require understanding of complex theory, such as the human error approach.

In sum, RCA as a package actively captures allies and interests by virtue of its discursive and methodological nature. It operates as an active source of agential power, although such performative capability is different from the one we usually attribute to humans as no intentionality is involved. The right image here would be that of a virus which attaches itself to vulnerable cells (cells without the appropriate receptors are not susceptible to viruses). RCA is a viral innovation capable of attaching itself to a sufficiently large number of actors, thanks to its discursive nature and narrative working. It carries and is carried around by some of the most powerful narratives of modern times: rationality, science, technology, and the USA. An irresistible package indeed.

8.5 Discussion and Conclusion

In this chapter we examined the global travel of an innovation—RCA. We found that the success RCA can be partly explained with reference to its content, that is, its being specifically framed as an "anxiety-reassurance" package (Fujimura, 1992). In all the countries we examined what traveled was not only a structured methodology for investigating incidents (RCA), but a more complex discursive package. This package concomitantly highlighted and amplified the uncertainty and dangers of medical practice and offered a reassuring solution, a set of techniques and practices promising control of uncertainty and producing safer healthcare services. RCA fed on the broader discourse of the "risk society," amplified by the work of a number of moral entrepreneurs that reiterated the dangers of the healthcare service. The very anxiety created by the discourse around RCA found its resolution in the methodology itself: RCA reassures that if correctly implemented, hospitals will learn from clinical incidents and healthcare services will become safer. RCA mobilizes the discourse of engineering and its "modernist" focus on controllability through rational deliberation and technique.

RCA constitutes thus a "standardized theory-method package" (Fujimura, 1992). The idea of a standardized package combines some of the intuitions behind the notion of "boundary objects" (Star and Griesemer, 1989) with the idea of "translation" (Latour, 2005). It suggests that the process through which "an innovation becomes the ruler over a realm" includes a number of typical steps such as: the labeling of the innovation, the establishment of the innovation as an obligatory point of passage, the emergence of the innovation as a distributed center of authority, the establishment of mutual interest within the network, the search for and the enrolment of new allies, the standardization of the innovation, the closure of the translation and the institutionalization of the relative performative composite entity (called the actor-network because of its capacity to make things happen).

We suggest, however, that particular attention needs to be paid to the rhetoric and discursive nature of the package itself. Unlike boundary objects, RCA is not an empty (or semi-empty) signifier or something that can be used as a projective surface by different groups with only partially overlapping interests. On the contrary, RCA is a very "full signifier" which operates as a rhetorical mechanism, capturing interests and practitioners thanks to its capacity to actively mobilize local interests and connect these to wider circuits of accountability (in our case, the global shift toward the risk management of everything).

The story of RCA suggests that much is to be gained if we find ways of opening the black box of some modern innovations and study whether there is indeed a "ghost in the machine." Albeit we are unlikely to find such a ghost, we will end up gaining a much better understanding of the inner persuasive and rhetoric workings of innovations. By addressing the circulation in terms of "active packages" we contribute to rectifying an imbalance in the current theorization of the travel of ideas in terms of "translation." The translation approach traditionally rejects the idea that innovations are propelled by their perceived novelty and superior performance, and travel thanks to their inherent innovativeness, as in the diffusion paradigm (Rogers, 1995). On the contrary, the spread of ideas is driven by actors' imitation of others as they pursue their own interests (Czarniawska and Joerges, 1996; Czarniawska and Sevón, 2005b). While this approach has the historic merit of providing an alternative to the diffusion approach, it has tended to see innovations (or rather a textualized version of them) as intermediaries that actants pass to each other. Although the theory postulates that the central ideas change as they travel, the focus is firmly on the users and their interest rather than the innovation itself.

We suggest that this focus on actors and their interests prevents us from asking whether innovation plays an active role in making itself relevant and compelling for all those touched by it. While for commodities the answer is likely to be "no," our case suggests that matters may be different for more complex innovations and other artifacts that are packaged as "rhetoric" and "persuasive machines." A focus on innovations as active packages of theory/discourse and methods/practice allows us to recover the performative role of innovations without reverting to the notion that innovations are diffused thanks to their innovative essence. We argue that in so doing we address an imbalance in translation theory and respond to Latour's exhortation that sociology should populate the world with more active mediators and less inactive intermediaries (Latour, 2005).

Acknowledgments

The chapter is based on the results of the project "Improving the Capacity of Healthcare Organizations to Act on Evidence in Patient Safety (PTOC21)" funded by the Warwick International Manufacturing Research Centre and the Engineering and Physical Sciences Research Council (EPSRC).

Notes

1. The "myth of the ghost in the machine" is an expression used by philosopher Gilbert Ryle (1949) to ridicule Descartes' view that volitional acts of the body must be caused by volitional acts of the mind, that is, that mind and body are separate entities and that the functioning of the former has control over the latter. The

traditional diffusion approach to the circulation of innovations (Rogers, 1995) makes more or less the same mistake in that the perceived "innovativeness" of the new products or practice is supposed to cause its diffusion and take-up. Our tenet here is that the process translation theory at times goes too far, so that consequential features of the innovation end up being overlooked.
2. We intentionally use the neutral terms "circulation" and "travel" as the ideas of transfer, transmission and diffusion are already heavily theory-laden.
3. The Centers for Medicare and Medicaid Services, which in 2008 also officially adopted RCA as a mandatory approach to apply with serious clinical incidents.

9

Mobilizing Knowledge in the Ecology of Healthcare Innovation

Maxine Robertson and Jacky Swan

CHAPTER SUMMARY

This chapter analyzes healthcare innovation, in particular the development of novel drugs and therapeutics, as an example of a networked innovation process occurring within a complex ecology of organizations. Existing research has identified the ways in which characteristics of the "landscape" (network relationships, institutionalized practices and epistemic logics) of the organizational ecology influence knowledge mobilization in innovation projects in the health sector. The chapter introduces the notion of an ecology "timescape" to more fully explain problems of knowledge mobilization in healthcare innovation projects. The timescape comprises the (different) temporal orientations that agents within the ecology—including commercial firms, clinicians, regulators, and financiers—draw upon to guide decision-making and the pace of their activities. The analysis demonstrates the considerable challenges posed to knowledge mobilization by both the ecology landscape and timescape and the importance of overcoming these challenges through appropriate forms of governance.

9.1 Introduction

Innovation in healthcare involving the development of new and improved forms of drugs and therapeutics has improved the lives of millions of people and clinical research is a critical aspect of any healthcare system. This entails mobilizing knowledge from scientific research into new, commercially viable drugs and treatments, typically via clinical trials that are designed to test their safety and effectiveness. Drug development is depicted in the sector as a linear process involving clinical trial "phases" starting with Phase I small groups of patients (to establish safety), through Phase II trials (testing safety and efficacy), much larger Phase III trials (establishing safety and efficacy in large populations), and Phase IV, post-market assessments (to evaluate adverse events). In reality, however, the knowledge mobilization process is far from linear (Styhre, 2006; Styhre et al., 2010). Trials often reveal unexpected results that require the underlying scientific premises to be revisited and high uncertainty is endemic throughout the process (Nightingale, 2000; Newell et al., 2008).

Developing drugs is also, without doubt, an expensive and risky business—development costs have risen from $179 million in the 1970s to $2.6 billion in the 2000s, the average time to develop a drug is estimated at more than ten years, and the percentage of drugs entering clinical trials resulting in an approved medicine at less than 12 percent (PhRMA, 2015). While many failures result from problems with the underpinning science, which only become evident from trials results, many other challenges are attributed to difficulties of managing and organizing clinical research and, in particular, linking commercial scientific research to clinical practice. As the PhRMA report concludes "addressing those challenges will require partnerships among all members of the biomedical innovation ecosystem, including the engagement and involvement of patients" (PhRMA, 2015: 56).

Often led by a biotechnology or pharmaceutical firm, executing clinical research entails coordinating work across an array of groups and organizations including; clinicians other medical specialists (e.g. clinical research nurses), specialist clinical research organizations (CROs), university scientists, manufacturing firms, regulators and R&D officers, investors/funding bodies and, not least, patients. The knowledge and effort required is widely distributed, with each party—or "agent"—having their own interests and agendas. Innovation can be characterized, then, as a highly networked process, which unfolds within a complex "ecology" of organizations (Dougherty and Dunne, 2011, 2012). Understanding how knowledge is mobilized in this ecology requires attention to the ways in which the actions and interactions across agents influence the ability of development teams in firms to execute clinical research projects at the local level.

In this chapter, we use the example of clinical research to identify and explore key institutional, organizational, and temporal barriers to the mobilization of knowledge for innovation in the healthcare sector. By drawing upon, and further developing, an *ecological* view, we show how institutionalized beliefs, expectations and "epistemic logics" concerning how knowledge "should" be produced, and for what purpose, can pose significant challenges. This we refer to as the ecology *"landscape."* In addition, we argue that the ecology comprises a *"timescape"* (cf. Adam, 2003), which is constituted through each agent's different "time reckoning system" (Clark, 1978) and "temporal logic" (Adam, 2003). This timescape influences the pace and rhythms of activities of agents within the ecology during the innovation process. Because of the high level of interdependency that exists across agents, the timescape also generates particular challenges for knowledge mobilization, with temporal misalignments leading to problems of coordination and knowledge flow. The chapter highlights the importance of considering distributed time, along with distributed knowledge and interests, in order to more fully understand—and ultimately improve—knowledge mobilization in healthcare innovation.

9.2 The Ecology of Clinical Research Projects

Clinical research determines the safety and effectiveness of new drugs, devices, diagnostics, and treatment regimes. In the UK and elsewhere, scientists and industrialists have expressed concern about the decline of the clinical research base and the "translational gap" between scientific research and innovations that will actually benefit patients. It has been repeatedly emphasized that "clinical research has not kept pace with the advances in basic scientific discovery and this disadvantages patients" (AMS Report, 2003: 7). In this chapter we focus on knowledge mobilization within early phase drug development (Phase I/II trials)—a phase that is seen as the "linchpin" for innovation and has been identified as being in particular jeopardy (AMS Report, 2003; PhRMA, 2015). This early phase is characterized by severe uncertainty—even "unknowability"—because the knowledge and resources that are needed are indeterminate and widely distributed across different organizations and professional groups (Newell et al., 2008; Swan, Robertson, and Newell, 2016).

Clinical trials are a major aspect of knowledge mobilization in early development and entail a complex set of interrelated activities. For example, "first-in-man" Phase I studies may be led by biotechnology firms or by public research organizations (e.g. trials units based in universities or hospitals). These lead organizations must collaborate closely with clinicians and other healthcare professionals in order to recruit patients that may benefit from the treatment. Or, firms may outsource trials to a CRO. At the same time, ongoing collaboration with university-based academic scientists is needed in order to understand the underlying science. Lead organizations must also work with manufacturing firms to produce quantities of the new drug, or compound, in the formula and dosage required to give to patients in trials. All the time, finance needs to be raised to secure future development, which may come from Venture Capital (VC) and/or some form of partnering/licensing arrangement with a pharmaceutical firm (Pisano, 2006, 2010). Potential investors will consider the relative opportunities and risks of the innovation and will assess the firm's ability to deliver according to promised timescales. Development is also subject to a very tightly prescribed governance regime of ethical and regulatory approval. Agents, such as regulators or financiers, while not *directly* engaged in development, nevertheless remain pivotal to the process, with delays in securing required approvals often being held responsible for significant delays in development (Swan, Robertson, and Evans, 2009; Swan, Robertson, and Newell, 2016).

In this complex ecology, the lead development team—usually in a small biotechnology firm in the early phases—may have little, if any, formal influence over other agents external to their organization (e.g. clinicians). Yet, they depend closely on these other agents to actually produce the knowledge necessary to progress development. Hence they must co-ordinate their work and activities and "co-produce" knowledge with these other agents (Swan et al., 2007a, 2010). This early phase of drug development can be viewed conceptually, then, as a "networked innovation" process; that is, innovation that occurs through agents' ongoing interaction and negotiation, which is not driven wholly by market-based or hierarchical mechanisms of control (Swan and Scarbrough, 2005; Hardy, Phillips, and Lawrence, 2003).

Networked innovation can be distinguished from a conventional R&D-oriented model of innovation in a number of ways, summarized in Table 9.1. In the R&D model the firm is the locus for knowledge production and mobilizing knowledge entails the transfer of knowledge from producers (R&D labs) to end users. This linear "diffusionist" model (Rogers, 2003) has proven increasingly ineffectual in complex innovation ecologies such as the

Table 9.1. Models of the innovation process

Model of innovation	R&D model	Networked Innovation model
Key actors	R&D scientists, engineers, technology experts, technology transfer offices	Managers, intermediary groups (clinical research providers/CROs), academic and clinical communities
Forms of knowledge	Scientific and technological knowledge	Heterogeneous forms of knowledge, including highly situated knowledge
Forms of governance	Hierarchical and market institutions	Heterarchies, involving networked governance, hierarchical and market institutions
Locus of innovation	Focal organization within a sectoral context (e.g. BIOTECH firm)	At interstices of group/organization boundaries within a trans-sectoral context (including BIOTECHs/pharma, hospitals, public research organizations, clinical research organizations)
Focus on knowledge mobilization	Transfer of knowledge into and out of R&D function, with social networks acting as information channels	Translation and transformation of knowledge among interacting agents with social networks building social communities of practice

Mobilizing Knowledge in the Innovation Ecology

health sector (von Hippel and von Krogh, 2006; Greenhalgh and Wieringa, 2011). This is because networked innovation involves the creation and mobilization of multiple forms of knowing, including situated and more explicit forms, and the translation and transformation of knowledge through ongoing negotiation across heterarchically coordinated groups, organizations and "communities of practice" (see D'Andreta and Scarbrough, Chapter 7 this volume). Networked innovations typically encompass market-based and hierarchical relationships among agents (e.g. licensing arrangements between biotechnology and pharmaceutical firms), but they entail more than the sum of these exchanges, for the locus of innovation lies within the network itself—at "the interstices" of the collaborating groups and organizations (Powell, Koput, and Smith-Doerr, 1996). In short, knowledge is "co-produced" through collaboration itself. Knowledge mobilization therefore entails "orchestrating" the collaborative, and sometimes competitive, relations, interests, and understandings of different agents within the ecology (Dougherty and Dunne, 2011; Newell et al., 2008).

Conceptualizing clinical research as networked innovation means that knowledge mobilization needs to be theorized at the level of the ecology, not just in terms of the elements (e.g. firms) within it (Dodgson, Gann, and Salter, 2005; Dougherty and Dunne, 2011). This means developing theory that recognizes the dynamic interplay between knowledge flows within innovation projects, the political interests of the various agents involved, and the constraints imposed by powerful institutions such as regulators and funding bodies (Swan et al., 2007a, 2010). It is important to note that such ecological theory is not the same as, more established, "territorial innovation" theories—for example, those that focus on industrial clusters or sectoral innovation systems (e.g. Pavitt, 1984). Rather, the term "ecology" denotes a distinct heterarchic, often highly distributed, form of social organization that "despite dense patterns of interaction, is less systematic and less coherent than more established territorial models...Temporary collaboration in project ecologies, in contrast (to territorial models), preserves the identities of a diverse spectrum of practices and organizational forms" (Grabher, 2002: 246). From this ecological perspective, the unit of analysis becomes the innovation process within the ecology, not individual firms or pre-defined sectors.

Other research on networked innovation in healthcare—including chapters in this book seen in Theme 3—has focused on the ways in which interprofessional boundaries and epistemic differences influence knowledge mobilization and emerging social relationships (Martin, Currie, and Lockett, 2011; McGivern and Dopson, 2010; Currie, El Enany, and Lockett, 2014; McGivern et al., Chapter 1 this volume). These studies highlight the contestation that arises from differences in knowledge and power—differences that are deeply entrenched and/or institutionalized. Here, we develop our ecological view of knowledge mobilization through an analysis of this "landscape" of biomedical innovation—which takes account of institutional practices and epistemic differences—but add to it an analysis of the different understandings of time applied by agents within the ecology. Attending to this "timescape," we argue, helps to further explain why there often appears to a lack of coordination across the ecology and seemingly perverse decision-making in innovation projects, both of which challenge knowledge mobilization.

In the following sections, we build on existing literature, in combination with insights based on one of our own empirical studies of clinical research, to develop our ecological model of knowledge mobilization in healthcare innovation. The latter formed part of a wider study of drug development in the UK and USA and is outlined next.

9.3 Empirical Context

We conducted longitudinal, qualitative case studies of ten clinical research projects led by biotechnology firms (six in the USA and four in the UK) going through the early phases of developing particularly novel therapeutics (see Swan et al., 2007b; Swan, Robertson, and Evans, 2009; Newell et al., 2008). In each case, the project had been ongoing for at least two years and was followed for thirty months. This was adequate time to trace what progress (if any) occurred and what factors facilitated or hindered innovation, compared to expectations. A minimum of four fieldwork visits per case were conducted (at approximately six-monthly intervals) where core development teams were asked to review progress and whether this had matched their expectations in the prior period, to tell us about knowledge mobilization challenges, and to indicate their expectations for the forthcoming period. Board-level managers were also interviewed in order to assess wider strategic priorities and how projects fitted within their overall product portfolio. Interviews were complemented with extensive documentary data (including companies' reports, inter-agent correspondence, contracts, and meeting minutes) and observational data (including non-participant observation of project team meetings, strategy meetings, and advisory board meetings). Challenges of mobilizing knowledge across the project ecology, leading to delays in development, were found across all our cases. Here we draw upon an exemplar case—BIOTECH[1]—in order to illustrate and analyse these challenges. The issues that were faced by the development team in this study epitomize many of the challenges that were experienced across all ten cases in the study.

9.3.1 BIOTECH (Allergy Project)

BIOTECH was a medium-sized firm that had developed a core technology to develop monoclonal antibodies. The technology was heavily protected so other firms licensed the technology for their own projects. This provided BIOTECH with a revenue stream to resource early development initiatives. The initiation of the Allergy project, aimed at developing a therapeutic that would offer long-standing protection against asthma, occurred as a result of a previous project failure that had been in late Phase III trials, when BIOTECH had attempted to do everything themselves. As a result of the massive expense incurred, and now aware that they did not have the expertise or financial resources to perform large later-phase trials, senior management were determined to find a partner for the Allergy project early in development in order to minimize future risk.

On this basis, a development plan was produced aimed at delivering "good results" as quickly as possible, to ensure a lucrative partnering deal. The project and plan were graphically depicted in the firms' product pipeline and uploaded to the website. This is common practice in the industry whereby quasi-Gantt charts are depicted for each project a firm is currently working on, focused upon the various clinical trial phases/stage gates of the regulatory process, with projections, extending many years ahead, about when development milestones will be delivered.

The basic science was quite advanced and the firm had announced positive results from an initial Phase I safety trial. They had just gained regulatory approval for a further, larger-scale Phase I multi-dose safety trial and also for a Phase II trial aiming to demonstrate efficacy. The latter would involve inducing a severe asthma attack in mild asthmatics and then treating with the new (as yet unproven) drug. BIOTECH was now working, as they put it, "flat out" to identify a partner. Aiming to secure positive data that would attract potential partners faster, they decided to "push ahead" with the more risky Phase II trial. The team managed to engage the interest of several leading clinicians with asthmatic patients and scaled up manufacturing almost immediately, even though actual patient enrolments had not been confirmed. This was very risky and, ultimately, a very costly strategy because the trial had to be abandoned. Perhaps unsurprisingly, given the design, clinicians could not, or would not (upon reflection) recruit sufficient numbers of patients for the trial. A significant amount of the product (which had a very short shelf-life) was therefore wasted.

BIOTECH's clinical team was now under pressure to come up with a new trial plan that would not jeopardize partnering negotiations, which were, by now, at quite a late stage. They needed to be able to demonstrate progress and positive results according to the overall schedule depicted in the original pipeline that had been shared with potential partners. They also had to consider the costs involved. The following excerpt from a project meeting illustrates these conflicting demands. The team debated a trial that would be more desirable from a scientific point of view but was also deemed higher risk in terms of the potential for producing negative results. After some heated discussion, they opted for a less risky but also less optimal study design, for the sake of keeping to the timelines projected in the pipeline, cognisant of the need to avoid negative results. The Clinical Trials Manager concluded:

> Scientifically we know what we'd like to know best, but there's a business case... For this particular program, what we want to do is to partner. So we're not interested in taking this all the way through to market. If that was our idea, we might take a different philosophy on risk. What we want to do is have a data package that is attractive to a partner. If they then, are willing to take on a very high risk study, that's their choice... if we were going to take it all the way through ourselves as a company, we would do it very differently because we would probably be much more likely to take a scientific approach because what that gives you is the ability to kill the project early if it's really not going well. But we don't want to kill it early until someone's given us a fat cheque.

At the same time, BIOTECH decided to try to expedite the low-risk Phase I trial that had been approved, working with just one clinician who had a good reputation for patient enrolment. In their rush to progress, the development team overlooked the fact that unique patient labeling on the bags of the drug solution could not be done by the unit in which the clinician worked. It was a hospital unit and did not have a manufacturing license, which was a regulatory requirement for labeling to occur therein. This caused significant frustration within the team, already under pressure to deliver following previous delays. As the clinical lead highlighted, "Any manufacturing manager would have known this – it's not the first time we've run a trial in a hospital!" The bags of solution had to be sent elsewhere for labeling and it took time to find a licensed facility that would do such trivial work. Recognizing that the project team was working (too) fast, the manufacturing manager thought it "best to double check" the solution after labeling, before the drug was sent for patient use. Unfortunately, granules were identified in the liquid and no-one had any idea why so the trial could not go ahead. BIOTECH scientists were asked to investigate and promised results within two weeks, although privately they admitted that it would "probably take that long to even know where to start."

9.4 The Landscape of the Innovation Ecology

This example illustrates the complex, social and political "landscape" of the ecology in which networked innovation processes unfold (Grabher, 2002; Engwall and Jerbrant, 2003). Grabher (2002) uses the metaphor of "landscape" to describe the architecture and layout of an industry ecology of which innovation projects are a part. It is important to understand the landscape because of "the interdependence between projects and the particular firms, personal relations, localities and corporate networks from which these projects draw essential resources" (Grabher, 2002: 246). This landscape is constituted by a multilayered, nested array of institutionalized practices, network relationships and localized firm/project-level knowledge and practices (Grabher, 2004). The network relationships and their effects on knowledge mobilization in the biomedical sector have been extensively researched and reported elsewhere (e.g. Owen-Smith et al., 2002; Owen-Smith and Powell, 2004; Murray, 2002). Hence here we focus specifically upon the way in which institutionalized practices occurring within the ecology influence the practices occurring at a local level in BIOTECH and how this constrains knowledge mobilization.

9.4.1 *Institutionalized Practices across the Ecology*

Epistemic logics (i.e. differences in understanding how valued knowledge is produced and warranted—cf. Knorr-Cetina, 1999) and the taken-for-granted work ethos of different professionals involved in development work are an important aspect of institutionalized practices. These are tied to divisions of knowledge and associated professional identities, work practices and epistemic "stances" (see McGivern et al., Chapter 1, this volume). Sometimes referred to as "epistemic communities," we prefer to use the term "epistemic collectivity" to describe this aspect of the landscape (Lindkvist, 2003; Grabher, 2004), because the latter captures the transient alignments and often loosely coupled, or even conflicting, interests commonly seen in networked innovation settings.

Conflicting knowledge and interests in the epistemic collectivity have been found to be important in seeding innovation by generating "creative abrasion" among those involved (Grabher, 2004). However, they also pose, significant challenges to coordination and knowledge mobilization across groups that have competing epistemic logics (McGivern and Dopson, 2010; Currie, El Enany, and Lockett, 2014). This can clearly be seen in the Allergy project where hospital-based clinicians/clinical investigators, whose work ethos is driven primarily by the need to promote patient wellbeing, on balance, chose not to recruit patients into the Phase II trial even though they had agreed in principle to do so. Literature in this area highlights a general reluctance on the part of clinicians and patients to participate in trials, generated by several factors, including the time involved in participating for uncertain, potentially harmful patient outcomes (Sandberg et al., 2002; Ashar et al., 2004; Fayter et al., 2006; Hackshaw et al., 2008). The actions of clinicians in Allergy, therefore, are not unusual given that it was an early stage, high-risk trial. This trial (with safety measures in place, of course) would, however, have been the most robust trial to run from the point of view of the development team in BIOTECH because, assuming positive results (which is the default assumption of any development team), it would have helped to demonstrate efficacy, which would have been a major step to securing a lucrative partnering arrangement and future of the project.

Different perceptions of risk across among agents in the ecology also influence how, when, and even whether, they are prepared to collaborate, which can have a significant effect on knowledge mobilization efforts. Clinicians, who are ultimately responsible for the welfare of their patients, tend to have a lower tolerance to risk as compared to their industry collaborators (Hackshaw et al., 2008). Thus while BIOTECH had an ambitious plan regarding when enough patients would be enrolled to deliver results on their Phase II trial, and had already manufactured the drug needed, clinicians actually spent a lot more time than expected assessing what they considered to be the risks involved and deciding whether or not to enroll their patients in the study. By definition, trials of novel therapeutics always entail some degree of risk but in principal these risks should be minimal because of the stringent regulatory process. However, in practice clinicians were not prepared to rush recruitment to meet BIOTECH's timescales because they were unconvinced of patient safety and/or of their ability to convince patients to participate.

Institutionalized practices around regulation and approvals also play a critical role in knowledge mobilization in the ecology. Regulatory authorities, impose a strict sequencing of activities, for any new trial, or modification to an existing protocol. Their primary concern is with safety and they can stop, or place on "clinical hold," trials that are not seen to meet standards. However, our study suggested that institutionalized practices around regulation are not just "contextual factors" that permit (or prevent) certain types of research. They also play a critical role in shaping the ways in which knowledge is actually produced within innovation projects themselves.

Firstly, the bureaucratic machinery (e.g. forms, templates, etc.) that is used when seeking/granting approvals inscribes a set of norms that is based on the notion that "good" science can only be produced through the randomized control trial (RCT) design. Whilst BIOTECH's drug in development was largely aimed at asthma prevention, it was easier to design an RCT to determine efficacy than attempt to submit something to the regulator that did not "fit" the RCT model. However, in so doing, clinicians were not convinced that risks were minimized. The "one-size-fits-all" approach of the RCT design is seen as a significant constraint on knowledge production efforts because it is more difficult to obtain "non-standard" trials approvals and the approvals process takes longer (Swan, Robertson, and Evans, 2009).

Secondly, trial managers develop their own sets of expectations about what is most likely to be approved based on prior experience and hearsay. Cognizant of the need to promote investor confidence, which rightly or wrongly means designing trials that will produce quick results, their expectations are framed around the kinds of study that regulators will more readily approve and they shape their designs accordingly. To illustrate, we observed a project meeting where the Allergy team were discussing the number of patients to recruit in their next clinical trial. After some debate the project manager concluded: "The magic number for subjects to be exposed (to antibodies) needs to be around 50... you might as well stick your finger in the air as to how many patients you need.... It's our guess against their [the regulator] guess, so let's stick with 42 – it's the answer to everything isn't it." Prior to arriving at this decision, it had been unanimously agreed that, from a scientific perspective, the trial could be carried out with as few as twelve patients, and at significantly less cost. However, an number of forty-two was eventually chosen, not just because it was "the magic number" (with reference to Douglas Adams' book *The Hitchhiker's Guide to the Galaxy*), but because this was the sample size that the team believed would convince regulators, a priori, of the possibility of obtaining statistically significant results and hence be quickly approved. This, in turn, would (they believed) ease approvals of further, larger-scale studies in the future.

9.4.2 *Local Project and Lead Firm Practices*

The example above illustrates how local project practices are nested within, and invoke, broader, institutionalized practices. In early development the lead firm on projects is often a small biotechnology firm. As shown in BIOTECH, these small firms often lack internal resources and expertise and have to work with a range of other agents within the ecology in order to actually mobilize the knowledge needed to deliver their projects. At the same time, however, as trying to drive the scientific research forward through clinical trials, they are also typically looking for further investment (venture capital funding, licensing deals, etc.) to support future development plans.

Juggling these conflicting demands often posed major challenges for knowledge mobilization. For example, the clinical team in BIOTECH, whose remit was to design trials for Allergy that were scientifically robust, struggled to comprehend and deal with BIOTECH's business development managers, who were focused on securing a good financial deal with a partner. Moreover, partnering negotiations, which are naturally shareholder sensitive, are highly secretive to the point that the clinical team in BIOTECH was not even privy to information on who was to be the partner. Thus, over several meetings the clinical team debated how best to design trials that would secure the future development of the project "in the dark," only being able to speculate as to who they would actually be working with. They needed to speculate because they were attempting to develop a trials plan that took account of the expertise of potential partners in taking the project forward and what potential partners would want to see in terms of trials design. Eventually, as highlighted, they opted for a trial design that was not ideal, had they been taking "a scientific approach," but one that would pose less risk to the ongoing partnering deal. This had paradoxical effects. Whilst it would generate knowledge and potentially secure resources needed for development in the future, this decision, in effect, increased the chances that the project would take longer overall in development because a more conclusive, but risky trial (from a scientific point of view), would not be carried out.

Raising investment in a context where the science is still very early stage and there is extremely high risk of failure is an ongoing challenge. Failure rates for early phase development are estimated anywhere in the region of 85 to 95 percent and development typically takes anywhere from ten to fifteen years (Hay et al., 2014). Even though only a very small percentage of products ever become "blockbusters," firms in the sector survive on the basis of their ability to convince investors that their products have this potential. To do so, firms have to convince financial markets, and potential partners, that they are capable of managing the massive risks and uncertainty involved in development.

Given the significant risks associated with any one project, the typical strategy to secure the firm's viability into the future is to develop a portfolio of projects at various stages of development (Gino and Pisano, 2006). The product portfolio is published in company reports and on firms' websites, usually in the form of Gantt charts for all "live" projects, with a schedule of the clinical trials planned in each quarter stretching years ahead. In the absence of evidence that products will eventually be successfully be commercialized, the pipeline is laid out according to regulatory milestones (see Figure 9.1). Therefore this pipeline is the major artifact, used across the sector, to publicly display progress to the outside world and attract potential investors. As such, development times and milestone achievements in the pipeline are often highly optimistic. In going public with this information it becomes imperative that firms attempt to adhere (in broad terms) to the schedules depicted. This is despite the fact that, in this highly complex, networked innovation setting, progress is highly uncertain as unexpected results almost inevitably occur. Forward projections thus prove difficult, if not impossible to meet (Dougherty and Dunne, 2011). This often causes additional pressures for development teams. In BIOTECH, project managers, under pressure to "make up lost time" on Allergy after abandoning the Phase II trial, neglected to notice an "obvious" problem in their next trial, which was that their chosen hospital

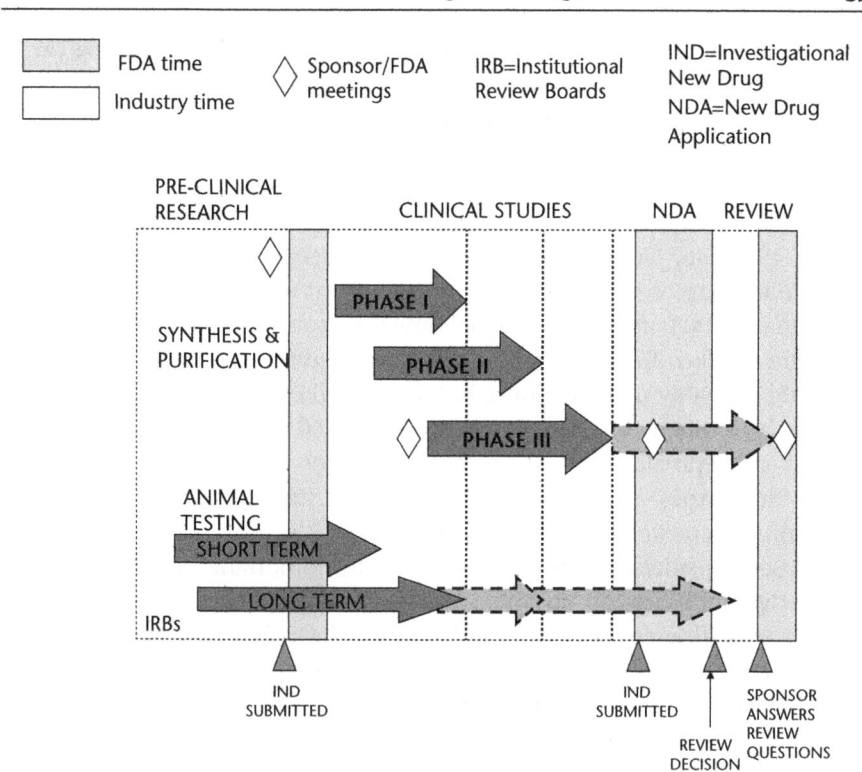

Mobilizing Knowledge in the Innovation Ecology

Figure 9.1 The drug development process[2]

Note: adapted from the Centre for Drug Evaluation and Research (CDER) Handbook

partner was not licensed to label the bags of solution. These kinds of "errors" or oversights were common in all our case studies, where we observed, despite the very lengthy times projected for development, a frantic pace of work within the teams, which often led to things being overlooked and costly mistakes being made. To understand these issues further, we turn next to the timescape of healthcare innovation ecologies which help explain further the challenges of knowledge mobilization across the ecology.

9.5 The Timescape of the Innovation Ecology

While it is recognized that networked innovation processes are distributed across space *and* time, the temporal dynamics of knowledge mobilization are rarely considered. Yet time is an important driver of the actions of particular groups. As Rifkin (1987: 1) observes, "Time is our window on the world. With time we create, order and shape the kind of world we live in." The ancient

211

Greeks had two words for time; *chronos*, which refers to chronological or sequential time, and *kairos*, which refers to a moment of indeterminate time in which events happen. Put simply, the former (often called "clock time") refers to time dictated by the clock/calendar as to when tasks begin or end, whereas the latter ("event-based" time) refers to the time experienced subjectively "in the events, and events are defined by organizational members" (Clark, 1985: 36). For example, the time may seem to "flash by" or "stand still" depending on one's experience of an event in context. Following this vein, Adam (2003) argues that "social time forms and integral part of the deep structure of taken-for-granted, unquestioned assumptions. As such it shapes not only everyday understanding but also the theories that social scientists develop to explain their world" (Adam, 2003: 60). Therefore, "Without an explicit conceptualization of the contemporary dromosphere—or, in my terms, 'timescapes'—it is difficult to understand full the human-technology-environment constellation" (Adam, 2003: 68).

A closer consideration of time is especially important in understanding knowledge mobilization in the innovation ecology because it helps to explain why different agents hold diverging views, both about the purpose of their work, but also about the pace at which it is/should be carried out. Differing projections regarding the future may also play an important role in influencing development in the present day. A number of organization scholars outside healthcare have examined the role of time in achieving co-ordination (e.g. Orlikowski and Yates, 2002; Evans, Kunda, and Barley, 2004; Ancona and Chong, 1996; Clark, 1978). Orlikowski and Yates (2002), for example, demonstrated how, in globally distributed communities, shared "temporal structures" may emerge among participants. They show, further, how temporal symmetry and co-ordinated action can be achieved across multiple communities through "entrainment"; that is the temporal alignment of pace and practices *across* communities (Ancona and Chong, 1996). They also acknowledge that, in more complex settings, varying conceptualizations of time that particular agents hold may influence, and potentially disrupt, the temporal patterns of activity of others, highlighting this as an area for future research.

This previous research has largely focussed on settings where groups are working directly together, with the focal unit analysis being a single project (Bourgeon, 2002), organization (Andersen-Gough, Grey, and Robson, 2001; Dubinskas, 1988) or occupational/professional community (Orlikowski and Yates, 2002). A smaller number of studies, in contrast, have explored the role of time in more complex inter-organizational settings. Clark and Maielli (2009), for example, showed how different conceptions of time influenced conflict between industrial engineering and marketing-design groups in car manufacturing. Pitsis et al. (2003) examined the way in which a time-oriented strategy was used to encourage knowledge sharing and collaboration amongst heterogeneous stakeholders involved in the development of the Sydney 2000 Olympics infrastructure. In these studies agents are working towards the same broad objective (e.g. build a stadium by a certain date). However, in the ecology of healthcare innovation, as seen in BIOTECH, the agents involved have quite different objectives (e.g. to establish safety, cure a patient, make a profit) and some (e.g. venture capitalists, clinicians) are simultaneously engaged in multiple other work projects (Newell et al., 2008). Regulators, for example, directly influence the pace of the work of a development teams in a commercial firm via the approvals process, but do not share a political agenda with the firm.

The very lengthy process involved in developing new treatments also entails extremely complex "temporal modalities" which blend clock/calendar time and event-based conceptions of time (cf. Clark 1978, Clark and Maielli, 2009). In the development "pipeline," for example, time is expressed in a linear sequence of key events—such as Phase I, II, and III trials—displayed across years and broken down into months or quarters (i.e. according to clock time, as shown in Figure 9.1). This is a key resource that lead firms construct, not only to schedule their work, but also, as we have highlighted, to secure financial resources from investors for existing and *future* development work. At the same time, development work is stretched across time, happening in response to past and projected-future events, such as the trading of intellectual property by venture capitalists (Pisano, 2010) or the anticipation of future partnering arrangements (as seen in BIOTECH). Here, then, time is not an exogenous or "contextual factor" that influences innovation but is an essential dimension of innovation itself—"a form of social action.... that trades, in a very engaged sense, on a proactive reconfiguration and contestation of the present in order to increase value in the future" (Hellstrom and Hellstrom, 2002: 408).

The role of time in knowledge mobilization can be further probed with reference to Clark's (1978) notion of "strategic temporal reckoning systems" (STRS). This highlights the varied ways in which different, and often contested, conceptualizations of time can exist across different stakeholders and, in so doing, influence activities in the present. STRS are defined as a "shared set of rules in which locally identifiable sequences of *anticipated* (emphasis added) events are constituted into socially prescribed blocks which are given a durational interpretation" (Clark, 1978: 406). The lead firm's project pipeline, which largely mirrors the Food and Drug Administration (FDA) regulatory process (Figure 9.1), is a good example of the firm's STRS as it applies the rules—represented as stage gate milestones across each phase of trials (I, II, III, etc.)—as prescribed by the regulator for drug development. Clark demonstrated that the enactment of a firm/agent-specific STRS involved the selection of trajectories or sequences of events, based on an assessment of vast arrays of previous, present and future events. His research highlighted, further, how in particular sectors the enactment of STRS by different agents privileged some STRS over others and influenced firm-level decision-making. For example, here the regulator holds a linear, events-based STRS—the Phase I event must be completed after an approval and before a Phase II event, for example. This dominates the sequencing of activities although not necessarily the *pace* of each activity. The latter may be influenced, for example, by clinicians' wary, risk-avoidant approaches when recruiting patients, or by a firm's urgency to secure funding.

The timescape of the innovation ecology can be further characterized drawing on Adam's (2003) concept of temporal logics, or principle beliefs about time. She identifies these principle beliefs according to, what she refers to as, the five "Cs"—creation, commodification, compression, control, and colonization. She has demonstrated that these have become embedded as cultural practice in industrialized societies. In particular, she suggests that the creation of clock/calendar time—and the control of it—emerged as an important force in the regulation and organization of social and economic life. Created as a means of gaining control over the more unruly, unpredictable, context-dependent rhythms of nature, clock-time became "naturalized"; that is, understood as given and unalterable. In the case of health innovation this control by clock-time is manifest in the pipeline that presents an orderly and linear progression. Adam argues, further, that the naturalization of clock-time as a societal norm brings with it other temporal logics upon which industrialization is built. Whilst she identifies four such logics, two—commodification and compression—are particularly illuminating in explaining challenges of knowledge mobilization in this context. First, the commodification of time entails the attachment of economic values (decontextualized as "money") to calendar/clock units of time: "when 'time is money', then time costs money and times makes money" (Adam, 2003: 65). Any time unaccounted for is also considered "a waste of time." The second is time compression, which is the intensification of the pace of work because time is money. As Adam puts it, "When time is money, then faster means better.... Speed is vaporized as an unquestioned and unquestionable good. Naturalized, the valorization of speed overshadows other social or environmental considerations" (Adam, 2004: 66).

Next we combine these insights with consideration of the STRS and temporal logics that different agents apply when mobilizing knowledge and coordinating their work in healthcare innovation and argue that these, in combination, shape the pace of each agent's activities in the present. Characterizing the timescape of the ecology in this way helps to explain, further, that challenges of mobilizing knowledge in this complex innovation system.

9.5.1 Strategic Time Reckoning Systems and Temporal Logics of Agents in the Ecology

To characterize the timescape shaping knowledge mobilization we outline different agents' rationales for engagement (briefly discussed in subsections 9.4.1 and 9.4.2 above), their strategic time reckoning systems, and their temporal logics. These are summarized in Table 9.2. As we have already highlighted, risk predominates within the landscape given the inherent uncertainty which characterizes the development process and we argue that this also influences the timescape, since risk will naturally play a significant role in

Table 9.2. The timescape of the healthcare innovation ecology

Stakeholder	Rationale for engagement	Strategic Time Reckoning System	Dominant Temporal logic(s)	Pace of activity
FDA	Patient safety	Healthcare innovation is abstract, linear and event based (e.g. trial phases) Present temporal orientation and risk averse	Control	Pace of activity determined by events (outcomes of trials) and calendar based (responses offered in pre-defined number of days)
Clinicians	Patient wellbeing	Healthcare innovation is abstract, linear, and event based Present temporal orientation and risk averse	Commodification	Engagement in trials peripheral to professional practice and time limited for such activity so pace is relatively slow and unpredictable
VC/Financiers	Generate wealth for clients	Healthcare innovation is calendar-based (around short financial cycles of 1–2 years) and event-based (around trial results) Future temporal orientation (ROI) and risk managed	Commodification and compression	Pace of investment activity (e.g. funding rounds) predictable within an investment cycle, based on outcomes in development
Commercial firm e.g. BIOTECH— core development team	Develop commercial healthcare innovation	Healthcare innovation is calendar-based with an emphasis on micro-time (days/weeks), event based and nonlinear Future temporal orientation (focused on successful outcome) and risk taking	Commodification and compression	Frantic pace of activity aiming to adhere to optimistic product pipeline schedules

determining the selection of trajectories of past, present, and future events that different agents draw upon when making decisions.

Time commodification features prominently in the temporal logics of commercial firms in the ecology. A common parlance across the sector is that every day "saved" in bringing a blockbuster drug to market is worth at least $1 million in sales (Burton, 2006). As one of our interviewees commented, "I don't know where this number comes from, but the number that is always quoted is every day you're not on schedule, it costs you a million pounds. So time is of the essence." This emphasis on time commodification leads firms to deploy careful time/cost-based calculations of performance on an ongoing basis. Thus all the biotechnology firms that we studied had developed numerous temporal metrics (e.g. around patients recruited, data collected, results analyzed, and regulatory submissions made by a certain date) upon which to judge progress against the clock/calendar times depicted in their plans. Time commodification also dominated negotiations between biotechnology firms and potential pharmaceutical partners and investors. Complex cost-risk calculations were performed; the better the clinical data that could be brought to the table in negotiations, the lower the perceived risk to partners/investors, and hence the potential for higher returns. These calculations influenced the bargaining process. However, being nearly always focused on short-term gains, they also had some perverse effects on the firm's willingness to share knowledge about their trials plans and data with other agents, as shown earlier in BIOTECH.

With time meaning money, time compression was very much in evidence, with project teams in lead firms often working at a frantic pace. For example, in BIOTECH, targets were agreed with senior management and reviewed against progress at approximately two-weekly intervals, despite the fact that little progress was likely to have occurred in that time. Meetings and project-plans highlighted the numerous activities that needed to be completed, scheduled in terms of weeks, days, or sometimes, as in the case of discussion agenda items at meetings, minutes. Only very rarely were activities discussed in terms of months ahead, despite development being projected to span many years. There was a heavy emphasis on the micro-management of time, characterized by the use of daily metrics and targets for team members. However, given that the scientific knowledge was still very uncertain, and complex interdependencies amongst agents existed (e.g. teams were dependent upon clinicians to enroll patients in trials), it was very hard to predict quite what would happen next.

When problems (unanticipated trial results, issues with manufacturing, poor patient recruitment, etc.) caused delays, as they did in *all* cases, project plans and Gantt charts would have to be revised. As one project manager commented, "I have this Gannt chart that is ten feet long and I'm constantly tearing it up." Deviation from the major milestones depicted in the pipeline was rarely entertained by senior management, however, because, symbolically, this might imply to external agents that the product was "failing," which would pose a risk to future investment. Therefore, often additional work would be squeezed into projects plans in order to claw back "lost" time. Hence the pace of work was driven by short-term deadlines in order not to "drift" from the overall pipeline, aiming to secure a longer-term future for the company. This often led to the taking of considerable risks in order to compress the time for activities, optimistically believing that everything would subsequently work according to plan. Manufacturing the product in advance of the patients being enrolled in the high-risk Phase II trial in BIOTECH is such an example. In project management discourse, this was also exemplified with jargon used such as "lock down time" and "drop dead time" which emphasized the importance of rapidly agreeing trial results so that this knowledge could be shared in the form of trials data with the regulator by self-imposed deadlines, even though regulators do not actually set deadlines for submissions (only for responses).

If targets were not being met, then costs were typically rising and, in principle, projects could be terminated. However in practice, projects were not terminated quickly even if they were experiencing significant problems because investment had been secured and therefore investors needed to be reassured that data (regardless of how poor or negative) was still coming through. This indicates important differences between the STRS of development firms as compared to those of investors. Given the very high risks involved, investment cycles in early phase development are typically very short (only one or two years at most) in order to minimize financial risks. VCs are mainly concerned, then, with relatively short-term returns, not with the returns from the product *if* it makes it to market (Pisano, 2006). In all our cases, in order to accommodate this short-termism, lead firms presented to others an overly optimistic scenario as to when (successful) trials would be completed. This, we argue, becomes a vicious circle of time compression as delays occur, serving to reinforce and amplify time compression across all activities, not just trials. It may also make it less likely that projects will be terminated even if they are going badly (Guler, 2007). As the clinical trials manager in BIOTECH noted, "... we don't want to kill it early until someone has given us a fat cheque."

The emphasis on time commodification and compression is also reinforced by many of the institutional agents in the sector including the US Pharmaceutical Research and Manufacturers of America (PhRMA), the UK Association of the British Pharmaceutical Industry (ABPI), and the regulators. They all apply a metric of "days saved" in trial set-up time, averaged across years, to assess clinical trial performance improvements across the sector. They too draw upon the heuristic that each day "saved" is worth a $1 million in revenue if the drug becomes a blockbuster. Whilst this figure clearly needs to be treated with caution, it nevertheless operates as a very powerful discursive device, serving to legitimate the emphasis on the commodification and compression of time in this sector and to convince investors that the sector is worthy of investment (Zider, 1998).

Turning to the STRS of regulators, these are underpinned by a linear, event-based conceptualization of drug development whereby certain stage gates (e.g. Phase I, II, III trials, etc.) must be navigated. Each stage-gate is also a significant milestone that symbolizes progress and a degree of "success" because, even though a particular project is still very likely to fail, statistically, on average, the chances of commercialization are known to increase after Phase II trials have been approved (Kola and Landis, 2004). These agents recognize that delays are costly and they look at time in development to assess sector-level performance. However, fundamentally they do not hold the same beliefs about the need to compress time; safety and efficacy override any concerns around delays and costs. Where development is concerned, they aim to take no risks at all in so far as possible.

Because of its governance role, firms must, in principal, conform to regulators' linear, event-based conceptualizations of time, despite the innovation process in practice being non-linear and highly iterative (Nightingale and Martin, 2004; Smith and O'Donnell, 2006). In order to reconcile tensions between the regulators' linear view of time and the nonlinear nature of scientific discovery (cf. Adam, 2003), project plans and Gantt charts are used to "fix," albeit temporarily, the development process in space and time. In this way lead firms draw upon the linear, event-based STRS of regulators in producing their own project plans. This invokes what we refer to as a form of "enacted entrainment", that is, their project plans emulate the event-based sequencing of the process defined by the regulator, which serves to legitimate their claims to be making progress (cf. Ancona and Chong, 1996; Swan, Robertson, and Newell, 2016). This enacted entrainment, however, reinforces attention to commodified time, driving project teams' efforts to further compress time and increase the pace of activities as far as possible.

Finally, the STRS of clinicians are largely rooted in the present. Whereas clinical research is aimed at benefiting populations of *future* patients, clinicians' overriding concerns lie with the wellbeing of their current patients. Hence clinical research is often viewed as peripheral to their practice and commercial interests may be perceived as at odds with primary clinical concerns (Montaner, O'Shaughnessy, and Schechter, 2001). Clinicians naturally prioritize avoiding risk of harm to patients. Should they actually decide to participate and to enroll patients in trials, they are often not motivated to proceed at the fast pace that the development teams seek, so patient recruitment often takes longer than envisaged (Swan, Robertson, and Evans, 2009). Clinical time is also compressed, but by different pragmatic concerns—being under increasing pressure to work more efficiently to meet ever more exacting targets and costs savings in the NHS, for example. Moreover, if working through the NHS system, development teams are entirely dependent on clinicians for patients so there is no real compunction for clinicians to alter the pace at which they work. This can result in delays in patient recruitment—seen in all of our projects—and an unwillingness on the part of clinicians to share knowledge with development teams. Whilst considerable policy effort has been aimed at encouraging more clinicians to participate openly in commercially led clinical research in the UK and the USA, this still continues to be a major barrier to innovation (Sahoo, 2007).

9.6 Conclusions

In this chapter we have sought to extend understanding of knowledge mobilization in healthcare by developing an initial ecological model. This is summarized schematically in Figure 9.2. We have focused on early phase development because this is a point where knowledge mobilization relies on significant collaboration and coordination of work among healthcare professionals and commercial firms, as well as with other agents such as regulatory bodies and investors. Public health services, in particular the UK NHS, are now under more pressure than ever to achieve dual imperatives of efficiency and innovation in order to improve treatments and services for patients. To achieve these imperatives will involve working more closely with commercial partners. By analyzing the ecology, in terms of its landscape *and* timescape, we are able to better understand the ways in which the ecology, and the institutionalized practices invoked within it, influence the ability to mobilize and "co-produce" knowledge in this domain.

Building on previous work, we have outlined how key features of the ecology landscape—epistemic logics and attitudes to risk—shape knowledge mobilization efforts. Moreover, by developing the concept of an ecology timescape (cf. Adam, 2003), we have drawn attention to the way different conceptions of time among agents drive the largely uncoordinated pace of their activities and capabilities for knowledge mobilization in this context. Marked differences in agents' STRS and temporal logics influence both their willingness to collaborate and the pace of their activities (Clark, 1978; Adam, 2003). These differences present significant challenges to mobilizing knowledge in the form of new drugs and treatments that will ultimately benefit patients, including the stopping of projects that are unlikely to yield results.

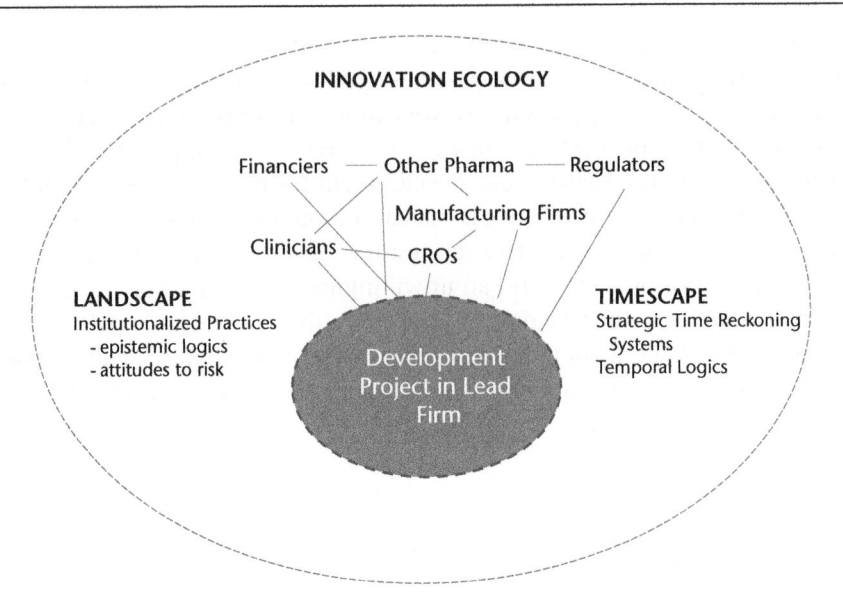

Figure 9.2 Ecological model of healthcare innovation

Our analysis has also demonstrated that, regardless of the core development teams' preferences, ultimately their frantic pace, and in some instances choices around trial design, are driven by the demands of investors or potential partners. Yet simultaneously they must adhere to the regulator's STRS governing the development process—which crucially controls the time *in* development. This can create further tensions for the development team. In the context of innovation in healthcare, clock/calendar time clearly provides the "invisible hand that rules" development work, as evident in the development pipeline. The ruling by clock time and time commodification (Adam, 2003) brings with it, somewhat paradoxically, an emphasis among development teams on micro-time planning (in the forms of project plans, meeting schedules, Gantt charts, etc.) and a rapid pace of work in the present when, inevitably, unanticipated events occur, projected plans are virtually impossible to adhere to, and development spans years.

Our ecological view also highlights the important, albeit previously neglected, role of regulatory authorities by considering the conceptions of time and risk that underpin their work. This role goes well beyond mere sequencing and approvals, actually influencing processes of knowledge production (e.g. decisions on what a trial should look like) in a real sense. By considering the interdependencies that exist between the core team and agents within the wider ecology as they attempt to mobilize knowledge, we have therefore demonstrated that many of these problems, whilst not necessarily insurmountable, nevertheless are deeply institutionalized in our society

(Swan et al., 2010). There is no doubt that the "constitutive agents" within this ecology (Grabher, 2002) each intend the development of new treatments to succeed, but their work activities are inextricably "nested" together. Their conflicting conceptions of time, along with more familiar aspects of the ecology, such as their differing epistemic logics (McGivern and Dopson, 2010) can, in practice, obstruct knowledge mobilization, even where there is a willingness to collaborate.

Our findings complement other studies of networked innovation, including those in Theme 3 of this book, by demonstrating the constraints on knowledge mobilization afforded, not just by network relations, but also by the particular features of the ecology. What is possible depends not only on spanning epistemic boundaries and coordinating knowledge and interests, but also on the particular constellation of the ecology. Borrowing from Clark (2000), we suggest that the landscape and timescape of the ecology together create a "zone of maneuver" that encourages certain aspects of knowledge production (e.g. staged development pipelines) and precludes others (e.g. longer-term partnering and knowledge exchange). Future research comparing different healthcare systems may shed further light on which feature of the landscape and timescape are particularly salient in this regard, and where there might be levers for change.

The practical implications of our chapter are several. First, it suggests that much more proactive attempts need to be made to incentivize clinicians to participate in clinical research. This could include, for example, novel forms of working that allow them to focus knowledge mobilization efforts on population needs rather than individual patients and/or to work more directly with industry for periods of time. Second, if invested partners could be persuaded to adopt a longer-term orientation toward collaboration, or at least address the issue of temporal alignment, then the frantic pace at which project teams' work, and some mistakes, might be avoided. Finally, while regulation is essential, this might take a more flexible approach that explicitly and practically recognizes that a "one-size-fits-all" linear model may be neither realistic nor desirable for certain kinds of development. These changes could, over time, produce a closer alignment of interests and expectations to enable knowledge mobilization. However, given ongoing commercial "imperatives," such changes would probably need to be driven, or at the very least supported, by policy and governance at the level of the ecology. As Fitzgerald and Harvey (2015) note, the impact of wider governance arrangements on the ability to mobilize knowledge locally in networked innovation settings is one area in need of further research, especially in the regulated healthcare context. We suggest, further, that this impact can only be understood by closer examination of the temporal differences and alignments that help or hinder knowledge mobilization in the healthcare ecology.

Acknowledgments

We would like to acknowledge the ESRC (Evolution of Business Knowledge Programme, project number RES-334-25-0005) and the ESPRC (Warwick Innovative Manufacturing Centre—project number EP/E002773/01) for funding of the primary research that informed the development of this chapter. We would also like to thank the following for their contributions to the cases studies in these funded projects: Mike Bresnen, Sue Newell, Ademole Obembe, Anna Goussevskaia, and Sarah Evans. The views and opinions expressed here are those of the authors and do not necessarily reflect those of the ESRC or EPSRC.

Note

1. This is a pseudonym, used to protext anonymity.
2. This figure was used previously in Swan, Robertson, and Newell, 2016.

Conclusions—Knowledge Mobilization: Moving On...

Jacky Swan, Sue Newell, and Davide Nicolini

The collection of chapters in this book adds to our understanding of the major challenges facing managers and organizations attempting to mobilize knowledge in healthcare. Presenting these studies in one place, foregrounds the rich seam of knowledge about knowledge mobilization that has already accrued in the fields of healthcare management and organization studies, both here and elsewhere.

The present collection sends a clear message about the need to move away from simple (and simplistic), linear models of knowledge transfer and utilization—a message declared also by other scholars. Such models paint an overly rationalistic and sanitized picture of the complexities of real life. The message alone, however, does not help actually guide healthcare practitioners, managers, or researchers as to what to do next. This is where this book makes its major contribution. Taken together, the chapters in this book start to build an alternative account of knowledge mobilization—broadly defined as *a proactive process that involves efforts to transform practice through the circulation of knowledge within and across practice domains* (see Introduction). More importantly, it shows us the practical insights that can be gained from a collective body of work that actually utilizes theoretically grounded, rich, qualitative empirical research studies and which focus on what is actually happening in the field. The chapters in this collection thus extend existing theory *and* provide concrete insights on ways to support (or prevent) knowledge mobilization and change.

The main contributions of individual chapters have been discussed in the introduction to the themed sections, and need not be repeated here. Instead, in this concluding chapter, we revisit the guiding framework outlined in the

Introduction and highlight, in brief, what this collection tells us about agency, the nested ecology, and processes/practices of knowledge mobilization. We finish with suggestions about a knowledge mobilization approach might usefully take us in the future. This is not a manifesto for change—there are probably too many of those in healthcare already—but, rather, some modest suggestions about future lines of research and avenues for practice.

C.1 Starting from Where the Agency Is

Seeing knowledge mobilization as a proactive, effortful process, necessarily points the chapters in this book toward different forms of agency; put simply as the capacity of "entities" to act and to exert influence over other agents. Importantly, the chapters show us that agency is collective, historically grounded, and dynamic; it does not arise solely from the behavior and choices made by individuals. Organizations and networks also acquire agency in their own right; they are not simply passive "structures" or communication channels, but also actively transform the way knowledge is mobilized by changing social relationships and practices (Clegg et al., 2016 forthcoming). As we see in Theme 3 (e.g. Chapter 7 by D'Andreta and Scarbrough) networked initiatives (the CLAHRCs in their case) create conditions that are favorable to the translation of research into practice by generating new social networks that link diverse professionals *and* allow deeper, task-focused knowledge sharing—what the authors call "ambidexterity." This favorable combination, however, also depends upon the strategic actions of participating managers and professionals and in particular in their capacity to set up formal role structures (e.g. knowledge broker roles) and to develop strategies to deal with the diverse concerns and interests of stakeholders (see Oborn et al., Chapter 5 this volume). Although networks necessarily operate through people, networks as such breathe life of their own into the process of knowledge mobilization.

Agency does not necessarily imply "freedom to act" though. In complex ecologies like healthcare there are always multiple agents involved, multiple forms of information, and power struggles at play (as seen in Newell and Marabelli's Chapter 6). For example, McGivern and colleagues (Chapter 1) and Nicolini and Korica (Chapter 2) clearly show how the agency of individual managers (including hybrid clinical/managers), in deciding what and when to use evidence and information, depends on it how fits with the dominant epistemic stance taken by their professional community and upon what forms of information are legitimate, and available, within their normal daily work. Clinical guidelines are more likely to be available to, and valued by, clinical practitioners than by commissioning managers, scientific reports by clinical researchers than by patients or carers, and so on. To make knowledge accessible to other groups, we need therefore to think about how they "practice" their own knowing and doing. We need to start from where they are rather where we (as academics) think they should be.

Recognizing that the agency of managers and healthcare professionals is constrained, as well as enabled, by the organizations in which they work, the professional networks with which they engage, and wider institutionalized practices, also runs through other chapters. In paying attention to agency, we naturally begin to understand that knowledge mobilization is a political act. Hence, "resistance," or "failure to adopt evidence," is quite a natural, not a deviant, state. And sometimes, practices of other agents (e.g. regulatory bodies, financiers) may reinforce ways of producing knowledge in local settings that are, in fact, counterproductive to healthcare improvement in the longer term (Chapter 9, Robertson and Swan).

C.2 The Complex, Nested Ecology

Tackling these issues concerning multiple forms of agency means an ecological view is valuable. Thus the chapters in the themed sections take as their focal point agency in different domains of the ecology—what we refer to as domains of action (managerial action, organizational capability, inter-organizational networking, and trans-local space/time—see Figure I.1). As seen in our Introduction, these are not hierarchically organized "levels of analysis" (as commonly assumed in studies of organization management) but are zones, or spheres, where actions unfold with each connecting to all the others. In more common parlance, each domain of action is "the context" for all the others.

The chapters in this book, then, bring to the fore the multiple ways in which knowledge mobilization in one domain (e.g. managerial decision-making) manifest in, builds upon and depends on what is happening, or has happened previously in other domains. Manifested in the ability, or willingness, of managers and healthcare professionals to use certain kinds of information, are for expectations about what knowledge is legitimate in their professional community (Chapters 1 and 2). The knowledge mobilization work of project teams in firms developing clinical research, manifests institutionalized expectations about how knowledge is produced, for what purpose, and at what pace (Chapter 9). The ability for innovations to circulate across contexts, manifests anxieties that healthcare managers have about their own ability to resolve problems (Chapter 8). The ability for organizations to develop learning capabilities and absorptive capacity manifests the regulatory environment of healthcare and managers' capacity for hands-on attention to nurturing positive social relationships (Chapters 3 and 4). The ability for networks to translate research into practice manifests the brokering activity of individuals, the boundary-spanning capacity of objects and the mechanisms used by professionals and policy groups to evaluate outcomes (Chapters 5, 6, and 7—see also Swan et al., 2010; D'Andreta et al., 2016 forthcoming).

Each chapter, then, speaks to not only a particular "level of analysis", as is common in research on organization and; it also foregrounds the embeddedness of any knowledge mobilization effort in nested ecologies of healthcare. This has important practical implications. It means that knowledge does not travel easily across different health systems. The reason for this is that the intricacies of each ecology are different. For example, we cannot simply "take" what has been done in one healthcare system and transport it into another, even though important lessons can be learned. As Chapter 8 by Nicolini et al. illustrates, circulation and reinterpretation go hand in hand, and to transfer is to transform. Also the ecology changes all the time. In the UK, for example, the introduction of Clinical Commissioning Groups, whereby commissioning decisions are led locally by groups of general physicians rather than centrally by regional authorities, fundamentally changes the landscape. While similar knowledge mobilization processes (e.g. absorptive capacity) remain important, the way they are configured may need to change. Mobilizing knowledge is always, therefore, an act of transformation, across space and across time.

C.3 Processes and Practices

The chapters in this collection demonstrate that the mobilization of knowledge is an emergent and political process. If healthcare improvements are to be achieved and sustained, then a processual view is essential. Knowledge mobilization is not a one-off event—nor can it just be left to happen. Rather, it is an ongoing, effortful process of generating, appropriating, implementing, and regenerating knowledge and learning such that it is able to sustain change in practice. This is a message that needs to be taken seriously by those practitioners, scholars, and policy makers who bemoan the lack of uptake of evidence—if effort is not given to the social processes that circulate knowledge and make it actionable, then any number of "evidence-based guidelines" will remain just that—guidelines about practice, not changes in practice.

The chapters, moreover, expose the many critical processes entailed in knowledge mobilization. Thus Croft and Currie showed us in Chapter 3 how the ability of an organization to learn and develop new services requires ongoing coordination capabilities to link the practices of design agencies (commissioners), general practitioners, and patients, so connecting population-level concerns with local experiences. The capabilities for organizations to learn also rest upon the development of generative (rather than toxic) spaces and emotional energy to impel people to contribute (Reay et al., Chapter 4). Developing these learning capabilities is, moreover, an ongoing accomplishment that requires continuous effort over time.

The chapters by Oborn et al. and D'Andreta and Scarbrough show how this applies to networked organizations whose purpose is to translate knowledge into practice. These organizations in fact develop ambidexterity (the ability to balance exploration and exploitation) through ongoing processes of structuring formal and informal relationships and knowledge brokering across the divides created by divisions of professional practice. The political processes entailed in how such networks actually work are revealed, further, by Newell and Marabelli (Chapter 6).

This attention to process also reminds us that knowledge is not just transferred en masse, but is transformed through use as its spreads within and across domains of action. The chapter by Nicolini et al. (Chapter 8) shows us new innovative ideas (in their case around patient safety) spread through particular discursive processes that generate both a thirst for the knowledge, and a departure from previous practices. Moreover, the development and spread of new ideas over time and space depend on the cycling of interactions between local processes of change and the actions of trans-local, field-level actors (e.g. regulatory agencies—Robertson and Swan, Chapter 9). This explains why even "proven" ideas can fail to spread, and also why "disproven" ideas (drug development projects that are doomed to failure, for example) can survive nonetheless (see also Scarbrough, Robertson, and Swan, 2015).

Some of the chapters (especially Chapters 2, 6, and 8) draw more explicitly on practice-based theory to delve further into what happens when knowledge is mobilized (see Nicolini, 2012 for an overview). While now quite well established in other disciplines, practice-based studies are still quite new to healthcare management and so comprise a novel addition to this book. These chapters show us that knowledge mobilization is always a socio-material accomplishment, performed by different kinds of agents (managers, organizations, networks) and objects, for particular practical purposes. The healthcare managers and clinicians designing new services in Newell and Marabelli's study (Chapter 6), or the senior managers dealing with multiple strategic challenges in Nicolini and Korica's (Chapter 2), collectively enact their practice. Managers' use of information and (what comes to count as) evidence stems from their relationships, their identity-based epistemic stances (McGivern et al., Chapter 1) and the material objects that they systematically make use of (e.g. the RCA in Chapter 8, or the SPOC tool in Chapter 6). How this is done is consequential for what happens next (Feldman and Orlikowski, 2011).

These chapters "zoom in" on what actually happens in practice and demonstrate why prevailing linear models of knowledge utilization are limited. This is because they stand back from what happens in real life, and so cannot hope to capture the many twists and turns entailed in actually transforming knowledge in practice. However, understanding practice is not just about micro-social phenomena. As the chapters by Nicolini et al. (Chapter 8) and Robertson and Swan (Chapter 9) amply demonstrate, local healthcare practices are shaped by—but may also reproduce and change—practices embedded in the wider ecology of organizations through which knowledge circulates (see also Dionysiou and Tsoukas, 2013).

C.4 Directions for Future Research

Thinking first about agency, we saw in the chapters how human agency operates in tandem with material objects and informational resources. New forms of technology—social media, mobile apps, management technologies, sophisticated online search tools, and "big data" analytical tools—are having an increasingly important role to play in knowledge mobilization. "Digital health," for example, is becoming an increasingly important topic in healthcare, with social events and media devoted to exploring how the better use of technology and data can enable the key developments needed to improve the health and care system (e.g. the King's Fund, Annual Digital Health, and Care Congress).

From a traditional knowledge transfer and utilization perspective, the role of such technologies can only be positive; after all, these are just new and better ways of transferring knowledge. From a knowledge mobilization viewpoint, however, things are rather more open and uncertain. Such technologies have the capacity to sustain and change social networks and transform practice. Hence, they may also exert agency, and may do this in ways that may not be wholly desirable for certain groups (cf. Latour, 1986). While some chapters say something about the role of various kinds of informational objects in shifting practice, this is certainly an area for further development. How might, for example, "big data" (already being used in the development of drugs) or "crowdsourcing" mobilize knowledge in healthcare settings? How will social media shift the circulation of knowledge (and power) between professional and patient groups? How might innovation and improvement in the delivery of healthcare be further informed through online communities? How will "big data" analysis—that seeks answers through connecting very many data points—be able to connect with clinical practitioners, who usually seek answers through hypothesis-testing and scientific method? What will "evidence" look like from these different epistemic stances? What are the social and ethical implications of using new informational objects such as "big data" in healthcare? These questions are becoming increasing important for future research on knowledge mobilization. They may also benefit from more practice-based studies that attend to the material affordances of new technology by zooming in and out on practice (Nicolini, 2009).

Given these questions, understanding more about how networks (both human and non-human) develop capacity for agency is increasingly important. While our chapters (especially those in Theme 3) say a lot about the ways networks shape transformations of knowledge, many more questions remain unanswered. For example, how do formal inter-professional networks established to translate knowledge into practice (such as the CLAHRCs) develop capacity for agency that goes beyond the lifetime and funding of formal initiative? What network structures work most effectively and in which conditions? How should these networks be governed? How do innovative practices spread beyond the formal network initiative? How do networks change over time—do they become more closed, self-contained groups, with their own identity, for example? What sort of leadership processes do they require? Network-level studies and analysis could help us to further understand these issues.

Regarding the nested ecology, there have been, and continue to be, major shifts in the ways health systems are organized. For example, just in the UK there have been recent moves toward centralization of the delivery of acute care, for example via large, tertiary centers, coupled with decentralization of primary care, with more decision-making powers being granted to Clinical Commissioning Groups. There is also increased blurring of public and private provision of healthcare via the increased use of private sector providers as well as shifts in the roles of major groups such as the National Institute of Clinical Excellence. Given what we have said about the essentially nested nature of the ecology, these shifts in the landscape are likely to have significant impact on how knowledge is mobilized and to what ends. Comparative study across different health systems would also help us to understand how different ecological arrangements impact upon knowledge mobilization. Practically, this kind of study would provide opportunities to learn from previous attempts and failures, albeit recognizing that any such learning needs to be appropriated to particular health systems.

Turning finally to processes and practice, we have seen that knowledge mobilization is an ongoing social process. However, we still need to understand better exactly how this process unfolds over time and why it takes some directions and not others. For example, we saw, in Chapter 4, that it is important to develop "generative spaces" for knowledge mobilization and, in Chapters 5 and 7, that developing ambidexterity is needed to be able to both innovate and translate innovative ideas into practical change. However, "generative spaces" might easily become "inert," if not "toxic," and ambidexterity may difficult to sustain. We have discovered, also, that the outcomes of efforts to mobilize knowledge across the research–practice divide are emergent and not always as intended. However, it is not wholly clear how things considered to be "outcomes" at any point in time feed back into processes. Nor is it clear what happens when different professional groups value different outcomes (e.g. patient outcomes, research results, individual vs. population improvement, cost reductions).

We have also seen that knowledge mobilization processes are multifaceted and may conflict with one another (e.g. creative processes of developing new knowledge may conflict with regulatory processes governing its use). Yet, our chapters say rather little about how this conflict plays out. For example, how do seemingly opposite, or conflicting, discourses and practices interact and even reproduce one another? How, and under what conditions, do local circulations of knowledge reproduce or change the wider circulation of knowledge across contexts? Such questions could be answered by accounts that take a more dialectical approach and consider how conflicting or opposing forces also drive knowledge mobilization.

While our chapters provide useful accounts of practice and process, most are set over a limited timeframe. More systematic, longitudinal, and/or historical analysis would help to explain why processes and practices shift in one direction or another, how they are sustained over time, and how they link to outcomes (intended or unintended) that are valued by those involved. This would allow us to understand better how knowledge mobilization might generate more sustained shifts in practice by changing, for example, the ways that people see their professional roles, identities, and careers (as "knowledge brokers," "hybrid professionals," and so on). This has practical implications, also, for how professional and managerial roles that support knowledge mobilization in healthcare might be developed and incentivized. Change in practice takes some time to embed, especially where practices are deeply invested (Carlile, 2002). Taking longer-term view, with an eye on the ecology, could help to avoid the costs (financial and social) of investing in knowledge mobilization initiatives that may otherwise stand little chance of sustained success (Swan et al., 2010).

References

Abebe, M., Angriawan, A., and Tran, H. 2010. Chief executive external network ties and environmental scanning activities: An empirical examination. *Strategic Management Review*, 4(1): 30–43.

Abraham, J. and Reddy, M. C. 2008. Moving patients around: A field study of coordination between clinical and non-clinical staff in hospitals. In Bo Begole and David W. McDonald (eds.), *Proceedings of the 2008 ACM Conference on Computer-Supported Cooperative Work*, pp. 225–8. New York: Association for Computing Machinery.

Abrahamson, E. 1996. Management fashion. *Academy of Management Review*, 21(1): 254–85.

Abrahamson, E. and Rosenkopf, L. 1997. Social network effects on the extent of innovation diffusion: A computer simulation. *Organization Science*, 83(3): 289–309.

Academy of Medical Sciences 2003. *Strengthening Clinical Research: A Report by the Academy of Medical Sciences (AMS)*. London: AMS.

Adam, B. 2003. Reflexive modernization temporalized. *Theory, Culture and Society*, 20(2): 59–78.

Addicott, R., McGivern, G., and Ferlie, E. 2006. Networks, organizational learning and knowledge management: NHS cancer networks. *Public Money and Management*, 26(2): 87–94.

Aguilar, F. I. 1967. *Scanning the Business Environment*. New York: MacMillan.

Albert, M., Laberge, S., Hodges, B., Regehr, G., and Lingard, L. 2008. Biomedical scientists' perceptions of the social sciences in health care. *Social Science and Medicine*, 66(12): 2520–31.

Amabile, M. 1996. *The Motivation for Creativity in Organizations*. Cambridge, MA: Harvard Business School Press.

Ambos, T. C., Mäkelä, K., Birkinshaw, J., and D'Este, P. 2008. When does university research get commercialized? Creating ambidexterity in research institutions. *Journal of Management Studies*, 45(8): 1424–47.

Amo, M. 1998. Root cause analysis: A tool for understanding why accidents occur. *Balance*, 2(5): 12–15.

Ancona, D. and Chong, C. L. 1996. Entrainment: Pace, cycle, and rhythm in organizational behavior. In L. Cummings and B. Straw (eds.), *Research in Organization Behavior*, 17, pp. 1–70. Greenwich, CT: JAI Press.

Andersen, B. and Fagerhaug, T. 2000. *Root Cause Analysis: Simplified Tools and Techniques*. Milwaukee, WI: ASQ Quality Press.

References

Andersen-Gough, F., Grey, C., and Robson, K. 2001. Test of time: organizational time-reckoning and the making of accountants in two multi-national accounting firms. *Accounting, Organizations and Society*, 26(2): 99–122.

Anderson, M. H. 2008. Social networks and the cognitive motivation to realize network opportunities: A study of managers' information-gathering behaviors. *Journal of Organizational Behavior*, 29(1): 51–78.

Andriopoulos, C. and Lewis, M. W. 2009. Exploitation–exploration tensions and organizational ambidexterity: Managing paradoxes of innovation. *Organization Science*, 20(4): 696–717.

Ansari, S. M., Fiss, P. C., and Zajac, E. J. 2010. Made to fit: How practices vary as they diffuse. *Academy of Management Review*, 35(1): 67–92.

Antonacopoulou, E. and Chiva, R. 2007. The social complexity of organizational learning: The dynamics of learning and organizing. *Management Learning*, 38(3): 277–95.

Ardichvili, A., Page, V., and Wentling, T. 2003. Motivation and barriers to participation in virtual knowledge sharing communities of practice. *Journal of Knowledge Management*, 7(1): 64–77.

Ardnt, M. and Bigelow, B. 2009. Evidence-based management in health care organizations: A cautionary note. *Health Care Management Review*, 34(3): 206–23.

Argote, L. 1999. *Organizational Learning: Creating, Retaining and Transferring Knowledge*. Boston, MA: Kluwer.

Ashar, B. H., Miller, R. G., Getz, K. J., and Powe, N. R. 2004. Prevalence and determinants of physician participation in conducting pharmaceutical-sponsored clinical trials and lectures. *Journal of General Internal Medicine*, 19(11): 1140–5.

Aube, C. and Rousseau, V. 2005. Team goal commitment and team effectiveness: The role of task interdependence and supportive behaviors. *Group Dynamics: Theory, Research and Practice*, 9(3): 189–204.

Auster, E. and Choo, C. W. 1993. Environmental scanning by CEOs in two Canadian industries. *JASIS*, 44(4): 194–203.

Baba, V. V. and Hakem Zadeh, F. 2012. Toward a theory of evidence-based decision making. *Management Decision*, 50(5): 832–67.

Bagian, J. P., Gosbee, J., Lee, C. Z., Williams, L., McKnight, S. D., and Mannos, D. M. 2002. The veterans affairs root cause analysis system in action. *JACO Journal of Quality Improvement*, 28(10): 531–45.

Baker, A. 2002. Receptive spaces for conversational learning. In A. Baker, P. Jensen, and D. Kolb (eds.), *Conversational Learning: An Experiential Approach to Knowledge Creation*, pp. 101–24. Westport, CT: Quorum Books.

Baker, A., Jensen, P., and Kolb, D. 2005. Conversation as experiential learning. *Management Learning*, 36(4): 411–27.

Bapuji, H. and Crossan, M. 2004. From questions to answers: Reviewing organizational learning research. *Management Learning*, 35(4): 397–417.

Barrett, M., Oborn, E., and Orlikowski, W. 2015. Performing business models in on-line health communities. Paper presented at *EGOS*, Athens, July 1–3.

Bate, P. 1994. *Strategies for Cultural Change*. Oxford: Butterworth-Heinemann.

References

Bates, M. J. 2007. What is browsing—really? A model drawing from behavioural science research. *Information Research*, 12(4), paper 330. Available at: <http://InformationR.net/ir/12-4/paper330.html> (accessed January 18, 2016).

Bates, M. J. 2010. Information. In M. J. Bates and M. N. Maack (eds.), *Encyclopedia of Library and Information Sciences*, pp. 2347–60. New York: CRC Press.

Bates, R. H., Greif, A., Levi, M., Rosenthal, J. L., and Weingast, B. R. 2000. Analytic narratives revisited. *Social Science History*, 24(4): 685–96.

Bateson, G. 1972. *Steps to an Ecology of Mind*. New York: Ballantine.

Battilana, J. and Casciaro, T. 2012. Change agents, networks, and institutions: A contingency theory of organizational change. *Academy of Management Journal*, 55(2): 381–98.

Baum, J. A., Shipilov, A. V., and Rowley, T. J. 2003. Where do small worlds come from? *Industrial and Corporate Change*, 12(4): 697–725.

Beck, U., Giddens, A., and Lash, S. 1994. *Reflexive Modernization: Politics, Tradition and Aesthetics in the Modern Social Order*. Stanford, CA: Stanford University Press.

Benner, M. J. and Tushman, M. L. 2003. Exploitation, exploration, and process management: The productivity dilemma revisited. *The Academy of Management Review*, 28(2): 238–56.

Berta, W., Teare, F., Gilbart, E., Ginsburg, L., Lemieux-Charles, L., Davis, D., and Rappolt, S. 2010. Spanning the know–do gap: Understanding knowledge application and capacity in long-term care homes. *Social Science and Medicine*, 70(9): 1326–34.

Beyer, J. M. and Trice, H. M. 1982. The utilization process: A conceptual framework and synthesis of empirical findings. *Administrative Science Quarterly*, 27: 591–622.

Beyes, T. and Michels, C. 2011. The production of educational space: Heterotopia and the business university. *Management Learning*, 42(5): 521–36.

Biernacki, P. and Waldorf, D. 1981. Snowball sampling: Problems and techniques of chain referral sampling. *Sociological Methods and Research*, 19(2): 141–63.

Blackler, F. and McDonald, S. 2000. Power, mastery, and organizational learning. *Journal of Management Studies*, 37(6): 833–51.

Bohmer, R. and Edmondson, A. 2001. Organizational learning in health care. *Health Forum Journal* (March/April): 32–5.

Borgatti, S. P., Everett, M. G., and Freeman, L. C. 2002. *UCINET 6 for Windows*. Harvard, MA: Analytic Technologies.

Bourdieu, P. 1977. *Outline of a Theory of Practice*. Cambridge: Cambridge University Press.

Bourdieu, P. 1991. *The Political Ontology of Martin Heidegger*. Stanford, CA: Stanford University Press.

Bourgeon, L. 2002. Temporal context of organizational learning in new product development projects. *Creativity and Innovation Management*, 11(3): 175–83.

Bouwen, R. and Hosking, D. M. 2000. Reflections on relational readings of organizational learning. *European Journal of Work and Organizational Psychology*, 9(2): 267–74.

Boxenbaum, E. and Battilana, J. 2005. Importation as innovation: Transposing managerial practices across fields. *Strategic Organization*, 3(4): 355–83.

Boxenbaum, E. and Pedersen, J. S. 2009. Scandinavian institutionalism—A case of institutional work. In T. B. Lawrence, R. Suddaby, and B. Leca (eds.), *Institutional*

References

Work: Actors and Agency in Institutional Studies of Organizations, pp. 178–92. Cambridge: Cambridge University Press.

Brennan, T. A., Leape, L. L., Laird, N. M., Hebert, L., Localio, A. R., Lawthers, A. G., Newhouse, J. P., Weiler, P. C., and Hiatt, H. H. 1991. Incidence of adverse events and negligence in hospitalized patients: Results of the Harvard Medical Practice Study I. *New England Journal of Medicine*, 324(6): 370–6.

Brown, J. S. and Duguid, P. 1991. Organizational learning and communities of practice: Toward a unified view of working, learning, and innovating. *Organization Science*, 2(1): 40–57.

Brown, J. S. and Duguid, P. 2000. *The Social Life of Information*. Cambridge, MA: Harvard Business School Press.

Brown, J. S. and Duguid, P. 2001. Knowledge and organization: A social-practice perspective. *Organization Science*, 12(2): 198–213.

Buckland, M. K. 1991. Information as thing. *JASIS*, 42(5): 351–60.

Burnett, G., Besant, M., and Chatman, E. A. 2001. Small worlds: Normative behavior in virtual communities and feminist bookselling. *Journal of the American Society for Information Science and Technology*, 52(7): 536–47.

Burt, R. S. 1992. The social structure of competition. In R. Swedburg (ed.), *Explorations in Economic Sociology*, pp. 65–103. New York: Russell Sage Foundation.

Burt, R. S. 1997. The contingent value of social capital. *Administrative Science Quarterly*, 42(2): 339–65.

Burt, R. S. 2000. The network structure of social capital. *Research in Organizational Behavior*, 22: 345–423.

Burt, R. S. 2005. *Brokerage and Closure: An Introduction to Social Capital*. Oxford: Oxford University Press.

Burton, A. 2006. Speeding up cancer drug development. *The Lancet Oncology*, 7(10): 798.

Cameron, K. S. 2008. *Positive Leadership: Strategies for Extraordinary Performance*. San Francisco, CA: Berrett-Koehler.

Cameron, K. S., Bright, D., and Caza, A. 2004. Exploring the relationships between organizational virtuousness and performance. *American Behavioral Scientist*, 47(6): 766–90.

Cameron, K. S. and Caza, A. 2004. Contributions to the discipline of positive organizational scholarship. *American Behavioral Scientist*, 47(6): 731–9.

Cameron, K. S., Dutton, J. E., and Quinn, R. E. 2003. *Positive Organizational Scholarship*. San Francisco, CA: Berrett-Koehler.

Caplan, N. 1979. The two-communities theory and knowledge utilization. *American Behavioral Scientist*, 22(3): 459–70.

Carlile, P. R. 2002. A pragmatic view of knowledge and boundaries: Boundary objects in new product development. *Organization Science*, 13(4): 442–55.

Carlile, P. R. 2004. Transferring, translating, and transforming: An integrative framework for managing knowledge across boundaries. *Organization Science*, 15(5): 555–68.

Carroll, J. S. 1998. Organizational learning activities in high-hazard industries: The logics underlying self-analysis. *Journal of Management Studies*, 35(6): 699–717.

Carroll, J. S., Rudolph, J. W., and Hatakenaka, S. 2002. Lessons learned from non-medical industries: Root cause analysis as culture change at a chemical plant. *Quality Safety Health Care*, 11(3): 266–9.

References

Chakravartty, A. 2011. A puzzle about voluntarism about rational epistemic stances. *Synthese*, 178(1): 37–48.

Chalkidou, K., Walley, T., Culyer, A., Littlejohns, P., and Hoy, A. 2008. Evidence-informed evidence-making. *Journal of Health Services Research and Policy*, 13(3): 167–73.

Chen, X., Yao, X., and Kotha, S. 2009. Entrepreneur passion and preparedness in business plan presentations: A persuasion analysis of venture capitalists' funding decisions. *Academy of Management Review*, 52(1): 199–214.

Chia, R. 2003. From knowledge-creation to the perfecting of action: Tao, Basho and pure experience as the ultimate ground of knowing. *Human Relations*, 56(8): 953–81.

Chung, Y. and Jackson, S. E. 2013. The internal and external networks of knowledge-intensive teams: The role of task routineness. *Journal of Management*, 39(2): 442–68.

Ciborra, C. 2006. The mind or the heart? It depends on the (definition of) situation. *Journal of Information Technology*, 21(3): 129–39.

Clark, P. 1978. Temporal inventories and time structuring in large organizations. In J. T. Fraser, N. Lawrence, and D. Park (eds.), *The Study of Time III*, pp. 391–416. New York: Springer-Verlag.

Clark, P. 1985. A review of the theories of time and structure for organizational sociology. *Research in the Sociology of Organizations*, 4: 1–32.

Clark, P. A. 2000. *Organizations in Action: Competition Between Contexts*. London: Routledge.

Clark, P. A. and Maielli, G. 2009. Making and missing the evolution of timed-space: How do you analyse longitudinal recursiveness and transformations? In R. Roe, M. Waller, and S. Clegg (eds.), *Time in Organizational Research*, pp. 255–75. London: Routledge.

Clegg, S., Josserand, E., Mehra, A., and Pitsis, T. (eds.) 2016. The transformative power of network dynamics: A research agenda. *Organization Studies*, 37(3): 277–91.

Clegg, S. R. 1989. Radical revisions: Power, discipline, and organizations. *Organization Studies*, 10(1): 97–115.

Cohen, W. M. and Levinthal, D. 1990. Absorptive capacity: A new perspective on learning and innovation. *Administrative Science Quarterly*, 35(1): 128–52.

Coleman, J. S. 1988. Social capital in the creation of human capital. *American Journal of Sociology*, 40(5): 95–120.

Coleman, J. S., Katz, E., and Menzel, H. 1966. *Medical Innovation: A Diffusion Study*. New York: Bobbs-Merrill Company.

Cook, S. and Yanow, D. 1993. Culture and organizational learning. *Journal of Management Inquiry*, 2(4): 373–90.

Cook, S. D. and Brown, J. S. 1999. Bridging epistemologies: The generative dance between organizational knowledge and organizational knowing. *Organization Science*, 10(4): 381–400.

Cooksey, D. 2006. *A Review of UK Health Research Funding*. London: HM Stationery Office.

Cramton, C. D. 2001. The mutual knowledge problem and its consequences for dispersed collaboration. *Organization Science*, 12(3): 346–71.

Crilly, T., Jashapara, A., and Ferlie, E. 2010. *Research Utilisation and Knowledge Mobilisation: A Scoping Review of the Literature*. National Co-Ordinating Centre for NHS Service

References

Delivery and Organization RandD (NCCSDO). Available at: <http://www.nets.nihr.ac.uk/__data/assets/pdf_file/0004/82408/ES-08-1801-220.pdf> (accessed December 30, 2015).

Crilly, T., Jashapara, A., Trenholm, S., Peckham, A., Currie, G., and Ferlie, E. 2013. Knowledge mobilisation in healthcare organizations: Synthesising evidence and theory using perspectives of organizational form, resource based view of the firm and critical theory. NIHR Health Services and Delivery Research Programme. London: NIHR.

Cunliffe, A. 2008. Orientations to social constructionism: Relationally responsive social constructionism and its implications for knowledge and learning. *Management Learning*, 39(2): 123–39.

Currie, G., El Enany, N., and Lockett, A. 2014. Intra-professional dynamics in translational health research: The perspective of social scientists. *Social Science and Medicine*, 114: 81–8.

Currie, G., Finn, R., and Martin, G. 2007. Spanning boundaries in pursuit of effective knowledge sharing within networks in the NHS. *Journal of Health Organization and Management*, 21(4/5): 406–17.

Currie, G., Finn, R., and Martin, G. 2008. Accounting for the dark side of new organizational forms: The case of healthcare professionals. *Human Relations*, 61(4): 539–64.

Currie, G. and Suhomlinova, O. 2006. The impact of institutional forces upon knowledge sharing in the UK NHS: The triumph of professional power and the inconsistency of policy. *Public Administration*, 84(1): 1–30.

Currie, G. and White, L. 2012. Inter-professional barriers and knowledge brokering in an organizational context: the case of healthcare. *Organization Studies*, 33(10): 1333–61.

Czarniawska, B. 2007. *Shadowing and Other Techniques for Doing Fieldwork in Modern Societies*. Malmö: Liber AB.

Czarniawska, B. and Joerges, B. 1996. Travels of ideas. In B. Czarniawska and G. Sevón (eds.), *Translating Organizational Change*, pp. 13–48. Berlin: de Gruyter.

Czarniawska, B. and Sevón, G. 1996. *Translating Organizational Change*. Berlin: de Gruyter.

Czarniawska, B. and Sevón, G. 2005a. *Global Ideas: How Ideas, Objects and Practices Travel in the Global Economy*. Frederiksberg: Liber and Copenhagen Business School Press.

Czarniawska, B. and Sevón, G. 2005b. Translation is a vehicle, imitation its motor, and fashion fits at the wheel. In B. Czarniawska and G. Sevón (eds.), *Global Ideas: How Ideas, Objects and Practices Travel in the Global Economy*. Frederiksberg: Liber and Copenhagen Business School Press.

D'Andreta, D., Marabelli, M., Newell, S., Scarbrough, H., and Swan, J. 2016. Dominant cognitive frames and the innovative power of social networks. *Organization Studies*, 37(3): 293–321.

D'Andreta, D., Scarbrough, H., and Evans, S. 2013. The enactment of knowledge translation: a study of the Collaborations for Leadership in Applied Health Research and Care initiative within the English National Health Service. *Journal of Health Services Research and Policy*, 18(3 suppl): 40–52.

Dahl, R. A. 1957. The concept of power. *System Research and Behavioral Science*, 2(3): 201–15.

References

Damanpour, F. and Schneider, M. 2009. Characteristics of innovation and innovation adoption in public organizations: Assessing the role of managers. *Journal of Public Administration Research and Theory*, 19(3): 495–522.

Darzi, A. 2007. *Our NHS, Our Future, NHS Next Stage Review: Interim Report*. London: Department of Health.

de Alwis, G., Majid, S., and Chaudhry, A. S. 2006. Transformation in managers' information-seeking behaviour: A review of the literature. *Journal of Information Science*, 32(4): 362–77.

DeSteno, D., Petty, R. E., Rucker, D. D., and Wegener, D. T. 2004. Discrete emotions and persuasion: The role of emotion-induced expectancies. *Journal of Personality and Social Psychology*, 86(1): 43–56.

Dezso, C. L. and Ross, D. G. 2012. Does female representation in top management improve firm performance? A panel data investigation. *Strategic Management Journal*, 33(9): 1072–89.

Dhanaraj, C. and Parkhe, A. 2006. Orchestrating innovation networks. *Academy of Management Review*, 31(3): 659–69.

Dhillon, G. 2004. Dimensions of power and IS implementation. *Information and Management*, 41(5): 635–44.

Dionysiou, D. D. and Tsoukas, H. 2013. Understanding the (re)creation of routines from within: A symbolic interactionist perspective. *Academy of Management Review*, 38(2): 181–205.

Dirks, K. T. and Ferrin, D. L. 2002. Trust in leadership: meta-analytic findings and implications for research and practice. *Journal of Applied Psychology*, 87(4): 611–28.

Dobbins, M., Robeson, P., Ciliska, D., Hanna, S., Cameron, R., O'Mara, L., DeCorby, K., and Mercer, S. 2009. A description of a knowledge broker role implemented as part of a randomized controlled trial evaluating three knowledge translation strategies. *Implementation Science*, 4(23).

Dodgson, M., Gann, D., and Salter, A. 2005. *Think, Play, Do: Markets, Technology and Organization*. Oxford: Oxford University Press.

DoH (Department of Health) 2000. *An Organisation with a Memory: Report of an Expert Group on Learning from Adverse Events in the NHS*. London: The Stationery Office.

DoH (Department of Health) 2001. *Doing Less Harm. Improving the Safety and Quality of Care Through Reporting, Analysing and Learning from Adverse Incidents Involving NHS Patients*. London: DoH.

DoH (Department of Health) 2010. *Equity and Excellence: Liberating the NHS* (Cm7881). London: HMSO.

Dopson, S., Bennett, C., Fitzgerald, L., Ferlie, E., Fischer, M., Ledger, J., McCulloch, J., and McGivern, G. 2013. *Health Care Managers' Access and Use of Management Research*. National Institute for Health Research Service Delivery and Organization Programme. Final report. Available at: <http://www.netscc.ac.uk/hsdr/files/project/SDO_FR_08-1808-242_V06.pdf> (accessed December 30, 2015).

Dopson, S. and Fitzgerald, L. 2005. *Knowledge to Action? Evidence-Based Health Care in Context*. Oxford: Oxford University Press.

Dopson, S., FitzGerald, L., Ferlie, E., Gabbay, J., and Locock, L. 2002. No magic targets! Changing clinical practice to become more evidence based. *Health Care Management Review*, 27(3): 35–47.

References

Dougherty, D. and Dunne, D. 2012. Digital science and knowledge boundaries in complex innovation. *Organization Science*, 23(5): 1467–84.

Dougherty, D. and Dunne, D. D. 2011. Organizing ecologies of complex innovation. *Organization Science*, 22(5): 1214–23.

Dreyfus, H. 1991. *Being in the World: A Commentary on Heidegger's Being and Time, Division 1*. Cambridge, MA: MIT Press.

Dreyfus, H. L. and Kelly, S. D. 2011. *All Things Shining: Reading the Western Classics to Find Meaning in a Secular Age*. New York: Free Press.

Dube, L., Bourhis, A., and Jacob, R. 2006. Towards a typology of virtual communities of practice. *Interdisciplinary Journal of Information, Knowledge, and Management*, 1: 70–92.

Dubinskas, F. 1988. Cultural constructions: The many faces of time. In F. Dubinskas (ed.), *Making Time: Ethnographies of High-Technology Organizations*. Philadelphia, PA: Temple University Press.

Dutton, J. and Ragins, B. 2006. *Exploring Positive Relationships at Work: Building a Theoretical and Research Foundation*. San Francisco, CA: Berrett-Koehler.

Dutton, J. E. 2003. Breathing life into organizational studies. *Journal of Management Inquiry*, 12(1): 5–19.

Easterby-Smith, M. and Araujo, L. 1999. Organizational learning: Current debates and opportunities. In M. Easterby-Smith, J. Burgoyne, and L. Araujo (eds.), *Organizational Learning and the Learning Organization: Developments in Theory and Practice*, pp. 1–22. London: Sage.

Easterby-Smith, M., Crossan, M., and Nicolini, D. 2000. Organizational learning: Debates past, present, and future. *Journal of Management Studies*, 37(6): 783–96.

Easterby-Smith, M., Graca, M., Antonacopoulou, E., and Ferdinand, J. 2008. Absorptive capacity: A process perspective. *Management Learning*, 39(5): 483–501.

Easterby-Smith, M. and Lyles, M. A. 2011. *Handbook of Organizational Learning and Knowledge Management*. Oxford: John Wiley and Sons.

Edelman, L. F., Bresnan, M., Newell, S., Scarborough, H., and Swan, J. 2004. The benefits and pitfalls of social capital: Empirical evidence from two organizations in the United Kingdom. *British Journal of Management*, 15: S59–69.

Edenius, M. and Yakhlef, A. 2007. Space, vision and organizational learning: The interplay of incorporating and inscribing practices. *Management Learning*, 38(2): 193–210.

Edmondson, A. 1999. Psychological safety and learning behavior in work teams. *Administrative Science Quarterly*, 44: 350–83.

Eisenhardt, K. 1989. Building theories from case study research. *Academy of Management Review*, 14(4): 532–50.

Emerson, R. M. 1962. Power-dependence relations. *American Sociology Review*, 27(1): 31–41.

Engwall, M. and Jerbrant, A. 2003. The resource allocation syndrome: The prime challenge of multi-project management? *International Journal of Project Management*, 21(6): 403–9.

Estabrooks, C. A. 1999. The conceptual structure of research utilization. *Research in Nursing and Health*, 22(3): 203–16.

Evans, J., Kunda, G., and Barley, S. 2004. Beach time, bridge time, and billable hours: The temporal structure of technical contracting. *Administrative Science Quarterly*, 49(1): 1–38.

References

Evans, S. and Scarbrough, H. 2014. Supporting knowledge translation through collaborative translational research initiatives: "Bridging" versus "blurring" boundary-spanning approaches in the UK CLAHRC initiative. *Social Science and Medicine*, 106: 119–27.

Fahy, K. M., Easterby-Smith, M., and Lervik, J. E. 2014. The power of spatial and temporal orderings in organizational learning. *Management Learning*, 45(2): 123–44.

Fayard, A., Gkeredakis, E., and Levina, N. 2016. Exploring IT-enabled opportunities for crowdsourcing innovation: An epistemic stance perspective. *Information Systems Research*, forthcoming.

Fayter, D., McDaid, C., Ritchie, G., Stirk, L., and Eastwood, A. 2006. Systematic Review of Barriers, Modifiers and Benefits Involved in Participation in Cancer Clinical Trials. Centre for Reviews and Dissemination Report 31, University of York.

Feldman, M. S. and March, J. G. 1981. Information in organizations as signal and symbol. *Administrative Science Quarterly* 26(2): 171–86.

Feldman, M. S. and Orlikowski, W. J. 2011. Theorizing practice and practicing theory. *Organization Science*, 22(5): 1240–53.

Ferlie, E., Crilly, T., Jashapara, A., and Peckham, A. 2012. Knowledge mobilisation in healthcare: A critical review of health sector and generic management literature. *Social Science and Medicine*, 74(8): 1297–304.

Ferlie, E., Fitzgerald, L., McGivern, G., Dopson, S., and Bennett, C. 2013. *Making Wicked Problems Governable? The Case of Managed Health Care Networks*. Oxford: Oxford University Press.

Ferlie, E., Fitzgerald, L., McGivern, G., Dopson, S., and Exworthy, M. 2010. *Networks in Health Care: A Comparative Study of Their Management, Impact and Performance*. Report for the National Institute for Health Research Service Delivery and Organization Programme.

Ferlie, E., Fitzgerald, L., Wood, M., and Hawkins, C. 2005. The non-spread of innovations: The mediating role of professionals. *The Academy of Management Journal*, 48(1): 117–34.

Fidel, R. and Green, M. 2004. The many faces of "accessibility": Engineers' perception of information sources. *Information Processing and Management*, 40(3): 563–81.

Fine, G. A. and White, R. D. 2002. Creating collective attention in the public domain: Human interest narratives and the rescue of Floyd Collins. *Social Forces*, 81(1): 57–85.

Fischer, M., Dopson, S., Fitzgerald, L., Bennett, C., Ferlie, E., Ledger, J., and McGivern, G. 2015. Knowledge leadership: Mobilising management research by becoming the knowledge object. *Human Relations*, 1(23) DOI: 10.1177/0018726715619686.

Fitzgerald, L., Ferlie, E., McGivern, G., and Buchanan, D. 2013. Distributed leadership patterns and service improvement: Evidence and argument from English healthcare. *Leadership Quarterly*, 24(1): 227–39.

Fitzgerald, L. and Harvey, G. 2015. Translational networks in healthcare? Evidence on the design and initiation of organizational networks for knowledge mobilization. *Social Science and Medicine*, 138, 192–200.

Foucault, M. 1978. *The History of Sexuality*, Vol. 1. London: Penguin.

Foucault, M. 1980. *Power/Knowledge: Selected Interviews and other Writings by Michel Foucault, 1972–77*, ed. C. Gordon. Brighton: Harvester.

References

Foucault, M. 1982. The subject and power. *Critical Inquiry*, 8(4): 777–95.

Fox, S. 2000. Communities of practice, Foucault and actor-network theory. *Journal of Management Studies*, 37(6): 853–68.

Freeman, L. C., 1977. A set of measures of centrality based on betweenness. *Sociometry*, 40(1): 35–41.

French, J. R. P. and Raven, B. 1959. The bases of social power. In D. Cartwright and A. Zander (eds.), *Group Dynamics*, pp. 150–67. New York: Harper and Row.

Frenkel, M. 2005. The politics of translation: How state-level political relations affect the cross-national travel of management ideas. *Organization*, 12(2): 275–301.

Frost, P. 2004. Handling toxic emotions: New challenges for leaders and their organization. *Organizational Dynamics*, 33(2): 111–27.

Fujimura, J. H. 1992. Crafting science: Standardised packages, boundary objects and "translation." In A. Pickering (ed.) *Science as Practice and Culture*, pp. 168–214. Chicago: University of Chicago Press.

Gabbay, J. and Le May, A. 2004. Evidence-based guidelines or collectively constructed mindlines? Ethnographic study of knowledge management in primary care. *British Medical Journal*, 329: 1013.

Gabbay, J. and Le May, A. 2010. *Practice-Based Evidence for Healthcare: Clinical Mindlines*. Abingdon: Routledge.

Gaventa, J. 2003. Power after Lukes: An overview of theories of power since Lukes and their application to development. Available at <http://www.powercube.net/other-forms-of-power/other-forms-of-power-resources/power_after_lukes/> (accessed June 28, 2015).

George, A. L. and Bennett, A. 2005. *Case Studies and Theory Development in the Social Sciences*. Boston, MA: MIT Press.

Gherardi, S. 2000. Practice-based Theorizing on Learning and Knowing in Organizations. *Organization*, 7(2): 211–23.

Gherardi, S. 2006. *Organizational Knowledge: The Texture of Workplace Learning*. Oxford: Blackwell Publishing.

Gherardi, S. 2012. Sociomaterial practices and technological environments. In S. Gherardi (ed.), *How to Conduct a Practice-Based Study: Problems and Methods*, pp. 77–102. Cheltenham: Edward Elgar.

Gherardi, S. and Nicolini, D. 2000. The organizational learning of safety in communities of practice. *Journal of Management Inquiry*, 9(1): 7–18.

Gibson, C. B. and Birkinshaw, J. 2004. The antecedents, consequences, and mediating role of organizational ambidexterity. *Academy of Management Journal*, 47(2): 209–26.

Gino, F. and Pisano, G. 2006. Do managers' heuristics affect R&D performance volatility? A simulation informed by the pharmaceutical industry. Harvard Business School Working Paper.

Gioia, D. A. and Chittipeddi, K. 1991. Sensemaking and sensegiving in strategic change initiation. *Strategic Management Journal*, 12(6): 433–48.

Gittell, J. H. 2001. Supervisory span, relational coordination and flight departure performance: A reassessment of postbureaucracy theory. *Organization Science*, 12(4): 468–83.

Gittell, J. H., Godfrey, M., and Thistlethwaite, J. 2013. Interprofessional collaborative practice and relational coordination: Improving healthcare through relationships. *Journal of Interprofessional Care*, 27(3): 210–13.

Gittell, J. H., Weinberg, D. B., Bennett, A. L., and Miller, J. A. 2008. Is the doctor in? A relational approach to job design and the coordination of work. *Human Resource Management*, 47(4): 729–55.

Gkeredakis, E., Swan, J., and Nicolini, D. 2014. Moral judgements as organizational accomplishments: Insights from a focused ethnography in the English healthcare sector. In F. Cooren, E. Vaara, A. Langley, and H. Tsoukas (eds.), *Language and Communication at Work Discourse, Narrativity, and Organizing*, pp. 293–324. Oxford: Oxford University Press.

Gkeredakis, E., Swan, J., Powell, J., Nicolini, D., Scarborough, H., Roginski, C., Taylor-Phillips, S., and Clark, E. 2011. Mind the gap: Understanding utilisation of evidence and policy in health care management practice. *Journal of Health Organization and Management*, 25(3): 298–314.

Gnyawali, D. R. and Madhavan, R. 2001. Cooperative networks and competitive dynamics: A structural embeddedness perspective. *Academy of Management Review*, 26(3): 431–45.

Golden-Biddle, K., GermAnn, K., Reay, T., and Procyshen, G. 2007. Creating and sustaining positive organizational relationships: A cultural perspective. In J. Dutton and B. Ragins (eds.), *Exploring Positive Relationships at Work: Building a Theoretical and Research Foundation*, pp. 289–305. San Francisco, CA: Berrett-Koehler.

Golden-Biddle, K. and Locke, K. 2007. *Composing Qualitative Research*. Thousand Oaks, CA: Sage.

Grabher, G. 2002. The project ecology of advertising: tasks, talents and teams. *Regional Studies*, 36(3): 245–62.

Grabher, G. 2004. Temporary architectures of learning: Knowledge governance in project ecologies. *Organization Studies*, 25(9): 1491–514.

Grandori, A. and Soda, G. 1995. Inter-firm networks: Antecedents, mechanisms and forms. *Organization Studies*, 16: 184–214.

Gratton, L. and Ghoshal, S. 2002. Improving the quality of conversations. *Organizational Dynamics*, 31(3): 209–23.

Greenhalgh, T. and Wieringa, S. 2011. Is it time to drop the "knowledge translation" metaphor? A critical literature review. *Journal of the Royal Society of Medicine*, 104(12): 501–9.

Greenwood, R., Hinings, C. R., and Suddaby, R. 2002. Theorizing change: The role of professional associations in the transformation of institutional fields. *Academy of Management Journal*, 45(1): 58–80.

Gulati, R. 1995. Does familiarity breed trust? The implications of repeated ties for contractual choice in alliances. *Academy of Management Journal*, 38(1): 85–112.

Guler, I. 2007. Throwing good money after bad: Political and institutional influences on sequential decision making in the venture capital industry. *Administrative Science Quarterly*, 52(2): 248–85.

Gupta, A. K., Smith, K. G., and Shalley, C. E. 2006. The interplay between exploration and exploitation. *Academy of Management Journal*, 49(4): 693–706.

Hackshaw, A., Farrant, H. M., Bulley, S., Seckl, M., and Ledermann, J. 2008. Setting up non-commercial clinical trials takes too long in the UK: Findings from a prospective study. *Journal of the Royal Society of Medicine*, 101(6): 299–304.

References

Hannah, S. T. and Lester, P. B. 2009. A multilevel approach to building and leading learning organizations. *The Leadership Quarterly*, 20: 34–48.

Hansen, M. T. 1999. The search transfer problem: The role of weak ties in sharing knowledge across organizational sub-units. *Administrative Science Quarterly*, 44: 82–111.

Hansen, M. T. 2002. Knowledge networks: Explaining effective knowledge sharing in multiunit companies. *Organization Science*, 13(3): 232–48.

Hardy, C. 1996. Understanding power: Bringing about strategy change. *British Journal of Management*, 7(S1): 3–16.

Hardy, C. and Maguire, S. 2016. Organizing risk: Discourse, power and riskification. *Academy of Management Review*, 41(1): 80–108.

Hardy, C., Phillips, N., and Lawrence, T. B. 2003. Resources, knowledge and influence: The organizational effects of interorganizational collaboration. *Journal of Management Studies*, 40(2): 321–47.

Hardy, C. and Thomas, R. 2014. Strategy, discourses and practice: The intensification of power. *Journal of Management Studies*, 51(2): 320–48.

Hargadon, A. 2003. *How Breakthroughs Happen: The Surprising Truth About How Companies Innovate*. Boston, MA: Harvard Business School Press.

Harvey, G., Skelcher, C., Spencer, E., Jas, P., and Walshe, K. 2010. Absorptive capacity in a non-market environment. *Public Management Review*, 12(1): 77–97.

Hay, M., Thomas, D. W., Craighead, J. L., Economides, C., and Rosenthal, J. 2014. Clinical development success rates for investigational drugs. *Nature Biotechnology*, 32(1): 40–51.

Hellstrom, T. and Hellstrom, C. 2002. Time and innovation in independent technological ventures. *Human Relations*, 55(4): 407–26.

Heracleous, L. and Jacobs, C. D. 2008. Crafting strategy: The role of embodied metaphors. *Long Range Planning*, 41(3): 309–25.

Hislop, D. 2013. *Knowledge Management in Organizations: A Critical Introduction*. Oxford: Oxford University Press.

Hislop, D., Newell, S., Scarbrough, H., and Swan, J. 2000. Networks, knowledge and power: Decision making, politics and the process of innovation. *Technology Analysis and Strategic Management*, 12(3): 399–411.

Hoffer Gittell, J. 2002. Coordinating mechanisms in care provider groups: Relational coordination as a mediator and input uncertainty as a moderator of performance effects. *Management Science*, 48(11): 1408–26.

Holbrook, M. B. and Batra, R. 1987. Assessing the role of emotions as mediators of consumer responses to advertising. *Journal of Consumer Research*, 14(3): 404–20.

Hornby, P. and Symon, G. 1994. *Tracer Studies: Qualitative Methods in Organizational Research: A Practical Guide*. London: Sage.

Hotho, J. J., Becker-Ritterspach, F., and Saka-Helmhout, A. 2012. Enriching absorptive capacity through social interaction. *British Journal of Management*, 23(3): 383–401.

Hunt, P. 2002. Patient safety: A major government priority. In S. Emslie, K. Knox, and M. Pickstone (eds.), *Improving Patient Safety—Insights from American, Australian and British Healthcare. Based on the Proceedings of a Joint ECRI and Department of Health to Introduce the National Patient Safety Agency*, pp. 3–9. Welwyn Garden City: ECRI Europe.

References

Hunter, F. 1963. *Community Power Structure*. Garden City, NY: Anchor Books.

Im, G. and Rai, A. 2008. Knowledge sharing ambidexterity in long-term interorganizational relationships. *Management Science*, 54(7): 1281–96.

Imison, C., Curry, N., and McShane, M. 2011. *Commissioning for the Future: Learning from a Simulation of the Health System in 2013/2014*. London: The King's Fund.

Janis, I. L. 1972. *Victims of Groupthink*. Boston, MA: Houghton Mifflin.

Janssen, O., Van de Vliert, E., and West, M. 2004. The bright and dark sides of individual and group innovation: A special issue introduction. *Journal of Organizational Behavior*, 25(2): 129–45.

Jansen, J. J. P., Van Den Bosch, F., and Volberda, H. W. 2005. Managing potential and realized absorptive capacity: How do organizational antecedents matter? *Academy of Management Journal*, 48(6): 999–1015.

Jansen, J. P., Vera, D., and Crossan, M. 2009. Strategic leadership for exploration and exploitation: The moderating role of environmental dynamism. *The Leadership Quarterly*, 20: 5–18.

Jarzabkowski, P., Bednarek, R., and Spee, P. 2015. *Making a Market for Acts of God: The Practice of Risk Trading in the Global Reinsurance Industry*. Oxford: Oxford University Press.

Johnson, B. and Hagström, B. 2005. The translation perspective as an alternative to the policy diffusion paradigm: The case of the Swedish methadone maintenance treatment, *Journal Social Policy*, 34(3): 365–88.

Kaelber, D.,C. and Bates, D. W. 2007. Health information exchange and patient safety. *Journal of Biomedical Informatics*, 40(6): S40–5.

Kanov, J. M., Maitlis, S., Worline, M. C., Dutton, J. E., Frost, P. J., and Lilius, J. M. 2004. Compassion in organizational life. *American Behavioral Scientist*, 47(6): 808–27.

Kaplan, R. and Norton, D. 1993. Putting the balanced scorecard to work. *Harvard Business Review*, 71(5): 134–47.

Kaplan, S. 2011. Strategy and PowerPoint: An inquiry into the epistemic culture and machinery of strategy-making. *Organization Science*, 22(2): 320–46.

Kepes, S., Bennett, A., and McDaniel, M. 2014. Evidence-based management and the trustworthiness of our cumulative scientific knowledge: Implications for teaching, research and practice. *Academy of Management Education and Learning*, 13(3): 446–66.

Kijkuit, B. and van den Ende, J. 2010. With a little help from our colleagues: A longitudinal study of social networks for innovation. *Organization Studies*, 31(4): 451–79.

Kimble, C., Grenier, C., and Goglio-Primard, K. 2010. Innovation and knowledge sharing across professional boundaries: Political interplay between boundary objects and brokers. *International Journal of Information Management*, 30(5): 437–44.

King's Fund 2011. *The Future of Leadership and Management in the NHS: No More Heroes*. London: The King's Fund.

Kislov, R., Harvey, G., and Walshe, K. 2011. Collaborations for leadership in applied health research and care: Lessons from the theory of communities of practice. *Implementation Science*, 6(64). Available at: <http://www.implementationscience.com/content/pdf/1748-5908-6-64.pdf> (accessed January 18, 2016).

References

Kitsuse, J. I. and Spector, M. 1973. Toward a sociology of social problems: Social conditions, value-judgments, and social problems. *Social Problems*, 20(4): 407–19.

Knorr-Cetina, K. 1999. *Epistemic Cultures: How the Sciences Make Knowledge*. Cambridge MA: Harvard University Press.

Knox, K. 2002. Emerging *lessons from implementing an organisation with a memory*. In S. Emslie, K. Knox, and M. Pickstone (eds.), *Improving Patient Safety—Insights from American, Australian and British healthcare. Based on the proceedings of a joint ECRI and Department of Health to introduce the National Patient Safety Agency*, pp. 21–30. Welwyn Garden City: ECRI Europe.

Kola, I. and Landis, J. 2004. Can the pharmaceutical industry reduce attrition rates? *Nature Reviews Drug Discovery*, 3(8): 711–16.

Kovner, A. R., Fine, D. R., and D'Aquila, R. 2009. *Evidence-Based Management in Healthcare*. Chicago: Health Administration Press.

Kovner, A. R. and Rundall, T. G. 2006. Evidence-based management reconsidered. *Frontiers of Health Services Management*, 22(3): 3–22.

Krackhardt, D. 1992. The strength of strong ties: The importance of philos in organizations. In N. Nohria and R. Eccles (eds.), *Networks and Organizations*, pp. 216–39. Boston, MA: Harvard Business School Press.

Landry, R., Amara, N., and Lamari, M. 2001. Climbing the ladder of research utilization evidence from social science research. *Science Communication*, 22(4): 396–422.

Lane, P. J., Koka, B., and Pathak, S. 2006. The reification of absorptive capacity: A critical review and rejuvenation of the construct. *Academy of Management Review*, 31(4): 833–63.

Lane, P. J. and Lubatkin, M. 1998. Relative absorptive capacity and interorganizational learning. *Strategic Management Journal*, 19(5): 461–77.

Latour, B. 1986. The power of association. In J. Law (ed.), *Power, Action, and Belief: A New Sociology of Knowledge?* London: Routledge and Kegan Paul.

Latour, B. 1994. On technical mediation. *Common Knowledge*, 3(2): 29–64.

Latour, B. 2005. *Reassembling the Social: An Introduction to Actor-Network-Theory*. Oxford: Oxford University Press.

Lave, J. and Wenger, E. 1991. *Situated Learning: Legitimate Peripheral Participation*. Cambridge: Cambridge University Press.

Lavertu, S. and Moynihan, D. 2013. Agency, political ideology and reform implementation: Performance management in the Bush Administration. *Journal of Public Administration Research and Theory*, 23(3): 521–49.

Lavie, D., Stettner, U., and Tushman, M. L. 2010. Exploration and exploitation within and across organizations. *The Academy of Management Annals*, 4(1): 109–55.

Lawrence, T. B., Mauws, M. K., Dyck, B., and Kleysen, R. F. 2005. The politics of organizational learning: Integrating power into the 4I framework. *Academy of Management Journal*, 30(1): 180–91.

Learmonth, M. 2006. Is there such a thing as "evidence-based management"?: A commentary on Rousseau's 2005 presidential address. *Academy of Management Review* 31(4): 1089–91.

References

Learmonth, M. and Harding, N. 2006. Evidence-based management: The very idea. *Public Administration*, 84(2): 245–66.

Levi, M. 2002. Modelling complex historical processes with analytic narratives. In I. R. Mayntz (ed.), *Akteure—Mechanismen—Modelle. Zur Theoriefähigkeit Makro-sozialer Analysen*, pp. 108–27. Frankfurt: Campus Verlag.

Levin, B. 2008. Thinking About Knowledge Mobilization. Paper prepared for an invitational symposium sponsored by the Canadian Council on Learning and the Social Sciences and Humanities Research Council of Canada, Vancouver, May.

Levina, N. 2005. Collaborating on multiparty information systems development projects: A collective reflection-in-action view. *Information Systems Research*, 16(2): 109–30.

Levina, N. and Orlikowski, W. J. 2009. Understanding shifting power relations within and across organizations: A critical genre analysis. *Academy of Management Journal*, 52(4): 672–703.

Levina, N. and Vaast, E. 2005. The emergence of boundary spanning competence in practice: Implications for implementation and use of information systems. *MIS Quarterly*, 29(2): 335–63.

Lewin, A. Y., Long, C. P., and Carroll, T. N. 1999. The coevolution of new organizational forms. *Organization Science*, 10(5): 535–50.

Lindkvist, L. 2003. Knowledge communities and knowledge collectivities. Different notions of group level epistemology. Paper presented at the 19th EGOS Colloquium, Copenhagen Business School, July 3–5.

Locke, K., Golden-Biddle, K., and Feldman, M. 2008. Perspective—making doubt generative: Rethinking the role of doubt in the research process. *Organization Science*, 19(6): 907–18.

Lockett, A., Currie, G., Finn, R., Martin, G., and Waring, J. 2014. The influence of social position on sensemaking about organizational change. *Academy of Management Journal*, 57(4): 1102–29.

Lomas, J. 2007. The in-between world of knowledge brokering. *BMJ*, 334(7585): 129–32.

Lukes, S. 1974. Power: A radical view. In J. Scott (ed.), *Power: Critical Concepts*. New York: Routledge.

McAneney, H., McCann, J., Prior, L., Wilde, J., and Kee, F. 2010. Translating evidence into practice: A shared priority in public health? *Social Science and Medicine*, 70(10): 1492–500.

McDonald, S. 2005. Studying actions in context: A qualitative shadowing method for organisational research. *Qualitative Research*, 5(4): 455–73.

McDonald, S. and Simpson, B. 2014. Shadowing research in organisations: The methodological debates. *Qualitative Research in Organizations and Management: An International Journal*, 9(1): 3–20.

McDonald, M. L. and Westphal, J. D. 2003. Getting by with the advice of their friends: CEOs' advice networks and firms' strategic responses to poor performance. *Administrative Science Quarterly*, 48(1): 1–32.

McEvily, B., Perrone, V., and Zaheer, A. 2003. Trust as an organizing principle. *Organization Science*, 14(1): 91–103.

References

McGivern, G., Currie, G., Ferlie, E., Fitzgerald, L., and Waring, J. 2015. Hybrid manager-professionals' identity work: The maintenance and hybridization of medical professionalism in managerial contexts. *Public Administration*, 93(2): 412–32.

McGivern, G. and Dopson, S. 2010. Inter-epistemic power and transforming knowledge objects in a biomedical network. *Organization Studies*, 31(12): 1667–86.

Maguire, S. and Hardy, C. 2009. Discourse and deinstitutionalization: The decline of DDT. *Academy of Management Journal*, 52(1): 148–78.

Maguire, S., Hardy, C., and Lawrence, T. B. 2004. Institutional entrepreneurship in emerging fields: HIV/AIDS treatment advocacy in Canada. *Academy of Management Journal*, 47(5): 657–79.

Mantere, S. and Ketokivi, M. 2013. Reasoning in organization science. *Academy of Management Review*, 38(1): 70–89.

Marabelli, M., Frigerio, C., and Rajola, F. 2012. Ambidexterity in service organizations: Reference models from the banking industry. *Industry and Innovation*, 19: 109–26.

March, J. G. 1991. Exploration and exploitation in organizational learning. *Organization Science*, 2(1): 71–87.

March, J. G. 1994. *Primer on Decision Making: How Decisions Happen*. New York: Simon and Schuster.

Marshall, N. and Rollinson, J. 2004. Maybe Bacon had a point: The politics of interpretation in collective sensemaking. *British Journal of Management*, 15: S71–86.

Martin, G. P., Currie, G., and Finn, R. 2009. Leadership, service reform, and public-service networks: The case of cancer-genetics pilots in the English NHS. *Journal of Public Administration Research and Theory*, 19(4): 769–94.

Martin, G., Currie, G., and Lockett, A. 2011. Prospects for knowledge exchange in health policy and management: Institutional and epistemic boundaries. *Journal of Health Services Research and Policy*, 16(4): 211–17.

Menz, M. 2012. Functional top management team members: A review, synthesis, and research agenda. *Journal of Management*, 38(1): 45–80.

Meyer, J. W. and Scott, R. W. 1983. *Organizational Environments: Ritual and Rationality*. Beverly Hills, CA: Sage Publications.

Miettinen, R., Samra-Fredericks, D., and Yanow, D. 2009. Re-turn to practice: An introductory essay. *Organization Studies*, 30(12): 1309–27.

Miles, M. B. and Huberman, A. M. 1994. *Qualitative Data Analysis: An Expanded Sourcebook*. Newbury Park, CA: SAGE.

Mintzberg, H. 1973. *The Nature of Managerial Work*. New York: Harper and Row.

Mintzberg, H. 1979. *The Structuring of Organizations*. Englewood Cliffs, NJ: Prentice Hall.

Miron, E., Erez, M., and Naveh, E. 2004. Do personal characteristics and cultural values that promote innovation, quality, and efficiency compete or complement each other? *Journal of Organizational Behavior*, 25(2): 175–99.

Montaner, J. S., O'Shaughnessy, M. V., and Schechter, M. T. 2001. Industry-sponsored clinical research: A double-edged sword. *The Lancet*, 358(9296): 1893–5.

Morrell, K. 2008. The narrative of "evidence based" management: A polemic. *Journal of Management Studies*, 45(3): 613–35.

Morris, T. and Lancaster, Z. 2006. Translating management ideas. *Organization Studies*, 27(2): 207–33.

References

Moynihan, D. P. 2006. Managing for results in state government: Evaluating a decade of reform. *Public Administration Review*, 66(1): 77–89.

Moynihan, D. P. and Hawes, D. 2012. Responsiveness to reform values: the influence of the environment on performance information use. *Public Administration Review*, 72 (S1): 95–105.

Moynihan, D. P. and Landuyt, N. 2009. How do public organizations learn? Bridging cultural and structural perspectives. *Public Administration Review*, 69(6): 1097–105.

Murray, F. 2002. Innovation as co-evolution of scientific and technological networks: exploring tissue engineering. *Research Policy*, 31(8): 1389–403.

Nag, R. and Gioia, D. A. 2012. From common to uncommon knowledge: Foundations of firm-specific use of knowledge as a resource. *Academy of Management Journal*, 55(2): 421–57.

Nambisan, S. and Sawhney, M. 2011. Orchestration processes in network-centric innovation: Evidence from the field. *The Academy of Management Perspectives*, 25: 40–57.

National Audit Office 1996. *HC 82 Session 1996–97, Health and Safety in NHS Acute Hospital Trusts in England*. Available at: <http://www.publications.parliament.uk/pa/cm199798/cmselect/cmpubacc/350ii/pa0203.htm> (accessed January 18, 2016).

Nemanich, L. A. and Vera, D. 2009. Transformational leadership and ambidexterity in the context of an acquisition. *The Leadership Quarterly*, 20(1): 19–33.

Nembhard, A. and Edmondson, A. 2006. Making it safe: The effects of leader inclusiveness and professional status on psychological safety in improvement efforts in healthcare teams. *Journal of Organizational Behavior*, 27: 941–66.

Newell, S., Edelman, L., Scarbrough, H., Swan, J., and Bresnen, M. 2003. "Best practice" development and transfer in the NHS: the importance of process as well as product knowledge. *Health Services Management Research*, 16: 1–12.

Newell, S., Goussevskaia, A., Swan, J., Bresnen, M., and Obembe, A. 2008. Interdependencies in complex project ecologies: The case of biomedical innovation, *Long Range Planning*, 41(1): 33–54.

Nicolini, D. 2009. Zooming in and out: Studying practices by switching theoretical lenses and trailing connections. *Organization Studies*, 30(12): 1391–418.

Nicolini, D. 2010. Medical innovation as a process of translation: A case from the field of telemedicine. *British Journal of Management*, 21(4): 1011–26.

Nicolini, D. 2011. Practice as site of knowing: Insights from the field of telemedicine. *Organization Science*, 21(4): 1–19.

Nicolini, D. 2012. *Practice Theory, Work, and Organization: An Introduction*. Oxford: Oxford University Press.

Nicolini, D., Gherardi, S., and Yanow, D. (eds.) 2003. *Knowing in Organizations: A Practice-Based Approach*. New York: M. E. Sharpe.

Nicolini, D., Korica, M., and Ruddle, K. 2015. Staying in the know. *MIT Sloan Management Review*, Summer: 57–65.

Nicolini, D. and Monteiro, P. 2016. The practice approach: For a praxeology of organizational and management studies. In H. Tsoukas and A. Langley (eds.), *The SAGE Handbook of Process Organization Studies*. London: Sage (forthcoming).

Nicolini, D., Powell, J., and Korica, M. 2014. Keeping knowledgeable: How NHS chief executives mobilise knowledge and information in their daily work. *Health Services*

References

and Delivery Research, 2(26) (August). Available at: <http://www.journalslibrary.nihr.ac.uk/__data/assets/pdf_file/0015/126114/FullReport-hsdr02260.pdf> (accessed January 18, 2016).

Nicolini, D., Scarbrough, H., and Gracheva, J. 2015. Communities of practice and situated learning in healthcare. In E. Ferlie, K. Montgomery, and A. Reff Pedersen (eds.), *Handbook of Health Care Management*. Oxford: Oxford University Press.

Nicolini, D., Waring, J., and Mengis, J. 2011. Policy and practice in the use of root cause analysis to investigate clinical adverse events: Mind the gap. *Social Science and Medicine*, 73(2): 217–25.

Nielsen, J., Mathiassen, L., and Newell, S. 2014. Theorization and translation in IT institutionalization: Evidence from Danish home care. *MIS Quarterly*, 38(1): 165–86.

Nightingale, P. 2000. The product-process-organization relationship in complex development projects. *Research Policy*, 29(7): 913–30.

Nightingale, P. and Martin, P. 2004. The myth of the biotech revolution. *TRENDS in Biotechnology*, 22(11): 564–9.

Nonaka, I. and Konno, N. 1998. The concept of "*ba*": Building a foundation for knowledge creation. *California Management Review*, 40(3): 40–54.

Nonaka, I., Toyama, R., and Byosiere, P. 2001. A theory of organizational knowledge creation: Understanding the dynamic process of creating knowledge. In M. Dierkes, A. Berthoin Antal, J. Child, and I. Nonaka (eds.), *Handbook of Organizational Learning and Knowledge*, pp. 491–517. New York: Oxford University Press.

Nonaka, I., Toyama, R., and Konno, N. 2000. SECI, *Ba*, and leadership: A unified model of dynamic knowledge creation. *Long Range Planning*, 33: 5–34.

Oborn, E., Barrett, M., Prince, K., and Racko, G. 2013. Balancing exploration and exploitation in transferring research into practice: A comparison of five knowledge translation entity archetypes. *Implementation Science*, 8(1): 104. Available at: <http://www.implementationscience.com/content/pdf/1748-5908-8-104.pdf> (accessed January 18, 2016).

Oborn, E., Barrett, M., and Racko, G. 2010. Knowledge translation in healthcare: A review of the literature. Cambridge Judge Business School Working Paper Series No. 5. Available at: <https://www.jbs.cam.ac.uk/fileadmin/user_upload/research/workingpapers/wp1005.pdf> (accessed December 30, 2015).

Oborn, E., Barrett, M., and Racko, G. 2013. Knowledge translation in healthcare: Incorporating theories of learning and knowledge from the management literature. *Journal of Health Organization Management*, 27(4): 412–31.

Oborn, E. and Dawson, S. 2010. Knowledge and practice in multidisciplinary teams: Struggle, accommodation and privilege. *Human Relations*, 63(12): 1835–57.

Obstfeld, D. 2005. Social networks, the tertius iungens orientation, and involvement in innovation. *Administrative Science Quarterly*, 50(1): 100–30.

Oliver, A. L. and Ebers, M. 1998. Networking network studies: An analysis of conceptual configurations in the study of inter-organizational relationships. *Organization Studies*, 19(4): 549–83.

Orlikowski, W. and Yates, J. 2002. It's about time: Temporal structuring in organizations. *Organization Science*, 13(6): 684–700.

References

Orlikowski, W. J. 2002. Knowing in practice: Enacting a collective capability in distributed organizing. *Organization Science*, 13(3): 249–73.

Øvretveit, J. 2005. *Effectiveness of Interventions to Improve Patient Safety: A Review of Research and Guidance*. Stockholm: Karolinska Institute.

Owen-Smith, J. and Powell, W. W. 2004. Knowledge networks as channels and conduits: The effects of spillovers in Boston biotechnology community. *Organizational Science*, 15(1): 5–21.

Owen-Smith, J., Riccaboni, M., Pammolli, F., and Powell, W. 2002. A comparison of US and European university-industry relations in the life sciences. *Management Science*, 48(1): 24–43.

Pavitt, K. 1984. Sectoral patterns of technical change: Towards a taxonomy and a theory. *Research Policy*, 13(6): 343–73.

Penley, L. E., Alexander, E. R., Jernigan, I. E., and Henwood, C. I. 1991. Communication abilities of managers: The relationship to performance. *Journal of Management*, 17(1): 57–76.

Pennebaker, J. W. 2011. The secret life of pronouns. *New Scientist*, 211(2828): 42–5.

Pettigrew, K. E. 1999. Waiting for chiropody: Contextual results from an ethnographic study of the information behaviour among attendees at community clinics. *Information Processing and Management*, 35(6): 801–17.

Pfeffer, J. 1981. *Power in Organizations*. Cambridge, MA: Ballinger.

Pfeffer, J. and Salancik, G. R. 1974. Organizational decision making as a political process: The case of a university budget. *Administrative Science Quarterly*, 19(2): 135–51.

Pfeffer, J. and Salancik, G. 1978. *The External Control of Organizations: A Resource Dependence Perspective*. New York: Harper and Row.

Pfeffer, J. and Sutton, R. I. 2006. Evidence-based management. *Harvard Business Review*, 84(1): 62–74.

PhRMA 2015. *Biopharmaceutical Research Industry Profile*. Pharmaceutical Research and Manufacturers of America. Washington, DC: PhRMA.

Pisano, G. 2006. Can science be a business? Lessons from biotech. *Harvard Business Review*, October: 114–25.

Pisano, G. 2010. The evolution of science-based business: Innovating how we innovate. *Industrial and Corporate Change*, 19(2): 465–82.

Pittinsky, T. L. and Shih, M. J. 2004. Knowledge nomads. *American Behavioral Scientist*, 47(6): 791–807.

Pitsis, T., Clegg, S., Marosszeky, M., and Rura-Polley, T. 2003. Constructing the Olympic dream: A future perfect strategy of project management. *Organization Science*, 14(5): 574–90.

Polanyi, M. 1962. *Personal Knowledge: Toward a Post-Critical Philosophy*. Chicago: University of Chicago Press.

Porter, K., Whittington, K. B., and Powell, W. W. 2005. The institutional embeddedness of high-tech regions: Relational foundations of the Boston biotechnology community. In S. Breschi and F. Malebra (eds.), *Clusters, Networks, and Innovation*, pp. 261–94. Oxford: Oxford University Press.

Powell, W. W., Koput, K., and Smith-Doerr, L. 1996. Interorganization collaboration and the locus of innovation: Networks of learning in biotechnology. *Administrative Science Quarterly*, 1: 116–45.

References

Power, M. 2007. *Organized Uncertainty: Designing a World of Risk Management*. Oxford: Oxford University Press.

Prince, K., Barrett, M., and Oborn, E. 2014. Dialogical strategies for orchestrating strategic innovation networks: The case of the internet of things. *Information and Organization*, 24(2): 106–27.

Quinn, R. and Dutton, J. 2005. Coordination as energy-in-conversation. *Academy of Management Review*, 30(1): 36–57.

Rafaeli, A. and Vilnai-Yavetz, I. 2004. Emotion as a connection of physical artifacts and organizations. *Organization Science*, 15(6): 671–86.

Reagans, R. and McEvily, B. 2003. Network structure and knowledge transfer: The effects of cohesion and range. *Administrative Science Quarterly*, 48(2): 240–67.

Reagans, R. and McEvily, B. 2008. Contradictory or compatible? Reconsidering the "trade-off" between brokerage and closure on knowledge sharing. *Advances in Strategic Management*, 25: 275–313.

Reason, J. 1995. Understanding adverse events: Human factors. *Quality in Health Care*, 4(2): 80–9.

Reay, T., Berta, W., and Kazman-Kohn, M. 2009. What is the evidence on evidence-based management? *Academy of Management Perspectives*, 23(4): 5–18.

Rich, R. F. 1991. Knowledge creation, diffusion, and utilization—Perspectives of the founding editor of knowledge. *Knowledge-Creation Diffusion Utilization*, 12(3): 319–37.

Rich, R. F. 1997. Measuring knowledge utilization: Processes and outcomes. *Knowledge and Policy*, 10(3): 11–24.

Rich, R. F. and Oh, C. H. 2000. Rationality and use of information in policy decisions: A search for alternatives. *Science Communication*, 22(2): 173–211.

Rifkin, J. 1987. *Time Wars*. New York: Holt.

Rivkin, J. W. and Siggelkow, N. 2003. Balancing search and stability: Interdependencies among elements of organizational design. *Management Science*, 49(3): 290–311.

Robertson, M., Swan, J., and Newell, S. 1996. The role of networks in the diffusion of technological innovation. *Journal of Management Studies*, 33(3): 333–60.

Rodriguez, C., Langley, A., Beland, F., and Denis, J. 2007. Governance, power, and mandated collaboration in an interorganizational network. *Administration and Society*, 39(2): 150–93.

Rogers, E. 1995. *Diffusion of Innovations*. 3rd edition. New York: Free Press.

Rogers, E. M. 2003. *Diffusion of Innovations*. 5th edition. New York: Simon and Schuster.

Rousseau, D. 2006. Is there such a thing as "evidence-based management"? *Academy of Management Review*, 31(2): 256–69.

Rousseau, D. 2012. *The Oxford Handbook of Evidence-Based Management*. Oxford: Oxford University Press.

Rousseau, D., Manning, J., and Denyer, D. 2008. Evidence in management and organizational science: Assembling the field's full weight of scientific knowledge through syntheses. *The Academy of Management Annals*, 2(1): 475–515.

Rousseau, D. M. and McCarthy, S. 2007. Educating managers from an evidence-based perspective. *Academy of Management Learning and Education*, 6(1): 84–101.

Runciman, B. and Walton, M. 2007. *Safety and Ethics in Healthcare: A Guide to Getting it Right*. Aldershot: Ashgate Publishing.

References

Runciman, W. B. 2002. Lessons from the Australian patient safety foundation: setting up a national patient safety surveillance system—is this the right model? *Quality and Safety in Health Care*, 11(3): 246–51.

Ryle, G. 1949/2009. *The Concept of Mind*. Abingdon: Routledge. Original edition, 1949.

Sackett, D. L., Rosenberg, W. M., Gray, J. A., Haynes, R. B., and Richardson, W. S. 1996. Evidence based medicine: what it is and what it isn't. *British Medical Journal*, 312 (7023): 71.

Sahlin, K. and Wedlin, L. 2008. Circulating ideas: Imitation, translation and editing. In R. Greenwood, C. Oliver, K. Sahlin, and R. Suddaby (eds.), *The Sage Handbook of Organizational Institutionalism*, pp. 218–42. London: Sage.

Sahoo, A. 2007. Patient recruitment and retention in clinical trials. Emerging strategies in the US, Europe and Asia. Business Insights Limited, June, p. 149. Report No.: RBI00152.

Saint-Martin, D. 2004. *Building the New Managerialist State: Consultants and the Politics of Public Sector Reform in Comparative Perspective*. Oxford: Oxford University Press.

Salge, T. O. 2011. A behavioural model of innovative search: Evidence from public hospital services. *Journal of Public Administration Research and Theory*, 21(1): 181–210.

Salge, T. O. and Vera, A. 2009. Hospital innovativeness and organizational performance: Evidence from English public acute care. *Health Care Management Review*, 34(1): 54–67.

Salge, T. O. and Vera, A. 2012. Benefiting from public sector innovation: The moderating role of customer and learning orientation. *Public Administration Review*, 72(4): 550–60.

Sandberg, J., Johnson, L., Robila, M., and Miller, R. 2002. Clinician identified barriers to clinical research. *Journal of Marriage Family Therapy*, 28(1): 61–7.

Sandberg, J. and Tsoukas, H. 2011. Grasping the logic of practice: Theorising through practical rationality. *Academy of Management Review*, 36(2): 338–60.

Sandelowski, M. 1993. Rigor or rigor mortis: The problem of rigor in qualitative research revisited. *Advances in Nursing Science*, 16(2): 1–8.

Savolainen, R. 2007. Information behavior and information practice: Reviewing the "umbrella concepts" of information-seeking studies. *The Library Quarterly*, 77(2): 109–32.

Scarbrough, H., D'Andreta, D., Evans, S., Marabelli, M., Newell, S., Powell, J., and Swan, J. 2014. Networked innovation in the health sector: comparative qualitative study of the role of Collaborations for Leadership in Applied Health Research and Care in translating research into practice. *Health Services Delivery Research*, 2(13). Available at: <http://www.journalslibrary.nihr.ac.uk/hsdr/volume-2/issue-13#abstract> (accessed January 18, 2016).

Scarbrough, H., Robertson, M., and Swan, J. 2015. Diffusion in the face of failure: The evolution of a management innovation. *British Journal of Management*, 26(3): 365–87.

Scarbrough, H. and Swan, J. 2001. Explaining the diffusion of knowledge management: The role of fashion. *British Journal of Management*, 12(1): 3–12.

Schatzki, T. 2012. A primer on practices: Theory and research. In J. Higgs, R. Barnett, S. Billett, M. Hutchings, and F. Trede (eds.), *Practice-based Education: Perspectives and Strategies*, pp. 13–26. Rotterdam: Sense Publishers.

Schatzki, T. R., Knorr-Cetina, K., and Savigny, E. V. 2001. *The Practice Turn in Contemporary Theory*. London: Routledge.

References

Schein, E. 1969. *Process Consultation—Its Role in Organizational Development*. New York: Prentice Hall.

Schultze, U. 2000. A confessional account of an ethnography about knowledge work. *MIS Quarterly*, 24(1): 1–39.

Shankar, P. R. and Subish, P. 2007. Disease mongering. *Singapore Medical Journal*, 48(4): 275–80.

Shipilov, A. V. and Li, S. X. 2008. Can you have your cake and eat it too? Structural holes' influence on status accumulation and market performance in collaborative networks. *Administrative Science Quarterly*, 53(1): 73–108.

Simsek, Z. 2009. Organizational ambidexterity: Towards a multilevel understanding. *Journal of Management Studies*, 46(4): 597–624.

Smith, C. and O'Donnell, J. 2006. *The Process of New Drug Discovery and Development* (2nd edition). New York: Informa Healthcare USA Inc.

Smith, J., Regen, E., Shapiro, J., and Baines, D. 2000. National evaluation of general practitioner commissioning pilots: Lessons for primary care groups. *British Journal of General Practice*, 50(455): 469–72.

Smith, K. G., Collins, C. J., and Clark, K. D. 2005. Existing knowledge, knowledge creation capability, and the rate of new product introduction in high-technology firms. *Academy of Management Journal*, 48: 346–57.

Solomon, R. C. and Flores, F. 2003. *Building Trust—In Business, Politics, Relationships, and Life*. Oxford: Oxford University Press.

Spender, G. 2008. Organizational learning and knowledge management: Whence and whither? *Management Learning*, 39(2): 159–76.

Spreitzer, G., Sutcliffe, K., Dutton, J., Sonenshein, S., and Grant, A. M. 2005. A socially embedded model of thriving at work. *Organization Science*, 16(5): 537–49.

Stadler, C., Rajwani, T., and Karaba, F. 2014. Solutions to the exploration/exploitation dilemma: Networks as a new level of analysis. *International Journal of Management Reviews*, 16: 172–93.

Star, S. L. and Griesemer, J. R. 1989. Institutional ecology, "translations" and boundary objects: Amateurs and professionals in Berkeley's Museum of Vertebrate Zoology, 1907–39. *Social Studies of Science*, 19(3): 387–420.

State Government Victoria, Department of Health. 2014. Lessons from the sentinel event case book. *RiskWatch* newsletter, 11(4): 1–2.

Stein, M., Newell, S., Wagner, E. L., and Galliers, R. D. 2014. Felt quality of sociomaterial relations: Introducing emotions into sociomaterial theorizing. *Information and Organization*, 24(3): 156–75.

Stewart, R. 1984. The nature of management? A problem for management education. *Journal of Management Studies*, 21(3): 323–30.

Strang, D. and Soule, S. A. 1998. Diffusion in organizations and social movements: From hybrid corn to poison pills. *Annual Review of Sociology*, 24: 265–90.

Strauss, A. L. and Corbin, J. 1998. *Basics of Qualitative Research* (2nd edition). Thousand Oaks, CA: Sage.

Sturdy, A. 2004. The adoption of management ideas and practices: Theoretical perspectives and possibilities. *Management Learning*, 35(2): 155–79.

References

Styhre, A. 2006. Science-based innovation as systematic risk-taking: The case of new drug development. *European Journal of Innovation Management*, 9(3): 300–11.

Styhre, A., Wikmalm, L., Olilla, S., and Roth, J. 2010. Garbage-can decision making and the accommodation of uncertainty in new drug development work. *Creativity and Innovation Management*, 19(2): 134–46.

Sveningsson, S. and Alvesson, M. 2003. Managing managerial identities: Organizational fragmentation, discourse and identity struggle. *Human Relations*, 56(10): 1163–94.

Swan, J., Bresnen, M., Newell, S., and Robertson, M. 2007a. The object of knowledge: the role of objects in biomedical innovation. *Human Relations*, 60(12): 1809–37.

Swan, J., Bresnen, M., Robertson, M., Newell, S., and Dopson, S. 2010. When policy meets practice: Colliding logics and the challenges of "Mode 2" initiatives in the translation of academic knowledge. *Organization Studies*, 31(9–10): 1311–40.

Swan, J., Clarke, A., Nicolini, D., Powell, J., Scarbrough, H., Roginski, C., Gkeredakis, E., Mills, P., and Taylor-Phillips, S. 2012. Evidence in Management Decisions (EMD)—Advancing Knowledge Utilization in Healthcare Management. NIHR Service and Delivery Research Programme. Final report. Available at: <http://www.netscc.ac.uk/hsdr/files/project/SDO_FR_08-1808-244_V01.pdf> (accessed January 18, 2016).

Swan, J., Goussevskaia, A., Newell, S., Robertson, M., Bresnen, M., and Obembe, A. 2007b. Modes of organizing biomedical innovation in the UK and US and the role of integrative and relational capabilities. *Research Policy*, 36(4): 529–47.

Swan, J., Robertson, M., and Evans, S. 2009. *Managing Clinical Research in the UK*. WIMRC Report. Coventry: University of Warwick.

Swan, J., Robertson, M., and Newell, S. 2016. Dynamic in-capabilities: The paradox of routines in the ecology of complex innovation. In J. Howard-Grenville, C. Rerup, A. Langley, and H. Tsoukas (eds.), *Organizational Routines: How they are Created, Maintained, and Changed (Perspectives on Process Organization Studies)*, vol. 6. Oxford: Oxford University Press.

Swan, J. and Scarbrough, H. 2005. The politics of networked innovation. *Human Relations*, 58(7): 913–43.

Swan, J., Scarbrough, H., and Newell, S. 2010. Why don't (or do) organizations learn from projects? *Management Learning*, 41(3): 325–44.

Swan, J., Scarbrough, H., and Robertson, M. 2003. The construction of "communities of practice", in the management of innovation. *Management Learning*, 33(4): 477–96.

Swan, J. A., Newell, S., and Robertson, M. 1995. The role of professional associations in technology diffusion. *Organization Studies*, 16(5): 847–74.

Swanson, E. B. 2012. The manager's guide to IT innovation waves. *MIT Sloan Management Review*, 53(2): 74–83.

Swanson, E. B. and Ramiller, N. C. 1997. The organizing vision in information systems innovation. *Organization Science*, 8(5): 458–74.

Szulanski, G. 1996. Exploring internal stickiness: Impediments to the transfer of best practice within the firm. *Strategic Management Journal*, 17(S2): 27–43.

Szulanski, G. 2000. The process of knowledge transfer: A diachronic analysis of stickiness. *Organizational Behavior and Human Decision Processes*, 82(1): 9–27.

Taylor, R. S. 1986. *Value-added Processes in Information Systems*. Norwood, NJ: Ablex Publishing Corporation.

References

Thomas, R., Hardy, C., and Sargent, L. D. 2007. Artifacts in interaction: the production and politics of boundary objects. Advanced Institute of Management. Research Paper No. 052.

Thomson, L., Schneider, J., and Wright, N. 2013. Developing communities of practice to support the implementation of research into clinical practice. *Leadership in Health Services*, 26(1): 20–33.

Thrift, N. 2008. *Non-representational Theory: Space, Politics, Affect*. London: Routledge.

Thüring, M. and Mahlke, S. 2007. Usability, aesthetics and emotions in human–technology interaction. *International Journal of Psychology*, 42(4): 253–64.

Timmermans, S. and Berg, M. 2003. *The Gold Standard: The Challenges of Evidence-Based Medicine and Standardization in Healthcare*. Philadelphia, PA: Temple University Press.

Todorova, G. and Durisin, B. 2007. Absorptive capacity: Valuing a reconceptualization. *Academy of Management Review*, 32(3): 774–86.

Tortoriello, M. and Krackhardt, D. 2010. Activating cross-boundary knowledge: The role of Simmelian ties in the generation of innovations. *Academy of Management Journal*, 53(1): 167–81.

Trinh, K. C. W. and Mitchell, W. 2009. Talk, think, read (if absolutely necessary): The impact of social, personal, and documentary knowledge on task performance. *European Management Review*, 6(1): 29–44.

Tsai, W. 2002. Social structure of "coopetition" within a multiunit organization: Coordination, competition, and intraorganizational knowledge sharing. *Organization Science*, 13(2): 179–90.

Tucker, A., Nembhard, A., and Edmondson, A. 2007. Implementing new practices: An empirical study of organizational learning in hospital intensive care units. *Management Science*, 53(6): 894–907.

Tuominen, K., Savolainen, R., and Talja, S. 2005. Information literacy as a sociotechnical practice. *Library Quarterly*, 75(3): 329–45.

Turner, N., Swart, J., and Maylor, H. 2013. Mechanisms for managing ambidexterity: A review and research agenda. *International Journal of Management Reviews*, 15(3): 317–32.

Tushman, M. L. and O'Reilly, C. A., III. 1996. Ambidextrous organizations: Managing evolutionary and revolutionary change. *California Management Review*, 38(4): 8–30.

Uzzi, B. 1997. Social structure and competition in interfirm networks: The paradox of embeddedness. *Administrative Science Quarterly*, 42(1): 35–67.

Vaara, E. and Whittington, R. 2012. Strategy-as-practice: Taking social practices seriously. *The Academy of Management Annals*, 6(1): 285–336.

Van de Ven, A. H. and Hargrave, T. J. 2004. *Social, Technical, and Institutional Change*. Oxford: Oxford University Press.

Van Den Bosch, F. A. J., Volberda, H., and de Boer, M. 1999. Coevolution of form absorptive capacity and knowledge environment: Organizational forms and combinative capabilities. *Organization Science*, 10(5): 551–68.

van Fraassen, B. 2002. *The Empirical Stance*. Yale: Yale University Press.

Vincent, C. A. 2004. Analysis of clinical incidents: a window on the system not a search for root causes. *Quality and Safety in Health Care*, 13(4): 242–3.

Vincent, C. A., Taylor-Adams, S., and Stanhope, N. 1998. A framework for the analysis of risk and safety in medicine, *British Medical Journal*, 316: 1–154.

References

Volberda, H. W., Foss, N., and Lyles, M. 2010. Absorbing the concept of absorptive capacity: How to realize its potential in the organization field. *Organization Science*, 21(4): 931–51.

Von Hippel, E. A. and Von Krogh, G. 2006. Free revealing and the private-collective model for innovation incentives. *R&D Management*, 36(3): 295–306.

Wald, H. and Shojania, K. G. 2001. Root cause analysis. In K. G. Shojania, B. Duncan, K. Mc Donald, R. Wachter, and A. J. Markowitz (eds.), *Making Health Care Safer: A Critical Analysis of Patient Safety Practices*. Evidence Report/Technology Assessment No. 43, AHRQ Publications.

Walsham, G. 1993. *Interpreting Information Systems in Organizations*. Chichester: Wiley.

Walsham, G. 2006. Doing interpretive research. *European Journal of Information Systems*, 15(3): 320–30.

Walshe, K. and Davies, H. T. 2013. Health research, development and innovation in England from 1988 to 2013: From research production to knowledge mobilization. *Journal of Health Services Research and Policy*, 18(3 suppl): 1–12.

Walshe, K., Harvey, G., Jas, P., and Skelcher, C. 2009. Responding to evidence of poor performance: Explaining public organization's capacity to deal with failure. ESRC End of Award Report, RES-166-25-0020. Swindon: ESRC.

Walshe, K. and Rundall, T. G. 2001. Evidence-based management: from theory to practice in health care. *The Milbank Quarterly*, 79(3): 429–57.

Ward, V., House, A., and Hamer, S. 2009. Knowledge brokering: The missing link in the evidence to action chain? *Evidence and Policy: A Journal of Research, Debate and Practice*, 5(3): 267–79.

Ward, V., Smith, S., House, A., and Hamer, S. 2011. Exploring knowledge exchange: A useful framework for practice and policy. *Social Science and Medicine*, 74(3): 297–304.

Waring, J. and Currie, G. 2009. Managing expert knowledge: Organizational challenges and managerial futures for the UK medical profession. *Organization Studies*, 30(7): 755–78.

Waring, J., Currie, G., Crompton, A., and Bishop, S. 2013. An exploratory study of knowledge brokering in hospital settings: Facilitating knowledge sharing and learning for patient safety? *Social Science and Medicine*, 98: 79–86.

Wears, R. L., Perry, S. J., and Sutcliffe, K. M. 2005. The medicalization of patient safety. *Journal of Patient Safety*, 1(1): 4–6.

Weick, K. E. 2005. Organizing and failures of imagination. *International Public Management Journal*, 8(3): 425–38.

Weick, K. E. and Quinn, R. E. 1999. Organizational change and development. *Annual Review of Psychology*, 50(1): 361–86.

Weick, K. E., Sutcliffe, K. M., and Obstfeld, D. 2005. Organizing and the process of sensemaking. *Organization Science*, 16(4): 409–21.

Wenger, E. 1998. *Communities of Practice—Learning, Meaning and Identity*. Cambridge: Cambridge University Press.

West, E., Barron, D. N., Dowsett, J., and Newton, J. N. 1999. Hierarchies and cliques in the social networks of health care professionals: Implications for the design of dissemination strategies. *Social Science and Medicine*, 48(5): 633–46.

References

Whittington, K. B., Owen-Smith, J., and Powell, W. W. 2009. Networks, propinquity, and innovation in knowledge-intensive industries. *Administrative Science Quarterly*, 54(1): 90–122.

Williams, A. P. O. 2001. A belief-focused process model of organizational learning. *Journal of Management Studies*, 38(1): 67–85.

Wilson, R. M., Harrison, B. T., Gibberd, R. W., and Hamilton, J. D. 1999. An analysis of the causes of adverse events from the quality in Australian health care study. *The Medical Journal of Australia*, 170(9): 411–15.

Wilson, R. M., Runciman, W. B., Gibberd, R. W., Harrison, B. T., Newby, L., and Hamilton, J. D. 1995. The quality in Australian health care study. *Medical Journal of Australia*, 163(9): 458–71.

Winnicott, D. W. 1971. *Playing and Reality*. London: Tavistock/Routledge.

Woloshynowych, M., Rogers, S., Taylor-Adams, S., and Vincent, C. 2005. The investigation and analysis of critical incidents and adverse events in healthcare. *Health Technology Assessment*, 9(19): 1–155.

World Health Organization 2010. *Framework for Action on Interprofessional Education and Collaborative Practice*. Geneva: WHO.

Wu, A. W., Lipshutz, A. K., and Pronovost, P. M. 2008. Effectiveness and efficiency of root cause analysis in medicine, *JAMA*, 299(6): 685–7.

Yanow, D. 2004. Translating local knowledge at organizational peripheries. *British Journal of Management*, 15: S9–25.

Yanow, D. and Schwartz-Shea, P. (eds.) 2006. *Interpretation and Method: Empirical Research Methods and the Interpretive Turn*. Armonk, NY: M. E. Sharpe.

Yin, R. 2003. *Case Study Research—Design and Methods* (3rd edition). Thousand Oaks, CA: Sage.

Zachariadis, M., Oborn, E., Barrett, M., and Zollinger-Read, P. 2013. Leadership of healthcare commissioning networks in England: a mixed-methods study on clinical commissioning groups. *British Medical Journal Open*, 3(2): e002112.

Zahra, S. A. and George, G. 2002. Absorptive capacity: A review, reconceptualization, and extension. *Academy of Management Review*, 27(2): 185–203.

Zbaracki, M. 1998. The rhetoric and reality of total quality management. *Administrative Science Quarterly*, 43(3): 602–36.

Zider, B. 1998. How venture capital works. *Harvard Business Review*, November: 38–44.

Zmud, R. W. 1978. An empirical investigation of the dimensionality of the concept of information. *Decision Sciences*, 9(2): 187–95.

General Index

abductive research 48
absorptive capacity 14, 61, 62, 66
  Clinical Commissioning
    acquisition of data 69–71, 80
    assimilation of evidence 71–2, 80
    exploitation process 74–6, 80
    GP involvement 73–4, 78, 80
    professionalized context 78, 80
    tracer study 68–9
    transformation processes 73–4, 80
  combinative capabilities 65, 66, 67, 68, 69, 76, 80
  conceptual outline 67–8
  coordination capabilities 65, 66, 67–8, 69, 70, 71, 74, 76, 79, 80, 81
  healthcare context 62, 79
  organizational learning *see* organizational learning
  potential vs. realized absorptive capacity 67
  socialization capabilities 65, 69, 72, 73, 76, 77, 78, 79, 80
  systems capabilities 65, 69, 75, 76, 77, 78, 79, 80
acquisition of data 69–71, 80
agency 3, 4, 9–10, 15, 224–5
ambidexterity *see* network ambidexterity
anxiety-reassurance 16, 177, 180, 194–6
assimilation of evidence 71–2, 80
authorization culture 87

ba 84, 85, 86, 89, 98
balanced scorecard 29, 30
best available information 4
best-practice transfer 21
big data integration 120, 228
BIOTECH 204–6, 207, 208, 209, 210, 213, 216, 217
brokerage 151, 152, 160–3, 164–9
  see also knowledge brokers
bureaucracy 77–8

Canada
  Dooly Hospital 132, 136–7, 147–50
    analysis of findings 142–7
    data collection 137–8
    from conception to start of pilot project (2008–10) 138–9
    pilot project (April 1, 2010–April 1, 2015) 139–42
    power in everyday practice 133–6, 142–6
  SEARCH *see* SEARCH Canada
CCGs *see* Clinical Commissioning Groups
Chief Executive Officers (CEOs) 14, 20–1, 149–50
  accountability 43, 59
  Dooly Hospital, Canada 141–2
  epistemic fit 30, 31, 32, 39
  healthcare settings 43
  information work 41–3
    academic interest in 44–5
    active information seeking 53
    centrality 58
    deliberate and non-directed heedful monitoring 54–5
    ethnographic study 47–9
    external sources of information 49–53
    keeping "in the know" 44, 56, 57, 58–9, 60
    monitoring practices 53–6
    unanticipated finding 55–6
CLAHRCs *see* Collaborations for Leadership in Applied Health Research and Care
Clinical Commissioning Groups (CCGs) 31, 66, 226, 229
  absorptive capacity
    acquisition of data 69–71, 80
    assimilation of evidence 71–2, 80
    exploitation process 74–6, 80
    GP involvement 73–4, 78, 80
    professionalized context 78, 80
    tracer study 68–9
    transformation processes 73–4, 80
clinical-managers 26
clinical trials 175, 199–200
  ecology of clinical research projects 201–4, 219–22
  institutionalized practices across the ecology 207–9
  landscape of innovation ecology 206–11
  local project and lead firm practices 209–11
  timescapes of the innovation ecology 211–19

General Index

clinical trials (*cont.*)
   empirical studies: BIOTECH 204–6, 207, 208, 209, 210, 213, 216, 217
   finance and further investment 209–10
closure 151, 152, 156, 160–3, 163–4
coaching 30–1, 100
Collaborations for Leadership in Applied Health Research and Care (CLAHRCs) 10, 12, 16, 34, 115–16, 127, 129, 151, 153, 158–9
   balancing competing priorities 118–19
   interplay between formal organization and social structures 163–9, 171
   managing engagement 116–18
   managing funding 118
   managing knowledge politics 119–20
   network ambidexterity 160–3, 170–1
   social network analysis 159–60
combinative capabilities 65, 66, 67, 68, 69, 76, 80
commissioners *see* Clinical Commissioning Groups
communities of practice 156
Cooksey Report 1
coordination capabilities 65, 66, 67–8, 69, 70, 71, 74, 76, 79, 80, 81
creativity 108
cultural fit 25
culture 25, 35, 62, 77, 79, 80, 86, 87, 96, 110, 114, 127, 129, 134, 136
   coaching culture 30–1
   epistemic culture 20, 24, 25, 26, 27, 29, 30, 31, 32, 33, 34, 35
   evidence-based culture 13
   research culture 8
   secrecy 187

data analytic tools 122, 138, 228
   legacy technologies 126
data collection 69–71, 80, 137–8
data privacy 121
decision-makers 80
diffusion 25–7, 174, 178, 179, 191, 202
drug development 16, 199–200, 211
   see also clinical trials

ecology 203
   clinical research projects 201–4, 219–22
      institutionalized practices across the ecology 207–9
   landscape of innovation ecology 206–11
   local project and lead firm practices 209–11
   timescape of the innovation ecology 211–19
   ecological modes of healthcare innovation 220
   nested ecology 3, 10–11, 14, 16, 19, 225–6
   see also timescapes
emotions 144–5, 149
epistemic clashes 26

epistemic collectivity 207
epistemic communities 27, 77, 207
epistemic cultures 20, 24, 25, 26, 27, 29, 30, 31, 32, 33, 34, 35
epistemic fit 13, 23–5
   case studies 29
      AHSC 30–1
      CLAHRC 34–5
      health policy think tank 34
      independent charitable trust providing specialist clinical services 29–30
      key features of management knowledge mobilization 35–7
      management consultancy 32–4
      PCT 31–2
      role of knowledge brokers 38–9
   diffusion, adaptation, and fit of management knowledge 25–7
epistemic logics 207
epistemic machinery 142
epistemic stances 13, 23, 24, 25, 27
epistemology of possession 6
epistemology of practice 6
evidence-based management 1, 5, 13, 19–20, 24
   quality of the evidence 53
evidence-based medicine 1, 4, 6, 19, 24
experiential knowledge 70
exploitation process 74–6, 80

feedback 75

generative space 83, 89, 91, 229
   assembling the right people 91–3
   developing positive social relationships 93–5
   focusing the conversation 95–6
   managing setbacks and frustrations 96–7
ghost in the machine 178, 196–7
GPs 73–4, 78, 80

healthcare commissioners *see* Clinical Commissioning Groups
healthcare networks *see* inter-organizational healthcare networks

identity work 26
implementation science 5
incident investigation 177, 181, 183, 184, 188, 189, 190
   human factor 186–7
   see also Root Cause Analysis
inert space 83, 89–90
information sources 49–53
innovation 16, 108
   diffusion 174, 178, 179, 191, 202
   drug development 16, 199–200, 202
   see also clinical trials

258

General Index

ecological model of healthcare innovation 220
literature review 109–11
mediation 180
R & D vs. networked innovation 202–3
standardized theory-method package 196
territorial innovation 203
transformation 73–4, 80, 175, 179
translation 178, 179, 191, 197
institutional context 174
intermediation 180
inter-organizational action 15, 63
inter-organizational healthcare networks 107–9, 111, 126–8, 132–3
 Canada: Dooly Hospital 132, 136–7, 147–50
  analysis of findings 142–7
  data collection 137–8
  from conception to start of pilot project (2008–10) 138–9
  pilot project (April 1, 2010–April 1, 2015) 139–42
  power in everday practice 133–6, 143
  see also SEARCH Canada
 CLAHRCs UK 10, 12, 16, 34, 115–16, 127, 129, 151, 153, 158–9
  balancing competing priorities 118–19
  interplay between formal organization and social network structures 163–9, 171
  managing engagement 116–18
  managing funding 118
  managing knowledge politics 119–20
  network ambidexterity 160–3
  social network analysis 159–60
 SEARCH Canada 111–12, 127, 128–9
  balancing competing priorities 114–15
  managing engagement 112–13
  managing funding 113–14
  managing knowledge politics 115
 TechFirm 120, 127, 129–30
  balancing competing priorities 124–5
  managing engagement 121–3
  managing funding 123–4
  managing knowledge politics 125–6

knowing-doing gap 1, 2, 6, 107, 152
knowledge brokers 24, 26, 31, 35, 38–9, 151, 155–6, 164, 166–8, 170
knowledge mobilization 2, 223–4
 absorptive capacity see absorptive capacity
 agency see agency
 definition 4–9
 developing learning capabilities over time 62, 63
 directions for future research 228–30
 ecological view see ecology
 healthcare context 62, 79

inter-organizational networks see inter-organizational healthcare networks
 networks see network relationships
 processes and practices see process/practice
 space see spatial context
 vs. knowledge utilization 7–8
knowledge politics 115, 119–20, 125–6
knowledge translation 1, 178, 179, 180, 191, 197
knowledge utilization 5–6
 vs. knowledge mobilization 7–8

leadership style 86, 100
linear models 1–2, 4

management consultancies 32
managerial action 13, 19–21, 99
 epistemic fit see epistemic fit
 hybrid managers 26, 30
 influences on managers' use of management knowledge 28–9
 research design and methods 27–8
 see also CEOs
mandated networks 151, 152, 154, 155, 169–72
mediation 180
mindlines 7, 24

nested ecology 3, 10–11, 14, 16, 19, 225–6
network ambidexterity 15–16, 105, 109, 152, 157–8
 balancing exploration and exploitation 107, 108, 109, 110, 126, 128, 129, 130, 131
 CLAHRCs 160–3, 170–1
 literature review 109–11
network closure 151, 152, 156, 160–3, 163–4
network relationships 15, 63, 103–5
 mandated networks 151, 152, 154, 155, 169–72
 see also inter-organizational healthcare networks; social network theory
networked innovation 202–3
New Public Management 77

organization studies 6
organizational action 14
 see also inter-organizational action
organizational capabilities 61–3
 absorptive capacity see absorptive capacity
organizational learning 82–4
 spatial context 14–15, 82, 83, 84–7, 88–9
  ba 84, 85, 86, 89, 98
  generative space see generative space
  inert space 83, 89–90
  receptive spaces 85
  relational spaces 85
  research findings 97–101

259

General Index

organizational learning (*cont.*)
   research settings and methods 87
   toxic space 83, 90
   transitional spaces 85
ownership 76

patient safety 177, 180, 183, 185, 187, 188
   clinical trials 208
   see also Root Cause Analysis
pharmaceutical companies 124, 200, 201, 216, 217
   see also clinical trials; drug development
political fit 25
positive organizational scholarship (POS) 85–7, 99
power relations 72, 73, 133–6
   power of continuous interactions 145
   power of emotion 144–5, 149
   power of objects 142, 143
   power of reputation 146
   power of symbols 145–6
   power of talk 142, 143
   power of text 142, 143
Powerpoint 142, 143, 144, 146
practitioner-scholars 104, 129
process/practice 3, 11–13, 226–8
professional bureaucracy 77–8
psychological safety 84, 85, 86, 99

quality improvement 65–6

rational decision makers 5, 20, 23–4, 25
rational fit 25
RCA *see* Root Cause Analysis
receptive spaces 85
relational spaces 85
reputational power 146
research-practice divide 1, 103–4, 229–30
   CLAHRCs *see* Collaborations for Leadership in Applied Health Research and Care
responsive adaptive behavior 5
risk management 186
   see also Root Cause Analysis
role modeling 100
Root Cause Analysis (RCA) 177, 180, 181–2
   anxiety-reassurance 194–6
   global travel
     Australia 186, 188, 189–91
     chronology 191
     origins: civilian and military industries 182–3
     translation vs. diffusion 191–4
     UK: NHS organizations 186–9
     US healthcare sector 183–6

scientific method 2
SEARCH Canada 111–12, 127, 128–9
   balancing competing priorities 114–15
   managing engagement 112–15
   managing funding 113–14
   managing knowledge politics 115
secrecy 187
silos 77, 78
small worlds 46, 60
social media 55
social network theory 151, 152, 153–5, 157
   brokerage 151, 152, 155–6, 160–3, 164–9
   CLAHRCs 159–60
   closure 151, 152, 156, 160–3, 163–4
social ties 155, 156
socialization capabilities 65, 69, 72, 73, 76, 77, 78, 79, 80
socially situated knowledge 2, 4, 6, 7–8, 14
sociology of translation 178, 179, 180, 191, 197
sources of information 49–55
spatial context 14–15, 82, 83, 84–7, 88–9
   ba 84, 85, 86, 89, 98
   generative space *see* generative space
   inert space 83, 89–90
   institutional context 174
   receptive spaces 85
   relational spaces 85
   research findings 97–101
   research settings and methods 88
   space and time 173
     see also timescapes
   toxic space 83, 90
   transitional spaces 85
   trans-local social spaces 16, 173
standardized theory-method package 196
status 87
strategic temporal reckoning systems (STRs) 213–19, 220
stress 87
structural holes 152, 155, 161, 170
suturing narratives 195
symbolic power 145–6
systems capabilities 65, 69, 75, 76, 77, 78, 79, 80

TechFirm
   knowledge mobilization through big data integration 120, 127, 129–30
     balancing competing priorities 124–5
     managing engagement 121–3
     managing funding 123–4
     managing knowledge politics 125–6
timescapes 16, 175–6, 199
   chronos/kairos 212
   clinical research projects 211–19

General Index

strategic temporal reckoning systems (STRs) 213–19, 220
toxic space 83, 90
transformational processes 73–4, 80, 175, 179
transitional spaces 85

translational gap 1
translation, sociology of 1, 178, 179, 180, 191, 197
trans-local social spaces 16, 173

whistle-blowing 190

Index of Names

Abebe, M., Agriawan, A., and Tran, H. 44
Abraham, J. and Reddy, M. 133
Abrahamson, E. and Rosenkopf, L. 193
Adam, B. 200, 201, 212, 214, 218, 219
Addicott, R., McGivern, G., and Ferlie, E. 154
Aguilar, F. I. 45
Albert, M. et al. 26, 37
Amabile, M. 108
Ambos, T. C. et al. 128
Ancona, D. and Chong, C. L. 212, 218
Andersen, B. and Fagerhaug, T. 181, 182
Andersen-Gough, F., Grey, C., and Robson, K. 212
Anderson, M. H. 42, 45
Andriopoulos, C. and Lewis, M. W. 15, 110, 131
Ansari, S. M., Fiss, P. C., and Zajac, E. J. 24, 25, 26, 35, 37, 38, 39, 178, 179, 192
Antonancopoulou, E. and Chiva, R. 83
Ardichvili, A., Page, V., and Wentling, T. 133
Arndt, M. and Bigelow, B. 24, 35
Argote, L. 83
Ashar, B. H. et al. 207
Aube, C. and Rousseau, V. 145
Auster, E. and Choo, C. W. 42

Baba, V. V. and Hakem Zadeh, F. 60
Bagian, Jim 184, 190, 191
Bagian, J. P. et al. 181
Baker, A. 85, 87, 98
Baker, A., Jensen, P., and Kolb, D. 85
Bapuji, H. and Crossan, M. 84, 99
Barrett, M., Oborn, E., and Orlikowski, W. 108
Bate, P. 35
Bates, M. J. 45, 46
Bates, R. H. et al. 181
Bateson, J. 45, 54
Battilana, J. and Casciaro, T. 158
Baum, J. A., Shipilov, A. V., and Rowley, T. J. 157
Beck, U., Giddens, A., and Lash, S. 195
Benner, M. J. and Tushman, M. L. 109, 126, 128
Berta, W. et al. 65, 66, 76, 77
Beyer, J. M. and Trice, H. M. 5
Beyes, T. and Michels, C. 85

Biernacki, P. and Waldorf, D. 68
Blackler, F. and McDonald, S. 87
Bohmer, R. and Edmondson, A. 87
Borgatti, S. P., Everett, M. G., and Freeman, L. C. 159
Bourdieu, Pierre 134–5, 136, 145
Bourgeon, L. 212
Bouwen, R. and Hosking, D. M. 83, 85, 98
Boxenbaum, E. and Battilana, J. 178
Boxenbaum, E. and Pedersen, J. S. 179
Brennan, T. A. et al. 183
Brown, J. S. and Duguid, P. 6, 7, 46, 84, 87
Buckland, M. K. 45
Burnett, G., Besant, M., and Chatman, E. A. 60
Burt, R. S. 155, 156, 157, 161
Burton, A. 216

Cameron, K. S. 86
Cameron, K. S. and Caza, A. 87
Cameron, K. S., Bright, D., and Caza, A. 85, 99
Cameron, K. S., Dutton, J. E., and Quinn, R. E. 85
Caplan, N. 154
Carlile, P. R. 10–11, 25, 128, 154, 230
Carroll, J. S. 183
Carroll, J. S., Rudolph, J. W., and Hatakenaka, S. 181
Chakravartty, A. 24, 27, 35, 39
Chalkidou, K. et al. 5
Chen, X., Yao, X., and Kotha, S. 144
Chia, R. 134
Ciborra, C. 144
Clark, P. 200, 212, 213, 219, 221
Clark, P. A. and Maielli, G. 212, 213
Clegg, S. R. 134, 136
Clegg, S. et al. 224
Cohen, W. M. and Levinthal, D. 66, 109, 126
Coleman, J. S. 156
Coleman, J. S., Katz, E., and Menzel, H. 156
Cook, S. and Yanov, D. 84, 87
Cook, S. D. and Brown, J. S. 2, 6
Cooksey, D. 154
Cramton, C. D. 171
Crilly, T. et al. 15
Crilly, T., Jashapara, A., and Ferlie, E. 28, 42, 154

Index of Names

Croft, C. and Currie, G. 14, 83, 100, 226
Croteau, Rick 183
Cunliffe, A. 84
Currie, G. and Suhomlinova, A. 154
Currie, G. and White, L. 133, 153, 155
Currie, G., El Enany, N., and Lockett, A. 26, 27, 128, 203, 207
Currie, G., Finn, R., and Martin, G. 154
Czarniawska, B. 47
Czarniaxske, B. and Joerges, B. 178, 179, 197
Czarniawska, B. and Sevón, G. 174, 178, 179, 181, 192, 197

D'Andreta, D. et al. 154, 226
D'Andreta, D. and Scarbrough, H. 15, 109, 203, 224, 227
D'Andreta, D., Scarbrough, H., and Evans, S. 158
Dahl, R. A. 134
Damanpour, F. and Schneider, M. 65
Darzi, A. 1
De Alwis, G., Majid, S., and Chaudhry, A. S. 42, 43–4, 44–5
DeSteno, D., et al. 144
Department of Health 187, 188
Descartes, René 197
Deszo, C. L. and Ross, D. G. 133, 148
Dhanaraj, C. and Parkhe, A. 111, 128, 130
Dhillon, G. 134
Dionysiou, D. D. and Tsoukas, H. 228
Dirks, K. T. and Ferrin, D. L. 161
Dobbins, M. et al. 156
Dodgson, M., Gann, D., and Salter, A. 203
Dopson, S. et al. 4, 6, 24, 42, 59
Dopson, S. and Fitzgerald, L. 4, 24, 26, 38, 39, 42
Dougherty, D. and Dunne, D. 10, 12, 16, 200, 203, 210
Dreyfus, H. L. 144
Dreyfus, H. L. and Kelly, S. D. 144
Dube, L., Bourkis, A., and Jacob, R. 148
Dubinskas, F. 212
Dutton, J. 86
Dutton, J. and Ragins, B. 86

Easterby-Smith, M. et al. 65, 66, 68, 76, 77
Easterby-Smith, M. and Araujo, L. 84
Easterby-Smith, M. and Lyles, M. A. 42
Easterby-Smith, M., Crossan, M., and Nicolini, D. 83, 84, 87
Edelman, L. F. et al. 87
Edenius, M. and Yakhlef, A. 85, 98
Edmondson, A. 10, 80, 84, 85, 99, 100
Eisenhardt, K. 28, 79
El Sawy, 45
Emerson, R. M. 134
Emslie, Stuart 188

Engwall, M. and Jerbrant, A. 206
Estabrooks, C. A. 5
Evans, J., Kunda, G., and Barley, S. 212
Evans, S. and Scarbrough, H. 154, 158

Fahy, K. M., Easterby-Smith, M., and Lervik, J. E. 85
Fayard, A., Gkeredakis, E., and Levina, N. 24, 27, 35, 39
Fayter, D. et al. 207
Feldman, M. S. and March, J. G. 45, 58
Feldman, M. S. and Orlikowski, W. J. 43, 46, 227
Ferlie, E. et al. 1, 2, 15, 16, 24, 26, 35, 37, 38, 66, 76, 77, 152, 154, 169
Fidel, R. and Green, M. 45, 47
Fine, G. A. and White, R. D. 195
Fischer, M. et al. 38
Fitzgerald, L. and Harvey, G. 1, 3, 6, 221
Foucault, M. 134, 135, 136, 142
Fox, S. 136
Freeman, L. C. 155
French, J. R. P. and Raven, B. 30, 134
Frenkel, M. 178
Frost, P. 90
Fujimura, J. H. 196

Gabbay, J. and Le May, A. 6, 7, 24, 35, 46
Gaventa, J. 135
George, A. L. and Bennett, A. 181
Gherardi, S. 46, 134
Gherardi, S. and Nicolini, D. 87
Gibson, C. B. and Birkinshaw, J. 110, 129
Gino, F. and Pisano, G. 210
Gioia, D. A. and Chittipedi, K. 58
Gittell, J. H. 86
Gittell, J. H. et al. 86
Gittell, J. H., Godfrey, M., and Thistlethwaite, J. 133, 149
Gkeredakis, E. et al. 1, 2, 6, 26
Gnyawali, D. R. and Madhuran, R. 156
Golden-Biddle, K. et al. 86
Golden-Biddle, K. and Locke, K. 28, 48
Grabher, G. 203, 206, 207, 221
Grandori, A. and Soda, G. 170
Gratton, L. and Ghoshal, S. 87
Greenhalgh, T. and Wieringa, S. 2, 203
Greenwood, R., Hinings, C. R., and Suddaby, R. 192
Gulati, R. 156
Guler, I. 217
Gupta, A. K., Smith, K. G., and Shalley, C. E. 110, 128

Hackshaw, A. et al. 207, 208
Hannah, S. T. and Lester, P. B. 86, 100
Hansen, M. T. 134, 155, 156

263

Index of Names

Hardy, C. 134, 149
Hardy, C. and Maguire, S. 136, 142, 148
Hardy, C. and Thomas, R. 136, 142, 148
Hardy, C., Phillips, N., and Lawrence, T. B. 202
Hargadon, A. 193
Harvey, G. et al. 66, 68, 76, 77, 81
Hay, M. et al. 210
Hellstrom, T. and Hellstrom, C. 213
Heracleous, L. and Jacobs, C. D. 146
Hislop, D. 42
Hislop, D. et al. 133
Hoffer Gittell, J. 171
Holbrook, M. B. and Batra, R. 144
Hotho, J. J., Becker-Ritterspach, F., and Saka-Helshout, A. 67
Hunt, P. 194
Hunter, F. 134

Im, G. and Rai, A. 110
Imison, C., Curry, N., and McShane, M. 66

Janis, I. L. 87
Jansen, J. J. P., Van Den Bosch, F., and Volberda, H. W. 68, 76
Jansen, J. P., Vera, D., and Crossan, M. 80
Janssen, O., Van de Vliert, E., and West, M. 157
Jarzabkowski, P., Bednarek, R., and Spee, P. 11
Johnson, B. and Hagström, B. 178

Kaelber, D. C. and Bates, D. W. 132
Kanov, J. M. et al. 86
Kaplan, R. and Norton, D. 29
Kaplan, S. 142
Kepes, S., Bennett, A., and McDaniel, M. 42
Kijkhuit, B. and van den Ende, J. 156
Kimble, C., Grenier, C., and Goglio-Primard, K. 133
Kings Fund 49, 59, 228
Kislov, R., Harvey, G., and Walshe, K. 156
Kitsuse, J. I. and Spector, M. 185, 194
Knorr-Cetina, K. 24, 26, 27, 128, 207
Kola, I. and Landis, J. 218
Korica, M. and Nicolini, D. 13
Kovner, A. R. and Rundall, T. G. 5
Kovner, A. R., Fine, D. R., and D'Aquila, R. 4
Krackhardt, D. 156

Landry, R., Amari, M., and Lamara, N. 5
Lane, P. J. and Lubatkin, M. 134
Lane, P. J., Koka, B., and Pathak, S. 68, 76
Latour, B. 135–6, 145, 147, 178, 179, 180, 196, 197, 228
Lave, J. and Wenger, E. 6, 7, 148
Lavertu, S. and Moynihan, D. 77
Lavie, D., Stettner, U., and Tushman, M. L. 109, 110, 128, 129, 131
Lawrence, T. B. et al. 134

Learmonth, M. 4, 6
Learmonth, M. and Harding, N. 4, 6
Levi, M. 181
Levin, B. 4, 7
Levina, N. 135, 149
Levina, N. and Orlikowski, W. J. 136, 148, 149
Levina, N. and Vaast, E. 46
Lewin, A. Y., Long, C. P., and Carroll, T. N. 109
Lindkvist, L. 207
Locke, K., Golden-Biddle, K., and Feldman, M. 48
Lockett, A. et al. 148
Lomas, J. 24, 26, 38, 39, 156
Lukes, S. 134

Maguire, S. and Hardy, C. 148
Maguire, S., Hardy, C., and Lawrence, T. B. 193
Mantere, S. and Ketokivi, M. 48
Marabelli, M., Frigerio, C., and Rajola, F. 126
March, J. G. 109, 181
Marshall, N. and Rollinson, J. 87
Martin, G. P., Currie, G., and Finn, R. 153
Martin, G. P., Currie, G., and Lockett, A. 26, 27, 203
Marx, Karl 134
McAneney, H. 153
McAneney, H. et al. 154
McDonald, S. 47
McDonald, M. L. and Westphal, J. D. 45
McDonald, S. and Simpson, B. 47
McGivern, G. et al. 13, 26, 30, 38, 42, 45, 52, 56, 58, 59, 203, 207, 227
McGivern, G. and Dopson, S. 24, 25, 26, 37, 203, 207, 221
Miettinen, R., Samra-Fredericks, D., and Yanow, D. 43, 46, 56
Miles, M. B. and Huberman, A. M. 28, 138
Mintzberg, H. 42, 77
Miron, E., Erez, M., and Naveh, E. 108
Montaner, J. S., O'Shaughnessy, M. V., and Schechter, M. T. 218
Morrell, K. 4
Morris, T. and Lancaster, Z. 178
Moynihan, D. P. 77
Moynihan, D. P. and Hawes, D. 77
Moynihan, D. P. and Landuyt, N. 65
Murray, F. 207

Nag, R. and Gioia, D. A. 58
Nambisan, S. and Sawhney, M. 130
National Audit Office 186
Nemanich, L. A. and Vera, D. 86
Nembhard, A. and Edmondon, A. 84, 100
Newell, S. et al. 20, 200, 201, 203, 204, 213
Newell, S. and Marabelli, M. 15, 154, 224, 227
Nicolini, D. 11, 12, 43, 46, 56, 59, 134, 178, 181, 227, 229

Index of Names

Nicolini, D. et al. 16, 227, 228
Nicolini, D. and Korica, M. 224, 227
Nicolini, D. and Monteiro, P. 12
Nicolini, D., Gherardi, S., and Yanow, D. 46, 56
Nicolini, D., Korica, M., and Ruddle, K. 59
Nicolini, D., Powell, J., and Korica, M. 8, 43
Nicolini, D. Scarbrough, H., and Gracheva, J. 10
Nicolini, D., Waring, J., and Mengis, J. 77, 180, 181, 193
Nielsen, J., Mathiassen, L., and Newell, S. 174
Nightingale, P. 200
Nightingale, P. and Martin, P. 218
Nonaka, I. and Konno, N. 84, 85, 89, 98
Nonaka, I., Toyama, R., and Byosiere, P. 83, 84, 85, 86, 98, 99, 100
Nonaka, I., Toyama, R., and Konno, N. 85

Oborn, E. et al. 15, 109, 126, 152, 224, 227
Oborn, E. and Dawson, S. 128, 154
Oborn, E., Barrett, M., and Racko, G. 2, 130, 154
Obstfeld, D. 156
O'Leary, Dennis 185
Oliver, A. L. and Ebers, M. 157
Orlikowski, W. 46
Orlikowski, W. and Yates, J. 212
Øvretveit, J. 189
Owen-Smith, J. et al. 207
Owen-Smith, J. and Powell, W. W. 170, 207

Pavitt, K. 203
Penley, L. E. 42
Pennebaker, J. W. 149
Pettigrew, K. E. 54
Pfeffer, J. 134
Pfeffer, J. and Salancik, G. R. 42, 134
Pfeffer, J. and Sutton, R. I. 42
Pisano, G. 29, 213
Pitsis, T. et al. 212
Pittinsky, T. L. and Shih, M. J. 86
Polanyi, M. 134
Porter, K., Whittington, K. B., and Powell, W. W. 157
Powell, W. W. and Koput, K. 155
Powell, W. W., Koput, K., and Smith-Doerr, L. 130, 203
Power, M. 195
Prince, K., Barrett, M., and Oborn, E. 111, 130

Quinn, R. and Dutton, J. 86

Rafaeli, A. and Vilnai-Yavetz, I. 144
Reagans, R. and McEvily, B. 15, 156, 157, 158
Reay, T. et al. 14, 227
Reay, T., Berta, W., and Kazmann-Kohn, M. 24, 35

Rich, R. F. 5, 6, 45
Rich, R. F. and Oh, C. H. 5
Rifkin, J. 211
Rivkin, J. W. and Siggelkow, N. 109
Robertson, M. and Swan, J. 10, 16, 227, 228
Robertson, M., Swan, J., and Newell, S. 26
Rodriguez, C. et al. 133, 148
Rogers, Everett 174
Rogers, E. 5, 9, 178, 197, 198, 202
Rousseau, D. 4, 5, 19, 42, 60
Rousseau, D., Manning, J., and Denyer, D. 24
Rousseau, D. M. and McCarthy, S. 5, 20
Runciman, B. 189
Runciman, B. and Walton, M. 181
Ryle, Gilbert 197

Sackett, D. L. et al. 4
Sahlin, K. and Wedlin, L. 178
Sahoo, A. 219
Saint-Martin, D. 32
Salge, T. O. 65
Salgo, T. O. and Vera, A. 65, 66
Sandberg, J. et al. 207
Sandberg, J. and Tsoukas, H. 59
Sandelowski, M. 49
Savolainen, R. 46
Scarbrough, H. et al. 2, 6
Scarbrough, H. and Swan, J. 192, 193
Scarbrough, H., Robertson, M., and Swan, J. 11, 227
Schatzki, T. 59
Schatzki, T., Knorr-Cetina, K., and Savigny, E. V. 46, 56
Schein, Edgar 30, 31
Schultze, U. 137
Shankar, P. R. and Subish, P. 194
Shipilov, A. V. and Li, S. X. 157
Simsek, Z. 110, 129
Smith, C. and O'Donnell, J. 218
Smith, J. et al. 66
Smith, K. G., Collins, C. J., and Clark, K. D. 110
Solomon, R. C. and Flores, F. 144
Spender, G. 84
Spreitzer, G. et al. 85
Stadler, C., Rajwani, T., and Karaba, F. 110, 111, 128, 129, 131
Star, S. L. and Griesemer, J. R. 136, 145, 196
Stein, M. et al. 144
Stewart, R. 42
Strang, D. and Soule, S. A. 5, 178
Strauss, A. L. and Corbin, J. 28, 138
Sturdy, A. 24, 25
Sveningsson, S. and Alvesson, M. 26
Swan, J. et al. 1, 2, 26, 37, 42, 59, 66, 108, 128, 146, 202, 203, 204, 221, 226, 230
Swan, J. and Scarbrough, H. 111, 130, 202
Swan, J., Newell, S., and Robertson, M. 10

265

Index of Names

Swan, J., Robertson, M., and Evans, S. 202, 204, 208
Swan, J., Robertson, M., and Newell, S. 12, 201, 218, 219
Swan, J., Scarbrough, H., and Newell, S. 154
Swanson, E. B. 174
Swanson, E. B. and Ramiller, N. C. 174
Szulanski, G. 134, 154

Taylor, R. S. 45
Thomas, R., Hardy, C., and Sargent, L. D. 147, 148
Thomson, L., Schneider, J., and Wright, N. 156
Thrift, N. 144
Thüring, M. and Mahlke, S. 144
Timmermans, S. and Berg, M. 35
Todorova, G. and Durisin, B. 79
Tortoriello, M. and Krackhardt, D. 158
Trinh, K. C. W. and Mitchell, W. 45
Tsai, W. 134
Tucker, A., Nembhard, A., and Edmondson, A. 84
Tuominen, K., Savolainen, R., and Talja, S. 46
Turner, N., Swart, J., and Maylor, H. 109, 110
Tushman, M. L. and O'Reilly, C. A. 109

Uzzi, B. 156

Vaara, E. and Whittington, R. 43, 46, 136
Van de Ven, A. H. and Hargrave, T. J. 5, 178
Van den Bosch, F. A. J., Volberda, H., and de Boer, M. 67, 77
Van Fraassen, B. 27
Vincent, Charles 186, 193, 195
Vincent, C. A., Taylor-Adams, S., and Stanhope, N. 187

Volberda, H. W., Foss, N., and Lyles, M. 68, 76
Von Hippel, E. A. and Krogh, G. 203

Wald, H. and Shojania, K. G. 181
Walsham, G. et al. 137
Walshe, K. 66, 76, 77, 81
Walshe, K. and Rundall, T. G. 4, 24, 42, 60
Ward, V. et al. 5
Ward, V., House, A., and Hamer, S. 156
Waring, J. et al. 2, 6
Waring, J. and Currie, G. 179
Wears, R. L., Perry, S. J., and Sutcliffe, K. M. 183
Weick, K. E. 48
Weick, K. E. and Quinn, R. E. 181
Weick, K. E., Sutcliffe, K. M., and Obstfeld, D. 58
Wenger, E. 35
West, E. et al. 157
Whittington, K. B., Owen-Smith, J., Powell, W. W. 133
Williams, A. P. O. 83, 84
Wilson, R. M. et al. 189
Winnicott, D. W. 83
Woloshynowych, M. et al. 181, 182

Yanow, D. 84, 87
Yanow, D. and Schwartz-Shea, P. 48, 49
Yin, R. 28

Zachariadis, M. et al. 108
Zahra, S. A. and George, G. 14, 66, 68, 76, 79
Zbaracki, M. 26
Zider, B. 218
Zmud, R. W. 45